THE BELFAST JACOBIN

Dedicated to the memory of
my loving parents.

Kenneth Dawson is a graduate of Queen's University Belfast. He was Head of History and Politics at Down High School, Downpatrick, 1997–2008, and has been Vice-Principal since 2008. He has been researching the United Irishmen for a number of years and is the author of numerous articles on the subject. He resides in Ballynahinch, County Down, close to the scene of the battle that took place there in 1798.

THE BELFAST JACOBIN

SAMUEL NEILSON AND THE UNITED IRISHMEN

Kenneth L. Dawson

Irish Academic Press

First published in 2017 by
Irish Academic Press
10 George's Street
Newbridge
Co. Kildare
Ireland
www.iap.ie

978-1-91102-475-0 (Paper)
978-1-91102-476-7 (Cloth)
978-1-91102-488-0 (Kindle)
978-1-91102-489-7 (Epub)
978-1-91102-490-3 (PDF)

British Library Cataloguing in Publication Data
An entry can be found on request

Library of Congress Cataloging in Publication Data
An entry can be found on request

Interior design by www.jminfotechindia.com
Typeset in Garamond Premier Pro 11/14 pt

Cover design by edit+ www.stuartcoughlan.com
Cover/jacket front: Samuel Neilson (1762–1803), *c.*1795, unknown 19th century (after Charles Byrne, 1757–1810), reproduced by kind permission of National Museums Northern Ireland.
Cover/jacket back: Front page of the *Northern Star*, 1795, reproduced by kind permission of the Linen Hall Library, Belfast.

Contents

Abbreviations

KHLC	Kent History and Library Centre, Maidstone (formerly the Centre for Kentish Studies)
LHL	Linen Hall Library, Belfast
NA	National Archives Kew, London
NAI	National Archives of Ireland, Dublin
NLI	National Library of Ireland, Dublin
NRS	National Records of Scotland, Edinburgh
PHS	Presbyterian Historical Society, Belfast
PRONI	Public Record Office of Northern Ireland, Belfast
TCD	Trinity College, Dublin
UM	Ulster Museum, Belfast
URIL	University of Rhode Island Library

ACKNOWLEDGEMENTS

I would like, at the outset, to thank the staff at the different libraries and archives visited for their unfailing assistance during the many years of research, which, for a busy teacher, was confined largely to school holidays. The librarians in the Irish and Reference floor of Belfast's Linen Hall Library deserve special thanks for their patience. I am also grateful for the help and advice given by staff at the Belfast Central Newspaper Library, the Presbyterian Historical Society, the former South-Eastern Education and Library Board headquarters in Ballynahinch, the Ulster Museum, the Public Records Office of Northern Ireland, Trinity College, Dublin, the National Library of Ireland, the National Archives of Ireland, the National Archives in London, the Kent History and Library Centre in Maidstone, and the National Records of Scotland. I am particularly indebted to Sarina Wyant and her colleagues in the University of Rhode Island Library for arranging to have the collection of Neilson Papers held there to be copied and sent to me. The excellent staff at Irish Academic Press, especially Conor Graham, Fiona Dunne and Myles McCionnaith, as well as those who proofed the text, have been a pleasure to work with, and I thank them for their constant support.

The task of writing about the life and times of Samuel Neilson was based firmly on the conviction that there was an important story to be told, and I would like to express my gratitude to those who were similarly convinced. In many respects, the idea was conceived by the late Reverend W.D. Bailie of Saintfield, County Down, whose knowledge of this period was remarkable. I am grateful to his daughter, Rosemary Young, for allowing me access to some of Dr Bailie's 1798 research material. As a newly arrived history teacher in County Down in the early 1990s, Horace Reid's articles on the 1798 Rebellion in the *Mourne Observer* newspaper got me well and truly hooked on this period. Horace's advice and friendship over many years are valued greatly. I am also grateful to Conor O'Clery for his generosity, encouragement and ideas, as well as a shared fascination with the *Northern Star*. Special thanks are due to Philip Orr for his thoughtful suggestions, great insight and unstinting friendship. Dr Michael Murphy read the manuscript and offered thoughtful suggestions that improved the text. His doses of humour kept my spirits up during the stressful editing stages. Dr Brian Turner is to be thanked for his sharp insight and keen eye for detail, while Dr Jonathan Wright provided much encouragement, support and positive feedback (not to mention sharing my enthusiasm for the importance of Belfast in the unfolding narrative of the late eighteenth century). A special word of thanks is extended to my sister, Karen Dawson; she was the first to read my manuscript with a critical eye and highlighted areas that required attention. Others who provided assistance include John McCabe, Robert McClure, Martin Hill from the *Belfast Telegraph* and Colin Campbell, who gave me a personal tour of Fort George. John Frazer advised me on all things masonic and has supported me throughout. Current and former friends and colleagues at Down High School have been a great source of encouragement over many years. Working with the most pleasant and interested students one could ever wish to teach has helped to maintain my love for the subject.

Finally, I would like to express my love and gratitude towards my wife Maureen, who has allowed Samuel Neilson to share our home for more years than she would care to remember and been a constant source of support throughout this process.

Introduction

Originator, Editor, Conspirator, Orchestrator

When the celebrated Irish patriot Theobald Wolfe Tone arrived in Belfast for the first time on 11 October 1791 at the invitation of the town's leading radicals, he found a group of political reformers known to him only by reputation. His knowledge of the north was limited to what he had been told by his great friend Thomas Russell, who had been posted there the previous year as an officer with the 64th Regiment of Foot. Russell's experience of Belfast and its most forward-thinking political activists would arouse the curiosity of the young Dublin lawyer. While Tone found the largely Presbyterian radical set interesting and politically advanced, he was concerned by their general lack of understanding of the increasingly strident Catholic Committee's call for the advancement of franchise reform and the right of Catholics to be elected to the Protestant-dominated Irish Parliament in Dublin's College Green.

Tone stayed in Belfast for around three weeks, during which he was present at the formation of a new political club, the Society of United Irishmen, and he later recorded this northern excursion as being 'perhaps the pleasantest in my life'.[1] Tone's entertaining journal about his stay in Belfast (or, as he termed it, Blefescu) introduces us to some of the town's prominent citizens, among them the more vocal campaigners who had already nailed their colours to the mast of reform through membership of the Irish Volunteers and their espousal of a more inclusive brand of politics that would include Irishmen of all religious outlooks. Tone's journal refers to many of these men using the soubriquets he applied to them, names that hint at their business interests (William Sinclaire is 'The Draper', Robert Simms 'The Tanner' and Dr James MacDonnell is 'The Hypocrite') or their politics (Thomas McCabe is 'The Slave', due to his resolute opposition some years before to any association of the town with the slave trade and the fact that the sign above his watchmaker's premises on North Street read

'An Irish Slave'). To the affluent businessman Samuel Neilson, the subject of this study, Tone assigned the name 'The Jacobin'.[2]

The French Jacobin Club was the most famous of the radical associations formed during the tumultuous early years of the French Revolution. Taking its name from the fact that it assembled initially in a Dominican convent in the Rue St Jacques, Paris, the Jacobin Club became a centre of progressive political discourse that called for a national constitution reflecting democratic principles and a polity based on the natural rights of man, with leaders ranging from Barnave and Mirabeau to the more republican and egalitarian Marat and Robespierre. As the revolution matured, the Jacobin Club would become renowned for its anti-aristocratic extremism, the Great Terror, and the promotion of the deistic cult of the Supreme Being as an alternative to traditional Catholicism. Tone's admiring description of Neilson predated the worst excesses of Jacobin rule and the label ignores the latter's strong attachment to an orthodox Presbyterian faith, based firmly on the scriptures. Nonetheless, Tone's appellation tells us something of Samuel Neilson's advanced political outlook. An enthusiastic organiser, propagandist and political agitator, he would become the director of Belfast's radical coterie and would, in time, take a leading role in developing republican principles across Ulster and beyond. By the time of his arrest in September 1796, Neilson was, in the words of the government informer William Bird, 'at the head of the conspirators'.[3]

This study of Neilson's life will attribute to him a very significant role in the origins, development and insurgency of the Society of United Irishmen, but, despite his importance, Neilson's contribution to Irish republicanism has often been overlooked and, in fact, derided. What might be termed as Neilson's semi-detachment from the pantheon of venerated United Irish figures can be attributed to the cloud of suspicion that formed over him in the years after the arrest and fatal wounding of the United Irishmen's commander-in-chief, Lord Edward Fitzgerald, in May 1798, on the eve of the rebellion. Previous to the unmasking of the barrister Francis Magan as Fitzgerald's betrayer, the songwriter Thomas Moore had constructed an analysis of Neilson as 'flighty and inconsiderate' in his role as one of Lord Edward's entourage. While not actually accusing Neilson of treachery, Moore's description of Fitzgerald's capture in a safe house impugned his character: 'There had now elapsed, from the time of Neilson's departure, not more than ten minutes and it is asserted that he had, in going out, left the hall door open.' Such was the strength of the implication that two of Neilson's daughters took active steps to prevent future histories from repeating the same account.[4] Furthermore, having experienced a significant deterioration in his health during a period of incarceration in Kilmainham Gaol from late 1796, his tendency to find solace in alcohol was highlighted in later accounts of the 1790s. Neilson's 'depraved habits which had lowered both the moral and intellectual tone of his mind' would lead him to damage the cause 'by his customary foolhardiness'.[5] Thomas Pakenham's influential narrative of the 1798 Rebellion, written in 1969 at a time when the primary sources were under-exploited, confirmed in the public mind the view that Neilson was, at best, a well-meaning liability to the cause, 'a huge shambling man and latterly a slave to drink', whose inebriation led to his arrest in Dublin on 23 May 1798 and, subsequently, the evaporation of any remaining plan for insurrection in the capital.[6]

More recent research has acknowledged Neilson's importance to the United Irish project, with historians such as Thomas Bartlett, Marianne Elliott, Kevin Whelan, Ruán O'Donnell and James Quinn placing him close to the core of the conspiracy. James Kelly has asserted that our understanding of the Society of United Irishmen will be enhanced by attending to Neilson's centrality to the organisation. Rising to that challenge is one of the primary objectives of this work.[7] His influence on the foundation of the Society of United Irishmen was profound. His proprietorship and editorship of the United Irish newspaper the *Northern Star* is another significant aspect of his contribution to the project. Furthermore, as the organisation developed towards a more militant position in the middle of the 1790s, his role in co-ordinating the conspiracy became marked.

* * * *

Wolfe Tone's visit to Belfast in 1791 was by invitation of a radical sub-set of the Volunteers, directed by Neilson, whose activities were, by necessity, kept confidential due to the fact that not all of the armed citizens of the town were as advanced in their thinking as he was. Moderate Presbyterian reformers were loath to countenance the empowerment of Catholics, fearing the latter's attachment to the dictates of their church rather than to the general will. For many northerners, Catholic theology was false and its fundamental laws were attacked in the Westminster Confession of Faith, which asserted Calvinistic doctrine, including the view that the Pope was the Anti-Christ. Neilson's own church, Third Belfast, was the most orthodox of the town's Presbyterian congregations, but while he would, on occasions, reveal a suspicion of Catholics, he was politically ambitious for this disempowered section of Irish society. Indeed, Neilson's secret committee of Irish Volunteers was, in many respects, the United Irishmen in embryo. Tone would refine and clarify the pre-existing views of these men; that a fundamental reform of Parliament, coupled with a unity of purpose among the three main denominations of Catholic, Protestant and Dissenter, was essential if Ireland was to achieve meaningful national independence. The existence of a radical society in Belfast, in harmony with Tone's own view, places Neilson at the heart of the debate on the origins of the United Irishmen.

As the United Irish vision developed, Neilson's abilities would become more vital still for the cause. The plans for a second newspaper in Belfast to counter the moderate reformism of the *News-Letter* were in full swing even before Tone's arrival in the town. From the first edition of the *Northern Star* in January 1792, edited by Neilson, the United Irishmen would have the means to influence, proselytise, criticise and demonise. This literary critique of the *status quo* would enable political education across Ulster and beyond, as Neilson built up an extensive network of agents who would take responsibility for the newspaper reaching all parts of Ireland, as well as larger towns in England and Scotland. The prospectus for the new paper emphasised the need for parliamentary reform based on a real representation of the people, and the new publication would circulate 'until the venal borough trade shall terminate, until corruption shall no longer at least be publickly [*sic*] avowed, and until the commons house of parliament shall become the real organ of the PUBLICK WILL'. The *Northern Star* would also promote the union of Irishmen and demand an end to Britain's 'griping hand of monopoly' prescribing Irish trade and manufactures. Neilson's appeal to the populace to support the new venture on the grounds of 'SPIRIT, IMPARTIALITY AND INDEPENDENCE' was well received. Indeed, even if his conduct in the unfolding narrative of the United Irishmen had not been significant, Neilson's leading role in promoting, printing and distributing the *Northern Star* would be worthy of biographical attention.[8] Neilson's *Star* editorials make up, to some degree, for the absence of his private papers, which had at various times been subject to confiscation, released to the family, sent to New York for safekeeping and then returned to Ireland only to be lost, it was alleged by the nineteenth-century historian R.R. Madden, when the *Shannon* was shipwrecked off the Donegal coast.[9] The *Northern Star* dedicated much of its content to news from Dublin, London and Europe, but Neilson's observations on political, social and religious issues offer considerable insight into his thinking, even if his comments were moderated in the interests of avoiding governmental persecution, a vain hope, as it turned out.

The outbreak of war between Britain and France in February 1793 sparked a concatenation of events that would accelerate a change in the *modus operandi* of the United Irishmen from constitutionalism to an insurrectionary-based strategy.

With their pro-French proclivities now deemed to be dangerous, the government took steps to marginalise the influence of the movement by arresting key figures, such as William Drennan and Archibald Hamilton Rowan, disbanding Volunteer companies, prosecuting the proprietors of the *Northern Star* (including Neilson) and effectively suppressing the United movement. With a clear message from the administrations in London and Dublin that the prospects for further reform were diminished, the United Irishmen reconstituted themselves, working at a clandestine level to adopt a more militant approach that would be augmented by French support, which was being courted at that time by Tone, who had made his way to Paris from his enforced exile in the United States. The grafting of a military organisation onto the existing United Irish structure in the mid-1790s went hand in hand with the careful cultivation of links with the Defenders, a Catholic secret society that, while acting in a self-interested way, was able – to some degree – to find common cause with the United Irishmen. Neilson was active in both of these areas, directing the affairs of Belfast republicans and playing a key role in the delicate building of relations with a movement that looked back to a golden age of native Catholic landownership more than it projected forward to a democratic and republican vision, uncontaminated by historical sectarian divisions. The pervasive influence of government informers, however, deprived Neilson of his freedom in September 1796, when he, Thomas Russell and the leading Defender Charles Teeling were whisked away to Dublin on suspicion of treacherous activity. With *habeas corpus* suspended, Neilson's imprisonment would prove long and difficult, his health deteriorating rapidly in the dark and damp conditions of Kilmainham Gaol. Despite the hardships, Neilson was still determined to carry on with the conspiracy and he was able to exert his influence over those inside and outside the prison as the plans continued apace.

Neilson was released on grounds of ill health in February 1798, but despite assurances that he would desist from returning to his seditious past, he soon re-engaged with a United Irish leadership that was weakened by the reports of informers and divided by differing views on how to proceed with the conspiracy. Alongside Fitzgerald, the errant son of the Duke of Leinster, Neilson organised the replenishment of a punctured military structure and, in the aftermath of the former's arrest and mortal wounding, attempted to unleash an uprising in Dublin – the intended prelude to a more ambitious assault upon the forces of the Crown. Neilson's intention may have been to facilitate the escape of Fitzgerald and Russell from Newgate Gaol, but he was arrested outside the prison on the evening of the 23 May, rendering almost useless the potential for a successful show of force by the Dublin rebels. The insurrection appeared doomed. A summer of atrocities and bloodshed ensued. Following a bloody and chaotic insurrection, he took the lead in trying to limit the spillage of more blood by seeking an arrangement between the state prisoners and the government, a controversial strategy then and since. Facing the prospect of trials and executions, Neilson promoted an initiative that would bring an end to the carnage, deliver limited information to the authorities and minimise the use of the gallows. While this plan gave rise to suggestions of co-operation and self-interest, the arrangement worked well for both sides, although the expected exile of the state prisoners was held up by the refusal of entry by the United States government to those who were not considered assets to the nascent American republic. An extended period of confinement followed for the most senior United Irishmen. Released eventually from Fort George in Scotland in 1802, Neilson departed for New York, only to perish within a year of the commencement of his new life, before his family could join him.

The material available to the historian offers an incomplete but tangible picture of a man who was determined, blunt, austere and not afraid to stand up to authority. Neilson was capable of sustaining warm friendships, but was also prone to outbursts of petulance that threatened to undermine those same close bonds. His flaws of character, which included a haughtiness that bordered on condescension, an impatient pedantry that saw him harangue even his closest political allies, an irascibility that alienated his friends and a tendency to drink to excess which prompted carelessness of action, are all mitigated by his years of isolation, ill treatment and poor health. He was a loving husband and father, but one never afraid to admonish and control, no matter how physically remote he was from his wife and children. In matters of religion, Neilson was not attracted to Thomas Russell's millennialist outlook, which allowed the latter's theological views to merge with his political vision to produce an explanation for the seismic revolutionary activity that erupted in the final years of the eighteenth century.[10] Certainly, though, Neilson's strong Christian faith – he was a church elder – defined his attitudes and behaviour and he was resigned to his fate being in the hands of God. Even in the midst of his despair in prison, he wrote to his wife that:

> my trust is still kept up by the hope that a Divine Providence will bring light out of all this darkness, and that the day is by no means remote when these important truths shall be manifest to all who will believe. In politics, my wish ever was the public good. So in religion, the desire of my heart is, that all mankind may be brought into the way of the Almighty, and that in his own good time.[11]

Neilson's political motivation can be explained variously. The influence of his older brother, John, one of the town's earliest Volunteers, was certainly important, as was the economic and cultural milieu in which he found himself as his economic, civic and political involvement increased. The infectious principles of the American and French revolutions, with their attack on exclusivity and corrupt practices, would certainly have influenced a young and energetic businessman whose social and religious background precluded him from accessing certain positions in civic life. As his economic and political interests developed, the hostile legal and military targeting of his *Northern Star* newspaper would certainly have pushed him towards more extremist views, a trend accelerated by the collapse of his business interests as he languished in prison with no prospect of having his day in court. Like many others, he would have been outraged by the military excesses committed across Ulster in the middle of the decade, provocative actions that pushed many into the swelling ranks of the United Irishmen or the Defenders. Bad faith, as he saw it, on the part of the government at the time of his release in February 1798 further affirmed his insurrectionary outlook as he set to work as a practical revolutionary, a role for which he – like so many others – was barely cut out.

Theobald Wolfe Tone would later refer approvingly to Neilson as 'an honest, a brave, and worthy fellow, a good Irishman, a good republican'.[12] It has long been acknowledged that northern Presbyterians were at the forefront of radical politics during these very turbulent years and yet Samuel Neilson remains largely unknown today among those who worship in the meeting house. He is often cited as one of the group of men who established the vision of a union of Irishmen in the socially progressive and economically prosperous town of Belfast, but few attempts have been made to unravel his contribution to this project. His newspaper did much to politicise a mass of people at a time of limited representation, but even the *Northern Star* remains relatively unknown in the region where it was conceived. In the uncertainty of the 1790s, Samuel Neilson referred to himself as 'an unfortunate, persecuted northern incendiary'. The following chapters aim to address the deficit of historical recognition and establish him as a significant player in the lives and times of the United Irishmen.

1

Son of the Manse

The parish of Drumballyroney in County Down lies in the shadow of the Dromara Hills, with the Mourne Mountains as its spectacular backdrop. Consisting of twenty-three townlands, the parish contains the town of Rathfriland, the ancient seat of the Magennis family, the expropriation of whose land in the aftermath of the 1641 Rebellion consigned that great Gaelic clan to a long period of rudderless uncertainty. The parish derives from the Gaelic *Drum Baile Ui Ruanadha*, meaning 'the ridge at the settlement of O'Roney'. Steeped in ecclesiastical and literary matters, the O'Roneys were closely associated with the powerful Magennis family and shared their fate as land-ownership patterns changed dramatically in the seventeenth century with the arrival of Scottish and English settlers. These denominational shifts saw the proliferation of Presbyterian meeting houses across what had been a strongly Catholic and Gaelic region.[1]

By 1708 the Presbyterian church in Rathfriland was too small to accommodate the large numbers of settlers and so a new meeting house was established in the village of Ballyroney in Lackan townland, with Mr James Moore ordained on 25 August 1709.[2] The fourth minister of this congregation was Reverend Alexander Neilson, who was born near Randalstown in County Antrim on 16 April 1714. Neilson was licensed by the Templepatrick Presbytery in 1750 and ordained by the Dromore Presbytery on 20 August the following year. Two months later, he married the 21-year-old Agnes Carson, a widow with a young daughter, Mary, from a previous marriage to one William Finlay.[3] The couple would have thirteen children, nine of whom would survive childhood. The first son, John, would die just weeks short of his third birthday and two more, both named James, died on 18 September 1768 and 29 April 1777 respectively. Another son, Robert, born in March 1776, would survive barely three months. A second son named John (born 18 February 1757) survived into adulthood and achieved success as a woollen draper in Belfast. Three of Reverend Neilson's other sons, Samuel, Alexander and Thomas, would follow John to Belfast and each of them made significant contributions to the commercial life of the town.[4]

Under the stewardship of Alexander Neilson, the Ballyroney meeting house was rebuilt in 1759 and would host services for the next seventy-three years.[5] The manse was situated at Ballybrick, McGilbrick's townland (*Baile Mhic Giolla Bhric*), close to what is now Katesbridge, which straddles the River Bann on the townland's eastern boundary.[6] One year after Reverend Neilson's death on 8 May 1782, William Fletcher was ordained as minister and served the congregation until 1824, although the Neilson brothers would remain freeholders at Ballybrick until financial circumstances dictated otherwise in 1798.[7] Samuel Neilson was born close to midnight on 17 September 1762 and baptised by Reverend John King, minister of the neighbouring Dromara Presbyterian church.[8] He was educated at home by his father and at a nearby school, probably in Rathfriland.[9] Like many young men, he was drawn to the industry of the expanding towns and so he moved to Belfast to serve as an apprentice in the woollen business established by his older brother, John, who would have a profound effect on Samuel's business and political development.

By the end of the eighteenth century, Belfast was a bustling port, benefiting greatly from the increase in trade and manufacturing that had been a consequence of the slow liberalisation of Ireland's commercial relationship with England. The pages of the *Belfast News-Letter* from the time reveal a vast array of occupations, but it was the capacity to import and export a range of desirable items that contributed most to the creation of a prosperous town that was both modern in outlook and capable of sustaining an affluent merchant class. Belfast had received its charter in 1613 and was the political preserve of the Chichester family, Colonel Arthur Chichester having been created the First Earl of Donegall in 1647, during the fateful reign of Charles I. As it was a parliamentary borough, the landlord could secure the election of two members of the Irish Parliament by virtue of the combined votes of a town sovereign and twelve burgesses, the latter appointed for life.[10] The extent of Belfast's population growth between 1782 and 1791 was measured by the town's High Constable, Robert Hyndman. By 1791, there were 18,320 people living in this busy port at the entrance to Belfast Lough, an increase of 5,000 on the 1782 figure. An additional 1,208 people resided at Ballymacarrett, an adjunct to the town on the far side of the River Lagan, across the impressive twenty-one arches of the Long Bridge, constructed in 1682.[11]

The growth of Belfast was managed by the establishment of a civic culture, dominated by the input of its 'respectable' citizens. The Poor House was opened in 1774 to give relief to the destitute and tackle the concomitant problems of begging and alcoholism. A banking enterprise was created and in 1783 the Chamber of Commerce was formed by some of the town's most reputable businessmen. This was a progressive act that placed Belfast's forward-thinking and innovative mercantile elite alongside that of Dublin and Glasgow, both much larger centres, where chambers of commerce had been founded in the same year.[12] A public subscription for the erection of a white linen hall to consolidate Belfast's position at the centre of Ulster's cloth trade raised the impressive amount of £17,750 and John Neilson's business contributed significantly to this.[13] The focus of commercial and recreational life was the Belfast Exchange, built in 1769 at the four corners of what are now Waring Street, Bridge Street, Rosemary Street and North Street. A second storey was added seven years later to provide the town with a tearoom and an assembly room, the venue for many important meetings and cultural events.

John Neilson's arrival in Belfast coincided with the beginning of an exciting era in Irish politics. The outbreak of the American War in 1775 caused some debate among Irishmen, especially in Ulster, as thousands had emigrated from Ulster in order to avail of the opportunities offered by a life in the New World. While there was considerable sympathy for the grievances of the Americans in their struggle against the injustices of British rule, the exodus of much of the garrison in Ireland was of more immediate concern, due to the age-old fears of invasion by one of England's traditional enemies, such as France or Spain, both of which had become involved in the war by 1779. A spirit of civic duty and service came to the fore, as it had done in the past, most notably during the Seven Years' War when there was a small French landing at Carrickfergus in 1760, and Volunteer companies, led by prominent Protestant personalities, were formed across the island. The first Volunteer unit was formed in Belfast, with the initial muster of the Belfast First Volunteer Company on St Patrick's Day 1778.[14] A second unit, the Belfast Volunteer Company (often referred to as the 'Blue Company' because of its distinctive uniform) was established shortly afterwards. The Volunteers gathered regularly and drilled in the manner of the English army so they would be ready to rally in the event of an invasion, as well as to act as a peace-keeping civilian defence body. The competence of the Volunteers in repelling hostile forces was never to be tested, but regular meetings occurred, often followed by dinners, toasts and political discussions, during which the grievances of many Irishmen, both within and without Dublin's College Green Parliament, were aired.

In existence since the thirteenth century, the Irish Parliament shared many of the characteristics of the Westminster model, with the king, the Lords and the

Commons providing the framework for administration. The king's wishes were represented by the Lord Lieutenant, who was assisted by the Chief Secretary, and the management of the legislature was carried out as effectively as possible through the use of patronage and pensions. The limitations of the Irish Parliament were obvious and related to the fact that since the passage of Poynings' Law in 1495 and the Declaratory Act (Sixth Act of George I) in 1720, legislation before the Irish Parliament had to be approved by the English Privy Council and was subject to English parliamentary control.[15] This weakness of the Irish Parliament was a grievance among many of the politically privileged Ascendancy class, which enjoyed a virtual monopoly in legal, political, military and civil matters as a consequence of the Williamite victory in 1691 and the resulting enactment of the penal laws, which created this elite Anglican minority. Their sense of injustice was articulated best in the writings of William Molyneux MP and Dean Jonathan Swift of St Patrick's Cathedral, Dublin. The emergence of this 'Patriot' viewpoint found support among those members of the Irish Parliament who were less likely to be seduced by the rewards offered by the Lord Lieutenant. The Patriot voice in Parliament called for the easing of trade restrictions on Ireland and the granting of legislative independence, a measure that would, in the first instance, confirm the ascendancy of the dominant class.

The Volunteers sympathised with the reformers' demands, and leading exponents of the Patriot cause, such as Lord Charlemont and Henry Grattan, became the commanding figures within the movement. The First Volunteer Company would play a major role in the life of the town and contained some of its leading figures, such as the merchant Waddell Cunningham, reputedly the wealthiest man in Belfast. Looking resplendent in their scarlet uniforms with black velvet facings, the First Volunteer Company mustered and drilled on occasions such as St Patrick's Day, when military manoeuvres would be conducted before dining at the Donegall Arms on High Street, the most refined of Belfast's many hostelries.[16] Significantly, the Volunteers saw themselves as distinct from the operation of official military units. Purchasing their own uniforms and weapons and electing their officers, they regarded themselves as citizens with arms, independent and resourceful exponents of civic virtue and responsibility. A typical example of these Volunteer units was the Rathfriland company, formed just a couple of miles from Neilson's birthplace. Rejecting the disciplinary code of the regular military, the men refused to subject themselves to corporal punishment, pledging instead to pay fines set by a court martial composed of their officers and twelve privates, chosen by their peers. Fines would be imposed for absence from drilling or church services, lateness, drunkenness on parade and laughing or being disorderly in any way while under arms. Those in arrears with their dues would have their weapons recalled. Expulsion would require the assent of two-thirds of the company.[17]

The growth of the Volunteer movement throughout Ulster would boost the profitable textile trade in Belfast, with shopkeepers and manufacturers providing uniforms, flags and the numerous quasi-military decorations that would adorn the dress of the town's upwardly mobile citizens. For businessmen like John Neilson, the opportunities offered by the increasing numbers of Volunteer companies were central to the town's prosperity, despite the obvious trading difficulties caused by the American War. John had served his apprenticeship in the textile business under a James Crawford and commenced business on Waring Street, at its corner with Bridge Street, in July 1778. He also opened a shop at 19 New Row on Dublin's Thomas Street, where he sold pins and knitting needles.[18] John Neilson was himself a member of the Belfast First Volunteer Company, serving as one of twenty-three privates in the Light Infantry, alongside his future business partner James Hyndman.[19] He also provided the materials required by any volunteer officer, advertising a range of coloured cloths and supplying 'gentlemen in the army and Volunteer Companies, with every article in the REGIMENTAL WAY'.[20] He established the Irish Woollen Warehouse in partnership with Hyndman and traded from his prime site close to the Exchange. Additionally, he assumed control of a clothing shop on High Street, adjacent to the town's post office, succeeding his uncles John and James Carson.[21] John married Martha McClelland on 16 March 1780 and together they had five children, all baptised in the Third Belfast Presbyterian church in Rosemary Lane.[22]

In doctrinal terms, this congregation was the most orthodox in the town, dating back to 1721, when some members of the First and Second churches (both of which were non-subscribing) grew unhappy with the conduct of services and appealed to the Synod of Ulster for permission to form a new congregation. The Third congregation meeting house, built at a cost of £1,300, stood on the site currently occupied by the County Antrim Provincial Masonic Hall on Rosemary Street. Opposed to the New Light beliefs of the non-subscribers, who emphasised the inherent capacity of man for virtue rather than his total enslavement by original sin, the Third Presbyterian church was traditional in its theology and, unlike the other two congregations, subscribed to the Westminster Confession of Faith, with its disdain for the Roman Catholic hierarchy.[23] The committee book for the Third Belfast Presbyterian church reveals that John Neilson was both a member of the church session in 1784 and one of its trustees, while he later acted as secretary of the congregation.[24]

The achievement of free trade for Ireland in 1779 was one of the great victories of the extra-parliamentary campaign that was established to demonstrate support for the efforts of the Patriot cause in the Irish Parliament. Buoyed by this success, Grattan (at that stage the MP for Charlemont borough) campaigned for legislative independence and this was granted in May 1782 by a new administration in London under the Second Marquis of Rockingham, which amended Poynings' Law and repealed the Declaratory Act. Pressure from the Volunteers undoubtedly lent extra weight to the endeavours of Grattan and his parliamentary colleagues. Delegates from across Ulster had gathered at Dungannon the previous February and their resolutions included calls to end the continuing influence of Poynings' Law, as well as a general welcome for the relaxation of the penal laws against Catholics.

By this stage, the Volunteers had demonstrated an ability to guard Ireland's shores against attack and police the streets with a degree of efficiency. In July 1781, eighty-two corps descended on Belfast for a military review, prompting the progressive *Belfast News-Letter* to note that 'many of the corps exhibited a perfection of discipline which would do honour to the most experienced troops'.[25] Such active demonstrations of men in arms, combined with the proclamations of citizenship during events that became increasingly politicised, pushed many landowners to take a step back from the companies that they had been very keen to raise just a few years before. Grattan himself was satisfied with the concessions gained in 1782. His response to a message from the Belfast First Volunteer Company thanking him for his efforts in helping to secure legislative independence but questioning whether the Westminster Parliament had, in fact, renounced in perpetuity its right to legislate for Ireland was politely rebuffed. Grattan had perceived their concerns to be 'ill founded'.[26] John Neilson's company sided with Henry Flood, Grattan's rival for the leadership of the Patriots, who used the so-called renunciation dispute to steal a march on his rival. On 6 July 1782, Flood responded to a letter sent to him by Waddell Cunningham on behalf of the unit, expressing gratitude for its acknowledgement of his claim that the simple repeal of the Declaratory Act was inadequate and did not confirm the independence of the Irish Parliament. The Belfast First Volunteer Company duly admitted Flood as a member of the corps, an act that prompted the warm response that 'You render Belfast more dear to me than ever.'[27]

A Renunciation Act, confirming the British Parliament's concession to the Irish legislature, was finally passed and while it seemed that the Volunteer moment was ending, the citizens of Belfast would find it difficult to dispense with the voice that gave expression to its political, commercial and civic aspirations. A further grievance was the disputed election at Carrickfergus in 1783, when Waddell Cunningham triumphed over Lord Donegall's nominee, only to be unseated after a successful petition alleging corruption and malpractice among the supporters of the Volunteer captain. The resentment that this caused added to the frustrations already felt by those progressive individuals in Belfast who were opposed to the planting of candidates in boroughs that were influenced by powerful landowners. In August 1783, John Neilson added his name to a list of members of the reformist Constitution Club, which included Cunningham (as well as men like Thomas McCabe, Henry Haslett and Robert Simms, who would later have United Irish connections). Members sought to show 'their determination to support the cause of Liberty, and more particularly the freedom of Election on the borough of Lisburn'.[28] In the election of that year, Lisburn returned two members with Volunteer connections, William Sharman and William Todd-Jones, in what was a startling defeat for the borough's patron, the Earl of Hertford. The inability of any independent candidate to challenge the control of the Chichesters in the closed parliamentary borough of Belfast would remain a frustration for the Volunteers of that town, who threw their influence behind Sharman and Todd-Jones. While the Lisburn victory was noteworthy, it was a chink of light in an otherwise chastening period for the supporters of reform. While a second Volunteer convention was held in Dungannon in September, there were fewer delegates in attendance than the previous year. A national convention in Dublin's Rotunda in November revealed divisions in the ranks and a diluted series of proposals calling for reform was rejected by the Irish Parliament, with many MPs believing that the extra-parliamentary pressure group, which had brought moral and political force to the campaign for legislative independence the previous year, was now threatening to usurp the power of the legislature itself.

While the momentum for reform was subsiding in many parts of the country, Belfast continued to seek redress of the grievances that stemmed from the political control exerted by the Donegall family. A second newspaper, *The Belfast Mercury; Or, Freeman's Chronicle*, was established in 1783 to provide an outlet for the reforming instincts of a frustrated merchant class that was accumulating large fortunes but which seemed incapable of overcoming the political obstacles placed before it. The paper was printed by John Tisdall, a member of the Belfast First Volunteer Company's band, from his print shop at No. 28 Bridge Street. The *Mercury* adopted a patriotic and reformist tone and would have enjoyed the support of many in the town for whom 1782 marked the beginning, and not the end, of the campaign for political change. In January 1784, public meetings were called to demonstrate impatience with the system of electing the town's two MPs and support for the Volunteers was affirmed. John Neilson was among those reformers who called for a meeting to show their approbation for the removal of men 'whose principle and conduct was inimical' to the Crown, the Lords and the people.[29] This was undoubtedly a reference to the departure of the Earl of Northington from the viceroy's office and there were false reports that the popular George Townshend would return to the post he had held some years before. John Neilson would be asked to serve as secretary of the committee charged with organising the annual Belfast review scheduled for the Twelfth of July commemoration of King William's victory at the Boyne. The Williamite triumph had guaranteed not just a Protestant succession but a monarchy that was circumscribed by an ebullient English Parliament, which had removed the Catholic King James from the throne in 1688. The review would be an occasion for the celebration of liberty and, despite falling numbers across Ireland, the Volunteer companies of Belfast were hopeful that an encouraging turnout would be achieved, although the deadline for confirming attendance had to be extended to 1 June.[30] In a bold statement underlining its tolerant outlook, the Belfast First Volunteer Company announced that men of all ranks and religious views were to be allowed to acquire knowledge and use of weapons.[31] Notwithstanding their commemoration of the Jacobite defeat, Volunteer units marched to attend the celebration of the Mass on 30 June and, having raised considerable sums to pay for the building of the town's first Catholic church in Crooked Lane, were warmly welcomed by the parish priest, Hugh O'Donnell.[32]

The liberalism that pervaded Belfast in the aftermath of legislative independence was a product both of its free-thinking, democratic Presbyterian tradition and the fact that there were so few Catholics in the environs, allowing the town's dissenting majority to express sympathy for the plight of Catholics without feeling threatened in any numerical sense. This was in contrast to the rather more complex sectarian geography of places like County Armagh, which would become all too apparent in the future. In the days before the review, this progressive population was treated in the Belfast playhouse to Mr Rowe's portrayal of the Swedish patriot-king Gustavus Vasa, a performance which 'went off with that gust of applause which might naturally be expected from an assemblage of patriots, feeling alive to the animated sentiments of LIBERTY which the above play is so admirably calculated to inspire'.[33] The review itself was held just outside Belfast and was attended by companies from Killinchy, Donaghadee, Ards, Whitehouse, Banbridge, Killead, Larne and Ballymena. Outside the White Linen Hall, four pieces of artillery sounded the salute to Lord Charlemont, the commander-in-chief.[34]

While John Neilson was establishing a reputation as an affluent businessman and as one of the foremost reformers in Belfast, his younger brother, Samuel, was learning his trade and familiarising himself with the array of goods that were available for purchase. There is no record of his involvement in political meetings or Volunteer activities before late 1784, although in the weeks before the review in July, the *Belfast Mercury* reported the existence of a 'patriotic furor [*sic*] which now pervades the spirited young men of this town' and that the local Volunteer units were being infused with the energy of no less than one hundred active recruits.[35] This may have been the occasion of Samuel's graduation into political activity. He was now 21 years of age and had served his apprenticeship, freeing him up to play a more active role in matters of public interest, at a time when the declining Volunteer movement was seriously addressing the questions of parliamentary reform, an end to corruption and the empowerment of Catholics. In October, the town's inhabitants met to elect delegates to a national congress to be held in Dublin. The refusal of some towns and counties to send any deputies to a gathering that bore many of the hallmarks of an alternative assembly and which had incurred the hostility of the Attorney General John Fitzgibbon is an indication of the divisions that existed among those who had been keen to pursue greater change after the Constitution of 1782 and those who were satisfied with the progress that had been made. The Belfast meeting agreed to send the Lord Bishop of Derry (who was unable to attend due to illness), Counsellor Alexander Stewart, Robert Thomson, Henry Joy junior and Rev. Sinclare Kelburn, the minister to the Third congregation. The congress itself was of limited consequence, but the town meeting marked Samuel Neilson's introduction into the political life of Belfast as he was one of the signatories who had called for the gathering.[36] Neilson was rubbing shoulders with Tisdall, the printer William Magee, Thomas McCabe, Robert and William Simms and Robert Getty, all prosperous businessmen with aspirations that would, in due course, see them all embark on a more radical political trajectory.

Of more immediate importance was Samuel Neilson's romance with Anne Bryson, the daughter of William Bryson, a wealthy merchant who was a member of the third division of the First Volunteer Company and one of the commissioners who would regulate the affairs of the Third congregation, the church which both Samuel and John Neilson attended. The couple were married on 3 October 1785 and five children, Agnes (commonly called Anne), Sophia, Jane, William and Mary, would survive infancy.[37]

John and Samuel Neilson continued to develop their business interests in partnership with James Hyndman and, in July 1786, the Irish Woollen

Warehouse moved into premises next to the Waring Street sugarhouse, opposite the Exchange.[38] In an advertisement placed in the *Belfast News-Letter* the previous month, John Neilson had indicated that they were still servicing the needs of Volunteer companies, providing epaulettes and other dress in advance of the seventh annual Twelfth of July review. The First Company marched to Holywood in advance of the proceedings to practise manoeuvres and although the absence of Volunteer units from Armagh and Lambeg was regretted, the impressive level of military discipline demonstrated by the thirty-nine corps that attended the Belfast event was proof that the movement had not completely dissolved.[39]

Aside from political matters, the philanthropic tendencies of townspeople provided the means for Belfast's first Sunday School, which met under the auspices of the Amicable Society in March, with over one hundred children being admitted. The cost of establishing this provision for the poor was raised by public subscription. By the end of the year, it was hoped that the school would become permanent and one of the Neilson family (possibly Samuel) was appointed to a committee with this remit.[40] A spirit of commercial co-operation was witnessed towards the end of the year when Samuel Neilson took responsibility for raising money to compensate the losses incurred by John Cunningham, a carman from the town who had saved merchandise belonging to traders after a fire broke out in the stables of one Isaac Moore near Drogheda. Cunningham's bravery in rescuing the goods being brought north, even though three of his own horses were killed, moved his fellow businessmen into a show of solidarity, allowing the unfortunate man to recommence his enterprise.[41]

The success of the family business interests was dealt a savage blow with the death of John Neilson on 6 July 1787. He died aged just thirty-one, leaving a widow, Martha, and five children, the youngest only two months old.[42] The *Belfast News-Letter* noted that he had been 'zealously attached to the liberties of mankind' and his body was accompanied by the First Volunteer corps with its artillery division, as well as the officers and men of the Blue Company, to Knockbreda churchyard for interment.[43] The Irish Woollen Warehouse would be carried on by Samuel, who set about the task of organising the company finances to the satisfaction of the executors. John Neilson's shop on High Street would be continued in the interests of his children under the name of Thomas Neilson and Company. Like Samuel, Thomas had also served as an apprentice to his late brother and had conducted the shop's business for several years before going into partnership with Martha.[44]

The Irish Woollen Warehouse continued to thrive under Samuel Neilson's stewardship and in February 1788 the partnership with James Hyndman was dissolved by mutual consent. The debts owed to the company would be paid to Neilson, who resolved to continue the business as before, in the interests of John's children as well as for his own financial benefit. By May, he had diversified, having been supplied with an extensive range of pins by an eminent Dublin manufacturer.[45] Trading under the name Samuel Neilson and Co., he was (according to the nineteenth-century historian Madden) able to amass a personal fortune of around £8,000 over the next few years.[46] He would also continue to play a significant role in church affairs, serving on a committee to regulate and conduct congregational matters, and as a commissioner, along with his father-in-law, during 1789. Neilson travelled with Rev. Kelburn to Lurgan in June as a representative elder to the annual meeting of the General Synod of the Presbyterian Church, during which the latter would stand unsuccessfully for the position of Moderator.[47]

By the end of the decade, Samuel Neilson was an established businessman with a record of good works and a strong commitment to his church. He was undoubtedly influenced by his late brother John and had followed him into the dwindling ranks of the Volunteers at a time when political change seemed further away than ever, despite the obvious limitations of legislative independence, which served only to enable the Irish Executive's control over the Irish Parliament in the form of the Lord Lieutenant. Yet within a year, the political landscape was transformed and Neilson became radicalised by the startling events in France, which, for him, served to accentuate Ireland's own servitude under an exclusive form of government that became the target of his considerable energies.

2

Belfast Politics, 1790–1

The relatively settled nature of Irish politics at the end of the 1780s would be tested by the revival of Patriot feeling over the issue of the Irish Parliament's status at the time of the regency crisis. King George III had descended into madness by the end of November 1788 and the issue of whether the Prince of Wales should be confirmed as regent precipitated a political debate between Prime Minister Pitt and the opposition Whigs, with each hoping to secure an outcome favourable to their respective factions at Westminster. For its part, the Irish Parliament was keen to assert the political independence that it believed had been won in 1782 and so Charlemont, Grattan and other defenders of the Patriot tradition aimed to invite the Prince of Wales to act as regent at the behest of an independent legislature at College Green. Political discussions were conducted at Charlemont's Dublin townhouse in Rutland Square in early February 1789, with the purpose of composing an address to the prince, asking him to assume his father's powers as regent in Ireland.[1] Although parliamentary support for such a move was secured with limited opposition, the Lord Lieutenant, the First Marquis of Buckingham, refused to communicate the request to the Prince of Wales, deeming it to be contrary to his oath of office.[2] A constitutional crisis loomed and was averted only by the sudden recovery of the monarch, who was sufficiently strong to take a two-hour early morning airing on 11 March before breakfasting with the queen at Kew Palace.[3]

The Prince of Wales was known to be well disposed towards the Whig interest at Westminster and a change in administration would have meant a new viceroy. Despite this, Belfast seemed to be relatively unexcited by the controversy and when the First Volunteer Company met to commemorate its eleventh anniversary on St Patrick's Day 1789, the monarch was toasted with enthusiasm. A sad note, on this occasion, was that one of the town's young inhabitants was found suffocated in his bed as a result of intoxication, which was a result of the general celebration of the king's recovery. One week later, the people of Belfast sent their best wishes to George III on the occasion of his restoration to good health.[4]

The spirit of the Volunteers had been retained in Ulster more than anywhere else and the sense of an imminent progressive political era is suggested in a poem entitled *The Patriot Soldier: or Irish Volunteer*, written and published in April 1789 by a member of the First Volunteer Company and dedicated to Lord Charlemont:

> I feel I feel the glorious reign commence,
> Laws form'd on right, and loyalty by sense;
> All sects uniting, partial creeds forsake.

Among the listed subscribers to this short publication were members of the company, such as Waddell Cunningham, but also future United Irishmen, like John Caldwell, David Bigger, Thomas Cruise, Robert Hunter, Rowley Osborne and Henry Joy McCracken. Samuel Neilson purchased six copies. An advertisement for his Irish Woollen Warehouse appeared just beneath one for the poem in the *Belfast News-Letter*, suggesting that he was possibly the author.[5]

Events in Paris and not London would capture the public's attention as the year progressed. Irish newspapers printed accounts of the unfolding political drama in France, noting the catastrophic state of the nation's finances and the nobles' revolt before the historic recall of the Estates General, its first session since 1614. By July, the *Belfast News-Letter* was reporting on the disturbances in Paris and noted that a number of French aristocrats were making their way to England. The term 'revolution' was now being used to describe a political crisis that saw 'the power of the King daily abating'.[6] The abolition of feudalism by the National Constituent Assembly on 4 August 1789 was a remarkable statement of political radicalism as the French Third Estate – that is, the segment of the population that was neither aristocratic nor clerical – came of age. The publication of *The Declaration of the Rights of Man and of the Citizen* at the end of that month was a bold encapsulation of all that had been achieved, reflecting Enlightenment principles in its bold assertion that the law of the land was to be an expression of the general will of the people. However, it would take some months before Irish reformers began to view the events in France as instructive. For the time being, the unprecedented political innovation there would be viewed only as news and the newspapers began to devote more and more space to stories of *émigrés* and English witnesses who had been present in Paris as the crisis erupted. The moderate *Belfast News-Letter* was at pains to stress the progressive nature of events in France in its editorials, pronouncing that the French Assembly was adopting the constitutionalism of England and Ireland, whereby one was innocent until proven guilty and all were equal under the law. The principles of Magna Carta were being upheld as France appeared to be embarking upon a path of political progress already trodden by England.[7] Meanwhile, Volunteer manoeuvres on the plains near Belfast in August were reviewed by Colonel Stewart Banks. Visiting companies contributed to the success of the day and it was noted that the spirit of volunteering was beginning to revive in Lisburn with the formation of a new corps, the Lisburn Rangers. The newly formed Downpatrick Company drilled impressively, belying its nascent state.[8]

By the autumn of 1789, leading Irish parliamentarians like Charlemont and Grattan were at the head of the newly proclaimed Whigs in College Green, taking their name from the enlightened and progressive faction at Westminster. The Whigs advanced the claim that the Irish Parliament's independence was inviolable, although the importance of the connection with Great Britain was equally upheld. An Irish Whig Club set out positive resolutions that underlined the need for Parliament to stand up against executive encroachment and, by the end of the year, Charlemont's desire for a similar club to be established in the north was reaching fruition, due largely to the influence of his friend Dr Alexander Haliday, a Belfast physician. The members of the Northern Whig Club were men of means; many of them, such as Charlemont, Francis Dobbs, Matthew Forde of Seaforde, the Earl of Moira and Gawin Hamilton of Killyleagh, were landed gentry, while William Sinclaire and Samuel McTier were prosperous Belfast figures, the former a linen merchant and the latter a notary-public and brother-in-law of the medical doctor and political author William Drennan.[9] The club's uniform, worn at meetings, reflected the affluence of its membership. It consisted of a dark blue coat with gilt buttons stamped with the Irish crown and harp. Underneath this, members wore a buff-coloured waistcoat with blue edging and cloth buttons. A blue velvet cape with gold lacing completed the ceremonial dress.[10]

This liberal spirit was highlighted during a meeting in Belfast in March 1790, with William Sinclaire's brother, Thomas, in the chair. The citizens of the town adopted a programme that complied entirely with that proposed by the Dublin Whigs – namely, annoyance at the attempts by Westminster to erode the independence of the Irish Parliament, opposition to placemen in political positions and the sale of peerages, resentment at high levels of taxation and a determination to uphold trial by jury against encroachments.[11]

Although the unfolding events in France and the establishment of the Northern Whig Club offered some hope to those desirous of political change, the main dynamic in terms of reform politics was the general election of that year, which saw closely fought contests in the county seats of Antrim and Down, if not in Belfast, with its two MPs elected by Donegall's appointed burgesses and town sovereign. Samuel Neilson was unable to vote in the latter contest, but as a freeholder in both Antrim and Down, he was entitled to exercise his franchise in those constituencies. The family land at Ballybrick enabled him to participate in the bitterly fought election in Down between the newly elevated Lord Hillsborough, son of the freshly appointed Marquis of Downshire, representing conservative instincts, and Robert Stewart (later Viscount Castlereagh), standing for the independent interest alongside Edward Ward. Neilson's holding at Skegoneill, north of Belfast, rendered him eligible to vote in County Antrim as well, where the conservative candidates James Leslie and Edmund McNaghten were pitted against Hercules Rowley of Langford Lodge and John O'Neill of Shane's Castle, both of whom had been returned uncontested in the election of 1783.[12] Many other Presbyterian residents of Belfast were able to vote for candidates in these counties and the reform-minded citizens of the town rallied around the independent ticket. On 31 March, Ward, Stewart, Rowley and O'Neill were entertained over dinner and resolutions were passed in their favour.[13]

As election fever mounted, a committee, chaired by Alexander McManus of Mount Davis near Cullybackey, was established to support 'the Candidates of the People' in the County Antrim poll. McManus was a member of the Northern Whig Club and a Volunteer. In an advertisement placed in the *Belfast News-Letter*, he called for friends of the cause to communicate any information that may be useful to the campaign by letter either to himself or to Samuel Neilson, who was chosen as the secretary of the committee managing the independent interest in the county. The committee met at the Donegall Arms in Belfast on Monday, 3 May. A second body was established to support Stewart and Ward in County Down and its secretary, George Warnick, expressed concern about corruption in the election, offering a five-guinea reward for information about bribes being given or received.[14] William Drennan's brother-in-law, Samuel McTier, was assisting the independent cause in Down, where the Londonderry interest was spending a huge amount of money in order to get Robert Stewart elected at the first time of asking. The desire to humiliate Hillsborough and his father, or, as Drennan put it, 'that the ass will at length throw the old man and his son into the dirt', maintained the popular candidates in the county and ensured that Stewart would receive assistance from reformers like Reverend William Steel Dickson of Portaferry, who would later be associated with the United Irishmen. It was said of Dickson that he had ridden one horse to death and reduced another's value by half in pursuit of the cause.[15] Robert Stewart would later follow a very different political path than that of many of his supporters, playing a leading role, as Lord Castlereagh, in the suppression of the rebellion in 1798.

Neilson's brother Thomas and other shopkeepers benefited from the public interest in the poll, advertising ribbons of all shades that could be made into election cockades.[16] On Sunday, 16 May, Rowley and O'Neill were received in Belfast by the committee that Neilson was helping to manage in support of their campaign and the candidates set out for Carrickfergus with Samuel and his colleagues at the front of the procession, followed by a band and then a number of electors on horseback. The assembled marchers wore blue cockades emblazoned with the words 'Rowley and O'Neill – the faithful representatives of the people'. At an election meeting in Carrickfergus, the two men announced their manifesto, which sought to better represent the people by abolishing rotten (or corrupt) boroughs that sent two MPs to College Green with the endorsement of only a small number of electors and by preventing placemen and pensioners from being present in Parliament.[17]

The extent of support for the independent interest in the County Antrim election is evidenced by the confident advertisement placed in the *Belfast News-Letter* as the twenty-one-day poll reached its halfway stage, with Rowley and O'Neill in the lead. The entry, possibly written by Neilson in his capacity as organising secretary, referred to the dispersal of the 'cloud of disgrace' that had resisted the claims of the people: 'The Sun of liberty breaks out with native splendour ... The hearts of Freeholders beat high in the cause of freedom.'[18] It is very likely that a published poll list advertised in the *Belfast News-Letter* on 25 June was compiled by Neilson, who was cited as the contact for those who wished to purchase it at a cost of two shillings. This may have been his first foray into printing and publishing, a full year before he conceived of his newspaper, the *Northern Star*.[19] In an age before the advent of the secret ballot, this list of voters offers a valuable insight into public attitudes in Belfast and elsewhere in the county. While conservatives such as Robert Gage, the landlord on Rathlin Island, voted for Leslie and McNaghten, Belfast merchants David Bigger, Gilbert McIlveen Jun., Thomas McCabe, William Tennent, William McCleery, Robert Simms and William Sinclaire (all future United Irishmen) endorsed O'Neill and Rowley. Of the figures associated with the establishment of that society, only John Caldwell, originally from North Antrim, supported Leslie and McNaghten, who were his acquaintances. Caldwell later recalled that he 'in consequence incurred considerable odium from my many Belfast friends'. At a meeting held in the Donegall Arms on 11 June, the committee established to manage the independent campaign opined that pressure from the aristocracy had resulted in the voting for O'Neill and Rowley being below the level expected. It was duly noted that 'We trust that the few independent gentlemen who were induced to desert their standard on the present election will, on cool reflection, see that they were betrayed into a support of their antient [*sic*] adversaries.' It was further stated that only around half of the gentlemen of Belfast who were eligible to vote actually did so, while landed supporters of the independent ticket had failed to register their freeholds and convince tenants to support the cause. It was stated that landlords who were supporters of reform should have been more proactive in granting leases to those whose electoral loyalty could be called upon.[20]

Samuel Neilson voted on 9 June, the last day of the election. The independent candidates emerged victorious, with John O'Neill topping the poll with 1,927 votes, followed by Hercules Rowley, who secured 1,855. The victorious candidates were announced in Carrickfergus and carried from the courthouse to Blaney's Inn and thence to Belfast, accompanied by a large crowd of electors, some on horseback and others in carriages in a procession extending about 2 miles. Close to the town, the returned Members were placed in a triumphal car led by six horses and fronted by a model of Hibernia with a wreath in one hand and a cap of liberty in the other. The Belfast Volunteer Artillery Company fired a nineteen-gun salute as the train arrived. The independent committee, with Neilson at the fore, dined at the Donegall Arms and the town was illuminated that evening by bonfires lit in Market Place and at the summit of the Cave Hill. Neilson would have felt extremely satisfied by the outcome of an election in which he had played such a significant role. Like other bourgeois merchants of Belfast's 'Third Estate', he revelled in the fact that he had 'an opportunity of showing that the same talents which have so much contributed to the wealth and prosperity of the North of Ireland, can be exerted with equal spirit in the cause of liberty'.[21] The election of Stewart in County Down (alongside the more conservative Hillsborough) was an additional boost to the cause of reform. Stewart was a member of the Northern Whig Club and his victory at the end of July, after a marathon three-month poll, was of equal consequence to the victory in County Antrim, especially given the power of the House of Downshire.[22]

Despite the success of the reform interest, there was some dissension in the ranks. William Sharman of Moira Castle, formerly MP for Lisburn, was disappointed by the declarations of the committee set up to manage the election campaign for the independent interest in County Antrim, of which he was a member. Sharman was absent from the Belfast meeting on 11 June and took exception to some of the published pronouncements. He wrote to Neilson, the committee secretary, in August to complain about the absence of public virtue and liberty from the committee's deliberations. Calls to manage the voting, he said, were tantamount to voters surrendering their free agency to landowners (no matter how reform-minded these landlords might be) and thus being bound into electoral slavery. Pursuing their stated goals would result in the independent interest assuming the aristocratic tendencies of subjugation that it condemned, rendering the right to exercise conscience obsolete.[23] The election provoked recrimination on the conservative side as well, with Henry O'Hara, the chair of the committee supporting the campaign of James Leslie, complaining that his candidate's prospects were undermined by 'a chain of unconstitutional influence, a system of intimidation, oppression, tyranny and the perfidy of some who recently appeared among your most attached friends'.[24]

The public fascination with the elections allowed the first anniversary of the fall of the Bastille to pass almost unnoticed in Ireland. The developing situation in France made it difficult for contemporaries to align themselves with the radicals for fear of being branded treacherous. The *Belfast News-Letter* did report on a commemorative event held in the Crown and Anchor public house in London, attended by well-known democrats such as Pitt's brother-in-law Lord Stanhope, the playwright and Whig MP Richard Brinsley Sheridan and the radical John Horne Tooke. The 600 in attendance were entertained by the sight of one of the waiters standing on a table with a fragment of the Bastille placed upon his head and Tooke stated cautiously that while the events in France were being commemorated, this did not mean that an identical change would be welcomed in England, whose constitution was sound; a display of moderation that drew 'hisses and howlings' from the floor.[25]

Neilson continued to devote his considerable energies to the civic life of Belfast, a town that was not without its social problems. A young girl of four had died after consuming bottles of spirits that had been left lying about by her parents, while a poor man thrown out of his lodgings was found dead the next morning under the market house on High Street, where he had sought shelter from the inclement weather. The *Belfast News-Letter* noted that children as young as six or seven were being employed in manufacturing because they were considered a burden to their parents, yet there was no significant development in the provision of Sunday Schools to attend to their moral and religious education.[26] The Belfast Charitable Society had been opened in 1774 to tend to the poor and destitute. Neilson was a member of the committee that administered the poor house, as was the vicar of St Anne's church, Reverend William Bristow, who was also the sometime town sovereign of Belfast. Other notable members of the committee included Robert Simms, Gilbert McIlveen Jun. and William

McCleery, all Volunteers and future United Irishmen. Neilson was concerned about the increasing numbers of poor people in the town, a consequence of the population growth generally associated with a prosperous centre of industry. The lack of money to absorb this problem forced the committee of the poor house to seek additional funds and the payment of all debts owing to the society. Indiscriminate begging had become a problem as new and transient inhabitants were given money directly, thus affecting subscriptions to the society.[27] The level of social concern shown by Neilson and his colleagues was typified by the decision in February 1791 to double the amount of outdoor relief to mitigate the effects of the harsh winter. However, such measures pushed the committee's resources to the limit and so attempts were made by this mainly Presbyterian body to 'wait on some of the respectable Roman Catholics of this town in order to know why their congregation contribute nothing to the Society – & to inform them that we make no distinction of religions in our Distributions'.[28] In March, Neilson was one of eight signatories to a request for Bristow to convene a meeting of the townspeople with the purpose of establishing a coal yard where the poor could be supplied with coal at moderate prices during times of scarcity. It was decided that wealthy subscribers to this fund would pay twelve guineas each to the Charitable Society in the form of an interest-free loan that would be repaid in May of each year.[29]

The records of the Charitable Society's committee reveal that Neilson's attendance at meetings throughout the rest of 1791 was poor. This was no doubt due to the increasingly active role that he was taking in the political life of the town and not just his devotion to the commercial success of the Irish Woollen Warehouse. Three main initiatives – the revival of Volunteering, the preparations for a second newspaper in Belfast and the establishment of the Society of United Irishmen – were making substantial claims on his time.

The approach of the second anniversary of the fall of the Bastille was awaited expectantly by the more progressive citizens of Belfast. The *News-Letter*'s detailed accounts of the events in France had convinced the town's Presbyterian politicos that the subjugation of tyranny and the spreading of liberty and general happiness were worthwhile goals and the coming of age of the Third Estate had obvious lessons for Ireland, with its flawed system of representation and the endemic corruption that was the inevitable accompaniment of vice-regal power. The increasingly radical merchant classes in Ulster viewed their political position as analogous to that experienced by the Third Estate under the *Ancien Régime* and, as July approached, Belfast became increasingly Francophile. In June, the Northern Whig Club, with Dr Haliday in the chair and Henry Joy (the editor of the *Belfast News-Letter*) acting as secretary, met to finalise its plans for an event that would demonstrate Belfast's devotion to the cause of liberty. The parallel Volunteer committee appointed to plan events that would commemorate the fall of the Bastille resolved that several of the corps would parade in full uniform on 14 July and would fire together 'in commemoration of that great event' before retiring to the White Linen Hall to publish resolutions to mark the occasion. Neilson was a member of this organising committee and intense efforts went into making the day a success.[30]

Even more significantly, Neilson was actively involved in establishing a secret committee of Volunteers that was pursuing a more active political agenda, one that was not likely to be published or distributed for the foreseeable future. The late historian A.T.Q. Stewart cited a document dated 1 April 1791 and signed by Neilson, John Robb, Alexander Lowry, Thomas McCabe and Henry Joy McCracken:

> That we the undersigned do solemnly declare ourselves in favour of the proposal by Samuel Neilson, a merchant of this town whose name is firstly subscribed hereto, to form ourselves into an association to unite all Irishmen to pledge ourselves to our country, and by that cordial union maintain that balance of patriotism so essential for the restoration and preservation of our liberty, and the revival of our trade.[31]

Herein lay the genesis of the Society of United Irishmen. This secret committee met clandestinely at the public house owned by Peggy Barclay in Sugarhouse Entry, which connected Waring Street to High Street and was located just behind Neilson's home and workplace. The first part of Thomas Paine's *Rights of Man* was, by this stage, in circulation in Belfast. In this powerful and at times vitriolic rejoinder to Edmund Burke's damning indictment of the French Revolution published the previous year, Paine denounced governments and institutions that were based on heredity and perpetuated by the denial of man's inalienable rights.

Neilson was not the only one to conceive of a new political association at this time. William Drennan, the son of Reverend Thomas Drennan (the former minister of the First Belfast congregation), had, as early as 1784, raised the possibility of creating an institution that would achieve the complete liberation of the country and promote the public good. Drennan's vision was for the establishment of a society similar to the Freemasons, although his ambition achieved nothing, articulated as it was in the aftermath of the Dublin Volunteer Convention, which had exposed divisions between that movement and the Irish Parliament. In May 1785, Drennan outlined his plans further when he was informed by Reverend William Bruce of the formation of a reformist Whig Club. Drennan argued that, 'Ten or 12 conspirators for constitutional freedom would do more in a day than they would do in ten. I should like to see a constitutional covenant drawn up, solemnly recapitulating our political creed, and every man who chose shd. subscribe his name to it. This would be a breaking down club – yours is but a switch, a rattan.' He later went further, suggesting that a small but dedicated band of reformers, mysterious as Freemasons, should separate itself from more moderate opinions and he hoped 'that such a constitutional conspiracy ought to take place as a means of perpetuating the best and noblest of political objects in the minds of the best and noblest men in the country'.

The scope of Drennan's reform plan was not new: the debates at the Volunteer Convention in November 1783 had revealed ambitious political goals, but these had been diluted in the interests of unity. The period after 1785 was politically quiet, although calls for political change re-emerged in the years after the outbreak of the revolution in France.[32] Drennan, by this stage practising in Dublin, warmed to his theme again in 1791 in a letter to his brother-in-law Samuel McTier. On 21 May, he suggested a secret society named the Brotherhood, the object of which would be the propagation of the rights of man and the greatest happiness of the greatest number. In a departure from the rhetoric of even the most radical activists, Drennan espoused the principles of real independence and republicanism. But his dream of 'a benevolent conspiracy – a plot for the people' was exactly that: a dream that required practical drive and support. It is significant that Drennan's letter pre-dates the birth of the United Irishmen by several months, but it is also noteworthy that in an earlier, rarely quoted, paragraph, he notes that he had met the previous day with Samuel Neilson ('a very smart young man') at the Dublin home of Counsellor Dunn. It is, therefore, quite possible that Neilson, supported from Belfast by McTier, had influenced Drennan's thinking and that this 'Brotherhood' was his own vision for a Dublin-based society that would in some way mirror developments in Belfast.[33] In early July, McTier wrote to Drennan to ask for some resolutions to be forwarded on the occasion of the Bastille commemoration. McTier had clearly passed his brother-in-law's sentiments on to his fellow Volunteers because he noted that 'If your club brotherhood takes place we will immediately follow your example.'[34]

The sequence of events that led to resolutions being prepared for the 14 July commemoration was in many ways fortuitous. The 64th Regiment of Foot was despatched to Belfast in June 1790 and in September a young officer called Thomas Russell, who had been living on half pay since his return from India three years previously, was called to the town to serve as a full-time ensign.[35]

Russell left the contented company of his devoted friend, the Dublin lawyer and political radical Theobald Wolfe Tone, and travelled to Belfast, a town that he quickly warmed to, due in no small measure to the personalities he encountered there.[36] Russell's personal journal from his time in the town reveals that he was well acquainted with members of the radical set, such as Neilson, Thomas McCabe and William Sinclaire, with whom he drank in the numerous public houses that were an obvious attraction for a young and unmarried soldier. He recorded that there were 'strong ideas of having a sort of whig [*sic*] club among the tradesmen'.[37] Russell was aware that while the Belfast reformers were advanced in their attitude towards kings and constitutions (in part a product of Presbyterian disabilities under the penal laws), there remained a palpable suspicion of Catholics. French Catholics had proved receptive to the anti-clericalism that was a feature of the French Revolution and this had impressed the northern Dissenters, who were doctrinally opposed to the hierarchy and falsehood that they believed to be the defining characteristics of that faith. As long as the Catholic majority was kept at arm's length by the Presbyterians, any prospect of reform in Ireland was hampered. Russell wrote about these suspicions in his journal and also communicated his insights to Tone, who had long since recognised the necessity of uniting all creeds in favour of fundamental reform.[38] Tone had been recommended as a political author to the northern radicals by Drennan, and Russell was urged to ask his friend for proposals that would receive support from those due to assemble to celebrate the fall of the Bastille. Tone's talents as a political polemicist are clear from the rapidity with which he was able to produce three resolutions that were sent north in time for the commemoration. His first resolution was critical of the extent of English interference in Irish affairs, an injustice that would be rectified by a 'more equal representation of the People in Parliament', which was the focus of his second. Implicit in his third proposal was the belief that only Catholic inclusion in any political and franchise reform would suffice, a view that was ultimately rejected by the town's Presbyterian-dominated Volunteers, not all of whom were as advanced in their political thinking as Neilson.[39]

The *News-Letter* detailed Belfast's commemoration of the storming of the Bastille on the 14 July. A parade assembled outside the Exchange at the Four Corners at two o'clock and the impressive spectacle of the procession commenced one hour later. This consisted of the Belfast Volunteer Company, Neilson's First Company, a troop of Light Dragoons and two artillery corps pulling four brass six-pound guns. Portraits of Hibernia, Mirabeau (the recently deceased president of the French National Assembly and advocate of constitutional monarchy) and the attack on the Bastille were carried.[40] Beneath Mirabeau's picture were the words, 'Can the African slave trade, though morally WRONG, be politically RIGHT?', connecting the Volunteer interest to the campaign of abolitionists such as Thomas Clarkson and William Wilberforce, despite the fact that Belfast imported vast quantities of goods that were the product of slave labour and that Waddell Cunningham, the captain of the First Volunteer Company, owned a West Indian plantation that he had named 'Belfast'. The town's attachment to the abolitionist cause coincided with the visit to Ireland of the freed slave Olaudah Equiano, who would later lodge with the Neilsons and use the Irish Woollen Warehouse as a sales point for his famous *Interesting Narrative*. Equiano noted that he had been 'exceedingly well treated, by persons of all ranks' in Ireland and found the people of Belfast to be particularly hospitable. Neilson brought Equiano to a meeting of the Belfast Charitable Society on 17 December 1791 and, given his own experiences, it is certain that he would have been impressed by the degree of civic culture.[41]

The celebrations in the White Linen Hall produced twenty-eight toasts and loud applause for Paine, George Washington, the abolition of the Popery Laws, the recently deceased Dr Franklin, Grattan and the end of the slave trade. Messages of support were sent to the French National Assembly (replies were later received from Friends of the Constitution groups in both Nantes and Bordeaux) and great satisfaction was expressed at the healthy turnout of the town's Volunteer units.[42] However, the reluctance of some in Belfast society to accept Tone's verdict that only Catholic enfranchisement would remedy Ireland's political ills was to prove critical in his decision to offer an exposition of his thinking in the celebrated pamphlet *An Argument on Behalf of the Catholics of Ireland*, which was published in August. Tone asserted that, contrary to common perception, Catholics were in fact fit for liberty because their capacity for both rejecting the anomalies of their faith and embracing change had been demonstrated in France, where the Church had been stripped of its powers and its erstwhile adherents empowered by the dramatic events that had made them less likely to be blindingly loyal to the dictates of the Vatican. Tone's pamphlet sold remarkably well in Belfast (its intended target) and anti-Catholic prejudices there would erode over the next number of months.[43] Tone was elected as an honorary member of Neilson's First Volunteer Company, an honour that had previously been bestowed on Henry Flood when he put his head above the political parapet on the Renunciation issue back in 1782.[44] This corps had always been open to Catholic membership and its most advanced members were convinced by the need to unite all denominations behind a banner of parliamentary reform.

Tone's pamphlet also alerted the recently re-enervated Catholic Committee, a body that had been in existence since 1760 but which had become more strident by this time as a consequence of an emerging leadership that was less deferential towards the patronising attitude of the Ascendancy. This new leadership included John Keogh, Richard McCormick and John Sweetman, all of whom would feature in the attempts to create a nexus between the United Irishmen and representatives of the Catholics. That the Belfast Presbyterians knew little of the Catholic Committee and its work was a state of affairs that Tone hoped to alter when he was invited to Belfast in October 1791 for the inauguration of a new society which would further the aims of the secret committee of Volunteers that had been working under Neilson's direction. Tone quickly discerned that the political leanings of the committee were more advanced than he had thought in July. He and Russell dined and drank with William Sinclaire, in the company of the visiting American Thomas Attwood Digges, a figure of controversy on both sides of the Atlantic, who had become part of the politically radical set in the town.[45]

Tone's journal records his immediate enjoyment of Belfast and its people. On Friday 13th, he met Samuel Neilson who approved of the resolutions that Tone had drawn up for the new club, which would be named the Society of United Irishmen. The following day, Tone met the entire committee for dinner and the procedures of the new society were agreed. It would assemble for the first time on 18th with Samuel McTier in the chair and Sinclaire moving the resolutions that would define the nature of the organisation. Neilson would be responsible for arranging the printing of these resolutions. Before this inaugural gathering, Tone dined with Neilson and the two men walked to the Crown Tavern off High Street for the meeting, during which Tone and Russell informed the twenty-eight members present of the attitudes of Catholic representatives in Dublin.[46] Tone's resolutions were accepted unanimously. They were:

> *First, Resolved,* That the weight of English influence in the Government of this country is so great as to require a cordial union among *ALL THE PEOPLE OF IRELAND*, to maintain that balance which is essential to the preservation of our liberties and the extension of our commerce.
>
> *Second,* That the sole constitutional mode by which this influence can be opposed, is by a complete and radical reform of the representation of the people in Parliament.

> *Third*, That no reform is practicable, efficacious, or just, which shall not include Irishmen of every religious persuasion.

Tone's journal account of his visit to Belfast reveals that he spent considerable periods of time in the company of Digges, Sinclaire, McTier and, of course, his close friend Russell. His contacts with Neilson were limited at this stage and confined to business and it is likely that the invited Dubliner deferred to the man considered the main driver of the secret committee. For his part, Neilson was possibly wary of Tone's pro-Catholic agenda. Moderate political figures, like Alexander Haliday, Reverend William Bruce (the minister of the First Presbyterian Church) and Waddell Cunningham, were reluctant to empower Catholics unless it was a gradual and safe process. Neilson, however, was undoubtedly convinced of the need to seek representative government and was wholly in favour of the demand to remove all religious distinctions on the island, but as an orthodox Presbyterian, he was sceptical of the capacity of Catholics to deliver their side of the bargain, which would have involved eschewing the teachings of their church, which, to him, endorsed hierarchy rather than democracy and loyalty to an external power, the Vatican. This tension between his optimistic political ambition for Irish Catholics and an innate suspicion of them reappeared at several times during the decade, when he would be frustrated by their reluctance to step up to the radical mark.

Tone departed Belfast on 27 October 1791 and returned to Dublin with the determination to establish such a club there. His *Argument* had left an indelible impression on the minds of many, due in no small part, according to Haliday, to his proselytising activities. Haliday was unaware of who the members of this new society were, but he was certain that Tone had played a central role in it.[47] Neilson would have no direct influence on the formation of the Dublin United Irishmen. He was left to contemplate the political direction that the most progressive of the Belfast Volunteers had taken. If the exciting new programme was to spread, a second newspaper that would provide an alternative analysis to the moderate editorial position of the *News-Letter* became a necessity and so it was to this purpose that he turned his attention.

The *Belfast News-Letter* had enjoyed an almost uninterrupted monopoly in Ulster since its inception in 1737, with the exception of the brief period during which the *Belfast Mercury* was in circulation under the stewardship of first John Tisdall and then William Magee between 1783 and 1786. Henry Joy's *News-Letter* was by no means a reactionary paper in 1791, welcoming the winds of political change that were blowing from France: indeed, its owner was a Volunteer and member of the Northern Whig Club. But his opposition to the immediate enfranchisement of Catholics was enough to deem him a conservative in the eyes of those of a more radical mindset who had come to realise that change in Ireland would be irresistible if Catholics were to become part of the nation's political life. The desire to pursue a more innovative programme convinced Neilson and his secret committee of the need to disseminate their principles through the printed word, taking advantage of a literate Ulster public and a culture of reading rooms to propagate the message of union and reform.

Significant progress had already been made on the proposed newspaper by the time Tone came to Belfast as an invited guest in October. Subscribers had been sought and a meeting held on 23 September at the home of Thomas McCabe on the northern edge of the town. A number of well-known radicals were in attendance, men who would enrol as members of the Society of United Irishmen barely one month later. The details of this meeting survive in the National Archives of Ireland and are set out in McCabe's handwriting. The gathering consisted of William Magee (who had purchased the *Mercury* from John Tisdall in May 1786 and had begun publishing it at the Bible and Crown on Bridge Street), William Tennent, Robert Caldwell, John Haslett, Gilbert McIlveen Jun., Henry Haslett, Thomas Milliken, William Simms, William McCleery, McCabe and Neilson. They unanimously appointed McCabe as the chairman and agreed to reach all major decisions by ballot. Where disagreement did exist, matters would be settled by a simple majority vote. The subscribers agreed to meet every fortnight and a committee of three was elected to keep detailed records of the meetings. Neilson came top in the ballot with ten votes, followed by eight each for Caldwell and Robert Simms (who does not appear to have been at the meeting). Two votes each were registered for Henry Haslett, McCabe, Tennent and Magee.[48]

Neilson, Caldwell and Simms immediately set about the task of gauging the level of interest for a second newspaper, sending canvassing letters to influential figures across Ulster, asking them to identify possible subscribers in their vicinities. Replies started to arrive by early October and while some doubts were expressed about the likely success of the enterprise, considerable approval was registered. By 6 October, Thomas Walsh of Armagh, David McComb of Dromore, Will Forsythe of Larne and Thomas Armstrong of Richill had all offered support for the venture, the latter declaring that he would be happy 'to be of service to any of my good friends in Belfast'.[49] Caldwell's association with the project was enough to convince Nicholas Browne of Dungannon to endorse the plan.[50] The residual loyalty that certain correspondents felt for Joy's *News-Letter* led to some notables rejecting the call for support. John Moore of Carrickfergus was one such figure and, with some foresight, he advised the three signatories to 'Caution your editor against admitting anything harsh or virulent, such language may irritate but will never convince.' John Boyd of Ballymoney informed Neilson, Caldwell and Simms that while he would certainly purchase the new paper, he would not wish to be listed a subscriber, adding that high prices would put off the lower orders, who, while eager for news, were generally reluctant to pay. The Lisburn physician Alexander Crawford also declined, although he wished the proprietors well in their attempts to 'cultivate a knowledge of the rights of man'. The Reverend Thomas Ledlie Birch, minister of Saintfield Presbyterian Church, would later become a staunch United Irishman who was court-martialled and forced to leave Ireland for his role in the rebellion of 1798. However, he rejected the call to subscribe to the project because he was on a friendly footing with Joy, who 'wishes well to the cause of liberty and intends to publish strictures occasionally in his paper'. Birch would not take subscriptions for this 'noble and virtuous pursuit', but said that he would procure a Mr John McWilliam to do so.[51] One new subscriber, Robert Hyde from Fivemiletown in Fermanagh, was pleased to have a competitor for the *News-Letter* 'on acct. [*sic*] of being mostly filled with advertizements and not delivered regular'.[52] The most negative response came from George Dickson from Portadown in County Armagh, an area known for the tensions that existed between Protestants and Catholics. He rejected the idea of a second newspaper with an ambition to repair the religious divisions in Ireland, arguing that 'instead of promoting unanimity and concord amongst Irishmen, [it] will tend to promote anarchy and discord'.[53] Despite objections and the obvious reservations of some respondents, the majority of those who answered the initial trawl of opinion were positive about the new project and, armed with this enthusiasm and promised support, Neilson began to take his plans for an organ of radical opinion to the next level. This would involve raising the capital required to lease premises, acquiring printing technology and employing compositors and printers to produce the newspaper.

The second meeting of the committee responsible for the establishment of the new paper was held in the Donegall Arms on 13 October, the day before the secret committee met with Tone and Russell to formulate plans for the Society of United Irishmen. Tone made no reference to this meeting in his journal – he was neither a resident of Belfast nor a subscriber, although he was no doubt aware of the plans. The notes at this meeting were taken by McCleery and it was reported by Neilson that Milliken and McCabe were willing to resign their interest in order to allow the experienced printer John Tisdall into the enterprise. This was agreed and the subscribers were then asked to release a quarter of the money that they had pledged so that the business could be advanced.[54] The title of the new paper, the *Northern Star*, was possibly Neilson's idea. It affirmed Ulster as the cradle of a politicised mass, with Belfast as the pole star guiding the spirit of reform.

Neilson was in Dublin in November, meeting an approving William Drennan, who, despite not liking the name of the paper, thought that his visitor was 'a man of the right stamp'. Neilson had asked for Drennan's help finding a motto for the banner of the proposed newspaper. The latter's suggestion (with which he was not pleased) was adopted: 'The Public Will our Guide – The Public Good our End'.[55] The prospectus was published on 18 November. Addressed 'TO THE PEOPLE', Neilson and his fellow proprietors announced that their object would be parliamentary reform based on a real representation of the people:

> To this great object the efforts of the *Northern Star* will continue to be exerted, until the venal borough trade shall terminate, until corruption shall no longer at least be publickly avowed, and until the commons house of parliament shall become the real organ of the PUBLICK WILL; then and then only shall the labours of the *Northern Star* in this great national business cease.

Additional objectives were that the union of Irishmen should be effected and the newspaper would point out any obstructions to Irish free trade and commerce, whereby England was attempting to 'impiously prescribe their intercourse with three-fourths of the habitable globe'. It was asserted that American and French news would feature heavily in the pages of the new enterprise, which was hardly surprising given how radicals in Ireland had been inspired by events in those countries. Thus, the proprietors hoped that the *Star* would become a viable concern and they appealed for support on the grounds of 'SPIRIT, IMPARTIALITY AND INDEPENDENCE'.[56]

Neilson's plans were stalled briefly due to the death of his brother Alexander, an apothecary and paint seller, in December.[57] However, he quickly returned to the enterprise, audaciously using the *News-Letter* to advertise his new Belfast paper, which would be published twice weekly on Wednesdays and Saturdays, 'with a view to the better dissemination of useful intelligence'. In a subsequent advertisement, headed pointedly 'To the People', it was announced that the *Northern Star*'s subscription price was to be 16*s* 3*d* per annum.[58]

The year 1791 had represented a seismic shift in the nature of politics in Ulster. Samuel Neilson was at the forefront of this process, influencing the revitalised Volunteers in both their Francophilia and their embracing of Catholic claims to citizenship, as well as laying the foundations for the Society of United Irishmen with an emphasis on parliamentary reform and the removal of the religious distinctions that had hitherto prevented the unity of all Irishmen. The development of this project would be hampered by numerous obstacles in the years ahead, but there was a palpable mood of optimism as the new year dawned, characterised by a commitment to the principles of liberty, representation and brotherhood. Practical issues of effecting political change were placed to one side as the lofty idealism of Neilson, Drennan and Tone offered the prospect of progress for Ireland's own beleaguered third estate. The torch had been lit.

3

Printing, Processions and Papists, 1792

The first edition of the *Northern Star* appeared on Wednesday, 4 January 1792, priced at two pence.[1] Printed at newly acquired premises in Wilson's Court, which connected High Street to Ann Street, the *Star* soon generated considerable excitement among the politicised population of Belfast. While plans to circulate the newspaper more widely were initiated some months earlier, the precise nature of its distribution had still to be confirmed and, at a meeting of the proprietors held the following day, Neilson was asked to wait upon a Mr Darby to endeavour to finalise with him the logistics for dispersing the paper across Ulster. John Tisdall and William Magee were deputed to agree terms and salaries with those compositors and printers employed at the office.[2] Tisdall would be responsible for printing the first few issues of the paper, but he soon withdrew from the enterprise, requesting the return of his printing press and types. The edition published on 28 January would have John Rabb's name at the foot of the page.[3]

The merchants of Belfast readily supported the paper by placing advertisements on the front page, reflecting both the varied and competitive economic interests upon which the town's prosperity was built and the extent of their support for the new enterprise. Much of the *Star's* content would relay news that was published elsewhere, with regular updates on events in Dublin, London and Paris. Writing in the nineteenth century, the historian of the United Irishmen, R.R. Madden, was critical of the *Star's* reliance on French news, 'copied, in most cases, verbatim from French papers; and so intent did its managers seem on filling their columns with the proceedings of the National Assembly, and Jacobin and other democratic clubs, that they seldom inserted leading articles of their own, or any original matter, except an occasional letter or some very indifferent verses'.[4]

Madden's assessment of the quality of the *Northern Star* is demonstrably unfair, in that the same criticism can be levelled at the *News-Letter* and most newspapers of the day and his comments ignored the fact that numerous contributors provided levels of political literacy, satire and propaganda that were unprecedented in such a medium in Ireland. Furthermore, the opportunities for discussing the significant matters of the day in the editorial space allowed Neilson to comment on matters in Europe as well as advocating changes to the political landscape at home. The possibilities offered by the publication of an alternative newspaper to the *News-Letter* in Belfast were intriguing, and a contributed article in the second edition, signed 'O', asserted that printing assumed the highest rank in the discoveries that have led to improvement in society:

> till the happy era of printing, the inert multitude has been immersed in ignorance, and its frequent attendants, slavery and superstition. The compositors' types and his form, are the talisman which has dispelled this ignorance, acting upon the uninformed mass, like the breath of animation on chaotic confusion ... When sections of Europe that have long slept under the torpid influence of despotism, are now awoke to liberty; it is time for this country to rouse from a more absurd vision that has ever frightened the imagination of infancy or dotage ... a large majority of the Irish people are aliens in their own country, and another respectable sect indulged only in a malignant precarious toleration; suffering under a rapacious and insolent establishment; the fruits of their industry devoured and their school lands monopolised by a useless hierarchy.[5]

Such sentiments set down a clear marker. Not only was the *Star* supportive of ending the hegemonic position of Anglicans in Ireland, it also welcomed the assertion of Catholic rights in tandem with the confident articulation of their political aspirations by Ulster Presbyterians. As such, it was a powerful exponent of United Irish ideology, celebrating the creation of new societies and delineating the programme of reform that was viewed as desirable by its enthusiastic readership.

However, such an enterprise would prove expensive and, at a meeting of the proprietors on 27 March, it was deemed necessary to raise the capital needed to run the newspaper to £1,600. At this meeting, his colleagues proposed that the absent Samuel Neilson take charge of the business of running the newspaper and that he be offered a 25 per cent share in the project, with a salary of £100 per annum.[6] A more formal and binding partnership was finalised in July, by which time the stock in trade had increased to £2,000, divided into forty shares of £50 each. Neilson, in company with William Magee, Robert Caldwell, William Tennent, Gilbert McIlveen Jun., Henry Haslett, William McCleery, John Haslett,

John Rabb, William Simms, John Boyle and Robert Simms, agreed to commit to publishing the *Northern Star* for a period of twenty-one years. Neilson was allocated three shares plus a further ten in recognition of a £500 advance by the new manager and editor.[7]

Neilson's editorials reveal much about both his political philosophy and the outlook of the radical coterie which signed up to both the Society of United Irishmen and the newspaper project. It was asserted confidently that the French Revolution had revived a moribund reformist instinct which had been suppressed since the early 1780s and that, as a consequence, the disenfranchised populace 'begin again to *feel* their chains'.[8] Events in Paris had created a climate in which it was feasible to question royal authority and challenge aristocratic power. Neilson proclaimed that the French people, having overthrown 'the tyranny of the Crown, the insolence of aristocracy, and the oppression of Judges', were now enjoying the mildest laws and the best-regulated government in Europe.[9] In the same month that the second part of the *Rights of Man* became available in Belfast, the *Star* questioned the competence and entitlements of an aristocracy spending its time on 'idle gratifications, and despicable pursuits, when the hereditary Legislators of a country shew no respect for public opinion' and stressed how it was no surprise that the masses were siding with Paine.[10] Of course, France was not a revolutionary template for most Irishmen at this stage. The powers of the monarchy had been clipped and while republican sentiment was growing there (France would be declared a republic in September), Volunteer and United Irish resolutions stressed loyalty to the king. There was indeed something of the Whig–Patriot tradition in United Irish politics at that time. This held that England's virtue had been disrupted by the invasion of William of Normandy in the eleventh century and, despite the foreign impediments placed on the political system, the country had enjoyed the benefits of constitutionalism since the diminution of royal power in the seventeenth century. However, the potential for corruption in Parliament remained large and so the solution for many radicals lay in the restoration of a once perfect polity that had been subverted over the years.[11] While the United Irishmen cannot generally be accused of lacking political foresight, there was an element of nostalgia in their attitude towards the governments of England and Ireland, with a stated affection for a contented golden age and a system that was 'laid by our Saxon ancestors, but which the Norman Conquest overthrew'.[12]

Neilson's political thinking would, of course, be transformed by circumstances in the 1790s, but his position in 1792 was essentially bourgeois and befitting his financial position. The violent attacks upon aristocratic indolence were motivated by a sense of injustice, whereby an unproductive stratum of Irish society enjoyed a virtual monopoly of power while an industrious merchant class, consisting of both Presbyterians and Catholics, was excluded from positions of political influence. Such a travesty could be corrected by the reforms suggested in the United Irish programme, which fell considerably short of revolution at this stage. For Neilson and others, a radical reform of the Irish Parliament and the removal of the religious distinctions between Irishmen would ameliorate the wrongs in Irish society, without 'unhinging the present form of government'. This would not empower the masses, for representative government was not the same as direct democracy, as Neilson was at pains to point out in this deconstruction of the ubiquitous terms 'liberty' and 'equality': 'A good many fools believe, and a good many scoundrels publish, that the meaning of these words is an equality of property – nothing more false and absurd – the meaning of EQUALITY, as practised in France – is an equality of rights not of property.'[13]

He continued this theme some months later, when, again in a *Star* editorial, he stated that 'nor is equality considered as implying the levelling of all property. These notions are artfully contrived and disseminated to bring into discredit that true principle of EQUAL RIGHTS which is the basis of British freedoms, by those who have personal reasons for wishing to perpetuate political abuse and corruption.' The definition of equality was therefore an Enlightenment and bourgeois one, and Neilson referred to Voltaire's view that equality was based on laws and their suitability for the defence of the weak against the ambitions of the powerful, not 'that absurd and impossible equality, by which the master and the servant ... are confounded together'.[14]

Neilson's business experience had helped shape his view of the masses. He was enlightened politically, but was not an equaliser of property. When a crowd of Belfast labourers assembled at the quay to complain about the rising cost of provisions and refused to disperse, his editorial referred to the protesters as 'a rabble of boys and blackguards'.[15] Earlier, in June 1792, Neilson's Volunteer corps had interceded in clashes involving weavers in Lisburn, around the same time that he and other affluent merchants asked the Belfast town sovereign for a meeting to discuss the worrying establishment of workers' combinations. The unrest caused by these developments came to a head on 14 June when working weavers were ready to launch an attack on those cotton workshops where the owners had failed to comply with their wage demands. The Volunteers were on full alert and Neilson's editorial bemoaned the fact that assembled mobs were intent only on mischief.[16]

In political matters, divisions between the moderate reformers, such as Haliday and Joy, and the radicals would be exposed during the year. The Whig

Club had been enthused by the events in Paris, but its members baulked at the idea of full Catholic citizenship. The vexing question of Catholic rights would also cause serious divisions in the ranks of the Volunteers. Radicals such as Neilson argued in favour of extending political rights to the majority, but many significant figures clung to the residual fears of Catholic disloyalty that had motivated the Irish Parliament to enact the penal laws in the first place. Lord Charlemont, the venerated commander-in-chief of the Volunteers, was certainly suspicious of any call to empower Catholics, whose lack of education and preparation for the responsibilities of government rendered them wholly unsuitable for the task. Writing to Haliday, he noted that, 'It would, in my opinion require a century at the least, of the best education, before our semi-barbarians could be brought to assimilate with their fellow subjects, or to a capacity of duly performing the functions of a citizen, before they could possibly provide themselves with bare freeholds of civilisation.'[17]

These fears surfaced during a meeting of the town's principal inhabitants in late January 1792, called after an advertisement was published in the *Star* lamenting the 'degrading state of slavery and oppression in which the great majority of our countrymen, the ROMAN CATHOLICS are held'. The call to discuss the position of Catholics was endorsed by a number of merchants, mostly Presbyterian United Irishmen such as Neilson, McCleery, Haslett, Robert Simms and McCabe.[18] The meeting was held on the 28th, with Reverend Sinclare Kelburn of the Third Presbyterian Church in the chair. The gathering discussed a petition to be delivered to John O'Neill (the Member of Parliament for whom Neilson had campaigned in 1790), who could then present it to the Irish Parliament. The resolution regretted the 'degraded' state of Catholics and asked the legislature to remove all disabilities, thus enabling them to achieve full citizenship rights.[19] The demand for the immediate granting of relief to Catholics was offensive to the moderates who attended the meeting. Haliday and his friend Reverend William Bruce, minister of the New Light First Presbyterian congregation, warned that only when the influence of priests over the laity had been reduced would the time be right to devolve political rights to the majority. They were also critical of the ideas of the United Irishmen, its radical oath and the emphasis on immediate Catholic enfranchisement, prompting Neilson to respond, proclaiming himself proud to be a member of that society. The radicals carried the day and a petition containing 800 names was presented at College Green by O'Neill (predictably to no avail). The demands were swiftly rebutted by Members, among them Sir Hercules Langrishe (Knocktopher, County Kilkenny), who was critical of the efforts being made on behalf of Catholics by their 'officious friends in the north'.[20]

Moderate reformers at the Belfast meeting, such as Waddell Cunningham, Henry Joy, Reverend William Bristow and Charles Brett, subsequently asserted that their sentiments differed from the majority only in terms of the pace and timing of inclusive reform, not its ultimate desirability.[21] Belfast Catholics met in April to thank their Protestant neighbours for their expressions of support, toasting their loyalty to the king and royalty, but also to Tone and a reform of Parliament, Kelburn, the Society of United Irishmen, Paine, and the memory of the storming of the Bastille.[22]

Neilson's new responsibilities as editor of the *Star* no doubt contributed to his decision to resign as treasurer of the Belfast Charitable Society. He was replaced by John Haslett. Neilson's brother Thomas was a regular attendee at committee meetings thereafter, maintaining the family record of contributing to the civic life of the town. He also advertised the availability of 'an elegantly finished house in an eligible situation in town, with suitable offices, to be let and entered upon immediately', suggesting that he was raising capital for the new publication.[23] The costs involved in printing and distributing a newspaper were not only financial. Just as attempts had been made to undermine the circulation of the *Belfast Mercury* during the 1780s, the *Star* too was being targeted. John Tisdall had offered a five-guinea reward back in March 1786 for information leading to the apprehension of two men who ambushed the *Mercury*'s delivery boy between Gillhall and Tandragee. He was convinced that the dastardly act was 'instigated by some malevolent person or persons in order to injure the circulation of this paper'.[24] In May 1792, Neilson too was forced to offer a reward for the capture of a thief who stole the horse belonging to the paper's carrier, as well as a bundle of copies destined for Doagh and Ballyclare.[25]

As July approached, the Volunteers once again turned their attention to the commemoration of the storming of the Bastille and this time the issue was complicated both by the fact that France was now at war with Austria and by the continuing divisions among northern reformers on the issue of Catholics. Tone had continued to impress leaders of the Catholic Committee and, alongside Drennan, was considered to be the most gifted literary proponent of the radical position. The agent to the Catholic Committee since the start of the year had been Richard Burke (son of the great parliamentarian Edmund), but his inability to inspire confidence led to his being sidelined by April and Tone was ready to fill the void. Neilson was invited to Dublin to attend the farewell dinner held in honour of Burke and responded to one of the toasts that spoke favourably of Belfast.[26] Virtually no evidence of Neilson's trip exists, but it is likely that he spent more time in Tone's company than had been the case the previous October, when the latter had come north to help found the Society of United Irishmen, because when Tone revisited Belfast in July 1792, the two men were collaborating closely on the issue of empowering Catholics.

As the anniversary drew near, Neilson advertised clothes coloured scarlet, blue and white (the French *tricolore*) and was one of a number of merchants selling breast medals of silver against a ribbon of the French colours. His brother Thomas was selling livery, buttons and uniforms in scarlet, green, blue and white with the aim, no doubt, of making the town's Volunteer corps look resplendent on their big day.[27] The plan for Saturday, 14 July, was that the infantry and artillery of the Belfast First Volunteer Company (now styled the 'green' company) would lead the procession under its captain, Waddell Cunningham, followed by the Belfast Volunteer ('blue') Company, commanded by John Brown. The Belfast Light Dragoons and the Union Regiment would then be followed by visiting companies from across Ulster. The parade would depart from High Street at 10am to march to the review ground at Falls, where the salute would be taken by the review officer, John Crawford of Crawfordsburn, County Down. The parade back to Belfast would end at the White Linen Hall, where a *feu de joie* was due to be fired, whereupon the officers would listen to resolutions before depositing their arms in advance of a celebratory dinner.[28]

The resolutions had been commissioned by the Volunteers and prepared by William Drennan and Tone. Drennan's motion, addressed to the French National Assembly, was supportive of its endeavours against foreign enemies. Tone addressed the second resolution to the people of Ireland, and his statement called for the inclusion of Catholics in the affairs of the nation. He offered nothing more radical than the United Irish-inspired petition in January. However, the moderate contingent (which included senior Volunteer figures such as Cunningham and Joy) was not prepared to be outmanoeuvred again and plans were afoot to derail Tone, who would arrive in Belfast on the 10th, soon to be followed by leading Catholic Committee members such as John Keogh.[29]

Tone's first day back in Belfast saw him join the First Company in military exercises and drink with Neilson and other radicals before retiring. The following two days were also spent in this company, although the absence from Belfast of Tone's close friend Russell (who had accepted the post of Seneschal to the Manor Court of Dungannon, County Tyrone) was a source of sadness for the Dubliner. Tone was persuaded to alter parts of the text of the Volunteer resolution in order to render it more generally acceptable, although the brooding presence of Joy and the scheming of Cunningham threatened to undermine the unanimity that Tone believed he had detected during his previous visit to Belfast. Neilson had grown increasingly suspicious of the moderation advocated by Waddell Cunningham and was angered to find that he had managed to procure an opportunity to impress anti-Catholic sentiments on some of the visiting Volunteer officers who were drinking in the Donegall Arms in the early hours of the 14th. With the resolutions due to be debated later that day, there was no time to be lost and Neilson tackled his commanding officer before waking Tone to tell him that the acceptance of his resolution was no formality and that their persuasive powers would be required in the morning.[30]

Belfast was ablaze with colour on the day of the review, with Volunteer companies processing through the town carrying banners depicting the free nations of Ireland, America, France, Poland and Britain. Portraits of Washington and Mirabeau were unfurled and the men of Carnmoney and Templepatrick carried a green flag with the motto, 'Our Gallic brother was born July 14 1789; alas we are still in embryo.' The reverse side of the banner reflected the United Irish tendency in this politically advanced area of County Antrim and its message ('Superstitious jealousy, the cause of the Irish Bastile [*sic*]; let us unite and destroy it') would have given heart to those like Tone and Neilson who were predicting a day of intense debate. There were worries that Tone's resolution might be defeated. His address to the people of Ireland called for parliamentary reform and the text had been altered by Neilson and Henry Haslett to replace the term 'Catholics' with 'Irishmen' in the hope of avoiding dissension. Earlier discussions had suggested that some more conservative country corps would reject any attempt to force the Catholic issue. As Neilson made his way into the Linen Hall, he must have wondered about the likely outcome of the discussions, for any sign of division would seriously undermine the campaign for reform and arrest the progress made by the United Irishmen in influencing the direction of the Volunteers.

Drennan's address to the French National Assembly was indeed passed without opposition. Tone's resolution recognised the theoretical excellence of the constitution but lamented the fact that some believed that reform was open to only some Irishmen. Any design to seek liberty for some while rejecting the claims of others would be tantamount to acquiescing in a system that was founded on the slavery of the majority. The sense of *bonhomie* and unity that had always been the hallmark of such assemblages was suddenly challenged by Joy's denunciation of the view that Catholics were ready for emancipation. He called for a more gradual reform that would allow the Catholics to demonstrate their fitness for liberty over a period of time and he was supported by Cunningham. Tone estimated that there were only around five dissenting voices. The original address was endorsed by Reverend Thomas Ledlie Birch of Saintfield, who declared that he would rather transport himself to Botany Bay than allow himself to abide in a country that allowed a large section of its people to remain enslaved. Neilson intervened after hearing one of the sceptics refer to the question of Catholics, declaring that the address 'no more presented a Roman Catholic question than a Church question, a Presbyterian, a Quaker, an Anabaptist or a Mountain question: the true question, if any, was, whether IRISHMEN SHOULD be FREE'. Supported in his reasoning by other radicals such as Kelburn, the solicitor William Sampson, Robert Getty and Reverend Steel Dickson of Portaferry, Tone's address was carried and the Volunteer officers retired to toast loyalty to the king, the French constitution, the success of the French armies, the United States of America, Polish constitutionalism, the *Rights of Man*, the union of Irishmen and the liberty of the press.[31] Tone was delighted by his victory and triumphed in the dejection of Cunningham, whose countenance resembled 'the Devil himself'.[32] As he became increasingly inebriated, he no doubt cheered the five-stanza song penned by Neilson to celebrate the anniversary of the fall of the Bastille:

> Gallia burst her vile shackles on this glorious day
> And we dare to applaud this great deed.
> We dare to exalt in a tyrant's lost sway
> And rejoice that a Nation is freed.
> For this we assemble, regardless of those
> Who wish to enslave the free mind.
> Our foes we are conscious are Liberty's foes,
> And our friends are the friends of mankind.[33]

Belfast was preoccupied not just with political matters in July 1792, but also with the festival of Irish music and culture that had been arranged for the Assembly Rooms by Dr James MacDonnell, a friend of Russell's and a member of the radical set. The Belfast Harp Festival attracted good crowds that were entertained by ten Irish harpists, nine of them male, and by a single, unidentified Welsh participant.[34] Tone's disdain for the festival is well documented. He was present in the Assembly Rooms on the 11th and described the playing as 'poor enough', noting that seven of the harpers were 'execrable'. He returned again on the 13th and the experience prompted his famous '*Strum strum* and be hanged' entry in his journal.[35] Tone's boredom was not the product of musical ignorance – he was an accomplished flautist – but his assertion that the harpers' festival did not in fact revive any of the lost music of Ireland's oral tradition was taken up by Neilson in the *Northern Star*, which commented that the lack of originality shown was proof that 'the Ancient music of this country is not suited to the genius and disposition of its present inhabitants'. Mozart had died the previous year and the progress in composition and orchestration that he represented had superseded ancient music and improved the performance of the players.[36] The *Star*'s questioning of the format, style and instrumentation of traditional Irish music is not a rejection of Irishness, merely an acknowledgement of advances in music. Neilson would indeed support the cultural revival in 1795 by printing an Irish-language magazine, *Bolg an tSolair*, which was edited by the Irish speaker and scholar Patrick Lynch, a friend of Russell's.[37]

The triumph of the Belfast radicals was interrupted by worrying accounts of sectarian strife in counties Down and Armagh. The precariousness of the region was caused by the delicately poised numbers of Protestants and Catholics there. Any increase in the power and status of one religious group was a threat to the other. Competition over land and employment in the burgeoning textile industry, as well as ancient sectarian feuds, was always likely to produce conflict and there existed an organised and increasingly politicised Defender movement that was determined to stand up for Catholic rights through the use of arms and direct action. The Defenders looked back nostalgically to the dominance of Gaelic families in the days before they had been displaced by the planter and one leading member of the movement, John Magennis of Ballela in County Down, declared himself the rightful chieftain of his clan and heir to its traditional territory. Exhibitions of Catholic strength, whereby Defender units would arm themselves and process in ways that would be deemed provocative, created considerable resentment among Protestants. Many of these joined bands of self-styled Peep o' Day (sometimes Break o' Day) Boys, who wreaked havoc on Catholic property and land at this time.[38] The west Down area fell under the influence of the House of Downshire and was augmented by the control exerted by minor landlords such as Lord Annesley, a well-known opponent of Catholics, who was, at that time, still closely linked to the Volunteers, although he was soon to become the scourge of Defenders and United Irishmen in the vicinity.

In truth, sectarian tension had been evident in the area for some time. John Magennis' parents were subjected to a terrifying attack on their Ballela home in March 1789, when a gang of 'Self-styled Break o' Day Men' fired shots into their bedroom and stormed into the house demanding access to weapons. Nothing was found and the men left, threatening to return.[39] The atmosphere had become decidedly worse by the late spring of 1792. The first historical narrative of the 1798 Rebellion was written by the loyalist and Orangeman Sir Richard Musgrave, whose blatantly one-sided account was considered something of an embarrassment because of its anti-Catholic bias. (The Viceroy Lord Cornwallis, to whom the book was dedicated, had asked for this tribute to be removed from the printed text.) Musgrave does, however, convey a sense of the sectarian disturbances in the south-west Down region in his description of a Catholic funeral procession which left Hilltown on Saturday, 6 May 1792. The cortège included large numbers of mourners 'decorated with ribands, carrying a flag and forming a kind of martial procession', who set out on the long walk to Ballyroney churchyard. The mourners were insulted and pelted with dirt by Presbyterians in Rathfriland and later, when the priests began to chant the requiem for the deceased at the graveside, the mourners were attacked with stones and clubs, forcing them to flee and leave the corpse unburied.[40]

This gruesome incident ignited a wave of sectarian incidents that threatened to engulf the area in civil war. The Reverend Samuel Barber, the minister of the Presbyterian Church in Rathfriland, was active in trying to quell the descent into violence. He reported in the *Northern Star* that a large amount of ammunition had been expended the following Monday and that a number of men had been killed. The next day, 'an army was assembled, consisting of many thousands, and everything ready for blood and carnage'. Barber and other local gentlemen rode to the army of Defenders and implored them to remain peaceful and the two sides agreed to forgive and forget past insults.[41] Notwithstanding this uneasy respite, the influential magistrate Robert Ross Rowan of Rathfriland was alarmed by the state of affairs, especially by the mobilising of Catholic Defenders in the locality, and wrote to Lord Downshire, the governor of the county, enclosing a copy of a resolution calling for more troops to be stationed there. Downshire's prompt response was a request to the Lord Lieutenant for three companies of foot for Newry, two for Rathfriland and one for Castlewellan in order to prevent the militarisation of Catholics: 'three to four thousand of those deluded people [who] regularly assemble every day and night training themselves in the use of arms and are purchasing such quantities of arms and ammunition insomuch that all sorts thereof in the town of Newry have been bot. [*sic*] up.'[42] Annesley was becoming belligerent, blaming the Catholics for the trouble and accusing them of becoming 'more insolent every day', purchasing every gun and piece of shot that they could lay their hands on. He also alleged that Catholics had procured the weapons they needed for an engagement with local Protestants two days before the Hilltown funeral and added anxiously that 'A Protestant can't leave the house but the bullets are flying about them.'[43]

The concerns about increasing sectarianism in the area must have been worrying for Neilson. His Ballyroney roots were strong and he still had contacts in the area, such as Reverend William Fletcher, his father's successor as Presbyterian minister and a subscriber to the *Northern Star*, who lived on the Neilson leasehold at Ballybrick.[44] Neilson considered it fortunate that several Catholic leaders had been in Belfast for the Bastille commemoration and he suggested that their good influence might be used to pacify the volatile mood in west Down. On 17 July, he offered to accompany John Keogh (a leading member of the Catholic Committee) to Rathfriland and a reluctant Tone joined the mission, resentful of the lost opportunity to make contact with Thomas Russell. They set off almost immediately, stopping for refreshments in Hillsborough before continuing to Linen Hill (at modern-day Katesbridge), the home of Alexander Lowry, a young radical with excellent contacts in both the United Irishmen and the Defenders. Lowry, a captain in the Ballyroney Volunteer Company, was a hospitable host.[45] The following morning, Neilson, Lowry and Tone set off for Rathfriland, where they met, among others, the Reverend Barber. The locals agreed that the Protestants had been the aggressors in recent clashes, but that the practice of arming and drilling Catholics was a nefarious one which was poisoning relations in the locality. The magistrate, Rowan, alleged a Catholic conspiracy with France and the imminent shipment of French arms, a possibility that was rejected by the meeting. Neilson proposed that the local Volunteer companies, commanded by Lowry, Barber and Cowan, would publish resolutions calling on their units to avoid confrontation with Catholics as they would with other denominations and requesting that Catholics refrain from such ostentatious displays of men in arms.[46] It was hoped that such an intervention would pacify the area and reduce the activities of both Peep o' Day Boys and Defenders. Local magistrates pledged that they too would 'act fairly against groups of whatever leaning'.[47]

Despite the gestures of goodwill, the problems flared up again in August and Tone departed Dublin on the 7th, having arranged to meet with Neilson in Rathfriland. However, he was astonished by the inhospitable reception that he and his companions received in the town, where they were refused food and accommodation at Murphy's Inn. The Peep o' Day Boys were active again and the atmosphere in the area was tense, so much so that Barber had actually advised against Tone, Keogh and Neilson going there.[48] Limited progress was made and by the 13th, Tone had arrived in Belfast, where he was hosted by the Neilsons and invited to dinners and drinking sessions, during which the political ills of the country were discussed. On the 16th, Neilson and Tone travelled to Hillsborough to meet Lord Downshire regarding sectarian unrest within his estate. The discussion was dominated by Downshire's son, Lord Hillsborough, who railed against both the accumulation of arms by the Defenders and the attempt by 'Dublin Papists and country Papists' to interfere in the disputes. Neilson and Tone argued that while Catholics had armed themselves, they were not the aggressors in recent incidents and that they could be assuaged by the granting of political rights on the same terms as Protestants. Frustrated, the two men then visited Ballynahinch and were entertained at Montalto House by the Whig magnate Lord Moira, who was considerably better disposed towards them than Downshire.[49]

The less deferential disposition of the reconstituted Catholic Committee under Keogh and Richard McCormick (assisted by Tone) was evidenced by the announcement in May 1792 of plans to assemble a Catholic Convention in Dublin at the end of the year. Keogh was deputed to act as a political missionary, travelling through the countryside to invite his co-religionists to send delegates to this eagerly awaited forum. Any lack of support for political reform from a traditionally conservative Catholic Church hierarchy was feared by Tone and his allies, who required unanimity if the government was to be persuaded to look favourably upon the calls for Catholic enfranchisement and trial by jury. Tone and the northern radicals hoped to convince Catholic delegates at the convention to ask for the extension of every political right, including the right to sit in Parliament. But given the incidents in west Down, it was necessary to repair any damage that had been done to relationships between Presbyterians and Catholics both there and elsewhere. Neilson's directing hand can, therefore, be sensed in the Belfast First Volunteer Company's ready participation in a Mass celebrated by Father O'Donnell in September, during which a significant financial contribution towards a new Catholic church was raised. Resolutions passed at a review in Dromore, County Down, attended by many of the Volunteers who had felt uneasy about Defender exercises in the area, emphasised that they were 'actuated by no hostile intention against our Roman Catholic fellow-subjects'. During October, Belfast's four United Irish societies published different resolutions that reached out the hand of fellowship to Catholics, recognising that three million people were 'degraded from the rank of Citizen and languishing in slavery'.[50]

As the convention approached, Neilson and the Belfast radicals were optimistic about the 'rapid progress of union' – that is, the United Irishmen – in the space of one year and were hinting at a measure of civil disobedience (refusing to pay hearth money or tithes) in order to pressurise the government into passing serious measures of reform. In a letter to Tone, Neilson recognised that not all Catholics had adopted the radical project just yet, but he was confident that one of the delegates for County Antrim, the Poleglass linen bleacher Luke Teeling, could be trusted to act in accordance with the wishes of the most advanced political actors in the county. Teeling dined with Neilson and other radicals on

22 November and the latter asserted that the Catholic delegate was coming 'to receive instructions; aye to receive instructions, for he says he will represent the county favourably'.[51]

Neilson's determination to influence the debate at the Catholic Convention from without was stepped up in the days preceding the event. He communicated to Tone, who was in Dublin, the views of a select group of Belfast United Irishmen, expressing concern about the rumours of an insipid Catholic petition that would fall far short of the more ambitious, emancipationist programme desired by the radical Dissenters. At this juncture and beyond, Neilson feared that the northern Presbyterians were taking risks for Catholics and that the latter were failing to acknowledge this. He hoped that the Catholic delegates would not 'run away' from the enemies of emancipation. The appeal from the north was that: 'In the present glorious era, we do expect that our Catholic countrymen have too high a value for the rights of man to be satisfied with anything short of them, the more so, as their Protestant brethren and fellow-citizens are determined to aid in the general recovery of those rights for all Irishmen.'[52]

In Dublin, Drennan was short of information on the mindset of Catholics on the eve of the convention, although he suspected that Neilson, whom he knew to be in contact with Tone, was one of the select few being kept informed of all the proceedings. As it transpired, this was not the case. Drennan was, however, updated by his sister Martha on the latest thinking of the inner circle of the United Irishmen through her husband Sam McTier. Drennan discovered that Neilson was not, in fact, informed by Tone about the precise mood of the Catholic leaders, a source of annoyance for both.[53]

The convention met in the Tailor's Hall in Back Lane on 3 December 1792 and the proceedings went better than expected, as delegates enthusiastically backed Teeling's call to demand full emancipation. The outcome was a vindication of the efforts made by Keogh and Tone to politicise Catholics during the previous months and plans were made to convey the wishes of the convention directly to London, ignoring the inevitable rejection that would come from Dublin Castle. However, Tone's preoccupation with events in Dublin infuriated Neilson, who had asked to be kept informed of their deliberations on a nightly basis. Neilson's personality, accessible in a range of sources, was amiable and generous. He was a gregarious individual, capable of sustaining warm friendships, but he was also prone to disputes with close friends who failed to align themselves to his way of thinking. Tone, Richard McCormick, Thomas Russell and Henry Joy McCracken would all fall foul of his temper at various times. On this occasion, Tone received a strongly worded note of disapproval:

> Slave, You have not done as I should have expected. You have, for five days of the most interesting crisis, kept us, your constituents, in the dark. We will never forgive you. We all waited, and searched, and laboured, to hear news from our friends. Then two nights – but not a word. The enemies have had abundance. Charges the most heinous are echoed against the Catholics, and we have no means of refuting them, thanks to our faithful representative.[54]

Notwithstanding the deficit in information, Neilson's *Northern Star* did report on the events of the convention and especially on its thanks to the Presbyterians of Belfast for leading the campaign for reform. The editorial noted confidently that 'the Union of Irishmen is complete' and that this would promote a new era of peace and harmony on the island. The Catholic delegation to London, which included Keogh and Tone, was greeted enthusiastically in Belfast as it took a somewhat tortuous route to the English capital. Heavy winds made it advisable to sail the short route to Portpatrick before beginning the long road journey to the city. The delegation breakfasted in the Donegall Arms and, to show their approbation of the ambition set out in the resolutions, the people of Belfast untied the horses and pulled the carriage across the Long Bridge before restoring them to the front of the coach.[55] Never one to miss an opportunity to criticise the radicals, Alexander Haliday noted dryly that when in Belfast, the Catholics had taken the opportunity to condemn the 'extreme violence' of the *Star*, which they believed would injure the cause rather than serve it. He also related (or perhaps invented) the rumour that several young men had in fact been hired to convey the carriage through the streets and huzza as the Catholic leaders departed for London.[56]

The radical agenda was now fully back on course and the northern vanguard welcomed the increased maturity of the Catholic leadership. Furthermore, a temporary truce seemed to have been established in the pressure cooker of south-west Down, the United Irish societies were growing in both Belfast and Dublin and the *Star* was mounting a serious challenge to the *News-Letter*'s erstwhile domination of the local market. But beyond the hubris, serious problems loomed on the horizon and these would depress and disillusion Neilson during the following year, throwing the entire project into jeopardy.

4

Trials and Tribulations, 1793–4

The increasingly radical state of political opinion in Belfast by the end of 1792 was viewed with serious concern both by the town's conservatives and the authorities in Dublin. The pronouncements of United Irish societies coincided with France becoming a republic and the inference made in Dublin was that the United Irishmen had become a seditious organisation bent on subverting the constitution. The emergence of a sinister association, the Irish Jacobins, in December was proof of the dangerous species of politics being embraced by some of Belfast's citizens. Chaired by Rowley Osborne (who later featured in many of the reports by government informers alleging the violent practices of the United Irishmen), the Irish Jacobins took their name from the French revolutionary club that assumed centre stage after the fall of the monarchy, advocating the execution of King Louis XVI and eventually endorsing the 'Reign of Terror' that was pursued by the club's most outspoken member, Maximilien Robespierre.

The Irish Jacobins of Belfast met on 12 December to articulate their ideas. These asserted that Ireland had no national government, that the penal laws were 'a disgrace to the land we live in' and that there should be a national convention of Scottish, English and Irish radicals with the object of achieving parliamentary reform. The secretary of the club was Samuel Kennedy, a compositor at the *Northern Star* who was intimate with Neilson and supportive of his politics.[1] Neilson's publication of these resolutions in the *Star* would contribute to the decision to prosecute the newspaper's proprietors, a legal fight which would seriously undermine the finances of the shareholders. A list of members of the Irish Jacobins can be found in the papers of Lord Camden, who became the viceroy in early 1795. This scrap of paper was most likely inherited by Camden, since it includes the name of Thomas Neilson, Samuel's brother, who died in April 1794. The list includes a number of radical figures in the town, many of whom were leading members of the United Irishmen: Osborne, Robert Orr, William Tennent, Henry Haslett, Robert Getty, William Sinclaire, William Sampson,

Dr John Campbell White, Isaac Patton, Robert Steel, Samuel McComb, Joseph Cuthbert and the minister of the Third Belfast Presbyterian congregation, Sinclair Kelburn (given the title 'Blunderbus' in the list of names).

It is uncertain whether Neilson was a member of the Jacobin Club in Belfast, although given the similarity of its aims with those of the United Irishmen, it is highly likely that he would have endorsed it. Tennent, Sinclaire, Haslett, Getty and Sampson were all men of means and intellect, so while Samuel Kennedy was a rung below his employer on the social ladder, it is difficult to regard the Irish Jacobins as an out-of-control working-class splinter organisation. Rather, as Nancy Curtin suggests, the Jacobins were part of the United Irish mainstream in Belfast, dabbling in advanced political rhetoric and acting as a 'stalking horse for extreme radicalism', while offering a degree of protection to the longer-established group. A list of the town's 'principal republicans' can be found in the Camden Papers next to the members of the Irish Jacobins. Samuel Neilson is at the head of the list.[2] It is worth remembering that Tone gave Neilson the sobriquet 'The Jacobin' in his journals, which would indicate that his views on Irish politics were advanced even by the standards of his colleagues. Martha McTier had become aware of Neilson's reputation, referring to him as 'a firebrand' and advising her brother William Drennan to keep his distance, lest any connection with Neilson land him in trouble.[3]

The idea of linking the Belfast Jacobins and United Irishmen with other radical groups in Scotland and England was not a new one. The *Northern Star* had been publishing reports on the meetings of several associations throughout 1792: the Friends of Liberty; the Society for Constitutional Information; the Friends of Universal Peace and the Rights of Man; the Friends of Freedom and the Friends of Liberty and the People, organisations which met in Edinburgh, London, Stockport, Manchester and Stirling respectively.[4] The infamous meeting of English and Irish residents at White's Hotel in Paris, during which hereditary peerage was condemned and Lord Edward Fitzgerald, the son of the Duke of Leinster, renounced his title and adopted the prefix '*Citoyen*' was also communicated to its readers.[5] Attempts to forge a nexus between radical groups across the two islands would become more significant as the decade progressed, placing the United Irishmen within a broader extremist movement, something which would alarm the administrations in both Dublin and London.

A town meeting in Belfast's Second Presbyterian Church on 26 December 1792 revealed the excitement and strength of feeling that existed in the aftermath of the Catholic Convention. Acting as secretary, Neilson recorded and published the opinions expressed, which included a damning indictment of the parliamentary system. During the discussions, Reverend Kelburn asserted that he could not approve of the House of Lords because 'wisdom is not hereditary'. Those present resolved that they held no ambition to ignite a revolution, 'deeming it the last measure of dire necessity, a measure to which no wise or good man would resort until every other means had been tried in vain'. This statement did not actually preclude the future possibility of revolution and the clear view expressed was that if such an undesired eventuality occurred, it would be precipitated by the inflexibility of the reactionaries. In Dublin, Drennan was impressed by the temerity of these sentiments, informing his brother-in-law Sam McTier that 'They speak more treason by the half than we dare to venture here.'[6] The Belfast gathering elected a committee of twenty-one to correspond with other opinion-formers about the prospects for meetings and conventions to formulate a programme for change. This committee included Sinclaire, Haslett, Kelburn, Getty, McTier, William Tennent, Robert Simms and Neilson and the endeavours of the committee would result in a Volunteer convention held at the symbolically important location of Dungannon in February 1793.[7]

The boldness of these statements was one of several signs which suggested that some of the more advanced radicals were prepared to step up their campaign. Firstly, a self-styled National Battalion of Volunteers, based on the republican French National Guard, had been raised in Dublin by James Napper Tandy, Archibald Hamilton Rowan and Oliver Bond, the latter a friend of Neilson's. The simplicity of the uniform contrasted with the expensive ostentation of northern Volunteer dress and weaponry, a point made in the *Star*, which noted: 'It is painful to see the rubbish of firearms which the Volunteers of this neighbourhood are dearly supplying themselves with, even at very high prices.' The National Guards would wear simple attire and carry cheap, but good-quality, consistent flintlocks. The First Belfast Regiment of National Guards comprised around 360 members of the different companies in the town and paraded to the Second Church in February 1793 wearing their green uniforms faced with yellow, white breeches, long black gaiters and leather caps.[8] However, the new corps quickly raised concerns at governmental level because of their similarity to the *sans culottes*, the shock troops of the French Revolution, and steps were taken to disperse them.[9] Secondly, while the control exerted over the Belfast Volunteer companies by Neilson and his colleagues meant that the United Irishmen did indeed have a *de facto* armed wing, this did not prevent society members in Lisburn writing to the movement's Dublin Corresponding Committee requesting permission to equip themselves with arms and ammunition. The committee's response was that the aims of the society could in fact be achieved without recourse to arms, but the inquiry itself is telling.[10]

Finally, the increasing radicalism of northern opinion was evidenced by the fact that the banner of the *Northern Star* had been altered, with the vignette of a harp and crown being replaced by one with a star over the harp.[11]

The apparent hardening of attitudes within the United Irish societies in Belfast (and to a lesser extent Dublin) made the intervention by government more likely and an obvious target for repression was the *Northern Star*, which had been provocative in its editorials from the outset. Haliday had been appalled by 'the many lying reports and inflammatory publications which it shamefully scatters abroad'.[12] Even moderates such as the clergyman father of William Tennent would comment that Neilson was sailing close to the wind with every edition and that newspapers should exist not to be 'partial', but to 'have both sides equally pointed out and let the public judge'.[13]

Rumours of an impending clampdown on the paper were rife in late December 1792 and Drennan suspected that action had been taken against Neilson when copies of the *Star* failed to arrive in Dublin. Martha rose above the numerous rumours of military action to inform him that two men had indeed come to Belfast with the intention of arresting Neilson and the other proprietors and that the editor wrote to the town sovereign (Reverend William Bristow) accusing him of inviting a party of Light Dragoons then stationed in Banbridge to Belfast to quell any possible disorder. Neilson was annoyed at any attempt by those in authority to calumniate either the proprietors or the inhabitants of the town, neither of whom had any intention of acting in an illegal manner. Bristow stressed that he had in fact interceded on behalf of the proprietors and it was agreed that, despite the existence of warrants, they would not be detained until clarification about bail could be obtained from Lord Chief Justice Clonmell. Neilson argued that it would be most unfair to take a large number of businessmen far away from their families and their economic interests. It was agreed that the men would not be apprehended that night but they would be expected to appear before Clonmell in due course to receive their conditions of bail.[14]

Neilson was certainly not cowed by the experience because the *Star* reiterated its position in the next issue. After celebrating the fact that its circulation was already more extensive than that of any other newspaper, his editorial pronounced, 'So long as a love of liberty exists in a people, that people will protect those who, with a single eye to the public good, publish IMPORTANT TRUTHS ... Countrymen, we embarked in YOUR CAUSE without any view to our own interest – WE WILL PERSEVERE.'[15]

The proprietors left Belfast for Dublin on Thursday, 5 January 1793, where they were received warmly by the radical set and lodged in apartments on Capel

Street. Each of the proprietors was bailed by one Catholic and one Protestant in a show of unity which repaired to some degree the dissatisfaction felt by Neilson about the lack of information conveyed north during the deliberations of the Catholic Convention. The following Monday, the northerners were entertained by the progressive Friends of the Constitution at a dinner in the Star and Garter on Essex Street, with Archibald Hamilton Rowan in the chair. Among the thirty toasts was one to the success of the *Northern Star* and its proprietors in the drive towards true liberty and equality.[16] By the end of the month, however, Neilson had been made fully aware of the nature of the charges against the owners. They had been indicted for publishing six offensive articles that the Attorney General had deemed to be seditious, among them the resolutions of the Belfast Jacobins.[17]

With no date for the trial having been fixed, Neilson could concentrate on the Volunteer convention being held in Dungannon Presbyterian Church on 15 February. Despite his steering of a secret committee of Belfast Volunteers, the movement was never homogeneous, especially on the issue of Catholics, and the dichotomy that was evident during the Bastille commemoration the previous July had not been fully resolved. The convention was held against a backdrop of rapid political change. The execution of Louis XVI on 21 January was deemed by Drennan to be right and appropriate if the revolution was to survive. The *Star* was in no doubt about Louis' 'evident criminality', but wondered whether it could have been possible to mitigate the punishment.[18] For many of the moderate Volunteer delegates, the effusion of royal blood was an excess that was in no circumstances to be endorsed. Furthermore, the outbreak of war between France and Great Britain on 1 February had a sobering effect on proceedings as there was no real desire to exhibit disloyalty at such a critical time. The convention was chaired by William Sharman, a long-standing Volunteer and former MP for Lisburn. The interests of the radicals were represented by delegates such as Reverend William Steel Dickson (Down), William Sinclaire, the Belfast United Irishman, and Dr James Reynolds, a member of the Dublin society, who represented Tyrone. To counter this, many of the counties had deputed Whiggish landowners to the convention and as the proceedings got under way it became clear that moderation would win the day. The fourteen resolutions included a declaration of loyalty to the Constitution, a rejection of republican forms of government, support for Catholic Emancipation and a call for parliamentary reform. Any moves to oppose Britain's involvement in the war against France were rejected as being divisive, although the call to establish a committee with the task of reconvening the convention when it was deemed necessary (giving the body the semblance of a parliament) must have alarmed the government.[19]

Neilson had been present in Dungannon, the '*mons sacer*' for the Volunteers, and he reported himself to be generally satisfied with the event, even though the meeting was dominated by the aristocratic interest in the counties. He noted that the 'peoples' spirit was infused into their resolutions' and while any condemnation of the war was not included in the list of resolutions, the delegates endorsed this view when it was raised separately. He summed up the long-awaited convention by saying that it was 'prudent and useful though not entirely up to my ideas'.[20] He was aware that Tone was rather cool on the resolutions and wrote to him two weeks later to offer his analysis. Still annoyed at the paucity of information coming north from the Catholics, Neilson noted that Ulster's position was clearly articulated at Dungannon, and he wished calls like these would emanate from the other provinces. The moderation witnessed during the convention was based both on a recognition by the delegates that the rest of the country was unprepared to stand by Ulster and the fact that the government had started to intimidate the northerners with a show of military strength. Neilson added that the radicals in Belfast were still uncertain about the deliberations of the Dublin United Irishmen and the Catholics: 'in short, that you leave us completely in the dark, at a time when a storm is obviously collecting round our devoted heads'. Neilson's frankness to Tone was, he said, the result of his being a 'plain and honest man' who liked to speak his mind without reserve to those he could trust.[21]

Despite his reservations about the moderation displayed at Dungannon, Neilson's public pronouncement in the *Star* that the convention 'demonstrated to the world that the whole province is ONE GREAT SOCIETY OF UNITED IRISHMEN' is a difficult one to sustain.[22] A.T.Q. Stewart has noted that County Armagh, the birthplace of plans for the original Volunteer convention at Dungannon in 1782, was now slow to respond to the call for delegates. This was a consequence of the peculiar sectarian geography that existed in an area where scuffles between Peep o' Day Boys and Catholic Defenders were commonplace. Armagh failed to send a full delegation to what was to be the last Volunteer convention and this, he argued, marked out 1793 as the year when disunity became a feature of Ulster Presbyterianism and when those based in the 'plantation frontier' were no longer prepared to stand shoulder to shoulder with their co-religionists from the less contaminated atmosphere of Belfast.[23] This trend would prove crucial in determining the fate of Ireland during the Rebellion of 1798. Nonetheless, the earlier divisions over the precise timetable for Catholic Emancipation did not manifest themselves at Dungannon and the very fact that there was even a debate on the virtues of republicanism suggests that the political vocabulary was changing. Drennan was an avowed republican by this stage and it is likely that Neilson, who felt that the convention did not measure up to his own position, was moving in this direction, even though he would never publish this in the *Star* at such a delicate time.

The storm referred to by Neilson posed a number of serious threats to the radical project. The government's legal attack on the *Northern Star* was just one method of derailing the United Irishmen and their potential Volunteer and Catholic allies. A Gunpowder Act made it illegal to import or deliver arms without a special licence, although the *Star* alleged that it would empower judges to 'enter and search any house, place, ship, boat or vessel where they may suspect any arms etc. to be deposited'.[24] Neilson's editorial on 2 March urged the Belfast Volunteers to secrete the artillery purchased by local units lest they be confiscated by the authorities, as had already happened in Dublin.[25] The implications of such legislation for the local companies and National Guard units were obvious. The Belfast United Irishman Robert Simms informed Tone that the Volunteers were taking steps to create stores for weapons, but the reality was that the authorities had determined to suppress the Volunteers and the raising of militia regiments (whereby young men in towns and counties would be selected for service by ballot) was planned to create a home defence force that could be both trusted and controlled by local conservatives.[26] The Volunteers opposed any such plans at Dungannon but were powerless to resist the initiative, which had the added advantage for the government of splitting the Volunteers by offering militia commissions to local landowners with a history of service in the movement. Also significant was the Convention Act, which outlawed meetings of any bodies that were designed to represent those who wished to alter the *status quo* in terms of church and state. This was a direct response to both the Catholic Convention and the tendency among northern Volunteers to promote periodic meetings that appeared to pose as alternative national assemblies, such as that at Dungannon.

The government seemed to be winning the day. This was confirmed by the fact that the administration, chivvied by Prime Minister Pitt, was now pushing for a Catholic Relief Act whereby Catholics would be entitled to vote on the same terms as Protestants, although they were still to be disallowed from sitting in Parliament. Again, this measure was designed to neuter the radicals by purchasing the loyalty of Catholics and limiting the potential of a dangerous alliance between them and the Presbyterians. Pitt hoped that further relief would help to ensure the security of the state at a time of war; the recruitment of Catholics to the army and navy was considered essential. An Irish Commons that had implacably opposed limited relief for Catholics the previous year was now enacting a piece of legislation that considerably increased the size of the electorate. Neilson was not slow to recognise the irony, noting how the Castle-influenced Dublin newspapers had lambasted the *Star* barely twelve to fifteen months earlier for daring to endorse Catholic Relief, only to back the measure passionately now. Asserting that Catholic loyalty had been bought, he stressed the limitations of a bill that 'removes only a *few* unjust grievances and restores that loyal and patient body to no more than a *portion* of their rights'.[27]

Of immediate concern to the advocates of political change in Belfast was the sense that the authorities seemed to be unleashing a system of terror and intimidation, drafting in troops and subjecting the residents to episodes of violence. On Saturday, 9 March, four troops of light dragoons arrived in the town from Hillsborough and Lisburn and, according to the *Star* editorial, ran amok, committing 'heavy depredations upon the houses of many of the inhabitants, and with their drawn sabres had dangerously wounded them'. One resident, Samuel Robinson, 'had his clothes cut through'.[28] The dragoons and some members of the 55th Regiment stationed in the town carried off a sign celebrating the French general Dumouriez (the hero of the battles of Valmy and Jemappes who, soon after, was to switch to the Austrian side) and attempted to detach the portrait of Benjamin Franklin that hung outside the door of the notorious tavern that was a United Irish meeting place, Peggy Barclay's Franklin Arms.

The cause of this unrest is difficult to discern, although it would seem that there had been unease in the town for some weeks. The authorities were in no doubt that the radicals constituted a threat. A short time earlier, Evan Nepean, the Under-Secretary of State for the Home Department, had written anxiously to the Irish Chief Secretary Robert Hobart, urging him to remove a quantity of weapons from the home of Lord Donegall for fear that they would be 'taken possession of by the disaffected party there'.[29] The troops stationed in Belfast under the command of General Richard Whyte maintained order in a manner that was not deemed offensive, but the dragoons did much to upset the delicate state of the town. The precise sequence of events was disputed by both the military and the townspeople. Whyte's official version was that the commotion was caused by a 'fiddler parading through the streets playing Ça Ira or as the dragoons termed it some rascally outlandish disloyal tune & desired God Save the King, the mob not allowing this and as the dragoons swear, damning the King and all his dirty slaves'. After being pelted with stones, the soldiers drew their sabres.[30] An alternative version was offered by representatives of the town. A committee of twenty-two gentlemen (including Reverend William Bristow, the town sovereign), five magistrates and the high constable attempted to remonstrate with the military chiefs. Their investigations revealed that some troops 'had avowed their intention of committing outrage against certain individuals who had been represented to them as disaffected'. The locals declared that there had been no provocation and added that the fiddler whose melodies were deemed so offensive was, in fact, blind. Bristow, who signed the written statement, declared that their argument lay with those who had stormed into the town, not with Whyte, whose conduct had hitherto been good and who was 'a friend'.[31]

Both Martha McTier and Robert Simms reported that the assailants were following written instructions provided by an enemy of the radicals who knew the town well, because among the houses and shops targeted were those of a milliner (who had provided uniforms for the Volunteer Light Horse), Kelburn, Haslett, McCabe and Neilson. Neilson's own account of the incident mentioned the attack upon McCabe's house but omitted any reference to his own loss. A large number of Belfast citizens, augmented by men from outside the town, met in Kelburn's church to organise resistance to the attack, but were prevailed upon by Bristow not to take action, advice the men were not prepared to heed. In a letter to Tone describing the affair, Neilson asserted that the Volunteers rallied to the defence of the town, forcing the rampaging soldiers to return to their barracks. Volunteer guards were mounted that evening and the homes of potential targets protected. Neilson informed Tone of how the offenders were 'permitted' to depart with their units on the Monday and that the Volunteers stood to arms as the military withdrew.[32] On the 11th, the Lord Lieutenant (Westmoreland) issued a proclamation condemning the role played by 'certain seditious and ill-affected persons' who were guilty of fomenting unrest: 'Bodies of men in Arms are drilled and exercised by Day and by Night, and that the declared object of the Said armed Bodies is Redress of alleged grievances, but that the obvious intention of most of them appears to be to overawe the Parliament and Government and to dictate to both.'[33]

This proclamation was, in effect, an order to suppress the Volunteers, a measure that would undermine the radical cause by depriving the United Irishmen of one of its greatest potential allies. General Whyte was confident that the spirit of the disaffected in Belfast had been broken with relative ease, noting how 'the leading men of sedition are greatly humbled'.[34] This appeared to be confirmed when the Volunteers remained inactive on St Patrick's Day, traditionally an occasion for drilling and celebrating (the First Company had been formed on that day in 1778). To add to the despair, the authorities in Dublin and Belfast moved quickly to arrest and charge leading United Irishmen, such as Simon Butler and Oliver Bond, the chairman and secretary of the Dublin society, who were indicted by the House of Lords for a supposed calumny on its practices after they alleged that its Secrecy Committee had changed itself into an inquisition, whose proceedings were 'illegal, unconstitutional and offensive'.[35] The men were fined and imprisoned in Newgate for six months, during which they were supported financially by their colleagues and entertained lavishly at banquets in the gaol. Help was guaranteed from Bond's friends in the north. His family placed a notice in the *Star*, advising customers that his business on Dublin's Bridge Street would continue operating during this difficult time. In the same edition, Neilson advertised the letting of Bond's cotton factory with all its machinery in the vicinity of Dublin, where 'the tenant need not lay out one shilling'. Further insult was added to injury when a Belfast tailor and ladies' habit-maker, Joseph Cuthbert, was charged with circulating an extract from a seditious pamphlet written by the Manchester academic and radical Thomas Cooper among members of the 55th Regiment, as well as shooting at an excise officer. Cuthbert was pilloried for one hour and confined in Carrickfergus Gaol for a year, from where he engaged a foreman to look after his business interests in Belfast.[36]

Neilson's own circumstances were being tested during these difficult times. In March, he advertised for a partner to invest 'about four or eight hundred pounds in business, where no personal attendance will be necessary'.[37] It is possible that he was preparing for the heavy costs involved in defending the integrity of the *Northern Star* in the courtroom, but it is more likely that the Irish Woollen Warehouse was suffering due to the economic dislocation created by the war. In his editorial on 11 May, Neilson wrote:

> Six months ago manufactures flourished, money was plenty and trade of every kind brisk, the people were strong and corruption shaken to its base; – a cry was made that government was weak and must be made strong; their hands were strengthened with a vengeance; – a gunpowder bill – a militia bill – an alien bill – a vote of credit – a vote of augmentation of the army, were passed – the volunteers were put down and the gaols were filled with patriots! – Behold the consequence! – see trade annihilated – money not to be had – the manufacturers starving – the Gazette filled with bankruptcies – and all public and private credit at the last gasp – such are the consequences of a strong government.[38]

Neilson's fortune had eroded during his years of active political involvement as he became distracted from his business interests. Furthermore, the newspaper enterprise had become a financial risk for all of the proprietors and, with legal sanctions looming, some were beginning to rethink their stake in the business. By the summer, the Belfast moderate Reverend William Bruce, minister of the

First Church, had intimated to Drennan that 'the *Star* people were all wishing to give up the paper, if they could dissolve their agreement ...'[39] The haemorrhaging of support for the radical project certainly became more pronounced in the months before the rebellion of 1798, when the consequences of sedition and the risk to personal wealth and industry became all too apparent. For now, however, there were decisions that needed to be made; to carry on with the newspaper in its current form would bring attendant risks. The alternatives were to close the newspaper or conform to the government's position. In June, the proprietors gave Robert Simms and Neilson the power to prepare their case for the courtroom or negotiate with the government with only one, John Haslett, dissenting.[40] Russell hinted that the proprietors were indeed 'in contemplation to sell the *Northern Star* to goverment [*sic*]' and that John O'Neill, the MP for County Antrim, was acting as an intermediary in a negotiation between the proprietors and the Castle, whereby the *Star* would avoid political controversy in return for the charges against the newspaper being dropped.[41]

The problems persisted. On Monday, 12 April, a party of artillery soldiers, accompanied by members of the 38th Regiment, rampaged through Belfast and spent a second night intimidating the local population. This time the signs above both the Franklin Arms (which had withstood the earlier attentions of the dragoons) and the *Northern Star* office were removed with the help of a rope.[42] Whyte had been expecting trouble, believing that the job of maintaining order in Belfast was comparable to the task of the British military in North America. He was, he wrote somewhat theatrically, 'in a situation pretty similar to that of my late friend Genl [*sic*] Gage at Boston and was daily threatened by the malcontents with a Bunker's Hill and a Lexington'.[43] While the incidents of military indiscipline were not sanctioned, the pressure applied on the town was deliberate and designed to cow its inhabitants. Trouble broke out again in May when it was alleged that soldiers had acted in an undisciplined manner and Clotworthy Birnie, a leading radical, received a stab wound in the back. Furthermore, the somewhat ill-timed performance of a play entitled *The Guillotine* created chaos in the theatre as the viewers clashed over the suitability of a plot that made reference to the recently departed 'Louis Capet', King of France. The female members of the audience fled the theatre, expecting the worst.[44] Martha McTier noted that there was a perception that the stridency of the *Star* had brought these acts of vengeance against Belfast and this too may have contributed to the sense of despair.[45]

Neilson, in low spirits, was in Dublin in April as an invited guest of the Catholic Committee, which was holding a dinner to celebrate the achievement of Catholic Relief. Toasts were drunk, including an expression of gratitude to the efforts of Belfast, but he was in no mood to rejoice and the granting of £100 for his use was scant consolation.[46] Despite the fact that Neilson felt that Catholics had given their approval to the Relief Act, a flawed concession, and thus betrayed the support given to their cause by the United Irishmen, Drennan believed he was working closely with the Catholic leadership and that he had brought other northerners, like Sinclaire, round to this way of thinking.[47] Neilson was, however, still brooding about the refusal of Catholics to grasp the opportunities that were open to that sector of Irish society. In the meantime, Belfast was persecuted and he found it difficult to be fully reconciled with Tone (who was, of course, firmly linked to the Catholic cause) and Thomas Russell, Tone's closest political ally. Neilson wrote to Drennan with the news that Russell had returned north and he now bored the radical set to such an extent that few of them listened to him any more. Most annoying for Neilson was his certainty that Russell corresponded with Tone almost daily and yet never communicated any news to him. He made it clear to Drennan that their positions were similar and that they should correspond. With reference to the pessimism that seemed to be enveloping Belfast, Neilson noted that while there were many in the town who were 'sick of politics' and disgusted at the 'scoundrel country' in which they lived, he was filled with enthusiasm for 'the fond hope of seeing my country free'. Despite suspicions that Neilson was losing his political appetite, his developing radicalism can be observed in his comments to Drennan. He suggested, somewhat optimistically, that the illumination of houses in Belfast the previous week to commemorate the king's birthday was not actually a demonstration of loyalty, but rather a tactical and prudent step designed to remove the pressure on the town. He also noted that while the war had a destructive effect on business, its continuation 'will work our salvation' because 'it was the scarcity of cash that demolished despotism in France'.[48]

Neilson's private sentiments contrast with the *Star*'s description of the town being 'brilliantly illuminated in honour of the king's birthday ... [which] highlights the wicked misrepresentation of the people of Belfast'. He also stressed the tranquillity of Belfast in comparison to those areas of the country that were disrupted by resistance to the Militia Act. Riots involving the Catholic peasantry in May were condemned in the *Star* and Neilson was quick to point out that Ulster Presbyterians had remained dignified in the face of adversity 'because the people there are better informed than the southern peasantry; and because they understand the difference between liberty and licentiousness'.[49] The newspaper was using its influence to defuse tension at a time when its editor, though disillusioned with the state of the project and the prospects for its success, was developing his ideological outlook.[50] Neilson would put his differences with Russell to one side when the latter returned to Belfast in August after a number of botanical and political excursions around County Antrim. The two men drank heavily together on the 21st and, although there is no record of their discussions, Neilson's subsequent written attack on the Catholic leadership was probably occasioned by something that had been said during that evening.[51] The strength of Neilson's feelings about their pusillanimity in the wake of the failure to push for the right to sit in Parliament was unabated and he wrote five days later to the leading Catholic representative and United Irishman, Richard McCormick, to register his annoyance. Neilson accused the Catholics of not taking advantage of their numerical strength and expecting Ulster Presbyterians to take all the risks. The project to promote unity had, he argued, been damaged severely by Catholics because of their desertion from the radical agenda. Neilson was indignant that the role of Ulster had been ignored by Catholics at a recent dinner in Dublin's Daly's Tavern, hosted by leading Catholics in honour of Lord Moira in August 1793, during which a range of toasts were offered but the contribution of Belfast to radical political discourse omitted. Neilson's letter is worth quoting at length because it does exemplify his lingering distrust of Catholic intentions:

> the Catholics of Ireland, if we are to suppose that their representatives know any thing of their sentiments, are decided in condemning us. For, not to speak of their refusal to include us among their friends when they were concluding their business as a convention, they could not, when assembled the other day in a festive capacity, omit insulting this province. Yes! I will repeat it, the meeting at Daly's insulted the province of Ulster; because, when ransacking the very dregs of royalty, aristocracy, and pseudo-patriotism for toasts, they tacitly condemned one fourth of their countrymen, the body who saved them, when deserted or opposed by all those whom they toasted on the 20th inst. Your prudence in overlooking Mr [Napper] Tandy, who has been destroyed in your cause; your wisdom in disregarding the sufferings of Mr Butler, Bond and [James] Reynolds, who were imprisoned for you, and your temperance in neglecting this town, which has been abandoned for four months past to martial law on your account, cannot be but highly gratifying to every true Irishman. But your omitting to mention the Dungannon convention, which represented one million and a quarter of your country-men, and which demanded the restoration of your rights in particular, as well as of the rights of Ireland in general, was such an act of ______ as will not in future be believed, and which I confess I can never forget.[52]

Neilson referred to himself both as 'an unfortunate persecuted northern incendiary' and a warm and honest Irishman who liked to speak his mind but who hoped not to be censured by McCormick for this outpouring of anger and betrayal. McCormick informed Tone of the 'unpleasant' letter and, while thinking parts of it exaggerated, confessed that it was 'in general too well founded'. Rather than responding in writing, he resolved to travel north to see Neilson in the hope of a *rapprochement*.[53]

As the expected trial of the *Star*'s proprietors approached, Neilson cast aside any thoughts of abandoning a newspaper that was now outselling the *News-Letter* and resolved to mount a sturdy defence of its position.[54] The minute book of the committee established to run the newspaper records that Neilson and his colleagues had set about forming a team of lawyers soon after the indictment, with Counsellor Alexander Stewart being hired and instructed to engage the services of Matthew Smith. By July, it was decided that the best option was to fight to defend the newspaper's reputation and all earlier thoughts of a climb-down were rejected as a ballot of the proprietors elected Neilson and Robert Simms (who gained nine and eight votes respectively) to manage the case and report back to their colleagues on a weekly basis.[55] The owners were well aware of the tactics that would be adopted by the government and reported that a hearth tax collector had been denigrating the newspaper during his rounds, attempting to undermine the credibility of the *Star* among the poorer classes, or, as Neilson termed it, implementing 'a systematic plan to poison the public mind previous to the ensuing trial on our impending prosecution'.[56] Another attempt to stigmatise the paper was revealed in August with the circulation of a letter threatening Rowland Jackson O'Connor, the distributor of stamps for County Antrim, with assassination. Neilson condemned the 'vile' letter, asserting that its intent was to harm the proprietors, and offered a fifty-guinea reward for anyone who could identify the culprit, a figure that was matched by O'Connor himself.[57]

However, constructing a case against the *Northern Star* that would stand up in court would not be a simple task and in early August it was revealed that the trial would be postponed. This was after the paper's agent in Dublin had been informed that the Crown would be serving notice of trial on only two of the alleged offending publications.[58] This notice was given on 19 July 1793 and the proprietors promptly contracted the services of the eminent barrister and MP John Philpot Curran. However, on 3 August, just five days before the assizes, the proprietors were informed that the trial would not proceed because the Crown case had yet to be finalised. The trial date was finally set for 19 May 1794 and a jury called, although the deliberations started only on the 28th.[59] In the days before the trial, a motion was made in the Court of the King's Bench on behalf of the proprietors against the printer of the pro-government *Freeman's Journal* for publishing 'a number of paragraphs tending to injure the proprietors in the minds of the public' in a manner that might be said to prejudice the outcome.[60] This was rejected and the long-awaited trial began, the proprietors appearing before Lord Chief Justice Clonmell and Mr Justice Downes. Their formidable legal team included Curran (who had unsuccessfully defended Archibald Hamilton Rowan against his recent charges of sedition despite a dazzling marathon three-hour speech during the summing-up), Francis Dobbs, John Dunn, Stewart and William Sampson. The proprietors were charged with:

> being wicked, seditious and ill-disposed persons, and being greatly disaffected to our said Sovereign Lord, the King, and his administration of the government of this kingdom, and wickedly, maliciously and seditiously intending, devising and contriving to stir up and excite discontent and sedition amongst the subjects of our Lord, the King ... wickedly and seditiously printed and published certain false, wicked, malicious, scandalous and seditious libel, of and concerning the government, state and constitution of this kingdom of Ireland.[61]

The delay in bringing the defendants to court was no surprise given the weakness of the Crown's case. Curran would easily refute the charges and the trial did not even merit a reference in the fond two-volume memoir penned by his son twenty years later. Despite this, the major shareholders (Neilson, Haslett and Simms) appeared to be preparing for a guilty verdict and a spell in Newgate Gaol, although another of the proprietors, William Tennent, was confident of success as the trial date finally approached, declaring that the owners had 'the best hopes'.[62] Much of the Crown's case centred on the notorious resolutions of the Irish Jacobins, which appeared in the edition of 12–15 December 1792, asserting that Ireland had no national government, that men of all religious persuasions had the right to constitute laws for their own welfare, that there should be universal male suffrage and that a national convention of Irish, Scotch and English should be established. The Attorney General, Arthur Wolfe, attempted to convince the jury that the proprietors were men who 'had no more to do with a newspaper than any other men upon earth', a charge that was not strictly true given that William Magee and John Tisdall had both been involved in the *Belfast Mercury* during the previous decade. He alleged that the *Star* was peddling inflammatory material and, since the newspaper was selling for a price that was below what was normal, it must follow 'that their only object was to excite sedition'.[63] Despite Tisdall's attempt to show that he had ceased to be a proprietor, the prosecution was arguing that there existed a collective guilt and that all those named as proprietors were culpable for the scandalous publications.

Curran's response was to assert that while the accused were identifiable as the owners of the newspaper, it did not mean that they were responsible for every article that appeared therein and likened this to blaming the entire crew of a ship for the errors of the navigator. Indeed, while there were affidavits to say that the named defendants were proprietors of the *Star* at its inception, no evidence existed that this was still the case and even if it were, proprietorship did not mean guilt in the act of publication. This point was conceded by Lord Chief Justice Clonmell and a verdict of not guilty was reached in relation to the proprietors, leaving the question of guilt to be centred on the printer John Rabb.[64]

Arguing the case for the defence, Francis Dobbs noted that the assertions by the Irish Jacobins could only be deemed libellous if the grievances identified did not actually exist. The fact that they did gave the newspaper a right to publish such assertions. Dobbs added that the Belfast group should not be judged by reference to the excesses of the French Jacobins, a point that was strengthened by the fact that the offending article was published before the more violent excesses of the French Revolution, events which could never have been predicted by Rowley Osborne, Samuel Kennedy and the Belfast radicals. Moreover, there was nothing seditious or libellous about alleging that there was no national government – after all, huge numbers of Irishmen were disenfranchised and a majority of Irish MPs were elected by less than ninety people. The Jacobins had called for the granting of the vote to Catholics and there was nothing seditious about that, since Parliament had subsequently passed an Act to that effect. Nor was calling for a national convention seditious because the Convention Act was not then on the statute book. In short, the pronouncements of the Belfast Jacobins were no more radical than those of Volunteer assemblies or Patriot MPs. Dobbs concluded by criticising the harassment of the proprietors by the authorities and accusing the prosecution of failing to spot that the north was tranquil compared to the rural violence that was ongoing elsewhere, a state of affairs that would not have existed had the *Northern Star* been genuinely seditious.[65] Lord Clonmell's response was to state that Rabb was guilty of sedition by printing the resolutions. To suggest that Ireland seriously had no national government was to disavow the legality of the king, Lords and Commons. Was this not seditious? The call for a national convention was an attempt to dictate to Parliament: 'To make a new government, or to destroy the present one seems to me to be the obvious meaning of that requisition.' Clonmell focused on the statement by the Irish Jacobins that they would 'exert every means' to achieve their end, interpreting this as 'an invitation to arms ... to effect change by force ... very little short of high treason – the most mischievous, inflammatory and wicked publication that I have ever read'.[66]

The jury was asked to consider whether Rabb, as publisher of the *Star*, had printed the resolutions with criminal intent. He was the sole printer and witnesses had verified that he was always in the newspaper office. Unless the resolutions were printed by mistake or unless he was ignorant of their insertion, John Rabb should be proclaimed guilty. Justice Downes agreed that there was indeed evidence to suggest that the article was libellous and the jury was sent to consider the case. After five minutes, they declared Rabb guilty but bailed him.[67] Tennent noted privately that the printer should 'stay out of the way' in order to protect his liberty; he subsequently broke his bail and fled to South Carolina.[68]

The proprietors celebrated their acquittal at a dinner hosted by the Catholic interest on the Saturday after the trial before returning north to resume their business interests.[69] The legal persecution of the United Irishmen would continue with the commencement of the trial of William Drennan in June. He had been arraigned as the author of an allegedly seditious paper, an address to the Volunteers by the Dublin Society (the distribution of which had already seen Hamilton Rowan confined in Newgate), but found not guilty after Curran successfully undermined the Crown case. In July, the *Northern Star* informed its readers that the proprietors were once again to be dragged away from Belfast to face charges of publishing the same contentious article, having had an information against them filed by the Attorney General.[70] The trial date was set for 17 November. In advance of this, Neilson thumbed his nose at the legal system by permitting the publication of Sampson's satirical *Trial of Hurdy Gurdy*, an intelligently savage critique of the state's propensity for trying reform-minded activists on flimsy evidence, on the word of unreliable witnesses and in front of packed juries.[71] Ironically, when the second trial commenced, one of the jurors was Luke Teeling, the Catholic Poleglass linen bleacher with radical connections, whose sons would all become active United Irishmen.

The Crown case against the proprietors was opened by Counsellor Ruxton, who charged them with publishing such material as would 'incite His Majesty's said subjects to tumult and anarchy and to overturn the established constitution of this kingdom and to overawe and intimidate the legislature of the kingdom by an armed force'.[72] It was alleged that the address was a call to arms made in the aftermath of the Lord Lieutenant's call for a militia and an end to associations that were deemed to be seditious. The Prime Serjeant addressed to the court his concern that the offending article was indeed rebellious because its call for a national convention of Volunteers was, in effect, an attempt to intimidate the Irish Parliament 'at the point of a bayonet'.

In his cross examination of the witness Rowland O'Connor (the distributor of stamps for County Antrim who was again subpoenaed to appear), Curran easily demonstrated that the controversial address had in fact been published in the *Belfast News-Letter*, considered a moderate paper, the day before its publication in the *Northern Star*.[73] Another Crown witness, a Mr McConnel, asserted that Rabb was always in the *Star* office when he purchased the copy of the paper ordered by the Right Honourable Charles Skeffington, the Collector of Belfast, who was monitoring its content. McConnel also saw Neilson and Haslett on occasions. Curran returned to the arguments of the first trial when he reminded the court that proprietorship did not mean that the accused could be charged with wilfully printing offensive material. To charge Neilson and Haslett because they happened to be present in the *Star* office was nonsensical, since O'Connor and McConnel could be accused of the same offence. Clutching at straws, the prosecuting counsel, J. Boyd, argued that by calling for a representative government, the United Irishmen were demanding the abolition of the monarchy and the Lords and so to print this implicated the proprietors. The motives of the *News-Letter* would never have been to harm the government, but the proprietors of the *Northern Star* were clearly involved in radical activity and their attempts to distance themselves from the content of the newspaper, leaving guilt to rest on the 'ragged printer', were both mendacious and unfair. The defence team, again comprising Curran, Dobbs, Stewart, Dunn and Sampson, had successfully exposed the meagreness of the prosecution case and the jury declared that the proprietors were guilty of publishing, but not with malicious intent, a verdict that did not satisfy the court. The jury retired again and returned a not-guilty verdict, prompting a large burst of applause in the courtroom.[74]

By the end of 1794, the *Northern Star* was still in print and its content had become emboldened due to the sense of persecution that had enveloped its owners. But although the battle had been won, Neilson's enemies would continue the fight against what was now firmly considered by the authorities to be a scurrilous rag and future campaigns against the newspaper would be determined in the barrack room rather than the courtroom. Neilson's considerable energies had been sapped by the trial, but tragic circumstances closer to home had made 1794 a difficult year in other ways as he attempted to balance his increasingly fraught political existence with his family and business affairs.

5

System of Eternal Silence, 1794–5

Samuel Neilson's political and business interests during 1793 and 1794 were undoubtedly affected by the range of governmental, legal and military measures that combined to alter both his perspectives and those of his colleagues in the United Irish movement. However, he would also be tortured by a series of personal tragedies and pressures and these too would have been uppermost in his mind throughout this turbulent period. Five children, Agnes (usually referred to as Anne), Sophia, Jane, William and Mary, would survive into adulthood. The first-born son (named Alexander, after Samuel's father) was born on 5 August 1790 and died, probably, in 1793 for in this year Neilson opened a burial plot in the parish graveyard of Knockbreda, adjacent to where his brother John had been interred some years previously. The gravestone also records the tragic loss of stillborn twins on 18 April 1794.[1] Shortly after this, Neilson's anguish was compounded by the death of his younger brother, Thomas, who, it was stated in the *Northern Star*, had suffered a 'tedious illness'. These losses coincided with the very difficult circumstances of the prosecutions of the proprietors of the *Star* and must have taken their toll. Neilson and William Simms served as executors for Thomas' estate and any uncertainty over his woollen drapery business was quickly resolved by the insertion of an advertisement asking those indebted to Thomas Neilson to pay outstanding dues to his nephew Alexander Gordon, who would run the business alongside two of the Neilson sisters. The public was duly informed when the new season's clothes arrived in September.[2]

The cost of defending the charges against the proprietors of the *Northern Star* during an economic downturn would surely have impacted upon Neilson's fortune. In September 1794, it was announced that he had brought Matthew Hughes, formerly his apprentice, into partnership in the Irish Woollen Warehouse, which would continue to trade under the name Samuel Neilson and Co.[3] Furthermore, distributing the *Star* to subscribers in outlying regions also proved difficult, especially if there was hostility towards the paper on the part of local officials such as 'the blaggard postmasters' in Armagh. The newspaper's account and distribution books for 1793 reveal a series of setbacks, with loose editions going missing in Enniskillen and individual subscriptions in places like Armagh, Lurgan, Ballyshannon and Newtownhamilton being cancelled because of the irregularity of deliveries. In one instance, insufficient newspapers were sent to Aughnacloy while in others money was simply not forthcoming. For example, the account of the landowner George Dowglass in Dromore was not fully paid in 1793 because his agent had spent the money given to him to pay the subscription.[4] The logistics of distributing a newspaper so extensively were proving difficult, especially as the *News-Letter* was responding to competition by altering the days of its publication, stealing a march by issuing editions on Tuesdays and Fridays, a day before the *Star*. Neilson responded by changing the days on which his paper became available, abandoning the original Wednesday and Saturday editions in favour of publishing on Monday and Thursday evenings, a manoeuvre that 'precludes the necessity of either printing or circulating on a Sunday', a point of detail that would have gone down very well in the Presbyterian heartlands.[5] In his Christmas editorial, Neilson lamented the fact that this change was necessary, affirming that the *Star* desired no malice and was not in the business of competing with the *News-Letter*, before publicly wishing its editor Henry Joy a merry Christmas and a happy new year.[6] Producing a newspaper with a trial looming cannot have been easy: in March 1794, William Drennan, himself due to appear before the bench on charges of sedition, noted that 'Neilson does not attend to his editorial duties as much as Joy', suggesting that he could have printed parts of the recently guillotined Jean-Paul Rabaut of St Etienne's much-acclaimed *An Impartial History of the Late Revolution in France*. Highlighting this omission was a harsh verdict in the light of the publication of original and intelligent satires such as *The Lion of Old England* in late 1793, penned by William Sampson and Thomas Russell as a damning criticism of England's historical legacy, and the former's *Trial of Hurdy Gurdy* (1794), which parodied the attempts to secure prosecutions against the radical interest.[7]

Concerned by the legal costs incurred by the trial, a subscription notice was placed in the *News-Letter* calling on 'all friends to the liberty of the press' to indemnify the owners. In the *Star*, Neilson responded that while the proprietors were grateful for the gesture, they were unaware of the plan and felt no need to accept money, preferring instead to '... consider the approbation of the patriotic part of the community as their best reward'. It would appear that this initiative originated in south Antrim. In a letter to Thomas Russell, then lodging with Dr James McDonnell in Belfast, Samuel Owens from the Holestone district near

Donegore (County Antrim) asserted that the enterprise had the support of 'a great number of people from Larne down Sixmilewater to Antrim' and that, while it was understood that the proprietors had no wish for financial support, it was not right for them to suffer 'in endeavouring to be useful to society'.[8] Neilson was, however, aware by this stage that the *Star* was running at a loss and this was acknowledged in print one week later.[9] The price of the paper was increased to two and a half pence at the start of 1795 in an attempt to claw back some of the deficit.[10] Despite the buoyant sales, war and the disruption to Irish trade meant that advertising revenue was falling. Belfast was suffering from the economic squeeze created by diminishing markets and well-established business ventures, such as the partnership between Clotworthy Birnie, Thomas McCabe junior and Thomas Milliken, were being dissolved; Neilson was one of two assignees charged to recover the debts owed to Birnie.[11]

The financial difficulties also affected Joy's *Belfast News-Letter* and in November 1794 the family business was put up for sale. This decision reflected not just the reduction in advertising revenue (although the announcement of sale stated that this was a considerable issue), but also the reality that the *Belfast News-Letter* was unable to compete with the *Star* as a reformist newspaper and Joy (a supporter of the Whigs) would find it difficult to present himself editorially as anything other than a reformer. If Belfast's second newspaper was to be wholly conformist, it could not have Joy at its helm. The paper would eventually be sold to Robert Allan of Edinburgh for £1,650, around a third of the original asking price.[12]

The outworking of the French Revolution had given rise to public debate in both England and Scotland. It has already been noted that the proceedings of reform groups were being published in the *Northern Star*, but the outbreak of war in February 1793 meant that any sympathy for the republican cause would be perceived as sedition. In the English Parliament, the small group of Foxite Whigs were sceptical of the war effort, while a number of extra-Parliamentary groups went further by expressing their outright opposition. Firm links with Scottish radicals had already been forged in December 1792 with the help of a printed address from the United Irishmen that was penned by Drennan and read to the Scottish Friends of the People Convention by the celebrated radical Thomas Muir. The moderate delegates were not, however, receptive to Drennan's political views and indeed Muir was arrested in January but released on bail. He visited Dublin in July 1793, where he was feted by the United Irishmen and Drennan wrote excitedly to his brother-in-law, Samuel McTier, that Muir was to visit Belfast before sailing for Scotland and that he would give him a line of introduction to Neilson.[13] There is no written record of such a meeting, but the following month the *Star* recounted Muir's sixteen-hour trial in some detail and he became something of a *cause célèbre* after the guilty verdict was delivered and he was sentenced to transportation for fourteen years.[14]

Another radical member of the Society of Friends of the People was James Tytler, a polemicist who, in an essay to the association entitled *To the People and their Friends*, launched a scathing attack on both the English House of Commons (which he referred to as a 'vile junto [*sic*] of aristocrats') and the moderation of some of his colleagues. Tytler's views brought him to the attention of the authorities and he was arrested on 4 December 1792 and bailed. He failed to appear in court for his trial in January because he had left Scotland for Ireland, settling in Belfast, where he lived for two years, joined by his second wife, Jean Aitkenhead. Tytler had achieved a degree of renown for his pioneering work as editor of the *Encyclopaedia Britannica* and for his experimentation in balloon flight, and he was soon welcomed by the radical set in Belfast.[15] There is a characteristic lack of documentation relating to Tytler's time in Belfast but the information provided to the authorities in 1796 by the informer William Bird (using the unimaginative alias John Smith) offers a sidelight into United Irish thinking at that time. Bird alleged that a man named 'Titler' [*sic*], who went by the assumed name of Donaldson, 'a man of genius but very poor', was indeed in Belfast after the Scottish convention and that the radicals wanted to use him as an emissary in Scotland. Bird wrote that the plan was that Tytler would traverse Scotland in the guise of a highland piper with the objective of raising Scotland in rebellion. If the Scottish people were ripe for insurrection, he would return to Belfast to advise the leaders there. Tytler was, by all accounts, slow to learn to play the bagpipes and when he was eventually ready to commence his mission he was recalled from his departure point in Donaghadee by the Belfast United Irishmen, who seemed to have had second thoughts about the enterprise.[16] Bird's evidence is interesting because it gives an insight into the thinking and direction of the Belfast United Irishmen in the 1793–5 period and the militant strategy being countenanced at such an early stage. It is clear from the information given that Neilson was central to these deliberations, being, in Bird's analysis, 'at the head of the conspirators'.[17]

Neilson's attempt to establish relations between radicals in Ireland and Scotland is confirmed by the reports of another informer, Thomas Collins, whose reporting of the deliberations of the Dublin Society of United Irishmen was a vital source of information for the Castle. A failed businessman, Collins was easily seduced by the prospect of pecuniary gain and his supply of names and the details of debates helped convince the government to take action against the organisation in 1794. Neilson appeared in Dublin in January of that year to prepare the case for the defence of the proprietors of the *Northern Star*, meeting at different times with Tone, Drennan and the legal team. Collins recorded that Neilson attended meetings of the Dublin society whenever he was in town. On one occasion, the assembled members would have listened carefully, perhaps in some cases in disbelief, as the northern visitor addressed the gathering. His message was rather too drastic for his audience. Neilson began by referring to his 'confidential friends' in Edinburgh and how he would be happy to forward papers and proceedings from Dublin to them. Neilson's awareness of Scottish reform politics would have been informed by Tytler and his enthusiasm for cultivating notions of brotherhood would remain foremost in his planning over the next few years. As he warmed to his theme, Neilson pledged that the northern radicals 'only waited for that time to come, when they will boldly shew themselves worthy of the name of freemen'. These sentiments were more explicit and extreme than the normal tenor of discourse at these meetings.

Ironically, given Collins' presence, Neilson asserted that the possibility of the society being infiltrated made it necessary for the United Irishmen in Dublin to follow the lead of the Ulster societies and adopt a less transparent appearance, whereby a small group of twelve, a committee of public welfare, would take the lead in shaping the direction of the body, with fewer meetings of the full society. His proposal must have stunned sections of this respectable gathering, hitherto unused to the conspiratorial sentiments that he had just delivered. Indeed, Simon Butler argued that open meetings were preferable since nothing illegal was being discussed. Collins' interpretation was that Neilson saw Ireland on the eve of a great event and that foreign assistance would be sought as the United Irishmen worked to achieve its goals.[18] Neilson's address indicated that the thinking of the northern societies had gone beyond the mere publication of resolutions and that a co-ordinated plot was required. The suppression of the Volunteers, combined with military repression in Belfast and the evident closure of the Catholic concession account, would certainly have led some there to consider altering the trajectory of the reform movement; or perhaps, as Nancy Curtin suggests, it was that the long and quietly held aspirations of the northerners were now being aired publicly. It was indeed the view of the government that the stated aims of the United Irishmen in 1791 were a smokescreen and that a more sinister motive was present from the earliest point. Neilson's political and publishing rival Henry Joy referred to these suspicions when he was preparing his history of Belfast. He viewed the *Northern Star* as a political incendiary that had a very clear purpose:

> From its earliest appearance, one of its principal objects was an union between Roman Catholics and Protestants and the establishment of the plan of United Irishmen ... the first year of its publication was devoted to prepare the minds of the populace and of all ranks for the rejection of regal government, and to excite a general expectation of a separation from Great Britain. Everything held valuable in the British constitution was by this paper artfully turned into contempt and the hereditary part of it into the greatest derision. The vulgar were taught to expect every happy consequence from some great and inevitable change, by which revolution was understood.

Joy noted that from the first edition of its second year of publication, the crown was omitted from the newspaper's banner.[19] Drennan's reference to 'Neilson's system of eternal silence' in Belfast would suggest that things were moving swiftly in Ulster and any hardening of attitudes there would surely have been accelerated by the pressure of the two trials of the *Northern Star* proprietors in 1794.[20] It is often accepted that the Society of United Irishmen was a constitutional organisation until its 'suppression' in 1794, after which an affiliated system was developed that was less public and therefore more difficult to penetrate. But in his evidence to the Secret Committee of the Irish House of Lords in August 1798, Neilson stated that the tightly structured organisation of the United Irishmen began in the spring of 1792 'and has gradually increased since that time'. As early as May 1793, an anonymous source (probably a magistrate) wrote from Dublin of the deplorable scheme planned by the Belfast republicans, whereby Catholics would be encouraged to press Parliament for changes which, if not forthcoming, would prompt local and provincial meetings to declare themselves representatives of the people. These assemblies would have 'invited the King and the Lords to have joined them but if they denied it, then to have declared both a nullity and to have introduced perfect French Politicks'.

According to the informant's melodramatic appraisal, Ireland was 'on the brink of everything that can be horrid to the mind of men'.[21] Neilson's secrecy and his quest for a tightly organised structure predated the commonly accepted view, acknowledged by the government itself, that the United Irishmen changed its direction through a structural overhaul and the introduction of a new test in 1795, which escalated demands for 'an impartial and adequate representation of the Irish nation in parliament' into 'an equal, full and adequate representation of all the people in Ireland'.[22] The northern radicals, under Neilson's leadership, had in fact been working hard to re-shape the project in the months before the often-accepted reasons for the acceleration of United Irish ambitions, namely the Jackson affair and the recall of Viceroy Fitzwilliam.

The arrest in April 1794 of Reverend William Jackson, an Anglican minister who had been despatched to Ireland by the French government to assess the state of the country and the potential for influence and intrigue, was the occasion if not the cause of the decision to apply added pressure on the United Irishmen. Jackson was captured in possession of documents that confirmed contact with the movement, a discovery that would implicate both Hamilton Rowan and Tone in the conspiracy. With the former already in custody, things were looking bleak for the aristocratic radical and his escape from Newgate Gaol in May added considerable weight to the view that the United Irishmen were indeed involved in a strategy that was deeply disloyal. Jackson was brought before the King's Bench in June to answer to the charges against him. These included high treason and landing in Ireland with treasonable intent. His communications referred to the staunch republicanism of Dissenters, the fact that the Defenders were in arms, the lack of coastline defences and the assertion that a French landing would be supported by a majority on the island.[23]

The following month, two sheriffs, accompanied by Aldermen Warren and Carleton and a number of Dublin police, launched a raid on the headquarters of the Dublin United Irish Society, confiscating its papers and effectively suppressing it in the way that the Volunteers had been closed down the previous year. Neilson's *Northern Star* was quick to add its satirical bite to the event, commenting on the seizure of papers '... among which it is said are discoveries – *new* – *wonderful* and of the highest *importance* to the State!!'[24] As Cullen has pointed out, the United Irish test was not illegal, nor did any of the confiscated materials feature in the trials of Drennan or Rowan.[25] The raid was of dubious legality, but the outcome was that the United Irishmen throughout the country would need to operate at a more clandestine level and this suited the purposes of Neilson and the northern leaders.

In some respects, the United Irishmen were moving into territory already occupied by the Defenders. Far from being the faction fighters they have often been portrayed as, the Defenders had played a politicising role during both the period when delegates were selected for the Catholic Convention in December 1792 and the period of debates over Catholic enfranchisement in the months preceding the Relief Act.[26] As early as March 1793, the Viceroy, Lord Westmorland, was reporting that large numbers of Defender 'banditti' were active in Louth and that they were plundering the houses of Protestants, searching for weapons.[27] The riots staged that year against the formation of the militia also led elements of the Defenders to seek ways of bolstering their position, while the unwillingness of local magistrates to take steps to prevent the targeting of Catholics by Peep o' Day

Boys in counties such as Armagh pushed the movement towards direct action. The leading soldier on the ground, General William Dalrymple, was predicting an increase in Catholic alienation, with the risk of outrages being committed by them.[28]

More alarmingly, Defender figures such as Father James Coigley had direct experience of Paris during the revolution and, despite Drennan's belief that Catholics (unlike Presbyterians) hated the newly secular France, there would seem to have been a degree of support for the revolution in Defender strongholds and even a hope of French assistance. In January 1794, during one of his perambulations, Russell encountered a young boy between Dublin and Dunshaughlin (County Meath) and their conversation hinted at the Defender position: 'He says the people in the county of Monaghan are in favour of the French. Says there are Defenders there. 300 armed. All for the French. That letters have come from France.' The following day, he was in Cavan, where an unidentified acquaintance, referred to as 'the Miller', exclaimed that the vast majority were sympathetic to the French.[29] Under-Secretary Edward Cooke wrote alarmingly that the lower classes in Leitrim and Roscommon, as well as in Cavan, were assembling in large bodies and raising arms, convincing him that the project 'seems universally to be a preparation to aid an invasion'.[30] Grievances included more immediate concerns such as evictions, the forced payment of tithes and the non-recognition of marriages by the state and these fed into the pro-French narrative in many rural areas.

The United Irishmen was a society that was in a state of some disrepair in the middle of 1794. The government clampdown on Belfast the previous year and the suppression of the Volunteers had undermined the confidence of the northerners and this dejection was compounded by the legal attacks on the *Northern Star*. Moreover, the failure of the Dublin radicals to endorse Neilson's more clandestine approach was a setback and the cause there was thrown into confusion by the moves to neuter leading figures such as Napper Tandy, Drennan and Rowan in the courts. The Jackson affair also placed the Dublin United Irishmen on the back foot. So while Neilson's secrecy provided a template for the society's continued existence, the potential for expansion without a popular cause behind it was bleak. It was at this point that the changing politics at Westminster produced a dynamic that would have a significant impact on Irish affairs.

William Henry Cavendish-Bentinck, 3rd Duke of Portland, had become Lord Lieutenant of Ireland back in 1782, helping to smooth the passage of legislative independence through the Irish Parliament. In 1794, his Whig faction joined Pitt's government and Portland's longstanding support for

Grattan's moderate cause in Ireland served to raise expectations that the reform purse would be reopened. With Portland himself in the Home Office, the 4th Earl Fitzwilliam was elevated to the position of viceroy, his first governmental position, and, like his uncle the Marquis of Rockingham (Prime Minister in 1782), he would have a significant impact on Irish politics. Staunch opponents of the excesses of the French Revolution and fearful of the possible impression that republicanism might make on Ireland, the Portland Whigs supported the war effort and fell away from the increasingly unpopular position held by Charles James Fox. It was Fitzwilliam's view that stability in Ireland would be achieved by both altering the corrupt nature of Ascendancy governance and by neutering any support for republicanism that the continuation of such a system might produce. In essence, this meant attaching Catholics more firmly to the *status quo*, especially at a time when rural unrest and Defender activity was causing concern. In what was a trademark policy of reforming to preserve, Fitzwilliam concluded that the best way to achieve this stability was to grant to Catholics that which had been withheld in 1793: the ability to sit in Parliament.[31]

Radical Belfast received the news of Fitzwilliam's appointment and his inclination to grant Catholic emancipation warmly and it was later rumoured that Lord Edward Fitzgerald might even be appointed to the post of Commissioner of Stamps and Impressed Accounts in the new administration.[32] The new viceroy also marginalised the mainstays of the administration, such as the revenue commissioner John Beresford (who, as a favourite son of the Westmorland administration, had been a dispenser of patronage) and Under-Secretary Edward Cooke, a well-known opponent of Catholic claims. The Whig figures of Grattan, George and William Ponsonby, Curran and the Duke of Leinster saw their influence increase and the new viceroy made encouraging noises about Catholics, whose expectations began to rise, resulting in a raft of meetings and petitions intended to push their political claims. In a letter to Portland which would have set alarm bells ringing in London, Fitzwilliam confessed, 'I tremble about the Roman Catholics, I mean about keeping them quiet for the session because I find the question already in agitation and a committee appointed to bring forward a petition for the repeal of the penal and restrictive laws.'[33]

In Belfast, more than 1,000 people signed such a petition, which was to be delivered to the Irish Commons by the two Antrim MPs, O'Neill and Rowley.[34] Grattan introduced a relief bill into the Irish Commons in early February, calling for the admission of Catholics to all state offices that were not ecclesiastical or regal. By this stage, the government in London was having second thoughts about Fitzwilliam's appointment, believing him to be at the mercy of an Irish

Whig faction drunk on the prospect of power, and Portland found himself in the difficult position of having to rein in his protégé. Immediate Catholic emancipation was considered too much of a risk and Fitzwilliam was recalled to London at the end of the month. The end of his brief tenure was greeted with shock and consternation by those well disposed to change. The Whigs in the Irish Parliament were despondent and large crowds gathered in Dublin to show their support for Fitzwilliam on the day of his departure. Neilson used the Dublin newspaper reports to inform his readers of the scene: shops were closed and the town was in a state of mourning, with its inhabitants combining their solemnity with anger, 'loud in their curses and execrations against the British government'. At College Green, a group of gentlemen dressed in black drew Fitzwilliam's carriage through the streets, moving the departing Lord Lieutenant to tears. The outcome was a triumph for conservatives such as Beresford and Cooke, who would soon be reinstated. The report added vitriolically that, 'We hear that the *Good Old System of Terror* dined yesterday at the Crown and Anchor in Earl Street to celebrate the event of the departure of earl Fitzwilliam and with him – IRISH INDEPENDENCE.' A meeting of Belfast Catholics, chaired by William Hendren, with Daniel Shanaghan (a very prominent United Irishman in the town) serving as secretary, lamented the recall of the liberal-minded viceroy and asserted that 'we must ever despise and detest those evil counsellors' who had helped to manoeuvre him out of office, pledging themselves 'to cordially unite with our Protestant brethren'.[35]

Fitzwilliam's recall united the dissatisfied mass against a system that was seen to be bent on perpetuating old inequalities and which was governed by sectarian attitudes. Catholic disappointment was difficult to contain and at a meeting on 9 April in Dublin's Francis Street chapel chaired by the leading Catholic John Sweetman, a series of speakers, including Edward Lewins and William James MacNeven, echoed the call from Belfast for a stronger union with Protestant malcontents and lambasted the British government for its handling of the emancipation issue. Neilson was in Dublin at the time and Drennan noted that he was due to attend the meeting, no doubt with the objective of forging closer links with the Catholics, thereby strengthening the hand of the United Irishmen.[36] Structured Catholic opposition to Fitzwilliam's recall was easy to rekindle because a similar mobilisation had taken place in the months before the Catholic Convention back in December 1792. One of the delegates from that time, Luke Teeling, chaired a meeting of Catholics in Antrim and again it was clear that the reaction against the government was likely to revive the flagging fortunes of the United Irishmen, with calls for a common cause to be made with the citizens in the town of Belfast and a resolution paying tribute to the immortal Volunteers passed with ease. Teeling's 16-year-old son, Charles, acted as secretary to the meeting. Within a year, he would be playing a major role in attempting to unite the Defenders and United Irishmen around a common cause.[37] There is little doubt that the crisis provoked a Catholic backlash against the system of government. For seasoned radicals like Samuel Neilson, there was little to be surprised at. His political thinking did not require Fitzwilliam's departure to ignite a more extreme programme. However, popular dissatisfaction with the government boosted the fortunes of the United Irishmen by radicalising a broader range of people and identifying the British government (which had engineered his dismissal) as a cause of Ireland's diminished condition. For many, the issue became one of separation.

The disdain for the new viceroy, John Jeffreys Pratt, 1st Marquess Camden, as he arrived at Dublin docks, was palpable. He was driven to the Castle to the sound of scoffs and hisses. Another 'Castle Ultra', the Lord Chancellor Fitzgibbon, was attacked with stones as he was driven through the city and he appeared the following day wearing an eye patch.[38] The repercussions continued: Grattan and the Whigs were reduced to sulking in the Irish Parliament and the recalled former viceroy came close to fighting a duel in London with John Beresford, one of the chief architects of his downfall, a political crisis that was averted only by the fortuitous arrival of a magistrate.[39] The new viceroy brought Thomas Pelham into the administration as Chief Secretary and promotions followed for Camden's brother-in-law Robert Stewart, Lord Castlereagh, who had triumphed as a reformer in the election of 1790 but who had now nailed his colours firmly to the reactionary mast. Another former Volunteer, Nicholas Price of Saintfield in County Down, who was also married to a sister of the viceroy, was elevated to the parliamentary position of Gentleman Usher of the Black Rod in a move that was bound to revive suggestions of nepotism.[40] Moderate reformers in the early part of the 1790s, these men adopted conservative positions as the decade wore on. Meanwhile, the brakes that had been applied to the reform agenda (for example, at the Volunteer convention in Dungannon in February 1793) were no longer going to frustrate those like Neilson whose radicalism knew fewer bounds.

With the new regime settling into Castle life, attention turned once again to Reverend William Jackson, the French government agent, who had been detained in gaol for the best part of a year. His trial in April 1795 produced the expected guilty verdict, but plans for an execution 'with great pomp and solemnity in front of the Parliament House in College Green' were thwarted by Jackson himself, who collapsed in the dock after taking poison and expired despite the efforts of Dr Waite and a druggist, Mr Kinsley, to revive him.[41] The principle of seeking assistance from the French had now been planted firmly in the minds of the leaders of the United Irishmen in Ulster and this part of the project was given an injection by Wolfe Tone's voluntary exile, whereby he would establish links with the French in the hope of an invasion.[42] Tone had agreed to depart Ireland as part of a deal that gave him immunity from prosecution for any part he had played in the Jackson conspiracy, something that the government would have difficulty proving anyway, given Rowan's escape from prison and the unlikelihood of Jackson himself betraying Tone. His plan to emigrate to America, where he would establish contact with the French minister, was discussed at Rathfarnham with the United Irishmen Thomas Addis Emmet and Russell during May 1795 and the strategy was later endorsed in Belfast. Tone felt that his deal with the authorities would 'extend no further than the banks of the Delaware' and that his role as a foreign emissary would 'enable us to assert our independence'. On the 20th, he set off for Belfast, his adopted home, where he would spend some time with those to whom he had become particularly close and where he affirmed his attachment to the revolutionary cause during his final days in Ireland. The development of United Irish strategy would be finalised during this time, and the authorities were not entirely oblivious to what was going on. Rowland J. O'Connor of the Stamp Office wrote (with considerable authority, as it turned out) that Tone's visit to the town was a significant one, that his exit for the United States would be temporary and that his ultimate destination was Paris. O'Connor asserted that:

> Tone has been paid the greatest compliments here and a subscription of £1,500 raised for him; Saml Neilson, Robt and William Simms, Couns Sampson, Dr McDonnell, John and William McCrackens [*sic*] and many others have had frequent private meetings with him and have often gone with him to visit different parts of the coast and taking plans of it ... the generality of the people here wish and are very ripe for a revolution.

O'Connor had summarised the next phase of the plot rather perfectly.[43]

Positioned at the southern end of the Antrim Plateau, the Cave Hill looms large over Belfast. One day in June 1795, Tone, Neilson, Russell, Robert Simms, Henry Joy McCracken and other leading United Irishmen climbed to McArt's Fort at its summit and surveyed the town where the society had been born and its spirit remained strong. There they pledged 'never to desist in our efforts until we had subverted the authority of England over our country', a covenant that meant as much to his colleagues as it did to Tone. On another day, the Neilson, Simms, McCracken and Tone families dined and played at the Deer Park to the north of the town. Tone also wrote nostalgically of a delightful trip to Ram's Island in Lough Neagh that he made with some of his friends, including Neilson, on 10 June. When the time came for his departure on board the *Cincinnatus*, his northern well-wishers provided him and his family with additional provisions for the journey.[44] Tone's departure coincided with the death of Sam McTier, Drennan's brother-in-law and one of the architects of the United Irishmen. It is unlikely that McTier, who chaired the society's first meeting, would have endorsed the project being undertaken by the most radical of the Belfast United Irishmen and, as Tone set sail, it appeared that the plot for the people had taken on a new dimension, one that eclipsed the constitutionalism of 1791.

Tone landed in the United States on 1 August and soon set to work on his task. Also in the new republic was James Tytler, who, unlike Tone, had endured a distinctly unpleasant voyage some time before. From Salem, Massachusetts, he wrote to Russell in September offering to become the medium of communication between France and Ireland, suggesting that such a plan had been in contemplation before Tone's exile. Tytler was planning to make his fortune by producing ink and he suggested that his next communication would be partly written in invisible ink, which could be displayed by dissolving 1 ounce of copperas (ferrous sulphate) in 6 ounces of water and adding 1 quarter of spirit of salt. Breathing over the invisible ink would render the writing readable. But Tytler's usefulness to the Belfast set had passed. Instead the radical coterie would await communication from Tone.[45] By September, he was in Philadelphia, where he met up with John Rabb, the former printer of the *Northern Star*, who had fled to the United States in the aftermath of the guilty verdict the previous year. Tone was not impressed by either America or Americans. In a letter to Russell, he referred to those he found as 'a selfish, churlish, unsocial race, totally absorbed in making money ... the most disgusting race'.[46] Tone left the US on New Year's Day 1796 and arrived at Le Havre in early February to embark on his stated quest to persuade the French to assist in the project to liberate his country. While Tone attempted to open a line of communication with the ruling French Directory, his colleagues in Ireland took steps to ensure that the populace would welcome assistance from a country with which England was at war.

More urgently, however, the sectarian nature of Armagh politics required attention. Neilson travelled to the county in September at the request of Charles Teeling, a leading Defender figure.[47] Teeling's call for assistance demonstrates the importance of Neilson to the plan of forming a nexus between the United Irishmen and Defenders; indeed, James Hope asserted that it was Neilson, in conjunction with Luke Teeling (father of Charles), who instigated this union.[48]

He had, of course, attempted to mediate in the disputes in the Rathfriland area in 1792, creating conditions that can be seen as the first steps towards establishing firm connections between the United Irishmen and the Defenders. The well-placed informer Leonard McNally reported that Henry Joy McCracken and Neilson had visited Armagh in 1795 to settle arguments between Catholics and Protestants and encourage unity between the groups.[49] The county – with its dangerous concoction of demography, economic rivalry between Protestant and Catholic, ancient Gaelic familial assertiveness and conservative Protestant landlordism – would be the crucible within which the United Irish programme would either succeed or fail.

Into this heady mix came a closely contested by-election for one of the county seats in Parliament after the death in October 1794 of the sitting MP, William Brownlow. His son, also called William, fought the election on a conservative ticket, something of a new departure given the Patriot/Whig reputation of his father, a former Volunteer and close ally of Flood. The election campaign itself coincided with the controversy surrounding Fitzwilliam's viceroyalty and contributed to the increasingly fragile state of affairs in the county. Brownlow won narrowly – by eighty votes – against the reform candidate Robert Cope, but the result was certainly concerning for the government because if Armagh had been lost to the Whig/Radical cause, as Down and Antrim were in 1790, it would have created a crescent of hostile constituencies in East Ulster and a significant boost to the morale of the United Irishmen.[50]

The situation in County Armagh was certainly volatile. The allegiance of many Catholics to the Defenders there was something of a given, with Anglican attachment to the banner of conservatism similarly assured. Lower-class Protestants would, moreover, find Orangeism an attractive proposition and the activities of the Peep o' Day Boys during 1795 were regular and, in many cases, brutal. An Orange festival was held on 12 July, during which the behaviour of the people was described by a senior army figure as faultless, suggesting a toleration of militant Protestantism by those in authority.[51] The key to the future of County Armagh lay with the disposition of the Presbyterians. The dominant Protestant interest was keen to absorb Presbyterians into the conservative and Orange camp, relying on the traditional and theological opposition to Catholicism. Meanwhile, the United Irish and Defender leaderships saw Armagh Presbyterians as crucial to their project and the energies of senior figures in both groups were being exerted to effect such a union. Leading personalities such as Neilson, Russell, McCracken and Alexander Lowry (from Linen Hill, near modern-day Katesbridge) were critical players in the forging of close ties with the Defenders. For their part, the leading Defender families, such as the Magennises of Ballela, the Teelings of Lisburn and the Coiles of Lurgan, were working hard to deliver their followers to the cause espoused by the radical Belfast Presbyterians. They had their work cut out. Regular clashes between Defenders and Peep o' Day Boys culminated in the formation of the Orange Order after a skirmish near Loughgall in September 1795. Orange lodges adopted the formality and symbolism of Freemasonry (as indeed did the Defenders) and their membership at first consisted of weavers and farmers. Neilson's visit, at Teeling's behest, to the Armagh area was a response to the violent activity that had helped to produce the Orange Order. The continuing conflict led to what is often referred to as the Armagh outrages, a systematic attack on Catholics designed to neuter the Defenders as a force and, in the worst excesses, remove Catholics from their homes. Catholics such as John Short in Tynan felt themselves to be in constant danger:

> Any of us that are Catholics here are not sure going to bed that we shall get up with our lives, either by day or by night. It is not safe to go outside the doors here. The Orangemen go out uninterrupted and the gentlemen of the county do not interfere with them but I have reason to think encourage them in their wickedness ... The Orangemen go out in large bodies by day and night and plunder the poor Catholics of everything they have, even the webs of linen out of their looms.[52]

The allegations of landlord collusion in the persecution of Catholics is not a difficult one to sustain when it is considered that sections of the aristocracy soon saw the potential of the Orangemen as a means of subjugating the United Irish and Defender union. The arrest and incarceration in Armagh Gaol of the leading Defender figure Bernard Coile later in the year was seized upon by Neilson's *Northern Star*. Coile was a prosperous muslin and cambric manufacturer who employed as many as 150 weavers; he was by no means a lower-class Catholic. In November 1795, Henry Joy McCracken and Joseph Cuthbert (a Belfast tailor who had been imprisoned for seditious practices in 1793) gave a bond plus expenses amounting to £60 to the Belfast-based Catholic solicitor James McGucken for any costs arising from proceedings instituted by them against the Armagh magistrate John Greer (who had been particularly active in the pursuit of Defender suspects) and any other found to be guilty of persecution. Those protected included Bernard Coile, Michael McCloskey, Paul Hannon, Patrick Hamill and Sicily Hamill, all victims of the Armagh outrages.[53] Neilson declared that Coile was arrested because he was accumulating evidence against the corrupt practices of local magistrates who were 'exciting the late disturbances' in Armagh. Coile's version of events was that he and one of his employees (Charles Neill) had been taken up because they had complained to the authorities about an attack on Neill's house and had named one Murray as being a leader of the mob. Murray remained at liberty while Coile and Neill were detained. Furthermore, it was alleged by Thomas Addis Emmet, one of those defending Coile, that Murray had been bribed £200 to lie to the court by claiming that the accused was the 'king' of the Defenders. Greer's credibility was further dented by the claim that he had ignored the complaints from a Catholic called McCluskey that a certain Nesbit had attacked his property. Nesbit was allowed to remain at liberty while McCluskey was detained twice by the magistrate. Coile was eventually acquitted in what was a vindication of United Irish allegations of legal bias, albeit a financially expensive one.[54] The movement continued to work hard to meet the costs of legal cases and Neilson attended a provincial meeting of the United Irishmen in the summer of 1796, during which members were asked to make further provision for the costs of persecuted Catholics in County Armagh, victims of what the movement would have regarded as a pogrom inspired by the Orange Order.[55]

By the end of 1795, the attempts to fuse the United Irishmen and Defenders into a common cause had progressed, due in part to the efforts of Neilson, Russell and McCracken. Government sources grew increasingly concerned by reports of political insolence in areas as far apart as Dublin and the Downshire estate in County Down, where some of the tenants merged with Defender groups. More alarmingly, there were suggestions that the disaffected were trying to induce soldiers away from their loyalty and rumours of an alliance with the French abounded.[56] The deepening threat of conspiracy necessitated a response by the authorities and the reinstatement in June of Edward Cooke as Under-Secretary by Camden ushered in a more co-ordinated approach to the collection of intelligence on the sinister developments in United Irish and Defender relations. Cooke's strategy was to create a network of spies to keep him abreast of the major developments within the radical societies and although the attendant risks were great, the Castle could rely on a significant number of informers, many of whom had turned either for financial reward or in order to escape prosecution.

One such figure was Michael Phillips, a Dominican friar from Coolavin in County Sligo, who provided quality information throughout 1795. Phillips alerted the authorities to the fact that the Defenders were more sophisticated politically than had perhaps been assumed and there was a concerted effort to connect them to the United Irishmen. Phillips' intelligence suggested that

Defender signs and codes were recognised across the island and sworn members were allocated a ticket with their number on it. He alleged that between sixty and seventy members of the society met weekly on a Sunday evening in Dublin's Thomas Street and, while there was an expectation of a French landing, it was thought that the Defenders would rise even without foreign assistance. Two-thirds of the militia, it was claimed, had taken the Defender oath.[57] Phillips stated that he had been present at discussions between the Defenders Peter Kearney and Michael McEvoy and a private from the Downshire Militia by the name of Christie. He was asked to go to Meath to meet with another member of the same regiment, Luke Cunningham, and an Anthony Daly in order to assess the number of men who could be called upon to seize the magazine in Phoenix Park, Dublin.

Phillips was reportedly recommended to a leading Defender in Newry called Terence McCann and to John Magennis, the head of the ancient Gaelic dynasty based in Ballela, County Down. Magennis would marry Luke Teeling's daughter in May 1796, a union which solidified his credentials and no doubt signalled a unanimity of purpose among adherents to these very powerful Defender figures. Phillips recounted how Magennis, alongside a Mr Fallon from Lisburn, had been distributing arms in the locality. Indeed, Magennis had collected one hundred pikes from Belfast for distribution among those in the Down area who were unable to afford their own weapon. He also purchased twelve guns and these too were made available to the Defenders. McCann and Magennis were well acquainted with the publican Robert Campbell from Grange in County Armagh, although it would appear that the latter's once dominant position in the Defenders had been taken by Magennis in what may have been a coup. One informant remarked how 'Magennis was the grand master and that no one in that county would acknowledge Campbell as president any more.' Indeed, Phillips claimed he had seen a letter from Campbell to Magennis in which the former deferred to his leadership.[58]

Towards the end of the year, Phillips gained access to the deliberations of Campbell and Magennis. At the County Down home of Patrick Callaghan, Magennis' trusted aide, Phillips reported that Callaghan had received communication directly from Neilson and that McCracken was also involved in the efforts to unite the United Irishmen with the Defenders.[59] This intelligence is corroborated by one of Downshire's correspondents, James McKey, who at one time resided close to Magennis' house at Ballela and observed that there were 'few days they had not meetings of the Belfast gentlemen Neilson, Russel [*sic*] and with the Teelings and others in the same clan'.[60] Phillips' high-grade information was aborted in January 1796, after his partly submerged body was found near the paperworks in Belfast's Cromac Dock, weighed down by a heavy stone in the pocket of his greatcoat. The hastily arranged inquest before the town sovereign, John Brown, recorded an improbable verdict of accidental death. Phillips was buried in Shankill churchyard, with the town authorities being aware only that he was a stranger who had probably come to Belfast from Dublin.[61] Once Phillips' information ceased to arrive with Cooke, the reality of what had happened began to dawn and General Carhampton, the commander-in-chief, acknowledged that foul play was the likely explanation.[62]

As the shift to a more insurrectionary strategy accelerated, the authorities were inundated with increasingly alarming reports of United Irish activity, with Belfast as the co-ordinating centre. The town's republicans met more secretively than before, gathering without ceremony and committing none of their deliberations to paper. While some of these reports may have been exaggerated, respected figures such as Captain Andrew MacNevin in Carrickfergus detailed how 'there is scarce a man in Belfast who is not furnished with a grape[shot] or some instrument of destruction' and that the societies there were working hard to deflect the soldiers from their loyalty to the state. The Carrickfergus postmaster, Nathaniel Johnston, warned of the dangerous levelling activities of the lower classes, whose objectives were to abolish royalty, end the tithe and support the French. They were directed by men from Belfast 'who have sufficient address to delude those poor people and at the same time to keep their own necks out of the noose'.

Rumours of large gatherings of men from different denominations in Cookstown and Toome, pledging to initiate rebellion and 'to imitate 1641', raised anxiety levels further, especially as arms had reputedly been acquired and concealed.[63] Johnston predicted that a rising was likely as early as July 1795, alleging that the numbers of United Irishmen in County Antrim, excluding Belfast, had reached 2,700. The influential rector Reverend Snowden Cupples expressed concern about the rumours that United Irishmen in the vicinity of Carrickfergus had been encouraged to procure and practise firing arms, with those without a gun being advised to acquire pitchforks with prongs closer together than would normally be the case. Blacksmiths were being employed to make pikes in what was a clear programme of militarisation.[64]

Neilson's political position was now considerably beyond that espoused by William Drennan, who had been cowed by his brush with the law the previous year and whose discomfort with Catholics made it unlikely that he could ever embrace the direction being pursued by the northern United Irishmen. Drennan confided to Martha that Neilson seemed to be in regular and confidential contact with Richard McCormick, the leading member of the Catholic Committee with whom he had been so frustrated back in 1792 and 1793. Martha too had discerned a difference in Neilson's aloof behaviour, that he was 'so on the keep off' and acting in a mysterious way. She observed that he had been 'heedless to a degree of incivility' when she approached him for some business assistance.[65] The truth was that Neilson had moved on, becoming a man of action and, therefore, perplexing to a man of letters. Radical Belfast in 1796 would become a centre of conspiracy, sedition and even murder. With Tone negotiating with the French to help deliver the outcome of the Cave Hill compact, Neilson the orchestrator worked the Defender axis and helped to prepare the United Irishmen for rebellion. It was a strategy that would soon deprive him of his freedom.

6

At the Head of the Conspirators, 1796

The developing radicalism of the United Irishmen during 1795 was not merely bombast on their part: the language of the *Northern Star* was becoming more defiant, the reaction against the administration of Lord Camden was growing increasingly strident and Wolfe Tone was embarking on a political journey that would subject Britain not only to a significant internal crisis but also to the possibility of invasion and conquest. Neilson continued to shape the United Irish agenda through his scathing attacks on both the injustice of minority government and Orange-inspired outrages in County Armagh. His editorials now began to exhibit greater levels of ebullience, a trend that would not have gone unnoticed among those who wished to terminate the paper's circulation.

The year 1796 was ushered in by the *Northern Star* with a celebration of the achievements of the French Revolution ('[a] system of hierarchical corruption banished; the state existing without a priesthood; without hereditary nobility; without a king!'), a thinly veiled template for the development of a new Irish polity.[1] The rejection of monarchy represented an evolution in the thinking of the most advanced Belfast radicals. Earlier proclamations of loyalty to the king had been toasted enthusiastically by Volunteers like Neilson in 1792. Four years later, however, classical republican notions of good government within existing but improved constitutional structures were being superseded by a modernist outlook which placed less value on the experience and wisdom of heredity. In Belfast's taverns, frequented by members of the radical set, the health of George III was often cheered in ironic tones ('George the Last') or in jest. On one occasion, Neilson and Russell were forced to drink to the health of the king by downing large bumpers of water, a punishment imposed upon them by their drunken associates. Leading Belfast republicans such as Joseph Cuthbert, Rowley Osborne and Daniel Shanaghan were reported as having evinced their hostility towards the monarch with, according to the informer William Bird, toasts worse than any that would be heard in a French camp.[2]

Furthermore, Neilson's invective against the human and economic impact of the continuing war was unceasing. In May, the *Star* had recounted how the body of a woman, the wife of a poor labourer, had been found in the Six Mile Water near Templepatrick in County Antrim. One of her sons had enlisted, the other had been pressed into the army and she had killed herself in a state of grief; 'one of the effects', wrote Neilson bitterly, 'of this *glorious and necessary war*'.[3] As the war continued to undermine economic confidence, Neilson's criticism would become even more strident; he pronounced his satisfaction with the victories of the French at Montenotte and Altenkirchen. In July 1796, the *Star* filled its front page with a map of the Rhine to enable its readers 'to form a correct idea of the great progress of the French'.[4] While other newspapers, such as the *News-Letter*, the *Dublin Journal* and the *Freeman's Journal*, were aligning themselves with Dublin Castle, Neilson and Denis Driscoll, the editor of the *Cork Gazette*, were adopting more critical (and, in the prevailing climate, it might be said nihilistic) positions that would see both men face periods of confinement. In May, Neilson paid tribute to those Dublin editors who were displaying courage by refusing to conform to the conservative position. His editorial considerations resounded with an almost autobiographical tone as he attempted to defend the integrity of the press:

> If the people were aware of the dangers and difficulties these intrepid men encounter ... they will esteem them more than they do. If we were to estimate the merit and services of those few individuals as highly as they deserve, we would find that no men in society have greater and better claims on the gratitude of their fellow citizens. How often do they expose their own bodies to the envenomed darts of the enemy – to the rude attacks of courtly panders and to the deadly weapons of corrupt and corrupting scoundrels, regardless of personal safety, so they can protect the people with the impenetrable aegis of the press? We have living instance of such generous men, who in shielding others, exposed themselves to wounds which are still fresh bleeding.[5]

The beginning of the year witnessed the highest tide in living memory and the newspapers reported that Belfast was subjected to unprecedented levels of flooding, with Waring Street and even parts of Bridge Street submerged.[6] It was also the high watermark of political radicalism in the town, as the Belfast leadership took steps to ensure that Ulster would be prepared for the outcome of Tone's project in France. Neilson was at the forefront of this development. His immersion in subversive politics had been presaged by Drennan, who noted that he was evasive on a recent visit to Dublin, preferring to communicate with leading Catholics like McCormick and calling only once to see him 'and at that time he appeared glad to get away, said he would call again and never did'.[7] Neilson's behaviour may also have been attributable to the poor state of his finances, a possibility suggested by Martha McTier, who noted that Neilson had disregarded her request for assistance in a business venture and that 'his rather embarrassed circumstances' were the most likely explanation for his behaviour.[8] Neilson's Irish Woollen Warehouse had been taken over by the businessmen Vance and McKenny, who were supplied by their Dublin enterprise in Pill Lane. The death of his partner, Matthew Hughes, was a blow to Neilson, who, along with James Hyndman, acted as administrator for Hughes' estate. By the beginning of September, Samuel Neilson and Co. had been dissolved and an attorney charged with calling in outstanding debts. To compound these business difficulties, Neilson needed to employ a collector to visit those subscribers and advertisers to the *Northern Star* who were in arrears with their payments and wrote that he hoped his 'friends will be so good as to save him the trouble of frequent calls'.[9]

His growing financial worries notwithstanding, Neilson continued to play a leading role in the unfolding conspiracy that was centred on Belfast. His importance to the project is evidenced by the regularity with which his name crops up in the reports produced for the government by the notorious informer William Bird, who was communicating the most intimate details of the plot to the authorities. Bird, a blanket merchant and swindler who had been enlisted for the fleet before escaping, had arrived in Belfast from England the previous September after the failure of a business venture and, as a man with connections to English radical groups such as the London Corresponding Society, he was welcomed by figures such as Thomas McCabe, Samuel Kennedy (Neilson's compositor in the *Star* office and the secretary of the Irish Jacobins in Belfast) and Daniel Shanaghan, a legal clerk who was one of the few Catholics to play a significant role in the town's United Irish coterie.[10]

Bird's positive mood towards his new-found friends in Belfast was soon soured after he was unsuccessful in his requests for financial assistance from his hosts and he offered his services to the authorities as a means of remaining solvent. He made contact with Charles Skeffington, the Collector of Belfast, stating his willingness to expose the seditious activities of his erstwhile friends. While Bird was prepared to go to Dublin to provide information to the Castle, he was not prepared to testify in court. Despite this, his information, while no doubt embellished by bravado, offers a fascinating (and often corroborated) insight into the inner workings of United Irish activity in its Belfast hub. Bird's opening gambit was to reveal his desire to incriminate the 'nest of vipers' by providing information that 'would make the boldest among them tremble' and by disseminating mistrust and jealousy in such a way that would 'divide and ultimately annihilate them'. The Under-Secretary in Dublin, Edward Cooke, welcomed the potential that Bird's boasts seemed to offer and the authorities awaited the high-grade information on Belfast which had been, until then, episodic and inconsistent.[11]

There was much to report. The achievement of a rebellion assisted by a French invasion required more than just intrigue in Paris, although if the government was uncertain about this aspect of the project, Bird was able to inform his handlers not only that there was a significant United Irish presence in the French capital, but also that plans were afoot for a French expedition and that there were agents in Holland.[12] His imprecise but still valuable information coincided with the visit to Switzerland to meet representatives of the French military by the future commander-in-chief of the United Irishmen, Lord Edward Fitzgerald, and the leading firebrand Arthur O'Connor, a Cork-born aristocrat and former MP who was now firmly attached to the republican cause. The latter's return to the British Isles after a meeting with Lazare Hoche (who would lead a military expedition to Ireland in December) took him through Holland. But it was the detail of the conspiracy in Belfast and its environs that would make Bird a valuable informant.

The acquisition of arms and materials would be an obvious priority for the United Irishmen in 1796. The Chief Secretary, Thomas Pelham, was already aware of attempts to import gunpowder by Irish agents in London who had placed large orders with a company whose offices were located close to the monument commemorating the Great Fire in the city. Pelham was asking his contacts at the Home Office to locate this company because no imports of gunpowder had arrived in Ireland under licence, making it likely that supplies had been landed clandestinely.[13] Bird stated that the United Irishmen had been involved in the production of saltpetre (potassium nitrate), a component in the manufacture of explosives and gunpowder, 'on mountains, in glens and unfrequented places' by burying animal and vegetable substances and adding sulphur and charcoals provided by United emissaries. A James Neilson was alleged to be one of the men entrusted with this function, alongside the tailor Joseph Cuthbert. Among those tasked with the production of shot was the Dublin iron foundry owner Henry Jackson, the father-in-law of Neilson's Dublin-based friend and business colleague Oliver Bond. Neilson and McCabe were said to be responsible for the procurement of guns, many of which had already been landed at different points around the country.[14]

The rapid arming of the United Irishmen would certainly have concerned the government and Bird's bulletins were corroborated by other sources. It was reported, for example, that 20,000 bags of saltpetre were sold at an auction of East India goods in the late summer and that much of this stock was purchased by brokers working on behalf of Irish merchants. Some of the saltpetre that had already arrived in Ireland was impounded by revenue commissioners.[15] Neilson's familiarity with the potential of saltpetre was probably enhanced by the fact that his late brother Alexander, a druggist, had stocked the commodity in his Belfast premises and Neilson would have been aware of its properties.[16] The Lisburn doctor and manufacturer, Alexander Crawford, a former Volunteer with close connections to the United Irishmen, no doubt cast suspicion on himself by appealing to the authorities for leniency in his attempts to acquire saltpetre, a crucial ingredient in the production of the sulphuric acid used as part of the linen-bleaching process. The government had established a procedure whereby ships carrying the material between Ireland and England could sail only as part of a convoy and this resulted in low supplies and frustrating waits. Crawford would later be imprisoned on the information of the notorious informer Edward Newell.[17]

Bird had informed the authorities in July that the United Irishmen were desperate for gunpowder and government supplies were likely to be targeted. In October, a raid on the military stores in Belfast delivered ten barrels into the hands of the conspirators, an act of daring that led the town sovereign, John Brown, to conclude that there had been collusion between the United Irishmen and sections of the military.[18] There was indeed a concerted attempt to attract members of the soldiery into the ranks of the United Irishmen. Figures such as Cuthbert, Daniel Shanaghan and Rowley Osborne were befriending troops in the taverns and spreading disaffection. Osborne, whom Bird described as 'a man of the first rank as a republican of the north', had served in the Volunteer artillery and written a treatise for his co-conspirators on the use of small arms.[19] On one occasion, Shanaghan showed Bird a small part taken from a cannon by one of the artillery militiamen, suggesting that the United Irishmen were encouraging military sabotage.[20] The large presence of militia troops at Blaris Camp near Lisburn provided the United Irishmen with an excellent opportunity to sow the seed of sedition. In April 1795, Neilson had informed his readers that it was the government's intention to establish a large military encampment there, capable of accommodating five or six thousand troops. It would be one of four such facilities, aimed at housing and training the militia regiments in preparation for service, the others being located at Loughlinstown (south of Dublin, with a view of protecting the capital in the event of a coastal invasion), Naul to the north of the city and Clonmel in Tipperary. The building of barrack huts in Dublin would delay the opening of Blaris Camp until July and when the troops had moved in, every effort was made to render the arrangements acceptable to the Catholic soldiers based there, with the camp commander, Major-General George Nugent, permitting troops to march to Sunday Mass in Lisburn chapel. Neilson was content to accept the advertising revenue that came from the district quartermaster's invitation to local producers to bring their goods to market on the promise that current prices would be offered.[21]

For Neilson and the republicans of Belfast, the presence of thousands of Catholic militiamen, many of whom (as the *Star* reported) had resisted their recruitment during the previous two years, was as much an opportunity as a threat. It became a central strategy of the United Irish conspiracy to infiltrate the militia regiments and swear troops into the movement, a task that was facilitated by the close links that had been cultivated with the Defenders. Bird alerted the authorities to this, pointing out that United Irish meetings were being held among the soldiery and that the whole of Blaris Camp was at the disposal of Belfast, an exaggeration certainly, but a cause of genuine concern. His advice was that the government should dissolve the militia since its artillery companies were 'filled with Republicans and Defenders'. Bird's connections with some of the leading radicals in Belfast allowed him to learn that 1,600 soldiers in the camp had allegedly been sworn in as United Irishmen, with 650 of these being 'up and up', that is, both United men and Defenders. After spending the day drinking with Shanaghan, Bird learned that he and Cuthbert, along with their wives, once hired a coach and four horses, complete with a coachman and footman in the finest laced liveries, to travel to Blaris to distribute seditious literature and money (five guineas) among the militia. [22]

The informer Leonard McNally was also aware of the importance of Blaris to the United Irishmen's project, alleging that he had it on good authority that the whole camp 'is organized and looks forward to such a revolution as will give Ireland a pure republican government and dissolve all connection between her and Great Britain'.[23] Information such as this was considered sufficiently important that it ended up on the desk of the Chief Secretary, Henry Pelham, who would have been alarmed further by the fact that officers in the Limerick City Militia were concerned about the loyalty of their men while members of the Queen's County Militia had been similarly compromised and, fully contrite, had asked the regiment's commander-in-chief, the Earl of Portarlington, to be allowed to serve as soldiers anywhere in Britain or beyond as a punishment.[24] Another informer, Newell, reported that one Alexander Kennedy was the most active agent at the camp and that 'he had made more soldiers United Irishmen than any other man in the province'.[25]

The military hierarchy would continue to grapple with the problem of disaffection among the militia and the discovery of United Irish cells within the Monaghan Militia in April 1797 by its colonel, Charles Leslie of Glaslough, led to the execution of four of its soldiers the following month. The problem of disloyalty within Blaris Camp was not ameliorated by the arrival of irregular troops from Scotland, with members of the Highland regiment, the Breadalbane Fencibles, being suspected of having been sworn in as United Irishmen. An exasperated General Lake, commander of the English forces in Ulster, would exclaim that 'Blaris Camp is the devil and all his ____ . I heartily wish they were all in hell.'[26] The conversion of the troops at Blaris was a crucial part of the United Irish plan. The negation of the Crown forces there would have had serious consequences for the prosecution of the counter-revolutionary strategy and provided the rebels with valuable manpower and weaponry in the event of an insurrection. Furthermore, the location of the camp at the junction of counties Antrim and Down offered the opportunity for the United Irishmen (in the event of a successful uprising with significant military support) to capture these two counties rapidly. As it turned out, however, the loyalty of the militia was not compromised in 1798 and the potential displayed two years earlier was never fulfilled, a calamitous setback for the United Irish conspiracy.

Bird's connections in Belfast were primarily with men of the second rank within the United Irishmen in the town. Although relatively prosperous, figures such as Shanaghan, Cuthbert, Osborne, Samuel Kennedy and Thomas Potts were hard-drinking republicans who were a rung below the likes of Neilson, Russell, Haslett and Thomas McCabe on the social ladder. Some of them became leading members of an assassination group that was active in the elimination of informers and spies during the latter part of 1796 and early 1797.[27] Bird admitted that one of his major difficulties was that these men would tend only to divulge information when intoxicated and that he would need to enter this state as well in order not to arouse suspicion. This brought with it attendant difficulties: 'There is one thing wherein they puzzle me, which is, that they seldom say much till they are nearly drunk, and by the time I get them in that plight, I am little better myself, and tho' they were to open their hearts ever so liberally, I stand a fair chance of forgetting it by morning.'[28]

The prize for Bird was to discover information about the leading radicals in the town. He admitted to knowing nothing about Thomas Russell, save that he was held in the highest regard by the men of Belfast and that his writings had done an essential service in the promotion of the United Irish project. Although he had been drinking with Henry Joy McCracken in the company of William Clarke and one Cunningham, he had nothing of substance to say about him.[29] His knowledge of Neilson was based largely on what he had been told by his associates. This remoteness from the leading players in Belfast does undermine his overall credibility as an informer. Samuel Kennedy had told him that Neilson and Shanaghan had been in Dungannon in July 1796 as delegates to a provincial meeting of the United Irishmen that focused on both its internal organisation and on the provision of financial aid to help pay the costs of defending leading Catholics in Armagh, such as Bernard Coile. It was John Young, a Belfast publican, who told Bird that Neilson had received letters in June from the United Irishmen in Dublin, Cork and Limerick, stating that they were ready to rise when the northern leadership deemed the time to be right.[30]

Bird spent little time in Neilson's company, but he did manage to obtain an invitation to dinner in his house through the auspices of Samuel Kennedy and he would pass on the details of this evening to the authorities. During their meal, Neilson was interested in Bird's connections with English radicals, although he observed dryly that while republicans there were in a very small minority, he considered the reverse to be the case in Ireland. He also criticised the openness of English radical societies, a transparency that made them penetrable. Neilson boasted, somewhat ironically given the status of his guest, that the United Irishmen were secure from infiltration because each branch was limited to thirty-five members and the strong test taken by them, coupled with the caution of the leadership, made the organisation difficult to break. Moreover, unlike the English societies, the United Irishmen committed nothing to paper. As the conversation developed, Neilson asserted that Irish independence would be a positive boost to the English economy because 'what England lost in prerogative she would gain in commerce'. When the conversation turned to Catholics, Neilson's longstanding concerns about their reliability in the political struggle can again be seen. While he acknowledged that there were enlightened and patriotic Catholics, he felt that the majority were scarcely to be trusted and he feared that 'the great mass were Bigots to monarchy' and, by implication, conservative by nature. He was of the opinion that Catholics (he specifically included the Defenders in his analysis) were useful to the project because of the sheer force of their numbers, but that they also were likely to undermine the cause of the United Irishmen because they lacked leadership and were 'nothing more than an undisciplined rabble'.[31] Neilson's quintessentially Presbyterian view of Catholics was that they lacked both the religious individualism to find ecclesiastical truth and the political imagination for republicanism.

He would adopt this theme in an editorial in June, when he criticised the control exerted over the Irish Catholic Church by the papacy, questioning why the Irish hierarchy would want to 'hug its chains' during such an enlightened period, when radicals were looking forward to the 'approaching downfall of the Pope'.[32] The evening was doubtless convivial and many toasts were drunk; Neilson raised a glass to show support for the French Republic. Toasts were also drunk to the success of the French army and navy, while Bird acclaimed General Pichegru (the French hero of the Fleurus and conqueror of the Netherlands). Bird also proposed that 'Liberty make the tour of Europe in a Triumphal Car'.[33]

In the one meeting he had with Bird, Neilson was circumspect and while he underscored his radical credentials, he said nothing that would implicate himself. Indeed, it would appear that Bird was viewed with suspicion from the outset 'as he gave uncommon seditious toasts after dinner such as put Neilson on his guard'. The stranger was to have dined with Haslett the following evening, but was not admitted because Neilson had passed on his concerns about the newly arrived Englishman with unconfirmed radical connections.[34] For his part, Bird's knowledge of Neilson was second-hand, provided by acquaintances like Kennedy, Shanaghan, Osborne and Young. He did, however, describe him as 'a man of the most rigid cast and a great affecter of consequence gloomy and pedantic. He is at the Head of the Conspirators [and] knows everything – but I am pretty certain he'll suffer death rather than tell anything.' Bird believed, however, that Neilson would be condemned if any of his associates were to turn informer.[35]

The upsurge in military activity (including the raising of a loyalist yeomanry that was considered more reliable than a militia vulnerable to republican infiltration) and the emergence of Orangeism, combined with the worries about the United Irishmen being undermined by spies and informers, pushed its members into more furtive activity as secrecy became paramount. There had long been a commonality between Freemasonry in Ulster and the United Irishmen; the resolutions published in the *Northern Star* from some lodges in 1792–3 indicated that there was an ideological affinity between Freemasonry, volunteering and the United Irishmen that centred on truth, justice, liberty and the rights of man.[36] While the rules of freemasonry, enunciated in the *Constitutions of Freemasonry or Ahimon Rezon*, published in several editions after 1723, stated that 'Polemical or political discussions shall not, under any pretence whatever, be permitted in any

Masonic assembly', it is clear that some Masonic lodges provided the environment for debate on matters constitutional, be they supporting or opposing the radical position.[37] In August 1796, Bird informed Cooke that it was a deliberate policy of the United Irishmen to establish a connection between the movement and the Freemasons. With typical flourish, he asserted, 'There is scarcely in the North a United Irishman who is not a Mason ... so that they have opportunities of meeting just as often as they please.' It was also expected that those Masons who were not United men would refrain from informing on their brethren because of the strength of the oaths taken. Bird alleged that the republican strategy of using the lodge room as a cover for sedition was a successful one and the United Irishmen pursued the order avidly, with few failing to comply. He reported that Thomas McCabe had recently joined the brotherhood.[38]

The largest Freemasons' lodge in Belfast was the 'Orange' Lodge, Number 257, revived in the 1780s by Amyas Griffith. The membership had traditionally been eclectic, with the Earl of Hillsborough and his son, Lord Kilwarlin, taking their seats in the lodge room alongside more liberal figures such as Griffith. The leading United Irishmen Henry Haslett and William Tennent joined Lodge 257 as early as 1791 and it is interesting to note that in 1796 prominent republicans from the town, such as William (brother of Henry Joy) McCracken, William Boyd, James McGucken and Robert Hunter, would all be sworn in. Neilson joined the Lisburn Lodge 193 in June 1796, a choice perhaps motivated by the fact that an awareness of the United Irish dynamic in the vicinity of Blaris Camp would assist with strategic planning for the unleashing of a rebellion.

Other members of this lodge included the apothecary Samuel Musgrave (later arrested on the same day as Neilson in September 1796), Henry Monro, the commander of the United Irish forces in County Down in 1798, and Bartholomew Teeling, one of Luke's sons who would later be executed for his part in the French military expedition in the west of Ireland in the year of the rebellion, during which he served as aide-de-camp to General Humbert.[39] Neilson's membership of a Lisburn lodge allowed him to be in close proximity to the Defender leadership that centred on Luke Teeling's Poleglass bleach works. Under the cover of Freemasonry, United Irish emissaries would be free to traverse the province inculcating radical ideas. Neilson's nephew, John Gordon, whose central role in the conspiracy would become clear during the period from late 1796 to the outbreak of the rebellion, was identified as being present in County Tyrone in October with the purpose of 'planting societies in different parts'. Information coming to Thomas Knox in Dungannon indicated that Gordon travelled under the pretext of selling muslins and that he was a Freemason.[40]

By the late summer of 1796, Bird had become fearful for his life. He had aroused suspicion because he was showing no visible means of supporting himself, despite having asked his new friends for financial assistance. The ever-astute Martha McTier would note later that Bird had been suspected and even hated in the town because he was 'sometimes poor at other times rich'.[41] While some friends who had seen his letters of introduction from radicals in England were happy to trust him, the rumours of his spying proved impossible to shake off and he departed the scene, petrified that he was going to be murdered by the 'Brown Square Boys'. He took a boat from Groomsport in County Down to the Isle of Man and thence to Liverpool, where he continued to make contact with his handlers in Dublin.[42] Taken as a whole, Bird's evidence is a combination of what Thomas Bartlett calls 'cheap tittle-tattle' (such as his relaying of information about late-night drinking and the personality traits of leading republican figures) and useful observations about the practical workings of the United Irishmen in its northern hub. He advised his handlers that the radicals were fearful of the threat posed by Orangeism and that the authorities should both officer and arm the Orange Order. He asserted that militia regiments were being infiltrated and also that there were United Irish links with the French. He suggested that the government's provoking of a premature rebellion would be a useful strategy because the United Irish leadership would become divided and open to betrayal. His analysis was that 'The men of B[elfast] are wealthy, wiley [*sic*] and avaricious – they are too tenacious of life and property to move themselves whatever they may effect by means of others, and however they may bravado they will never dare to act decisively till they are aided by the French.'[43]

This assessment efficiently sums up where the United Irishmen stood at this time: Neilson and his colleagues were preparing the ground for the fulfilment of Tone's plan to seek the co-operation of the French and the United Irish leadership would not contemplate precipitating a rising without the arrival of foreign troops – until, that is, the split between moderates and extremists within the Dublin leadership at the end of the following year. Moreover, the capitalist instincts of the Belfast merchants would see some of them retreat from their republicanism as the day of reckoning approached, including men such as Robert Getty, William Sinclaire and Gilbert McIlveen – all founder members of the United Irishmen. When the rebellion broke out in the early summer of 1798, Robert Simms, the appointed general for County Antrim, refused to commit because the French had not landed. However, some of those identified by Bird would become involved in the murky world of assassinations before the year was out, including Henry Joy McCracken, who would begin to exhibit the characteristics of a political fanatic.

Samuel Neilson was a wealthy businessman, but for him the political project had become more important than his business prospects, which he would lose along with his freedom in what was a clear contradiction to Bird's opinion of his former friends.

Worrying information from other sources was reaching the administration in Dublin. The United Irish activity in Belfast, Pelham was warned, was being directed by an executive group in the town, which called itself the Committee of General Welfare and oversaw the accumulation of arms, ammunition and pikes. (Military planning was shaped by the number of men in each society who had been Volunteers – marked as 'V' in membership lists.) None of the rank and file were aware of who actually served on this committee but it seems unthinkable that Neilson was not a leading light.[44] Another Belfast initiative was to assess the readiness of other parts of the country for an insurrection in the event of a French invasion. In the late spring and early summer of 1796, United Irish emissaries were sent to Dublin with letters of introduction from Neilson to leading strategists in the city, such as Edward Dunn and Richard Dry. It is likely that these emissaries were James Hope, the Templepatrick weaver and leading radical, and William Metcalf from the Purdysburn district, south of Belfast. Their job, in Hope's words, was 'to introduce the new United Irish system in the capital'.[45] At the same time, the Belfast United Irishmen Thomas Potts and Joseph Cuthbert were despatched to Glasgow with copies of the new United Irish constitution and they returned with positive news of support for the conspiracy in Scotland.[46]

By the time of Bird's hasty retreat in the late summer of 1796, the government had resolved to act and, while his refusal to testify in court was going to prove problematic, Lord Camden detailed the situation in the north (in what was largely a rehash of Bird's information) and recommended to Home Secretary Portland that the Belfast republicans be seized and *habeas corpus* suspended.[47] Plans for the arrest and detention of Neilson and his co-conspirators were set in motion. Oblivious to these preparations, Neilson continued to address his readership and respond to the challenges of distributing a radical newspaper in an increasingly polarised society. In early September, Neilson appealed to his subscribers in Armagh to excuse the irregularity of papers there, caused by the concerted attempts by Orangemen to disrupt its circulation: 'They have accordingly way-laid and abused several of our men and threatened them with instant death if they should ever return.' This was not simply *Northern Star* propaganda. General William Dalrymple, based in the county, informed Under-Secretary Cooke that 'At Richill, the Orangemen have almost killed the man who circulates the Northern Star.'

Despite the alternative delivery routes taken, the disruption to services was repeated barely three months later.[48] Of course, there were reciprocal attempts to stymie the delivery of the *Belfast News-Letter*, which, since Henry Joy had put the paper up for sale in late 1794, had been moving towards a conservative editorial position. A *News-Letter* carrier called Joseph McIlwaine was attacked in February 1797 on the road from Lisburn to Dromore and between 300 and 400 papers destroyed. A few days later, another delivery was halted and the newspapers thrown into a stream. Services in Dundonald and Portaferry were also disrupted during what became a newspaper war in just about every sense of the term.[49]

The feud between the two Belfast newspapers over the dates of publication had reared its head again in May 1796. In an editorial, Neilson attempted to argue that the change in publication dates from Monday and Thursday to Monday and Friday was in direct response to requests from advertisers and subscribers and the decision was taken after the *News-Letter*'s new editor, Charles Gordon, declined to reach an accommodation with the *Star*, which had hoped to avoid direct competition with its rival.[50] This was the third change in publication date since the *Star*'s inception in January 1792 and Neilson's decision provoked a critical response from Gordon, which Neilson responded to in his next edition, referring to the 'real or pretended ignorance' of his counterpart and pointing out that the *News-Letter* had adopted an aggressive attitude to the *Northern Star* and had twice before changed its release dates to precede the publication of the *Star*. Gordon responded by criticising Neilson's suggestion that the *News-Letter* be published on Wednesdays and Saturdays – these had, after all, been the *Star*'s original issue days and if they were so advantageous, he mused, why did Neilson not retain them?[51] Not one to be cowed, Neilson offered the following observation in his next edition: 'When the editor of that paper thinks proper again to commence an unprovoked attack upon us, it is to be hoped he will conduct it with more patience and consistency.'[52]

Although it is undeniable that the distribution of the *Star* was being targeted by its enemies, Neilson was attempting to plant the spectre of Orange violence in the minds of his readers while, at the same time, seeking to moderate the behaviour of those whose activities threatened to subject parts of Ulster to the draconian terms of the Insurrection Act passed that year by the Irish Parliament. This measure enabled local magistrates to request the viceroy to subject districts to military discipline and remove the rights of assembly. Rampant Defenderism was likely to alienate Presbyterians in some localities and drive them into the ranks of loyalism. Concerned that the planting of liberty trees and the beating of Orangemen would bring the full rigour of the law down on areas where United

Irish and Defender influence was strong, Neilson called on the promoters of such violent conduct to desist, arguing that 'These men are little aware that they may actually be accessory, by these silly pranks, to have the county put out of the King's peace. Outrages of every kind are both criminal and disgraceful, tend to no good purpose, and always defeat the object of their promoters.'[53] Neilson was thus able to demonstrate that he was a conciliatory influence, but it was in his interest to propagate the United Irish project to the maximum in areas that needed to remain free from military control.

The authorities continued to prepare to arrest the ringleaders of sedition, fearing that some sort of uprising was imminent. The United Irishmen were, at this time, grafting a military command onto the existing local and county structures and, according to Madden, Thomas Russell was appointed as the general for County Down around the autumn of 1796.[54] Government anxiety was heightened by reports of intensive United Irish preparations across Ulster. At the beginning of September, Cooke was informed of suspicious activity in Coagh, County Tyrone, where 'two genteel young men were in this town from Belfast the whole night with the society in place'. Lord Downshire's correspondents were sending him the alarming news that United Irish emissaries were astir in every quarter, while Viceroy Camden was expressing his concerns about a French invasion. Writing from Dublin, Robert Ross scribbled that 'We certainly have very alarming accounts from the Northern counties in particular, that is to say from Down, Armagh, Tyrone and Antrim, and from Belfast in particular. I am satisfied that if even a privateer and crew were to land, an insurrection would be the consequence.'[55]

These anxieties were not without foundation. The informer McNally would later make the authorities aware that in the period before Neilson's eventual arrest, 'a native of this country came from France where he had long resided'. The emissary spoke to the leading United Irishmen in the town and, 'in a long and eloquent speech', announced that the French 'intended to end Ireland's subordination to Britain as long as the people show an inclination to support France in the event of an invasion'. The address was received with 'general and loud applause' by the leading militants in Belfast.[56] Something close to panic was enveloping conservative circles. A purported United Irish oath pledging 'that they shall exterminate all Orangemen out of the kingdom' seemed to indicate that a wave of violence would soon engulf the country, corroborating (in the minds of the authorities) what Bird had been told by the Belfast republican John Simpson, who boasted that it was their intention to extirpate every Orangeman in Ireland and that lists of loyalists were being drawn up in advance of an insurrection.[57]

Given the rumours of disaffection in the militia, Camden asked Lord Downshire to return to his estate from London to exert his influence in County Down and requested significant reinforcements of artillery and gunpowder from the Home Secretary, the Duke of Portland, including four 18-pounders, ten medium 12-pounders, twenty light 6-pounders, four 8-inch howitzers and enough entrenching tools for 1,000 men.[58] In the vicinity of Lisburn, the leading Orangeman Reverend Philip Johnson, the vicar of Derriaghy, established a loyalist association to arm Protestants against the threat of sedition. Such action increased animosity in an area where United Irish and Defender activity was strong and within two weeks of this development Johnson reported to Castlereagh that one of his more vocal followers, 'a foolish talking fellow', had boasted in public about the establishment of the loyalist group. That very night, a number of the man's cows and horses were brutally attacked and had their ears and tails cut off.[59] In these deteriorating circumstances, it was considered necessary to take decisive action against those Belfast republicans who were regarded as the fomenters of such unrest. Bird's flight, not to mention his reluctance to testify, created an obvious problem for the authorities and the emergence of a potential new prosecution witness against Neilson in August turned out to be nothing more than a ruse. Clutching at straws, Justice Boyd received sworn evidence from one of Neilson's employees at the *Star*, James Manson, claiming that 88,695 newspapers had been printed on paper without stamps over recent months.[60] A Belfast weaver prevailed upon by the Ballynahinch informer Pharis Martin Jun. had rejected a financial offer to incriminate Neilson and his colleagues.[61] None of this was likely to secure the conviction that the authorities wanted and needed; a more decisive – if risky – approach was required. The scene was set for what the *Northern Star* would refer to as 'wanton bravado and [a] contemptible invasion of ... peace' in Belfast on 16 September 1796.[62]

The arrests of the United Irish leaders in Belfast were well planned, as they needed to be, given that the success of the government's action would be 'of very material consequence to the country', according to Major-General Nugent, who was to be part of the military party. Nugent had met with Lord Downshire, Crown Solicitor John Pollock and Lord Castlereagh at Hillsborough on Tuesday, the 13th, to check the details of their mission. It was decided at this meeting that detaining the suspects in Carrickfergus and Downpatrick gaols would not be appropriate because of concerns about the resolve of local magistrates. Accordingly, the arrest warrants were returned to Edward Cooke in Dublin with the request that the prisoners be taken there. Dragoons were despatched to Newry to form a military escort to Drogheda and thence to Dublin.[63]

Castlereagh's conversion to the side of reaction was not untypical among those gentry who had rallied to the patriotic cause in the 1780s and enlisted as Volunteers. The drastically changed context meant that the issues at stake by the middle of the 1790s were of fundamental importance to the survival of the state. As Robert Stewart, he had fought a bitterly contested election against Lord Hillsborough in 1790, standing as a liberal candidate and availing of the support of Reverend William Steel Dickson (the Presbyterian minister in Portaferry and later a leading United Irishman) and Neilson, who had campaigned hard for the election of O'Neill and Rowley in County Antrim the same year. Castlereagh was regarded as a major disappointment by those who had invested so much in his youthful potential. His role as a leading architect of the government's counter-insurgency strategy prompted an acerbic rebuke in the first *Northern Star* to be printed after the arrest of its editor. Castlereagh was painted as 'the youthful apostate, who betrays his friends and insults his benefactors ... At one time we were almost persuaded that this puppet was a real man.'[64]

Equipped with the amended warrants charging the sought men with high treason, the arresting party of Downshire, Castlereagh, Pollock and Lord Westmeath, accompanied by a large number of cavalry, arrived in Belfast on Friday morning at around ten o'clock in what the *Star* described as a 'shew of war'.[65] The warrants, signed by Justice Boyd, were not without errors: the document relating to Henry Joy McCracken bore the name James McCracken, while the warrant for Thomas McCabe erroneously identified him as John.[66] Neither of these men were detained, but others were, including the publican, John Young, Daniel Shanaghan, Samuel Kennedy, Rowley Osborne, Henry Haslett, Thomas Russell and Neilson. The house of the United Irishman and lawyer William Sampson was searched by the recently cuckolded Westmeath, whose wife, Marianne Jefferys, had had a scandalous affair that led to a well-publicised divorce earlier that year. Asked if Neilson was there, Sampson admitted he had visited earlier but that he had just left. Sampson registered surprise that the party had not seen Neilson in the street. As Westmeath continued his trawl, disturbing Sampson's wife as she lay in bed, the lawyer complained that she 'was not, as some other ladies are, in the habit of privately harbouring gentlemen'. The embarrassed peer made a hasty retreat and the *Star* delighted in informing its readers of this humorous interlude in what was otherwise a very dark day.[67] Westmeath was spared what Martha McTier referred to as the 'Belfast Laugh' by the more sympathetic Dublin newspaper editors.[68]

Aware that he was being sought, Neilson returned to his dwelling on Waring Street to see his wife Anne, before offering himself for arrest at the artillery barracks on Ann Street before Westmeath, who was reluctant to conduct the arrest because he was not in possession of the warrant. He eventually gave himself up to Pollock and Downshire at the premises of the Belfast Society for the Promoting of Knowledge, of which Russell was the librarian, and stated that all he would wish for was a speedy trial.[69] Neilson's calmness was no doubt based on a confidence that no evidence could be brought to bear against him and that the acquisition of a strong legal team would soon see him and his fellow detainees exonerated of all charges, as had been the case in 1794. The suspension of *habeas corpus* a short time later, however, showed that his optimism had been unfounded. The other suspects were rounded up, with one unsympathetic source saying that Rowley Osborne 'wept much' while Haslett was 'sullen'. An 'agitated' Russell presented his illustrious captors with a copy of his recently published pamphlet, *A Letter to the People of Ireland*.[70] At around three o'clock, a train of seven post-chaises departed the town *en route* to Dublin, with Castlereagh at the front of the procession and Captain Coulson of the artillery at the rear.[71] As the train departed, it was said that Anne Neilson acted like Brutus' wife Portia: a strong-willed woman, with perhaps a clear view of her husband's involvement in the conspiracy, she cheered him as the carriage was drawn along the street.[72] Haslett's wife would later take her revenge on Coulson, giving him a 'severe cudgelling in the street with her tongue'.[73]

Despite Neilson's earlier bravado, Martha McTier was aware of his vulnerability and wrote to her brother in Dublin, 'I hope there will be no irons. Neilson will be easily killed though he looks bluff.' She asked Drennan to call to see both him and Russell in prison and offered her assistance.[74] The Belfast prisoners were joined by other United Irish suspects who were arrested earlier that day in Lisburn, including Samuel Musgrave and Charles Teeling, the 18-year-old son of Luke, who was a leading figure in the establishment of the junction between the United Irishmen and Defenders. They were detained on the evidence given to the Reverend Johnson by Michael Lowry of Lissue near Lisburn. Lowry deposed that Teeling had sworn a man into the United Irishmen at the home of one Robert Brown in July and claimed that he had overheard a conversation involving the young republican, whereby the merits of an insurrection among the people of both Ireland and England were discussed.[75]

On arriving in Dublin on the Saturday evening, Neilson and most of the other suspects arrested in Belfast and Lisburn were committed to the new Kilmainham Gaol, which, despite having been opened only one month before, was a bleak place. At the outset, each prisoner would have his own cell, although this situation would change as the list of interned United Irish suspects grew longer.[76] Thomas Russell, Musgrave, Osborne and Young were taken to Newgate, an older and generally overcrowded prison where the inmates lived in complete squalor. The following morning, the men were brought before Justice Boyd to be committed formally. Teeling's subsequent account of this reveals Neilson as a swaggering ridiculer of the justice system, in line with the satire published in the *Northern Star* over several years. On being called forward, the following scene unfolded:

> Justice Boyd: 'Samuel Neilson.'
> Neilson: 'Here.'
> Boyd: 'You stand charged with high treason against ...'
> Neilson: 'Whom, my Lord?'
> Boyd: 'Suffer me to go on, sir.'
> Neilson: 'With great respect, I wish to set your Lordship right.'
> Boyd: 'I am right, sir.'
> Neilson: 'And sober too.'[77]

Neilson was rebuked for his levity by Russell, who had a regard for the etiquette of the courts, having been appointed as Seneschal to the Manor Court of Dungannon five years earlier.

The men were returned to gaol. Drennan related that he was refused access to Russell and visitors to Kilmainham had similarly been turned away. Rumour and speculation soon became rife and Drennan noted that it was said among the guards that Rowley Osborne, one of the arrested men, had turned informer.[78] A scribbled note on a copy of the arrest warrants made reference to the fact that Osborne knew everything about the Belfast conspiracy and was very frightened. The notes suggested that John Young, Shanaghan and Henry Haslett were also likely to 'peach'.[79] The *Northern Star* printed an angry denial of a rumour published in the London-based *Sun* newspaper, which suggested that Russell had turned informer.[80] The pro-establishment *Dublin Journal* added further spice to the mix by alleging that one of the Newgate prisoners had become deranged, with violent apprehensions of being assassinated by two of his fellow detainees who had been arrested on the same day.[81]

Meanwhile, an anonymous figure, signing himself 'A.B.', wrote to Chief Secretary Pelham offering to authenticate the handwriting of 'certain United Irishmen and newspaper printers' whose papers were confiscated, and awaited a government response through the medium of the *Dublin Journal*.[82] The prisoners were to be kept apart and deprived of pens, ink and papers. As the reality of confinement set in, both Neilson and Henry Haslett wrote to Edward Cooke requesting the privilege of allowing their wives to visit.[83] The women did indeed call upon their husbands and in October Anne Neilson was permitted to spend the night in the prison with Samuel. She remained close to him, staying at the home of James Dixon, a Catholic tanner and United Irishman who resided in the Kilmainham area of Dublin and could call upon the prisoners.[84] The Castle was being informed that the 'wives of some of the most respectable state prisoners' feared that their husbands would be killed by nervous guards, fearful of a rescue attempt from sympathisers on the outside.[85] Their friends, among them Drennan and Oliver Bond, were instead working hard to secure the services of the barrister Leonard McNally (who was in fact an informer, passing information to the authorities under the pseudonym 'J.W.') and John Philpot Curran, who had been part of the legal team working on behalf of Neilson and the proprietors of the *Northern Star* in 1794.[86]

Camden was confident of a conviction, detailing to the Duke of Portland in London that the United Irish leaders were guilty of treasonable correspondence and the propagation of seditious principles. 'Against some of these persons there is every reason to believe we shall establish guilt,' he claimed.[87] The suspension of *habeas corpus*, however, meant that the authorities were able to ride roughshod over their entitlement to a fair trial and so Neilson remained in Kilmainham, frustrated by his powerlessness to undermine the Crown case against him and concerned, no doubt, by the uncertainty over both the future of the *Northern Star* and the direction of the conspiracy back in Belfast.

As regards the conspiracy there, the authorities soon discovered that the removal of these state prisoners from the political scene there did not incapacitate the United Irishmen. Rather, the leadership of the society fell upon a younger and more militant grouping whose activities in the weeks before the arrests were such that the authorities simply had to take the initiative. Camden was soon convinced that the abilities of the detained individuals were to be feared less than the strength of the movement as a whole and while the arrest of Neilson, Russell and Haslett checked the progress of the United Irishmen, 'they soon again proceeded with as much system and more vigour than before'.[88] The mantle of leadership was assumed by figures such as Henry Joy McCracken, son of the respectable sea captain and cotton manufacturer John McCracken and his wife Ann Joy, whose father had established the *Belfast News-Letter* in 1737.

McCracken is not often mentioned in the accounts of the early business of the United Irishmen, although there can be little doubt that he was acquainted with its leading players. When the society remodelled itself in response to both a government clampdown and its own radicalisation, McCracken was sworn into the Third Society on 24 March 1795 by one H.M. Hull.[89] Possessed of similar democratic and egalitarian impulses to those of social reformers like Thomas Russell, McCracken felt at ease with those of a lower social standing who would have been welcomed into the Muddler's Club, a society that was aligned with the United Irishmen and acted as a forum whereby visitors to Belfast would be entertained and briefed on the progress of the plot. Neilson and Russell gave advice to its members and were no doubt present at many of its discussions in Campbell's public house in the Sugarhouse Entry.[90] McCracken was also a key figure in the attempts by the United Irishmen in Belfast to liaise with the Defenders. The previous year, Patrick Callaghan, a leading Defender in Down, told the informer Friar Phillips that McCracken 'had been chosen to visit different parts of the north to reconcile them to the principles of the Belfast society' and he had given a purse of gold coins to Callaghan to assist with this task.[91]

McCracken's associates in the maintenance of the United Irish conspiracy included two of Neilson's nephews, Alexander Gordon (one of his uncle's partners in the business that had been established in the aftermath of the dissolution of Samuel Neilson and Co.) and his brother John, Thomas Potts, Joseph Cuthbert, Thomas Storey and Charles O'Donnell. Under their influence, the United Irishmen in Belfast unleashed a system of terror on those who were suspected of being in the pay of the government, giving rise to accusations that the United Irishmen were operating a policy of assassination.

The evidence for this predates Neilson's arrest and helps to explain why Castlereagh and Downshire took the actions they did. On Sunday, 7 August 1796, a body was discovered in the River Lagan in the Strand Mills (Stranmillis) area south of the town. A court of enquiry before the sovereign, Stewart Banks, recorded a verdict of accidental death. It was observed that the injury to the man's eye and his broken nose were likely to have been caused by his fall, while his flesh wounds and blood-clotted face were the result of being fed upon by 'eels and other fish'. Papers found in the dead man's pocket identified him as Joseph Connolly, a private in the City of Limerick Militia. Earlier that summer, he had requested permission to leave his regiment for a period of thirty-one days in order to go to Belfast, where he said he could provide service to the authorities by identifying those colleagues who had been sworn as members of the United Irishmen, as well as making further discoveries about sedition there. Connolly had been invited north by a Corporal Burke, who had promised him employment at the *Northern Star* since he had previously worked in the printing industry. Burke had lured Connolly with the prospect of securing vital information against the United Irishmen, since 'he knew the conductors of that paper to be among the leaders of that Society'. Aware that Connolly had communicated his intentions to travel to Belfast to a number of his colleagues, his commanding officer, Colonel Prendergast, advised him against going because he would be murdered. The soldier disregarded the warning and Prendergast reluctantly granted him permission to leave. Connolly subsequently expressed concern for his safety during a conversation with an unnamed officer in Belfast, since the job in the *Star* office did not materialise and Burke's conduct since his arrival had concerned him greatly. Connolly was due to report to Major-General Sir George Nugent at Hillsborough on the day after his body had been found. The general knew what had really happened: 'I am thoroughly convinced that he was discovered and made away with in the same manner that poor Friar Phillips was.'[92] Connolly had, indeed, been killed and elements within the United Irishmen were responsible for his death. The subsequent evidence of the informer Edward John Newell, a Downpatrick-born miniature painter, suggested that Connolly had been thrown from a bridge into the river by Corporal Burke and that he had been aided by Alexander Gordon, John Gordon and John Young, all of whom had beaten the soldier.[93] While Newell's credibility can be questioned, there is no doubt that much of his information was sound and indeed supported by circumstance and other evidence.

In September, just two days after the Belfast arrests, Edward Cooke received important information from Reverend William Lambart, the Anglican rector at Edenderry on the King's County estate of Lord Downshire. Lambart had overseen the arrests of two men, Dennis Delaney and Thomas Butler, deserters from the Queen's County Militia. Several implicating items were found in Delaney's pocket book, including resolutions of United Irish meetings and a number of oaths that were to be administered to recruits for the cause. Also discovered was a pass, authorised by someone with the initials 'HJMcC', that was to enable the two men to access United Irish (or perhaps Defender) societies in County Kilkenny. Delaney and Butler had become emissaries and their role was to convert people to the republican cause.[94] One month later, Lambart informed Lord Downshire that he had received information confirming that the initials sanctioning their safe passage were those of Henry Joy McCracken, whom he alleged 'was instrumental in many murders and also in the attempt on Mr Johnson [i.e. Reverend Philip Johnson] of Lisburn on last Saturday'.[95] The two deserters were returned to their commanding officer, the Earl of Portarlington, at Blaris, where they confirmed that their introduction to the Kilkenny republicans had been underwritten by McCracken. Portarlington went on to record that 'Butler and Delaney informed me that it was in consequence of Cpl Smith of the Limerick City Militia writing to McCracken, I believe they said, that if a private of the Limerick Regiment [sent to Belfast to get information for the government] was not put out of the way, that everything would be blown.'[96]

Remarkably, one of the newly incarcerated state prisoners, Rowley Osborne, was aware that the two militiamen had sworn examinations implicating McCracken and a fellow conspirator, Thomas Richardson, and he attempted to communicate this information to Belfast by writing to his friend Samuel Hewitt. However, the town's postmaster, Thomas Whinnery, was in the habit of intercepting the mail and he duly revealed that Osborne had advised 'HJ McCracken and Thos Richardson to escape as 2 of the Queen's Co. Militia whose names are Butler and Delaney have sworn examinations of a very dangerous nature.'[97] By the time the earl wrote his letter, McCracken had already been arrested and conveyed to Kilmainham under a warrant prepared by Justice Boyd. He was being watched by the Belfast vicar and elector, Reverend William Bristow, High Constable Atkinson, Town Collector Skeffington and others, who had observed that McCracken was frequently sent out on missions to the country. Bristow wrote to Downshire on 9 October, informing him that McCracken knew he was being tracked and that when arrested, he would be sent to the care of Reverend Johnston. Bristow too was unaware at this stage that McCracken had been captured the previous evening and that Johnston had been shot.[98]

McCracken and other leading Belfast United Irishmen were also alleged to have been fully aware of the events surrounding the attempted assassination of John Lee, a sergeant in the invalid company based in Carrickfergus, as he was travelling to Blaris Camp on 19 August. The background to this incident was the apparent emergence of an informer, 'Robert Smith' from Carrickfergus, who had offered to testify against Neilson and the other leading conspirators. Lee claimed that he had used 'every art and stratagem' to get Smith to declare all he knew before Edward Cooke at the Castle. Smith had received a guinea up front, with the promise of twenty more before leaving Belfast for Dublin, where it was hoped that Cooke would provide an additional £300 to enable Smith to settle in America.[99] While the *Belfast News-Letter* stated that Lee was delivering pension bills to Blaris, he was, in fact, bringing his prize informer to the camp to identify militiamen who were involved in the conspiracy. Lee's suspicion had not been aroused by the fact that it was Smith who had demanded they go to Blaris. The pair were intercepted by a party of between twelve and fourteen men near Drumbridge on the road between Belfast and Lisburn. According to Lee's own account, Smith suggested that he ride behind his controller in order to appear as a servant and, presumably, avert suspicion. It was at this point that Lee was shot by

Smith. Lee struggled to return fire because his horse had taken fright. He rushed to the camp, where he was attended to by Surgeon Moore of the Cavan Militia.[100]

The informer Bell Martin, who worked in Christopher Campbell's public house in Sugarhouse Entry, one of the inns frequented by the United Irishmen, provided information to the authorities. She was well known to the conspirators and made a deposition before Dean Dobbs about the events on the night Lee was shot. Martin lived with a certain Robert McCrea, in whose house the conspiracy was planned. McCracken and Joseph Cuthbert, along with two other men, oversaw the loading of two pistols there before sending Bell to Campbell's for 'cherries' (which turned out to be musket balls) wrapped in a handkerchief. The men left McCrea's in separate parties and returned the following morning without having been to bed and carrying a great coat, which Martin understood to be Lee's. Bell Martin believed the conspirators to be McCracken, his brother Francis, Thomas Potts, Thomas Storey, Cuthbert, John Tennent (younger brother of William), Alex Kennedy, William Clark, Dr Nixon and Gordon, 'a supposed partner of Neilson'. She alleged that the person who actually shot Lee was called McGahan.[101] McCracken's involvement in assassination plots sheds light on a rather cryptic letter written to him in Kilmainham the following March by his sister, Mary Ann. In it, she wrote that a certain article causing him some concern in the lead-up to his arrest had been given to a trusted friend and buried in the country – 'its being found will not injure anyone'.[102]

The murders continued after McCracken's detention. On 19 October, a cotton spinner named William McBride was killed on North Street. In a move that was probably designed to deflect attention away from the notion of an assassination squad at a time when some leading republicans were in prison, several prominent United Irishmen (including William Sampson, Francis Jordan, Francis McCracken and Thomas McCabe) contributed generously to a public subscription offering a reward for the capture of the assassins. At the end of the month, the life of the Reverend John Cleland (a magistrate and later handler of the County Down informer Nicholas Mageean) was spared only because an assassin's gun misfired in Newtownards. The situation was getting out of hand and within days Camden was writing to the Duke of Portland to tell him that a system of terror had become entrenched in Belfast and surrounding areas and that magistrates had been unable to acquire information on the agitators. Consequently, Lord Carhampton, the commander-in-chief of the army in Ireland, was heading north into Antrim and Down and it was hoped that this, plus the proclamation of these counties under the terms of the Insurrection Act, would have a subduing effect.[103]

On 8 November, the body of a butcher, John Kingsbury, was found on the road to Lisburn, near Drumbridge. Carhampton believed that the murder was carried out by a gang from Belfast that followed Kingsbury because he and others had been singing loyal songs in a public house. He informed Pelham that apprehensions were imminent and the information provided by Sergeant Lee and Bell Martin contained sufficient grounds for this.[104] Arrests followed quickly, with Cuthbert, Potts, Storey, O'Donnell and John Gordon being rounded up on a charge of conspiracy to murder. An advertisement in the *News-Letter*, submitted by Colonel Lucius Barber, made a clear connection between the captured men (described as 'ruffians') and the murder of Kingsbury and there was an implication that the *Northern Star* 'seemed calculated to encourage such horrid proceedings'. Such an association was likely to jeopardise the chances of a fair trial and the *News-Letter's* editor, Charles Gordon, became aware of popular dissatisfaction with Barber's action, forcing him to publish an explanation of what had happened. He claimed that he had accepted Barber's printed notice for publication without reading it carefully and, once he had done this, he had sent a card to the colonel asking for alterations to be made. The editor argued that, while the advertisement did not reflect his own sentiments, he could not refuse its insertion.

The imprisoned men were not prepared to let the issue lie and a statement from them was published in the *News-Letter* and the *Star*, expressing their objection to the fact that they had been calumniated in such a public manner by 'treacherous insinuations' that prejudiced their case. The detained concluded that they 'earnestly look forward to the day when an impartial Jury in our country will pronounce our innocence'. The jurors involved in studying Kingsbury's death inserted a piece in the newspapers clarifying that while they had acknowledged that the dead man had received three stabs from a bayonet or a similar weapon, they had no evidence tending to involve any person with the murder.[105] The *Star's* position was clear – the auspices of the *Belfast News-Letter* had been used to condemn the men, who were arrested 'on the evidence of a common prostitute' (that is, Bell Martin). There was criticism too of the *Freeman's Journal* and the *Dublin Journal* for their reporting of the Belfast arrests. Faulkner's *Dublin Journal* had described the capture of four members of the assassination committee of Belfast, all heads of the United Irishmen.[106] Notwithstanding the arrests in Belfast, worries about assassination plots continued, and Lord Downshire reported to Camden in December that he too was at risk. The following month he was informed by one of his correspondents, the staunchly conservative landowner Lord Annesley, that a group of assassins had gathered at Kate McKay's Bridge (now Katesbridge in

County Down) in the hope of intercepting him as he journeyed from Rathfriland to Hillsborough.[107]

While Belfast was experiencing such dangerous levels of assassination attempts and counter-insurgency, Neilson was languishing in Kilmainham. The harassment and elimination of those whose testimonies could indict him and his fellow prisoners were probably considered unpleasant but necessary. Furthermore, when he was joined in Dublin by prisoners such as Cuthbert and his nephews, the Gordons, there was no obvious expression of disapproval of their actions. The reality was that the United Irish conspiracy, with Neilson at its head, had developed dramatically during the previous twelve months, and the appearance of a French fleet off the coast of Cork in late December was an indication of just how far the plot had advanced. There would be no turning back.

7

Within These Walls, 1797

The unity of purpose which characterised the northern United Irishmen in late 1796 was demonstrated by the remarkable solidarity shown towards the imprisoned leadership. During the harvest, the crops of those incarcerated were lifted in repeated acts of defiance that resembled military manoeuvres as much as agricultural routines. Exactly one month after his arrest, Neilson's potato crop on his Skegoneill farm was dug by over 1,500 people in around seven minutes, with additional gatherings in places such as Kells and Drumbo to assist other families affected by the government policy of detaining suspects without the need to produce evidence before the courts. Another high-profile prisoner, Rowley Osborne, had one of his holdings slated by volunteers who assembled at his Belfast home to carry out the repairs.[1] Responding sarcastically to loyalist descriptions of the United Irishmen as swine and reptiles, the *Star* was quick to remind its readers that the crowds who rallied to the assistance of their imprisoned colleagues exhibited behaviour that was disciplined, orderly and productive, unlike the Orangemen, whose depredations would 'drive innumerable families from their habitations and barbarously destroy many of their fellow creatures'.[2]

In October, 600 assembled to raise the oats of William Orr near Antrim a few days after the corn grown by a Mrs Clark from Swatragh (close to Magherafelt), whose son was in gaol for being a United Irishman, was cut in two hours. Reporting on this show of strength, the editors observed that 'These swine did not grunt at all when they were at work.'[3] With further activity in Doagh, Rashee, Killymoon, Lisburn and Coleraine (where '8,500 reptiles crept out of their holes'), it was becoming clear that these shows of United Irish strength threatened to stretch the magistracy to the limit, especially when combined with more sinister activity.[4] Writing to Downshire, the Bishop of Dromore recognised that the republicans were gathering to gauge their strength in different areas and that 'after the digging is over, they meet at night for the purpose of mustering, even drilling and training'.[5] In the Sperrin Mountains in County Derry, a loyalist landowner reported his concerns to Cooke in Dublin Castle, informing the Under-Secretary that the men assembled for potato digging carried their spades like muskets and gave the distinct impression that they could carry weapons with equal balance and precision.[6] Lord Carhampton's arrival in Belfast brought some assurance to the fearful, but even he acknowledged that while the United men were unlikely to meet for potato diggings close to areas where troops were encamped, some other means of assembling and drilling – most likely funerals – would be contrived.[7] In a show of strength near Lisburn on Saturday, 12 November 1796, the magistrate Reverend Philip Johnson, who had survived an attempt on his life weeks before, led a party of loyalists (presumed to be Orangemen) to disrupt a potato digging on the land of Jeremy Galway in Stoneyford. According to the *Northern Star*, a number of people were injured and only the intervention of two dragoons and a servant of Lord Downshire ensured that a massacre did not occur.[8]

Given the extent to which Neilson, McCracken and others had supported Defender prisoners such as Bernard Coile during their earlier incarceration, it is hardly surprising that republicans rallied to the aid of those United Irish leaders who were arrested in Belfast and Lisburn. Neilson's detention took him away from his business interests, chief among which was the *Northern Star* itself. Robert and William Simms, two of the proprietors still at liberty, were assisted by employees such as the chief clerk Matthew Smith, William Kean and William Templeton. Unsurprisingly, the immediate aftermath of the arrests saw a surge in support for the radical enterprise, so much so that Charles Gordon (the editor of the *News-Letter*) feared for the future of his paper as several merchants had organised a campaign to withhold advertisements, forcing him to look to the government for support.[9] Nevertheless, despite an increase in the *Star's* readership, the paper was in financial difficulty. In October, Smith had to sign a promissory note for £100 to an Alexander Blackwell, while in January 1797 agents were sent into a number of districts to collect unpaid subscriptions.[10] Just as worryingly, without Neilson's watchful eye, the quality of the paper began to suffer; the banner on the 28 November–2 December 1796 edition read *Star Northern*, while the new editors felt the necessity to offer an apology to their readers for the poor quality of the paper being used, a consequence of unpaid subscriptions and advertising debts.[11]

In February 1797, the office of the *Northern Star* was attacked by the military. The dispute between the newspaper and Colonel Lucius Barber over the arrests of those suspected of the murder of John Kingsbury at the end of the previous year was one factor that helps to explain this deliberate act of state persecution. A further reason was undoubtedly that the *Northern Star* had been adamant in telling its readers that the fleet assembling off Bantry in December was not, in fact, French. Once it was apparent that a French invasion force under General Lazare Hoche had indeed attempted to land, the *Star* defended his reputation as the suppressor of a counter-revolution in La Vendée, refuting accusations that he had been involved in atrocities there against opponents of the new regime.[12] In addition, the newspaper continued its *exposé* of loyalist atrocities and ran the satirical 'Billy Bluff and the Squire' series, produced by the wickedly humorous pen of Reverend James Porter from Greyabbey, which lampooned the local aristocracy in County Down. At this stage, loyalists such as Humphrey Galbraith, the customs officer in Groomsport, County Down, were asking questions about the legality of the articles being published and the impact of the paper's ability to print sedition with apparent impunity: 'If it were possible for government to suppress the infamous paper called The Northern Star of Belfast, it would produce a very happy effect, for it is that has poisoned the minds of the people with its rebelly [*sic*] and republican principles.'[13]

Furthermore, an address to the electors of County Antrim, written by the increasingly outspoken Arthur O'Connor (the former MP for Philipstown in King's County who had declared his intention to run for election to the Commons for County Antrim in 1797), had been published in the *Star* the previous October, arousing considerable hostility among conservatives. O'Connor's address declared: 'If union of Irishmen be treason and if to place the liberties of my country on its TRUE REPUBLICAN BASIS be treason, then I do glory in being a traitor.'[14] O'Connor had been in Hamburg with Lord Edward Fitzgerald in the summer of 1796 and met with Reinhard, the French minister there, before going to Switzerland and then to France to meet with Hoche to plan the military expedition. He was, by the end of the year, one of the five members of the newly established National Executive of the United Irishmen, along with Fitzgerald, Oliver Bond, Henry Jackson and William James MacNeven. O'Connor kept Belfast informed of his negotiations with Hoche and was residing 'at a country house Magee, the printer of the *Evening Post* lent me within a half a mile of Belfast' in preparation for the election.[15] He was joined in Belfast in December by his great friend, Francis Burdett, the famous English Radical MP, where they were reputedly entertained by the leading United Irishman, William Tennent.[16]

O'Connor was also present at the Belfast Exchange on 31 December 1796 when plans to establish a yeomanry company by leading moderates such as William Bruce, John Brown and Waddell Cunningham were derailed temporarily by a manoeuvre orchestrated by the prominent United Irishman William Sampson.[17] O'Connor's address was revised and re-published in January, touching a nerve in government circles so soon after the attempted landing at Bantry Bay. The presence of Lord Edward Fitzgerald in the town would also not have gone unnoticed. He met with Robert and William Simms, as well as with Sampson, and was apprised of the latest information on the conspiracy by O'Connor.[18] O'Connor's question, 'Could French invaders do worse than establish a system of corruption and unfairness as exists in Ireland already?' was seditious in the extreme and he was arrested in February 1797, with Viceroy Camden regarding the declaration so inflammatory that to do nothing would have opened the government to accusations of weakness. Camden informed his Chief Secretary that, in the light of the publication of O'Connor's address, warrants had been issued against the remaining printers of the *Northern Star*, Robert and William Simms.[19] The full fury of the government would descend once again on the *Star* and Barber reported to his superiors that the operation against the newspaper had been effected, with the Simms conveyed to Dublin and the printing office closed. A guard was placed at its door because the presses were too heavy to move. Barber advised Cooke that notice should be given that any future attempt to publish without having a registered printer would be a criminal offence.[20]

The response of Robert and William Simms was to complain bitterly to Cooke from their prison cell in Newgate, requesting that the presses be returned to the control of the remaining clerks and printers so that publication could continue despite the excesses committed by the military in what they described as an 'unprecedented act'. Their request for bail was denied and complaints about bad air and overcrowding ignored. Claims for an increase in their meagre daily prison allowance of five shillings – lower than that received by the other state prisoners – were similarly discounted.[21] The brothers, along with Neilson and Haslett, later lodged a claim for £5,000 compensation for the damage caused to the *Star* office by the 'swords, staves and bludgeons' of the military men who led the attack – Barber, Forster Coulson and William Fox – whose actions had prevented the proprietors from generating the means with which to pay off their debts.[22]

It was determined that, notwithstanding the barriers imposed by the military, the *Northern Star* would continue. Barber stumbled upon two printed handbills, one which praised Bonaparte's military achievements in Italy and a second (dated 10 February), which declared that the paper would be carried on as usual once a new printer received the authority to publish.[23] Despite the attempts by the Commissioner of Stamp Duties to prevaricate by refusing to issue a licence to print, the paper was revived and appeared again on 24 February with a stinging attack on those who were frustrating the proprietors from exercising their legal right. Within days, however, the situation had been resolved by the registration of Thomas Corbett as the new printer of the *Star*. His first publication requested that readers show patience as the new team came to terms with the intricacies of producing a twice-weekly newspaper: 'The plunder of the office – the consequent derangement of the Printing Materials – the imprisonment of ALL the proprietors and the inexperience of the Printer, will plead a powerful apology with a generous public, for any inaccuracies, mistakes or delays that may unavoidably occur in the management of the business.'[24]

These developments led to predictable outbreaks of violence against the men tasked with delivering both the *Star* and the *Belfast News-Letter* to their subscribers. The *News-Letter* informed its readers that future deliveries of the newspaper would be through the post office, necessitating a delay.[25] For its part, the *Northern Star* experienced renewed difficulties in its distribution, with its carrier being stopped in Hillsborough, detained overnight and threatened with imprisonment on board the prison tender that lay in Belfast Lough. This was in response to a biting remark about Lord Downshire in the edition of 17 March, when he was christened the Marquis of Upshire since his territory had once been Down but had now become 'Up' – that is, 'rebellious'. Copies of the paper were also stolen from the carrier on the road between Ballymoney and Coleraine in County Antrim.[26]

Despite the hyperbole, the newspaper project was in serious financial difficulty and Corbett warned readers that there would be no toleration of non-payment:

> The subscribers to the Northern Star are most respectfully informed that in future no papers will be forwarded to *any person whatever*, who does not pay in advance. The shameful conduct of many who have given our young men the trouble of a variety of calls (trifles to them, but when taken in the aggregate of some thousands, no trifles to the Proprietors) has been long overlooked: – but *now* that the National Banks have stopped payment – *now* that money is not to be had in any quantity, by those who have every exertion in their power – and *now* when ALL the proprietors, closely confined are deprived of the necessary means of expending any more of their property in support of that FREE DISCUSSION which has caused their imprisonment – it is to be hoped that every rational man will see the absolute necessity of this measure. Those who do not see it in this light will be so good as to pay what they owe and withdraw their names. The Northern Star will not go a begging. It requests no *favour* from the public. But it demands *Justice*.[27]

The *Star* remained critical of a government that it no longer viewed as legitimate, condemning a reverend magistrate in Derry for holding a young girl underwater until she had informed him of her father's whereabouts and suggesting that some magistrates had ordered prisoners be shot if attempts were made to liberate them. Alleged atrocities and excesses were reported, from drunken rampages of the militia in Loughbrickland to the dispersal of a wake in Newry. The Orangemen, 'those pillagers, burners and murderers', were depicted as villains whose activities were upheld by the state.[28]

General Gerard Lake, the commander of the army in Ulster, was convinced of the danger posed by Belfast and 'the seditious and diabolical wretches inhabiting that town'.[29] He was attempting to cultivate a positive relationship with those figures in the north who were opposed to the United Irishmen, such as the influential Waddell Cunningham, with whom he dined during the height of the crisis surrounding the *Northern Star* in February 1797.[30] Lake sought and received authorisation to take the fight to the conspirators who were causing such anxiety in loyalist circles in Belfast and throughout Ulster. On 1 March, Viceroy Camden informed his superior in London that Lake had been given orders 'to take the most effectual measures' to disarm all those not commissioned by the state.[31] Lake, a veteran of the American War and future commander-in-chief in India, took to the task with relish, informing Chief Secretary Pelham that he 'may rest assured that nothing but coercive measures in the strongest degree can have any weight in this country; the lower order of people and most of the middle class are determined republicans, have imbibed the French principles and will not be contented with anything short of a revolution – of this I am certain'.[32]

Lake's robust approach to the state of the province was refined by the suggestion of General John Knox, whose local knowledge of Tyrone and Armagh convinced him that the Orange Order could be harnessed by the state to eradicate the republican threat, a policy which, as Kevin Whelan argues convincingly, saw the government introduce sectarianism as a means of counter-revolution.[33] In this contaminated atmosphere, another attack on the *Northern Star* seemed a distinct possibility; this was acknowledged by Martha McTier at the end of the month.[34] Lake was certain of the need to shut down the newspaper that was criticising military policy in every issue. He wrote to Pelham: 'Surely the Northern Star should be stopp'd, the mischief that it does is beyond all imagination. May I be allowed to seize and burn the whole apparatus?'[35] But the reality was that the newspaper was operating legally, with stamp duty paid and a new printer registered with the government, so any attempt to close down the paper was likely to be challenged legally.

The termination of the *Northern Star* would occur soon enough, however, as circumstances in Belfast and the military camp at Blaris took a new and sinister turn. The informer Edward John Newell had managed to infiltrate the United Irishmen in Belfast and was able to deliver information to the authorities that would lead to the detention of those republicans who had become more prominent in the aftermath of the arrests of September 1796, when Neilson, Russell and others had been imprisoned on the basis of the information provided by Bird. Born in Downpatrick in 1771, Newell was a rootless philanderer who ended up in Belfast in 1796. A Defender and sometime United Irishman, Newell quickly found solace in the company of republicans in the town, being sworn into the United Irishmen in Mrs Magee's public house on Mill Street by John Gordon, Neilson's nephew, who was a clerk to John McCracken, one of the brothers of Henry Joy McCracken. Newell's political affiliation was betrayed by an acquaintance (a loyalist named Murdoch) and he became an informer after being transmitted to Dublin to meet with 'that arch betrayer of every honest heart ... the damned insinuating [Edward] Cooke'.

Upon returning north, Newell – in the disguise of a light horseman and with his face blackened – assisted the military in Belfast by identifying republicans for arrest. Newell's information singled out leading figures within the United Irish movement, such as John and Alexander Gordon, Joseph Cuthbert, Thomas Potts and Thomas Storey, all of whom were arrested and conveyed to Dublin in due course. Newell had also exposed a Corporal Reel from the Monaghan Militia (then stationed in Belfast) as a United Irishman and subsequent enquiries by the commanding officer, Colonel Charles Leslie of Glaslough, uncovered seventy members of the regiment as having taken the United Irish oath. Four ringleaders – Daniel Gillan, Peter Carron, Owen McKenna and his brother William – were executed after court martial in front of soldiers from the 22nd Light Dragoons, the Royal Artillery, the 64th Regiment of Foot (Thomas Russell's former regiment), the Light Infantry, the Monaghan and Carlow militias and the Breadalbane and Argyll fencibles. Lake believed that this very public display of zero tolerance would serve as an effective deterrent against further incidents of insubordination and the troops were made to march, in formation, past the bodies of the guilty men.[36] Camden was aware that this breakthrough in the attempt to undermine United Irish efforts to infiltrate the military was a result of Newell's information.[37]

One immediate consequence of the executions was the desire among members of the Monaghan Militia to demonstrate their loyalty and an easy target was the *Northern Star*. The paper's notoriety was increased further by the arrests of William Kean and William Templeton, two of its remaining employees, on the evidence of Newell. The loss of these young men pushed Corbett into issuing another apology to his readers, blaming any errors on the fact that experienced men had been replaced by strangers.[38] In an act of contrition, members of the Monaghan Militia attempted to place an advertisement declaring their loyalty and offering a reward 'for those who had propagated reports to their injury', but this was refused because a section of it impugned the reputation of Belfast and its citizens.[39] This rebuttal produced a backlash that would be final for the newspaper that had expended so much of Neilson's energies since 1791. On the afternoon of 20 May 1797, a number of men from the Monaghan Militia attacked the *Star* office and destroyed the types and presses, as well as books and papers that were stored there. Money was thrown from the window onto the street before the mob was returned to barracks after the intervention of Colonel Leslie.

One source published many years later asserted that those printing machines which were salvaged were purchased by two journeymen printers (named Simms and Dougherty) from the *Belfast News-Letter*, who were hoping to establish a business.[40] General Lake found it impossible to disguise his 'extreme satisfaction' at the demise of the newspaper that had for months published details of military excess. Writing to Knox, he recounted that, despite Leslie's action, 'As luck would have it the moment they were gone the recruits of the Artillery with some of the old hands rushed into the place and did lay about them most lustily and almost totally demolished the whole of the machines.' In contrast to Lake's hubris, Martha McTier noted soberly that a number of the paper's remaining employees, at some risk to their own safety, remained in the office long enough to identify some of the perpetrators.[41]

For Samuel Neilson, imprisoned in Kilmainham Gaol for the past eight months, the forced closure of the *Northern Star* would have been a devastating blow to his political agenda and to his finances. The suspension of *habeas corpus* had meant that the state prisoners in Dublin – and elsewhere – were being detained without trial, especially once it became clear that informers such as Bird and Newell were refusing to testify in open court. In the first instance, the state prisoners in Kilmainham were held in individual cells, had tablecloths at mealtimes and partook of food and drink that was of a decent standard – at least, that is, until the numbers of prisoners arriving from Belfast and other parts of Ulster became overwhelming.[42] But the rigours of confinement would soon undermine their mental and physical conditions. An agitated Henry Haslett wrote to Chief Secretary Pelham on 6 December 1796 to request that he be brought to trial or bailed. Within a week, his sister, who had been attending him in prison, died of measles and was buried in the family plot at Knockbreda, where, according to the

Northern Star, 'The tears of sad sorrow literally moistened the clay which covered the remains of this beautiful and accomplished young woman.'

By Christmas, Haslett was writing again to complain about the fact that his wife was not allowed to visit, even though he had been promised that she could.[43] Haslett's relationships with the other prisoners were far from harmonious and these deteriorated as repeated requests for trial were turned down by the authorities. Henry Joy McCracken recounted that Haslett struck him on the head with a pot of scalding hot water and proceeded to beat him with it. He suggested that most of the other prisoners had, at some stage, fallen foul of his temper.[44] The disagreements inside the prison were often the consequence of a group of frustrated young men living in such close proximity to each other, but there were also disputes about whether the families of individual prisoners should intercede on their behalf for release rather than all those detained acting on an 'all-for-one' basis. McCracken was in dispute with a number of fellow inmates, including Neilson, 'because [he wrote] I took notice of an impropriety (to give it the softest term) in their conduct'. This breakdown in relations was underlined by McCracken's assertion that 'You will say we see the worst side of man in jail, true, but I did not think he had so bad a side.' On the outside, Mary Ann McCracken and Anne Neilson were hoping to effect a reconciliation between the two men and had shared recent letters to confirm the sense of hurt felt by both. Mary Ann entreated her brother to make the first move to revive what had been a close friendship, with a suggestion that Neilson's sensitivities had been offended greatly by McCracken's accusations:

> Ought men of superior sense and virtue, who have long enjoyed mutual esteem and confidence and who never for an instant subjected each other's integrity, suffer themselves to be disunited, and their affections estranged, by the misrepresentations of fools or knaves, when it is so easy to come to a right understanding, by merely declaring the truth – if anything contrary to that, was requisite I would not urge you, for much as I regard his piece of mind, and much as I value his life, if both depended on it, I would be the last person in the world to wish you rather to either to utter or to sign a false hood if that were necessary to restore him ... it is the ardent wish of all your mutual friends to see you again united and on the same footing of esteem and affection if possible, as formerly. Is it not injurious to the cause of union when two men who from the first went hand and hand [*sic*] endeavouring to promote it, should set such an example of disunion betwixt themselves [?] ... the envenomed dart rankles in his bosom the wound can never heal, and it is

> in your power and yours alone to extract it. I therefore intreat [*sic*] you will seriously reflect on the subject and remember that an entire reconciliation between you is not only the earnest wish of all your friends but must be that also of every friend to humanity and Truth.[45]

The two men were finally reconciled in the light of the interventions from outside the prison.

The arrival of new prisoners from the north in April 1797 meant that Neilson was joined by his nephews, John and Alexander Gordon, who had been arrested on the evidence of Newell. McCracken was reunited with some of his co-conspirators, such as his brother William, Thomas Storey, James Burnside, Thomas Jackson, Joseph Cuthbert and Robert Neilson. The growing community of prisoners meant that McCracken now had to share a cell with Shanaghan as his room was to be occupied by two other detainees who were arrested on Newell's information: Dr Alexander Crawford and Reverend Sinclare Kelburn, minister of the Third Presbyterian Church in Belfast and clergyman to both him and Neilson.[46] McCracken was upbeat about this, pointing out that 'we will have a great garrison' and using the window of his new quarters to pass wine and provisions to other prisoners using a string.[47] The prisoners were able to disable the locks of their cells and would often congregate in the gaol's corridors when the guards were asleep. This deception was uncovered when it became clear that they were sleeping during the day and not availing of the time set aside for exercise.[48] Morale was maintained by holding regular parties in the cells for the prisoners and their visitors, during which seditious toasts were drunk and republican songs sung. There was dancing to the French revolutionary song, '*La Carmagnole*'.[49] During the daytime, they were allowed to play with a ball in the prison yard and it was not unheard of for money to be sent out of the prison for the purchase of racquets and balls.[50] The prisoners were able to use visitors such as James Dixon and Robert Black to deliver letters to relatives and friends back home, thereby evading the attention of the Belfast postmaster, Thomas Whinnery, who was aware that letters were being secreted north from William Simms and Rowley Osborne.[51] Despite these moments of levity, however, life and conditions for the prisoners were harsh. The gaoler at Kilmainham, John Richardson, was active in his persecution of his charges, threatening them with shackling irons in the evening, requesting permission from his political masters to punish the prisoners for their singing and, on one occasion, attacking Alexander Gordon, Neilson's nephew, with a knife.[52]

Martha McTier's concerns about Neilson's ability to withstand the rigours of confinement were well founded. Enforced separation from Anne and his children, the destruction of his business interests, the harsh conditions in Kilmainham and his loss of liberty at such a crucial time in the United Irish project combined to undermine his physical condition to an alarming degree. To seek redress by drinking was never going to ameliorate his condition, but many of the prisoners used part of their daily allowance to procure alcohol. The mixture of drinking and politics, as detailed earlier by the informer William Bird, was continuing in the prisons. Mary Ann McCracken chided her brother for drinking excessively, inquiring whether he would not 'find more amusement from reading than drinking now that you subscribe to a circulating library'.[53] In the early part of their confinement, spirits appeared to remain high, although this would change as a second winter approached.

Anne Neilson had visited her husband several times in Kilmainham, following a series of requests to the authorities. She too was one of several visitors (such as Francis Jordan, Luke Teeling and James Dixon) able to carry letters from the gaol for friends and family on the outside.[54] Neilson had requested visits from his wife but, as his confinement became more arduous, he expressed a preference that Anne should not visit, lest she become upset by the conditions and his declining state of health. He was particularly loath to expose her to the unpleasantness of prison life, where she would be 'shocked by the brutality of a turnkey ... [and where her pride would] be wounded by the insolence of a minion in office'.[55]

Despite the harshness and isolation of prison life, Neilson was able to oversee some of the United Irish activity in the north and even arrange for the legal representation of those prisoners awaiting trial at the assizes. In March 1797, a letter from Neilson was smuggled into Carrickfergus Gaol, where James Cochran of Hilden, James Fitzgerald from Sandy Bay (Lough Neagh) and William Orr from Farranshane were imprisoned. Orr was accused of administering a United Irish oath and hanged the following October on dubious evidence before a packed jury. Neilson's communication was headed 'Kilmainham bastille' and he concluded with the sign-off 'Last year of Irish slavery'. He indicated that he expected the men to be bailed and John Philpot Curran and Sampson arranged for their defence in the event of a trial.[56] According to Reverend John Cleland, the vicar of Newtownards and the agent of Lord Castlereagh, Neilson was continuing to play a central role in the conspiracy, acting as the medium through which the north would connect with the new Leinster-based leadership and outlining military strategy. Cleland was critical of the fact that the increasingly sick Neilson had been indulged by the authorities, who allowed him to take exercise outside the prison walls in the evenings, a privilege he had abused by using the time to conduct United Irish business. Cleland informed Castlereagh that Neilson was working alongside Reverend Arthur McMahon, a leading United Irishman who was, according to the information provided by the informer John Hughes, a member of the organisation's Ulster Executive. McMahon had stayed in Dublin from March until May 1797 while the insurrectionary strategy was being discussed and he issued instructions from Saintfield to the military leadership of the United Irishmen in County Down as he returned home.[57] McMahon was formerly the non-subscribing minister in Kilrea (where one contemporary report recorded him as being 'a most daring and pugnacious man, impatient of all defiance and opposition') before being called to the congregation in Holywood in 1794.[58]

John Hughes, whose late brother (Matthew) had been Neilson's business partner, was a bookseller in Belfast who had enrolled in the First Society of United Irishmen in 1793. Until his arrest in 1797, he had undertaken an important position in the organisation and was sent to Dublin in November 1796 on the instruction of Bartholomew Teeling, son of Luke and older brother of Charles. Bartholomew Teeling was a member of Neilson's Masonic lodge in Lisburn. In Dublin, Hughes met with the leading republican and emissary to France, Edward Lewins, who apprised him of the state of the United Irishmen in the city. Hughes returned to Dublin the following spring to secure the services of Curran at the northern assizes and was in the capital again in June at the request of Teeling and Alexander Lowry of Linen Hill. Before setting out for Dublin, he was sent for by John Magennis of Baleely (Ballela), the leading Defender figure in Down, who made him swear that he would not mention to any other party the names of those with whom he would come into contact. The Dublin meeting was designed to assess the state of readiness of the various counties for a rising, with Lowry and Teeling asserting that Down and Louth respectively were certainly prepared. The Antrim leaders were less enthusiastic and the plans for a rebellion in 1797 seem to have foundered both on that county's unwillingness to commit to the field without the French and the lack of preparedness in other areas.[59]

The governments of England and Ireland were anxious about the possibility of insurrection at such a critical point in the war against France. This was accentuated by the mutinies that occurred at Spithead anchorage and the Nore in the Thames estuary in April and May 1797, disputes which disabled parts of the king's fleet. While much of the disaffection centred on rates of pay and conditions of service, the fact that Richard Parker, the leader of the Nore mutiny, conspired to sail for France highlighted that there was a political motivation behind the actions of some of those who were prepared to disobey orders. The strategy of punishing United Irish sympathisers by despatching them to the fleet was practised widely in the aftermath of the passage of the Insurrection Act the previous year. Marianne

Elliott and Roger Wells have demonstrated how the Royal Navy was comprised of thousands of Irish sailors and that as much as 50 per cent of the crews of mutinous ships were Irish.[60] It is not surprising, therefore, that the United Irishmen would seek to infiltrate the navy as well as the soldiery. Lake was conscious of the danger and advised Pelham that the delivery of suspects would be better managed on land because 'the prisoners were rejoicing at the prospect of going to sea because they said that they would convert the crew'. In June, Cooke felt the need to warn the Foreign Secretary, Lord Grenville, that two Belfast surgeons and 'dangerous United Irishmen' (Telfair and Campbell) were endeavouring to gain positions in the fleet, adding that he had warned his political bosses a year earlier how republicans in Ulster had talked confidently of a mutiny in the British navy.[61]

Against this backdrop, there would appear to have been a degree of insurgent activity in mid-west County Down at the beginning of June 1797, when a large gathering of several hundred United Irishmen and Defenders mustered on Dechomet Mountain, near Magennis' centre of influence. According to an informant, Magennis and two of his allies – Dunkin and Savage – proposed an immediate rebellion, hoping to march on Castlewellan to seize yeomanry weapons and kill the ultra-loyalist landowner Lord Annesley before proceeding to Blaris Camp to enlist militiamen sympathetic to the cause. The action was halted by the intercession of a local doctor who convinced the majority of the assembled crowd to resist the call, much to the disgust of the firebrands.[62]

Around this time, two Irish officers in the French army, Colonel James Plunkett and his nephew Captain O'Gorman, were in Dublin to assist with plans for an insurrection. Plunkett had, some years before, been a delegate to the Catholic Convention and was present at the Dublin meeting attended by John Hughes in November 1796. Thereafter, the two officers came north to meet with William Putnam McCabe and Hughes and, in mid-June the following year, undertook a reconnaissance of the area surrounding Blaris Camp to assess its strength as a military fortification. Plunkett surmised that the United Irishmen could capture the artillery at Hillsborough and deploy it against the camp. The visitors also attended a meeting of the Ulster Provincial Committee of the United Irishmen at Randalstown with McCabe and Hughes, both of whom were Belfast delegates to the committee. At this meeting, the United Irish leadership in Antrim declared its reluctance to act in advance of a renewed French invasion. The Down leadership, represented by Alexander Lowry and McMahon, announced its readiness for the field.[63] Teeling, Magennis and Lowry then determined to meet with the colonels of Down and Antrim in Armstrong's Inn in Ballynahinch, County Down, but the failure of the latter county's representatives to attend convinced them that the intended insurrection could not happen at this stage and the men decided to leave Ireland, a decision that was entirely sensible, given that Lake was aware of the plot.[64] Lowry, Teeling, Magennis and McMahon, all of whom were well known to Neilson, departed in the middle of June, along with their closest allies, such as Robert Rollo Reid from Ballygowan and Hastings Mason, a close ally of Lowry and member of the Downshire Militia.[65]

The United Irish conspiracy continued to gather momentum and, notwithstanding the failed invasion at the end of 1796, negotiations between French and United Irish emissaries were continuing. It was assumed that the large fleet being assembled by France's Dutch allies at the mouth of the Texel was destined for Ireland. The rise to prominence within the United leadership of Arthur O'Connor and Lord Edward Fitzgerald had given further impetus to the project and it was reported that they were traversing the north valuing horses and making military preparations.[66] It is clear that a section of the United Irishmen was in favour of acting unilaterally rather than waiting for a French invasion. O'Connor and Fitzgerald epitomised this tendency, while other members of the leadership – such as Thomas Addis Emmet and William James MacNeven (supported by the majority of the Antrim leadership) – were committed to waiting for a successful landing. The unleashing of Lake's campaign in Ulster pushed elements there to contemplate action in order to prevent the defeat of the movement. Reports of trees being cut down for the manufacture of pikes became widespread but the flight of McMahon, Lowry and John Magennis, the main promoters of the United Irish–Defender axis in Ulster, would prove fatal to the cause, especially as their sponsors (Neilson, Russell and McCracken) were in prison.

The absence of this small but critical group of militants undermined any prospect of achieving the religious unanimity upon which the United Irish project was based. Hints of this can be detected in the intelligence that was being sent to the administration and its supporters. Buoyed by the information provided by the informer 'Farmer', the Bishop of Dromore wrote optimistically to Lord Downshire that recent events had 'occasioned a great jealousy between the Papists and Dissenters in this country', a view echoed by the information given to Cleland by the informer Nicholas Mageean.[67] Indeed, reports from County Armagh suggested that United Irish activity was on the wane and large numbers of men 'who were formerly united' (that is, United Irishmen) had embraced Orangeism and taken the oath of loyalty.[68]

While the fortunes of the United Irishmen ebbed and flowed, Neilson was adjusting to life behind Kilmainham's dark walls. The state prisoners received a number of visitors, some welcomed, others resented. Among those who visited was Lord Carhampton, the commander-in-chief of the government forces in Ireland, who made a midnight call to the men in Kilmainham. According to the account written by Charles Teeling, Neilson recognised Carhampton and addressed him by name, prompting the visitor to inquire how Neilson seemed to be fully acquainted with him. Neilson responded that Carhampton had been the reviewing officer at a Volunteer display some years previously, to which the latter replied, 'Stop, sir, stop; those days are gone by – these are not fit subjects for prison reflections; go to bed, sir, and dream of something else than Irish volunteers.'[69]

Madden's account of Neilson's life recounted how he was visited in prison by Lord Castlereagh, who, as Robert Stewart, had triumphed in the county seat of Down in the landmark election of 1790. As stated previously, Stewart had, at that time, campaigned as a reformer and was considered a darling of the liberal position before hardening his stance and aligning himself with the administration, much to the chagrin of his erstwhile supporters. Neilson's prominence in the campaign in Antrim meant that he was well known to Castlereagh, the man who had led the arresting party that descended on Belfast in September 1796 to seek him out. In response to Castlereagh's invitation to be of assistance, Neilson asked for the release of two innocent men – Pat Whelan and Martin Short – who were accused of stealing arms and confined in the gaol under sentence of death. Castlereagh seemed moved by their plight and reprieved them.[70]

A hostile source in March 1797 reported that the state prisoners had received a visit from Lord O'Neill, who was a moderate Member of Parliament for County Antrim until his elevation to the peerage in 1793. Neilson had served as secretary of the committee that co-ordinated O'Neill's election campaign in 1790, when he and Hercules Rowley triumphed over the conservative candidates. By this stage, Neilson's politics had advanced significantly beyond those of O'Neill and during their prison discussion he implored the peer not to support the draconian measures that were an affront to those who retained considerable faith in his outlook and abilities. It was reported that O'Neill was greatly affected by Neilson's words and moved nearly to tears. The prisoners left him in no doubt that the conspiracy was strong and not dependent on French assistance. For his part, Neilson railed against Chief Secretary Pelham and Edward Cooke, declaring, 'They cannot hurt me – I defy them – for if the halter was about me, such I would smile conscious it would be the signal for the regeneration of my country.'[71]

Neilson's physical strength, which, according to contemporaries, had been considerable, was undermined by the length and nature of his confinement. His initial confidence was dented by the fact that he was not arraigned for trial, while the onset of inclement weather towards the end of 1797 would bring him perilously close to breaking point. Several of the United Irish prisoners suffered from ill health during their time in Kilmainham, most notably McCracken (who would often be paralysed with rheumatism), Teeling and Thomas Storey, both of whom were afflicted with fever. It seems that Neilson was in reasonable health as late as September.[72] That conditions were harsher than they had been at the outset was probably attributable to the fact that more detainees had arrived in a gaol which had now become overcrowded. Moreover, the authorities were disinclined to treat the United Irish prisoners generously, given the deteriorating situation in the country and the constant fears of invasion. By October, the Kilmainham prisoners wrote a letter of complaint, detailing how the servings of food constituted barely a fifth of what they were entitled to and how supplies of porter and candles were low. Their worsening health was, they said, due to the fact that their bed linen had not been changed for two months.[73]

By the middle of the month, Neilson had fallen victim to a debilitating nervous fever. Drennan and another medical doctor named Plunkett visited him and wrote to the authorities to say that he was in a declining state of health for want of proper diet and care. They requested his release so that he might recover. Neilson's illness was confirmed by another doctor named McDowell and by a surgeon, George Stewart, who visited Neilson in prison at the request of the Lord Lieutenant. Stewart informed Cooke that Neilson was a little better but that he would benefit from exercising on horseback, 'an indulgence he very much desires'.[74] He was attended by the faithful William Kean, his former employee at the *Northern Star*, who would sit up all night with Neilson as the fever worsened.[75] By early November, the sickness threatened his life and Matthew Smith (chief clerk at the newspaper, who had been managing Neilson's interests since his confinement) was asked to travel to Dublin at Neilson's request to settle his affairs. William Simms also arrived at Kilmainham to see him but was refused access by Richardson, the gaoler. Neilson began to recover shortly afterwards and again urged the authorities to bring him to trial at the next assizes. While this request was not granted, Neilson was given permission to resume his brief excursions outside the prison walls, albeit 'a draught of fresh air in a carriage which will scarcely satisfy the longings of nature'.[76]

Neilson was convinced of the medical benefits of such a concession and, on Christmas Eve 1797, he wrote to Cooke that he wished to ride out in the company of a guard and, if this was inconvenient, he would ride alone and offer security for his return at whatever hour the authorities saw fit. Cooke had, of course, received information from Cleland that such concessions earlier in the year had seen Neilson embark on United Irish business. Obstacles were created which frustrated Neilson greatly and he urged Cooke to allow him to leave the gaol in the period before lunch and not at the time that was considered more convenient to Richardson. With no agreement reached, Anne Neilson returned to Dublin to wait on Cooke, imploring him to send an agent to ride with Neilson, whose health had deteriorated since the concession had been discontinued.[77]

The government was facing the dilemma of what to do with the state prisoners (many of whom were falling ill) in a scenario in which informants were reluctant to take to the stand. The suspension of *habeas corpus* meant that there were no legal impediments to their continuing detention but moral considerations and overcrowded gaols, combined with the fact that the north was being quietened by Lake's military campaign, meant that prisoners were being released. After eleven months in captivity, Charles Teeling was freed on bail security of £4,000, having fallen victim to fever. The Under-Secretary, Edward Cooke, was deemed to have acted with great humanity in this case, a fact later acknowledged by Teeling himself and by the United Irishmen in Ulster.[78] By the end of 1797, other prisoners, such as Henry Joy McCracken and his brother William, were liberated, leaving behind a hardcore of republicans, such as Neilson, his nephew John Gordon (who was considered the most likely to be prosecuted) and Thomas Russell, whose military experience meant that he would become the longest-serving United Irish prisoner.[79] Neilson was being arraigned for trial, but William Bird disappeared and the Crown case collapsed. Bird had been in the protective care of a state official named Dawes, but he wrote to Cooke informing him that he no longer wished to be part of a scheme that would associate him with the informers Newell and Frederick Dutton, whom he described as 'blood-stained, sanguinary cannibals'.[80] He claimed that his motives were entirely ethical and he had not been 'directly or indirectly applied to', although the informer and editor of the *Freeman's Journal*, Francis Higgins, believed that the leading United Irishman Matthew Dowling had shuffled Bird away on the instruction of Neilson, who had paid him £400 for his silence.[81] Bird wrote subsequently to Neilson, apologising for the hurt that he had caused and expressing that 'No man more fervently wishes you every blessing Providence can bestow, than the person who robbed you of all comfort on earth.' Bird then wrote to the viceroy, Lord Camden, demanding that he give orders for the release of Neilson and Russell or face the ignominy of having information published that would highlight the dubious methods used by the prosecution to secure convictions.[82]

On 22 February 1798, Samuel Neilson was released from Kilmainham after seventeen months of confinement. Prison had taken its toll on his once broad-shouldered and muscular frame and he moved into the residence of his friend, John Sweetman, a leading Catholic United Irishman and prosperous brewery owner. Earlier that month, Drennan had predicted Neilson's freedom, speculating that it was attributable either to squabbling among informers or to Neilson's conversations with Pelham and Castlereagh, during which he must have convinced them that he was not going to involve himself in politics or sedition in the event of his release. Drennan believed that Neilson had placed Russell's liberation as a condition for his own, but in the event, the former soldier would remain incarcerated in Newgate.[83]

The United Irish project was in a precarious state. The detention of leading figures such as Neilson (who had pushed the conspiracy in Ulster) notwithstanding, the military campaign in the north had done significant damage to the movement there. The strength of Orangeism was increasing daily and was now receiving overt support from the state – for example, General Lake reviewed 20,000 Orangemen at the Twelfth of July celebrations in Lurgan in 1797.[84] The intimidation of known republican strongholds was having a serious impact on morale. After his release from custody, Rowley Osborne returned to Belfast, which he described as being like a deserted village. Suspects were being rounded up by the loyalist yeomanry and regulars and lodged in the artillery barracks. Osborne himself was harassed by the yeomanry, while Francis Falloon (an innkeeper from Donaghadee) and Hugh McCormick from Bangor, two well-known United men, were arrested and taken to the guardhouse, where soldiers spat on their faces and wiped their feet on the prisoners' pantaloons.[85]

While the execution of William Orr on 14 October 1797 renewed the determination of many republicans to resist the regime, there was a growing realisation that French assistance was not imminent. France had overrun the Dutch Republic in 1795, establishing the Batavian Republic, with considerable popular support, as a client state. The gathering of a large fleet at the Texel had given hope for the United Irishmen that a second invasion was forthcoming and Tone was preparing once again to sail towards his native shores as part of a large expeditionary force. However, the defeat of the Dutch naval fleet under de Winter at the Battle of Camperdown on 11 October 1797 once again dashed the hopes of the revolutionaries and set back the cause of insurrection in Ireland by strengthening the faction of the United Irish leadership (represented by figures such as MacNeven, Robert Simms and Thomas Addis Emmet), which refused to rise until the French landed to offer assistance. This attitude was resisted by the more strident approach of Arthur O'Connor and Lord Edward Fitzgerald, who were increasingly of the view that Ireland was capable of unleashing a rebellion that need not be dependent on a French military presence on the island. The victory of the Royal Navy under the command of Admiral Duncan at Camperdown was received with delight in Belfast by Lake, who noted that 'It has annoyed the scoundrels of this town most completely.'[86]

As the year 1798 dawned, it was by no means certain that rebellion would break out at all, let alone be successful. A new five-member National Executive of United Irishmen had been appointed at the end of 1797, with O'Connor representing Ulster, but there were clear divisions in the organisation's leadership.[87] It was amid this state of confusion that Neilson would once again resume his place at the head of the conspirators.

8

The Northern Incendiary, 1798

The government's campaign against the United Irishmen was being undermined not only by the frustrating failure to accumulate witness evidence against Neilson and the other state prisoners, but by the crisis in military policy that blew up in early 1798 once the new commander-in-chief, Sir Ralph Abercromby, had surveyed the state of his troops. Appointed the previous November to succeed Lord Carhampton, Abercromby was alarmed by the irregular methods used by the soldiery as part of the crackdown initiated by his predecessor and carried out with particular enthusiasm in Ulster by General Lake. The use of the army to protect individual magistrates (thereby dispersing the forces that would be needed to withstand any French invasion), coupled with the ferocity of counter-insurgency tactics, convinced the new commander to rein in the excesses of those now under his charge. Consequently, Abercromby issued his famous general orders on 26 February 1798, declaring the army to be 'in a state of licentiousness which must render it formidable to everyone but the enemy' and ordering soldiers not to initiate action against suspected traitors unless under direct and unprovoked attack or with the express authority of a magistrate.[1]

The military and political upshot of Abercromby's order was profound because his damning indictment of the state of affairs that he had inherited was insulting not only to the army command but also to the Lord Lieutenant himself. Camden indicated his surprise at Abercromby's pronouncement to Home Secretary Portland and hoped that it could be explained away without the creation of a political storm. The viceroy was, however, critical of this 'injudicious and almost criminal order' and his first instinct was to publish his 'decided disapprobation', which he resisted only because it would provoke the general's resignation, allowing Whig opponents in Dublin to make considerable political capital out of the crisis.[2]

The succeeding weeks witnessed vitriolic attacks on Abercromby's character and fitness for the role of commander-in-chief as hard-line opponents of his approach, including Speaker John Foster and John Beresford, the Chief Commissioner of the Revenue and one of the so-called 'Castle Party' that shaped Irish policy during Camden's tenure, lined up to discredit him. Robert Ross, one of Downshire's correspondents, wrote from Dublin to denounce Abercromby's orders as 'offensive to the army, government and the gentlemen of this country', suggesting that either he or the Lord Lieutenant himself would have to go. Referring to the Scottish general's earlier posting in the West Indies, Ross stated witheringly that while Abercromby 'may be an excellent general in the field, he is a miserable politician. I wish he had stayed with the negroes in Martinico.'[3] Officers on the ground were also incensed by the commander-in-chief's orders. In Tyrone, Lord Abercorn offered his resignation as head of the Tyrone Militia, citing how Abercromby's instruction 'bitterly and indiscriminately censures an army that I think (with few exceptions indeed if any) have deserved everything of their country'.[4] Abercromby's offer to resign his position was, in the end, accepted by Camden and the offended conservative faction was assuaged by the appointment of Lake to the overall command. Within weeks, the military response had hardened and the country was deemed to be in a state of rebellion, with counter-insurgency measures being formalised. Camden had his reservations about Lake's ability in a crisis and was unsure whether he would be able to address the 'complicated nature' of the political and military situation. Nonetheless, his zeal in dealing with the 'very unpleasant business in the north' the previous year was deemed commendable and Camden was confident that the province, cowed by effective military action, had been restored to political tranquillity and a return to its traditional economic considerations.[5]

Leinster was now the hub of United Irish activity and an executive committee there had been in operation since the beginning of 1797, comprising (at different stages) of leading figures such as Lord Edward Fitzgerald, Arthur O'Connor, William James MacNeven, Oliver Bond, Henry Jackson, James Dixon and Thomas Addis Emmet, whose younger brother, Robert, would achieve renown as the architect of an insurrection in 1803. Beneath this, a provincial committee comprising delegates from county committees would help to prepare the insurrectionary strategy.[6] Treasurer to this committee was the silk mercer Thomas Reynolds (Wolfe Tone's brother-in-law), who had been sworn into the United Irishmen by Oliver Bond and moved quickly up the line of responsibility. Reynolds' financial delicacy was always likely to make him a suitable candidate for the role of informer and, sure enough, he was recruited by the Castle, providing the intelligence that allowed the authorities to arrest fourteen leaders of the Leinster leadership at the home of Oliver Bond on Dublin's Bridge Street on 12 March 1798. The arrests of Sweetman, MacNeven and Emmet followed promptly, making this a seminal moment in the development of the United Irish project.[7] The incarceration of the Leinster leadership, most of which was reluctant to unleash a rebellion without the arrival of French support, paved the way for a less cautious command structure to assume prominence. This group included Fitzgerald, Henry and John Sheares, and Neilson, who had quickly resumed his seditious activities following his release from prison.

Government fears had been heightened by the arrest in England of Fitzgerald's close associate, Arthur O'Connor, in February. Along with the leading Defender and Catholic priest, Father James Coigley, O'Connor stood accused of embarking on a mission to France and co-ordinating links between the United Irishmen and republican elements within the London Corresponding Society, as well as radical groups in other parts of England and Scotland. The authorities had long been aware of these attempts to forge such networks and the informer Leonard McNally had alerted the government to the increasing Irish influence in English and Scottish republican clubs, such as the striking similarity between the oaths of the United Irishmen and the United Britons. Coigley, O'Connor, Reverend Arthur McMahon and Benjamin Binns, who had been cultivating links between Irish and English republicans since moving to London with his brother John in 1794, were all known to the government as key movers within the London Corresponding Society.[8] The charismatic Lord Edward Fitzgerald had avoided arrest on 12 March and, while his capture became the ultimate prize for the authorities, his continued freedom remained the best hope the United Irishmen had of unleashing some sort of rebellion without French assistance. As Fitzgerald was moved through a series of safe houses in Dublin, friends of the government were ever vigilant. Indeed, his whereabouts became something of a national fascination, with false sightings and apprehensions reported in Newry, Stranraer, the Isle of Man, London and Chester.[9] In reality, Fitzgerald was shepherded through Dublin and its surrounding districts by figures such as Neilson, the surgeon William Lawless and William Putnam McCabe (a son of Thomas McCabe, the Belfast watchmaker who was, like Neilson, a founder member of the organisation that had now evolved to the point of revolution).

Neilson's precise movements subsequent to his release from Kilmainham are difficult to trace, although the reports submitted to the Castle by Cooke's web of informers provide some sense of his role in the planning of the rebellion. Neilson's freedom, which was subject to him not becoming involved in any treasonable practices, was facilitated by both his ill health and the collapse of the case against him by Bird's refusal to testify and his threat to discredit the legality

Samuel Neilson (1762–1803), *c.*1795, unknown 19th century (after Charles Byrne, 1757–1810), reproduced by kind permission of National Museums Northern Ireland.

John, 1st Viscount O'Neill of Shane's Castle (1740–1798), *c.*1780, by Francis Wheatley, reproduced by kind permission of National Museums Northern Ireland.

Captain Waddell Cunningham (1730–1797), *c.*1786, by Robert Home, reproduced by kind permission of National Museums Northern Ireland.

Theobald Wolfe Tone (1763–1798), by artist unknown, reproduced by kind permission of the National Gallery of Ireland.

William Drennan, MD (1754–1820), *c.*1790, by Robert Home, reproduced by kind permission of National Museums Northern Ireland.

Henry Joy McCracken (1767–1798), 1926, by Sarah Cecilia Harrison, reproduced by kind permission of National Museums Northern Ireland.

Mary Anne McCracken (1770–1866), photograph by John Gibson, reproduced by kind permission of National Museums Northern Ireland.

Lord Edward Fitzgerald (1763–1798), *c.*1798, by Hugh Douglas Hamilton, reproduced by kind permission of National Museums Northern Ireland.

THE Northern Star.

No. 11.] From SATURDAY, FEBRUARY 4, to WEDNESDAY, FEBRUARY 8, 1792. [Price Two Pence

Northern Star.

NUMBER 318.] FROM THURSDAY, JANUARY 15, TO MONDAY, JANUARY 19, 1795. [PRICE TWO-PENCE HALFPENNY.

Front pages of the *Northern Star*, 1792 and 1795, reproduced by kind permission of the Linen Hall Library, Belfast.

Henry Grattan (1746–1820), by Francis Wheatley, reproduced by kind permission of the National Portrait Gallery, London.

Robert Stewart, 2nd Marquess of Londonderry (Lord Castlereagh, 1769–1822), by Sir Thomas Lawrence, reproduced by kind permission of the National Portrait Gallery, London.

Fort George, Scotland. Photographs by the author.

The Neilson family grave in Knockbreda Cemetery, Belfast. Photograph by the author.

Samuel Neilson's grave, Poughkeepsie. Courtesy of Linda Silkworth and the Rural Cemetery, Poughkeepsie.

of the Castle's prosecution case. The Lord Lieutenant was of the opinion that Neilson had 'pledged himself to be forthcoming' upon release, a commitment he was to break.[10] Before his release, Edward Cooke was among those who visited Neilson in his cell, inquiring of him what measures would conciliate the people at this critical juncture. According to the informer Francis Higgins, Neilson replied that the release of prisoners and the granting of their demands would certainly be more constructive than the repressive policies that had served only to increase recruitment into the United Irishmen. This boldness in the face of Cooke's questioning was recounted by Neilson to his close confidante Oliver Bond, who communicated the conversation to a meeting of United Irish leaders, who resolved that, in the event of a rising being successful, 'Neilson should be the first object of reward and compensation from his country.'[11]

Writing to his wife on 17 March, Neilson complained that, while his health had improved, 'My limbs still refuse their office, and at times give me much pain.'[12] Neilson would eventually reside in the outskirts of Dublin, at the Dundrum residence of the St Stephen's Green brewer John Sweetman. According to his later testimony before the Secrecy Committee of the House of Lords on 7 August, Neilson was politically inactive until after the arrests at Bond's. Thereafter, he threw himself into the task of filling the vacancies that had been created at the apex of the United Irish leadership.[13] Neilson's re-involvement in the society's affairs was not entirely unexpected, given the militant solidarity that had existed among the state prisoners and the fact that he was apprised of key developments by visitors to Kilmainham, such as James Dixon and Arthur McMahon. The slow response to the arrests at Bond's prompted Neilson to complain two or three days later that the United Irishmen in Leinster were not as organised as those in Ulster, 'who instead of flying about the streets asking for news, would have quietly proceeded to fill up the places of the arrested delegates'.[14] This analysis was affirmed by a member of the Ulster provincial committee, a Belfast shipbroker called Robert Hunter, who opined that had it not been for Neilson, Robert Simms (the adjutant-general for County Antrim, who had been in Dublin to establish the state of the movement) and a half-pay military officer named Captain Ludlow, the entire Leinster project would have been completely disorganised.[15]

Madden describes an incident that allegedly took place shortly after the arrests at Bond's and was related by the son of the informer Thomas Reynolds. According to this account, Neilson accosted Reynolds early one evening in March 1798 and told him that Mrs Oliver Bond wished to have a word with him. Reynolds was led into a warehouse on Bridge Street (probably the premises owned by Bond) under the pretence of meeting with her. Reynolds was instead confronted by 'a stout ill-looking man' with pistols he had fetched for Neilson, who subsequently threatened to kill Reynolds, accusing him of being the man who had betrayed the arrested leaders. Reynolds seized Neilson by the collar and pushed him against his associate, who fell through a crane gate into the entry below. Reynolds prevented Neilson from falling as well and the latter attempted to turn the incident into a joke before leaving to check on the condition of his friend.[16] Reynolds's son, admittedly a hostile source, referred to Neilson as 'the most violent, determined conspirator among the associates [who] seemed to possess unbounded influence over the Dublin leaders'.[17] As Neilson immersed himself in the developing plot, he sought refuge in the house of John Jackson at Creeve, County Monaghan. Jackson was the brother of the iron founder and leading United Irishman Henry Jackson, whose daughter was married to Oliver Bond, one of Neilson's closest allies. Madden states how Neilson had on one occasion avoided arrest there by stealing out of a window at the back of the house and into an adjoining property after a military party had come at midnight to arrest him.[18]

For opponents of the United Irishmen, Neilson's release in February 1798 caused anger and not a little conjecture. His proprietorship of the *Northern Star* was sufficient grounds for many to have him imprisoned indefinitely, so his liberation seemed to offer the possibility that he was in the pay of the authorities, a difficult game given the fact that he was so strident in his abuse of the government. Francis Higgins, the editor of the *Freeman's Journal*, who was in regular communication with Edward Cooke in Dublin Castle, issued this advice to his handler: 'If Neilson is not bringing you information, he is a most dangerous person to remain here. He has dined, supped etc. among the entire of the party, and after dinner gave such lectures, advice and intelligence to shew them that their cause must shortly be successful and to leave the strongest impressions.' Higgins' own spy within the upper echelons of the United Irishmen, Francis Magan, also suspected that Neilson was a plant. Magan, a barrister eager to cover his own tracks, may have been attempting to make a scapegoat of Neilson in order to maintain his own anonymity and obviate the need to testify. After Neilson's arrest on 23 May, Higgins continued to float the idea that Neilson was in league with the government, referring to him in a letter to Cooke as 'your supposed *quondam* communicator'.[19]

It is indeed likely that Neilson's release in February was the result of a deal whereby he would stay out of trouble and recover his health in return for both the handover of his papers and terms of release being agreed for the other prisoners. One month after being freed, a disappointed Neilson wrote to Cooke, requesting that his papers and accounts be returned and reminding him about the deteriorating conditions in which the remaining Kilmainham prisoners were being held.[20] There is no doubt that Neilson now threw himself fully into the organisation of a rebellion and he became part of a cadre of rebel leaders that worked tirelessly to cultivate an insurgency across Dublin and its surrounding areas. Five years earlier, in an angry letter to the Catholic leader Richard McCormick, Neilson had referred to himself as an incendiary. In the spring of 1798, he toured the region and, in concert with Fitzgerald and the other rebel chiefs, decided when to strike the match. Still recovering from the effects of his long confinement, he wrote to his wife in March to tell her that he rarely stayed in the same place, moving from one safe house to another for fear of arrest and a return to his 'old lodgings'.[21] From his release to the outbreak of the rebellion, Neilson's old associate Henry Joy McCracken worked the axis between Ulster and Dublin, acting as a conduit of information and, according to a government agent, implementing Neilson's plan. According to the northern informer Nicholas Mageean, fourteen northerners (he named Neilson and Robert Orr) were in Dublin working most diligently for the cause. He reported that McCracken was in Neilson's company frequently and that the former's health had improved considerably, appearing 'what he did before he went to jail'.[22]

Despite Neilson's protestation that he was inactive until after the arrests of 12 March, evidence exists that he was, in fact, busy propagating the United Irish cause before this date. The informer Thomas Boyle, a publican, contacted Cooke on the 10th to update him on Fitzgerald's preparations for a rising. He added:

> A man by the name of nelson [*sic*] from Belfast and his family are supported by Sweetman of Francis Street or out of the stock purse, a horse is kept for him and he is constantly riding to different parts of the county Dublin, West, North and South. Very frequently goes to Fingal, Drumcondra, Ballybough &c. he was lately at Raheny, Clontarf and that Quarter visiting different parties and delivering instruction and advice, he speaks well, the lower orders much admire him.[23]

The concession of allowing Neilson to take exercise on horseback during his incarceration had served the purpose of preparing him for the role of insurgent missionary. Dennis Ryan was a Dublin stonecutter who had been sworn into the United Irishmen and elected to the rank of captain in the military structure. He was first introduced to Neilson at the home of Miles Duigenan, a Grafton Street grocer and leading United Irishman in the city. In subsequent conversations, he learned that Neilson had ridden 387 miles across Leinster and – interestingly –

Ulster and that his purpose was to secure the support of the Defenders for the project.[24] Neilson's credentials for this task were strong, dating back to 1792 and his attempts to mediate in the disputes between Presbyterians and Catholics in the Rathfriland area. He was also seeking to organise the United Irish leadership, fill vacancies by promoting officers and acquire vital funds for the cause now that Bond, who had organised the fundraising lottery, was in prison. Significant effort was expended in April trying to establish a new military committee to co-ordinate the plans for rebellion. At the start of the month, a group that included Neilson, John Sweetman's son and the merchant Thomas Braughall dined at Portrane House near Swords, the opulent country home of Hampden Evans, who had been associated with the United Irishmen for some time. One topic of discussion at this gathering was the proposed construction of portable barricades that would be placed across streets to protect the insurgents from government attack and allow them to fire their weapons in safety.[25] Securing a cohesive leadership committee was, however, proving difficult and, as the rebellion approached, it was reported that the Dublin executive had been changed three times in ten days.[26]

Links with Ulster were maintained, although the north's revolutionary potency was stultified by the influence of Robert Simms, the commander for County Antrim, who was strongly of the opinion that a successful rebellion could be accomplished only with French assistance. Nonetheless, Mageean's reports to the authorities indicated that Ulster chiefs were being kept informed of developments in Dublin and the ongoing discussions in France involving, at various times, the United Irish representatives Edward Lewins, McMahon and Bartholomew Teeling. Thomas Reynolds was provided with information which suggested that William Kean, one of Neilson's close associates in the *Northern Star*, had been in Dublin, had been fully briefed on the plans for rebellion and had received instructions for how the north should act. Kean would be a key figure in Ulster once the rebellion finally erupted, taking part in the action in both Antrim and Down and serving as the aide-de-camp to Henry Monro at the Battle of Ballynahinch. Kean was eventually captured but made a dramatic escape from the provost prison in Belfast, the Donegall Arms, and afterwards hid under a grate which covered the main street sewer. He later concealed himself before departing from Belfast for the United States dressed as a sailor.[27]

Neilson's defiance of the order to remain aloof from any proceedings of the United Irishmen meant that he was now sought by the authorities and every effort was made to apprehend him, especially as the intelligence appearing on Cooke's desk seemed to suggest that he was heavily implicated in the plans for a rising. Camden informed the Home Secretary that Neilson had made 'the worst use' of his freedom and the appropriate measures would be made for his return to custody.[28] There were opportunities for Neilson's capture, but he proved elusive. One such occasion was recounted in a deposition given to Town Major Henry Charles Sirr, the man in charge of policing the capital. The deponent stated that Neilson and Lord Edward had been taken by a patrol of artillery officers near Palmerstown. Lord Edward was disguised as a labourer and Neilson acted drunk. After being held for a period of time, they were released and rode off into the night on their 'common horses but good trotters'.[29] Francis Magan may have been referring to the same incident when he reported to Cooke that Neilson and Lord Edward had been detained for a time by a military party in the neighbourhood of Lucan and while he again hinted that Neilson was some sort of *agent provocateur*, he added tellingly that 'His absence I know at the present moment would be considered by many to be fatal to the cause in Dublin.'[30]

Another attempt to detain Neilson was instigated by a Castle messenger named Hyde, who had discovered Neilson's whereabouts and tried to lure him into accompanying him to see Cooke. Neilson refused to go to the Castle but, despite advice to the contrary, he agreed to breakfast at Hyde's house the following morning. On arrival, he noticed that there was movement in an adjacent guardhouse. Neilson gave orders for his horse to be readily available for him as he entered Hyde's residence before engaging in the pleasantries of breakfast. As Neilson got up to leave, he was obstructed and asked to remain in the house. Hyde is believed to have said, 'Do you not know I can now take you?' According to one informant who had heard Neilson's account of the incident, the fugitive declared, 'If you attempt it you shall have this sword and the contents of a case of pistols in your body.' Neilson stated that he had not come alone and he could summon assistance immediately if he was not allowed to retire from the scene. Hyde backed down and Neilson was on the run once again.[31]

Neilson's contact with the leading Whig Henry Grattan during this period aroused the interest of the authorities, who seized the opportunity presented as a means of discrediting the veteran politician. As plans for the rebellion developed apace, elements of the United Irish leadership sought to foster relationships with the reformist Whigs and in particular Grattan, traditionally the champion of progressive politics. Attempts to forge closer links were pursued during 1797, with the lawyer William Sampson (a regular contributor to the *Northern Star*) acting as the main go-between. Sampson's efforts were well received by the Whigs, one of whose leading spokesmen, John Philpot Curran, had worked with him during their defence of the *Star*'s proprietors at the time of the legal prosecutions three years earlier. Moderates in the United Irish leadership, such as MacNeven and

Emmet, were keen to exploit this opportunity and a joint resolution encompassing Whig, Catholic and United Irish sentiments had been agreed during a meeting in February. Grattan and his Whig supporters absented themselves from the Irish Parliament after the inevitable rejection of their call for parliamentary reform and in protest against the repressive nature of government and military policies.[32]

The United Irishmen had also found Grattan and Curran useful in the destruction of Bird's credibility as a potential witness against the state prisoners, paving the way for their expected release. In the period between the arrest of the Leinster Committee in March 1798 and the outbreak of the rebellion in May, elements of the United Irish leadership sought to gauge the position of Grattan and the Whigs in the hope that the weight of their influence might in some way be brought to bear. One informer, 'A.B.', who had arrived in Ireland from Lyons six years earlier and was a teacher of French, alleged that Curran would have been at Bond's house on the day of the arrests had the authorities delayed their actions and went on to state that Grattan himself was part of a large committee directing the activities of the United Irishmen, albeit with a watching brief. The credibility of this source is questionable (considering his evaluation of Thomas Addis Emmet as bloodthirsty and 'the blackest man in the world'), but Dublin and London were being presented with intelligence that the United Irishmen and elements of the Whigs were in cahoots.[33] As well as being a cause for alarm, such intelligence presented the government with a wonderful opportunity to undermine Grattan. The intelligence was provided through the evidence of John Hughes, the Belfast bookseller whose brother, Matthew, had been a business partner of Neilson before his death.

Hughes, who was a relative of Neilson, joined the United Irishmen in 1793 and took the oath under the new structure in 1796, eventually establishing his own society due to the outgrowth of one of the existing Belfast groups. Hughes travelled from Belfast to Dublin in 1797 at the behest of Bartholomew Teeling and returned to the capital in March 1798 and again in April, when he met up with Neilson, Fitzgerald and William Lawless. On 20 October 1797, Hughes had been arrested in Newry and sent to Belfast on a charge of high treason but he was liberated the same night. Hughes was now an informer and his information, presented to the Secrecy Committee of the Irish House of Lords in August 1798, proved damaging to both Neilson and Grattan, irrespective of its veracity. Giving evidence, Hughes stated that during the period he was in Dublin in April, he accompanied Neilson in Sweetman's carriage to Grattan's estate at Tinnehinch in County Wicklow. Hughes was given a tour of the gardens while Neilson and Grattan spoke privately for around half an hour, until Hughes returned to the house. In his evidence,

Hughes stated that Grattan had asked about the United Irishmen and the impact of government repression. After leaving the house, Hughes asked Neilson about what had been discussed and Neilson stated that he had asked Grattan to come forward in support of the United Irishmen and that he had sworn Grattan into the movement. Under questioning, Hughes said that he had seen a printed copy of the constitution of the United Irishmen on the desk in the MP's library and that Grattan had asked Hughes a number of questions about it.

When Neilson was later cross-examined by the committee of the Lords, he admitted that he had been to Tinnehinch on two occasions, in the company of Sweetman and Bond, to meet with Grattan and that their discussions had included references to the constitution. When asked, Neilson asserted that Grattan had not taken the oath. He did not refer to the visit paid to Grattan in the company of Hughes, but on returning to prison, he addressed a note to Lord Chancellor Fitzgibbon, correcting his evidence and stating that he had, in fact, taken a third trip to see Grattan and that he had been accompanied by Hughes. The information contained in the Lords' report caused something of a sensation, but privately Castlereagh noted that what was published went beyond what had actually been stated in Neilson's examination before the committee.[34] He was also sceptical of Hughes, 'a man not of the best character', but believed that Grattan was guilty of 'flirting with the traitors tho' not actively embarked with them'.[35]

In 1842, Grattan's son attempted to exonerate his father from any association with the United Irishmen by publishing the details as recounted to him:

> The conversation and interview with Neilson was nothing – it was quite accidental. I was in my study, and Neilson was shown up along with Mr Hughes who I did not know. They complained very much of the excesses in the north of Ireland, and the murders of the Catholics; and I remember Hughes saying that the phrase used by the anti-Catholics was, 'To Connaught or hell with you!' They stated their numbers to be very great, and I then asked, 'How does it come, then that they are always beat?' I did not ask the question with a view to learn their force, as the examination would lead one to believe, but in consequence of these two individuals boasting of the numbers of those men who could not protect themselves. Hughes went downstairs, and Neilson asked me to become a United Irishman. I declined. He produced the constitution and left it in the room. This was nothing new; I had seen it before and it was generally printed and published. Hughes then returned and they both went away. That was the entire of the transaction on which so much importance was attached.

The younger Grattan published two correspondences, one from the United Irishman William Dowdall, formerly Grattan's agent, and one from Neilson. In the former, Dowdall expressed concern at the attempts by Members of Parliament to malign Grattan, asserting that Neilson's published examination:

> ... has been miserably carved and patched to answer their own views; every artifice was used by the Chancellor and the Speaker to implicate you ... [Neilson] named you himself, positively asserting you were not a United Irishman to his knowledge; nor did he believe you such; that he made use of every argument to bring you forward in some manner, to save the country, as you were at that time so completely popular, that he never pointed out any particular manner to you, and that nothing could induce you to take any part, as you could not see a clear course to steer by which the country might be saved from tyranny on the one hand, or anarchy on the other. He also stated that the plan of reform prepared by you (called Mr Ponsonby's) would have satisfied the North at the time.

Dowdall persuaded Neilson, by this stage his fellow prisoner in Newgate Gaol, to communicate with Grattan the precise nature of the answers he had given to the committee, restating that he did ask Grattan to become a member of the United Irishmen in order to prevent the country from becoming 'shipwrecked on anarchy or despotism', but that the MP refused these advances. Hughes's assertion that Neilson had sworn Grattan as a United Irishman was false.[36]

Grattan still suffered for his meetings with the rebel leaders. Lord Cornwallis (who replaced Camden in June 1798, combining the roles of commander-in-chief and viceroy) explored the possibility of charging Grattan with treason, but felt that Neilson, who had already contradicted Hughes's evidence before the Secret Committee, would want his day in court and the prosecution might fail. Meanwhile, Castlereagh had sought and received permission from William Wickham, the Under-Secretary for the Home Department, to strike Grattan's name from the list of Privy Councillors. Drennan noted that Grattan's ignominy was further achieved by the removal of his portrait from the Examination Hall in Dublin's Trinity College and the Guild of Merchants declared publicly its intent to disenfranchise a number of named individuals who had been awarded the freedom of the guild. That Grattan was associated with United Irish leaders such as Napper Tandy, Rowan and Henry Jackson would have been particularly hurtful, forcing the veteran parliamentarian to publish a refutation of the accusation that he was in some way involved in the conspiracy.[37] Concerned by any cloud of suspicion hanging over Grattan and keen to clarify his own role in the answering of questions asked by members of the Lords and Commons, Neilson wrote to the editor of the *Morning Chronicle*, a London newspaper that had pioneered the publication of parliamentary debates as recalled by its reporters, defending Grattan's reputation and lambasting Hughes's evidence:

> SIR,
>
> It appears to be the occupation of a certain party to calumniate the State Prisoners; so far as their calumnies regard myself, I smile at them for the moment. Time rolls on and truth will one day be heard. In the meantime, I am, however, particularly called upon (by some recent publications) in vindication of a truly respectable character, whose conduct and principles have been basely vilified, to state this publicly, that not one word ever fell from me which could, in the most remote degree, tend to support the accusations made against him, as the Committees of the Lords and Commons well know, and I cannot but say that the coupling my name with that of a common informer, whose testimony was in direct opposition to mine, even as given in a celebrated Report, is but a clumsy pretext for the traduction of virtue.[38]

Having failed in the attempt to give credence to the United Irish project by harnessing leading political figures to its banner, Neilson stepped up his association with Fitzgerald and those planning a rising. Following his evasion from capture on 12 March, Lord Edward remained in the capital, staying in safe houses under the protection of sympathisers to the cause, first on Aungier Street and then close to the Grand Canal, at the home of a Mrs Dillon, where he stayed for around a month. Fitzgerald's next refuge was on Thomas Street, in the house of a feather merchant named Nicholas Murphy. He would also move between the houses of John Cormick and another sympathiser called Moore, both of whom also resided on Thomas Street.

The leadership of the National Executive was now determined on rebellion, although there were disagreements over how this might be staged. The brothers Henry and John Sheares proposed a coup centred on Dublin, involving a takeover of the Irish Parliament and other political and strategic locations, such as the barracks at Chapelizod and the military camp at Loughlinstown, with an expectation that the disaffected militia would rally to the standard of rebellion. Also considered at one stage was an attack on the College Green Parliament on 18 May, the day of the trial of the notorious Lord Kingston, who stood accused of the murder of Colonel Henry Gerald Fitzgerald, his half-brother, who had seduced Kingston's 16-year-old daughter. Kingston had chosen to be tried by his fellow peers, in accordance with his entitlement, and the Sheares saw this occasion as an opportunity to seize power by surrounding the chamber and capturing the key governmental figures (including Camden, Castlereagh and Lord Chancellor Fitzgibbon) who were expected to be in attendance. Fitzgerald and Neilson preferred the notion of a Dublin rising backed up by the establishment of a rebel cordon (consisting of United Irishmen from the neighbouring counties of Kildare, Meath and Wicklow) around the capital and the igniting of insurrectionary activity across the country, led by local leaders who had been instructed on how to act by the written and verbal communications to be transmitted by emissaries. The Fitzgerald–Neilson approach would arouse the strong opposition of the Sheares, who felt that such a strategy was likely to end in disaster because, in their view, the necessary levels of leadership and expertise were not present beyond Dublin, leaving the fate of the capital at the mercy of those outside of their control. The fissures that existed within the leadership of the United Irishmen can be seen in the information that reached Dublin Castle by the pen of one of Cooke's spies, Samuel Sproule. Sproule had been told of the plans to attack the military camps by one of his informants, a local silk mercer, and claimed that William Lawless and the Sheares were suspected of treachery by the rest of the leadership and so misinformation was communicated so that the authorities would be misled.[39]

Despite these difficulties, the United Irish executive continued to make preparations. As the commander of the rebels, Lord Edward drew on his military experience to compile lists of resources and strategies designed to prevail over the government forces. With the passage of time, these seem derisory. Papers found on Lord Edward at the time of his arrest included requisitions for scaling ladders and hooks for attacking the magazine, fifty chains and padlocks for the safekeeping of loyalist prisoners, 1,000 spike nails, cramp irons, hammers, 100 hatchets and 300 shovels. Also discovered, this time in Leinster House, were notes scribbled in a pocket book considering the efficacy of the pike against a mounted enemy engaged in narrow streets, the strategy of showering soldiers with stones and bricks from a height and the generation of noise that would render military orders worthless. Plans to erect barricades and disable the effectiveness of artillery and cavalry by removing paving from the streets formed part of the plan for urban warfare. The need to fight at close quarters in order to disrupt the order and discipline of the troops was deemed essential.

Central to the conspiracy was the need for large numbers of rebels in Dublin. A worried Camden wrote anxiously to London about the number of pikes that were being concealed in the capital. The loyalist *Dublin Journal* reported that 300 finished pikes had been discovered on Lord Edward's estate in Monasterevin, County Kildare.[40] By 11 May, the authorities were desperate to apprehend the charismatic Fitzgerald and a proclamation was issued by the viceroy offering a £1,000 reward for his capture.[41] A desperate search for insurgent leaders and arms was yielding some success. Following the confiscation of pikes at the Dundrum home of the imprisoned John Sweetman (where Neilson had stayed after his release from Kilmainham), his brewery on Francis Street was scoured by the military. During the search, Lieutenant Stewart of the Derry Militia was stabbed by an attacker who had drawn a sword from his cane. The attacker, a plasterer named Stringer, was injured as he escaped and was later apprehended and lodged in Newgate. The press reported that a seven-barrelled gun, capable of firing several shots simultaneously, was found in the brewery and delivered into the hands of Alderman Alexander. One government spy was under the impression that Neilson had been present in the brewery during the search and that he had, in fact, been the assailant.[42]

The search for Lord Edward was intensified. Cooke was receiving intelligence from Francis Higgins, whose agent, Francis Magan, was by now at the heart of the United Irish apparatus as a member of the ruling executive. On 1 May, Higgins told Cooke that Fitzgerald was in Dublin preparing to take command of the Leinster insurgents. Two weeks later, Cooke was informed that Fitzgerald was being moved between safe houses, protected by his armed bodyguards. Magan's information was high grade and on 18 May the authorities were able to concentrate their efforts on the rectangular area around Thomas Street, Usher's Island, Watling Street and Dirty Lane (now Bridgefoot Street). Cooke was informed that Fitzgerald would be in disguise ('he wears a wig, or may be otherwise metamorphosed') and intended to fight if challenged.[43] The authorities nearly achieved their prize on that Friday evening, with Town Major Sirr encountering Lord Edward's retinue on Watling Street on the fringes of the Liberties. Sirr was assailed by Patrick Gallagher, one of Fitzgerald's bodyguards, and knocked to the ground in the ensuing scuffle. In the confusion, Ireland's most wanted man escaped to the safety of Murphy's house on Thomas Street.[44] He was deprived of his liberty the following evening when the safe house was stormed and Fitzgerald mortally wounded in a struggle with Major Swan of the police, Captain Ryan (a yeomanry officer) and Major Sirr. Neilson had been at the house on two occasions that day, once at noon and then again around four.

Pakenham's assessment of Neilson as a helpless drunk, leaving the door of Murphy's ajar as he hurried away after dinner has tended to overshadow his importance within the United Irish leadership, but it was nothing compared to the damning verdict of Thomas Moore, the famous songwriter, whose widely read two-volume account of Lord Edward's life intimated that it was Neilson who had betrayed Fitzgerald. Writing in 1831, long before the outing of Francis Magan as the man who had informed the authorities of the rebel chief's whereabouts, Moore's narrative stated, 'There had now elapsed, from the time of Neilson's departure, not more than ten minutes and it is asserted that he had, in going out, left the hall door open.' The clear implication was that Neilson, who was considered to be mentally unstable, was responsible for this decisive blow to the designs of the United Irishmen.[45] Moore was not the first to cast suspicion on Neilson's role. As already noted, Higgins and Magan, while reporting Neilson's overtly militant stance to Cooke, were equally convinced that he must have been in the service of the government. On the 23rd, the day of his arrest, Samuel Sproule – in a typically hasty correspondence with Cooke – asserted 'Neilson is the traytor [*sic*] – all his conduct shows it.'

Rumours continued to circulate in the years following the rebellion. Lady Elizabeth Holland, husband of Henry Vassell-Fox (a cousin of the leading politician Charles James Fox) and a socialite with impeccable Whig connections, wrote about Fitzgerald's (another of her cousins) demise: 'Neilson was supposed to have given him up & McNevin [*sic*] was also a false friend.'[46] Such was the cloak of suspicion hanging over Neilson's reputation that two of his daughters, Mary Hancock Neilson and Sophia McAdam, contacted Madden in 1842 when they heard of his intention to publish his multi-volume account of the lives and times of the United Irishmen, urging him to reject any suggestions that their father had betrayed Lord Edward. It was their view that Moore had been deceived and that 'He was never suspected by friend or foe of having acted so base a part ... and we feel most anxious to guard you against falling into the same error in the forthcoming work.' Sophia had written to MacNeven in the USA in 1831, the year of the publication of Moore's book, hoping to 'repel the calumny and shield a father's memory from so unjust and abominable insinuation'. MacNeven arranged for two inserts into American editions of Moore's book, stating that Neilson was 'utterly so incapable of treachery to his friends or to his country', instead attributing his erratic behaviour to the 'constant agitation of his mind'.[47]

Fitzgerald's arrest was a devastating blow to the United Irishmen and a great coup for a government that was becoming increasingly anxious. The viceroy, Lord Camden, was made aware of the arrest while attending a production in the theatre, 'from whence I could not retire without giving rise to much conjecture'.

He reported to the Home Secretary that Fitzgerald was expected to survive and face trial and sought a special commission to be assembled for this purpose. The raid on Murphy's harvested clear proof of Lord Edward's position; a dark green uniform coat with purple facings and a seal with the motto 'Erin go Bragh' on one side and his cypher 'EF' on the other.[48] It is easy to look retrospectively on the rebellion and assume that the government had the situation fully under control, with soldiers in place and a network of spies and informers – like Magan – who were providing the intelligence that would disable the insurgency. As Thomas Bartlett makes clear, however, omniscience was never an advantage that the Castle would enjoy. For every success against the conspiracy, numerous individuals and designs went undetected and while leaders like Neilson could be accused of carelessness in their behaviour, others took great care in their personal conduct – for example, by employing coded language in written communication to frustrate the authorities.[49]

Deprived of their commander-in-chief, Neilson and the rump of the United Irish leadership attempted to carry on with the plan for rebellion, despite the differences that existed within the group. Henry and John Sheares were lawyers who had been part of the fabric of the society since their return from France in early 1793. In the wake of the arrest of the Leinster leadership at Bond's, they had stepped into the vacuum alongside Fitzgerald, Neilson and William Lawless, whose frustration with the divisions within the leadership saw him abandon the project on the eve of the rebellion. The Sheares were convinced that the military would rally to the republican cause and this belief had been affirmed by Captain James Warneford Armstrong of the King's County Militia, stationed at Loughlinstown camp, in whom they had confided in the mistaken belief that he was a sympathiser. Armstrong betrayed their trust and, on Monday, 21 May, Henry and John Sheares were arrested. They were subsequently executed on the ninth anniversary of the fall of the Bastille.[50] Evidence of the divisions within the leadership can be gauged from the contents of a letter from John Sheares to Neilson, found in the latter's possession at the time of his arrest. Sheares was already scathing about the plan to entrust the success of the rebellion to the actions of United Irishmen in surrounding counties and was of the opinion that only a strategic uprising, centred on the capture of key buildings and bolstered by the enlistment of militia support, would succeed. He was even more alarmed by the prospect of an assault upon Kilmainham Gaol to liberate the political prisoners confined there (among them Oliver Bond and Thomas Emmet) and his letter to Neilson, written before both his arrest and that of Lord Edward, was worded in the strongest possible terms:

> Sir—I have sought you in every direction, but unfortunately in vain. It is now too late to use many words upon the subject of our intended interview; let it suffice to say that I am acquainted with the destructive design you meditate, and am resolved to counteract it, whatever it may cost. Rest assured that nothing shall check a resolution which honour, private affection, and public duty unite to demand the immediate execution of; and that, however unwilling I may be at any other moment to take the only steps which your obstinacy may render necessary this evening for the preservation of my friends and of my country, I will without hesitation take them. The scheme you have undertaken I view with horror, whether its effects be considered as relating to my imprisoned friends, the destruction of whose property and lives must be the consequence even of your success; or as affecting Arthur O'Connor's existence, the precarious chance for which you thus cruelly lessen; or (what is superior to every other consideration) as ensuring the ruin of Ireland's freedom. In short, Mr., to be candid with you, the scheme is so totally destitute of any apology, even from the plea of folly or passion, that I cannot avoid attributing its origin to a worse cause, and nothing can convince me of the contrary but your immediately foregoing so pernicious an enterprise. In these sentiments I am not singular, nor in the resolution which arises from them; and, should you doubt me, you must purchase your conviction at a severe cost. My resolution and that of my friends is this: if you do not, by nine o'clock this evening, give us every necessary and sacred assurance that you will counteract and prevent the perpetration of this plot against all that you ought to hold dear, notice of it shall be given to the government without a moment's delay; for we do prefer that a few misguided (not to say guilty) individuals should perish, than that every remaining hope of our country's success, and the lives of our most valued friends, should be sacrificed by the accomplishment of a stupid, perhaps wicked, undertaking. Do not feed yourself with hope that any consideration shall deter me from fulfilling this threat. If every poignard you could command were at my throat I would do my duty. I did think well of you; I wish to do so still; you alone can prevent me. J. S.
>
> I dine at 52, Abbey-street, where I shall expect your answer before eight o'clock.[51]

Undeterred by the severity of Sheares' rant, Neilson now took the initiative in organising a rebellion without the charismatic commander-in-chief and against the backdrop of division and confusion within the leadership. According to Higgins, Neilson met with what remained of the military committee on Friday, 18 May, and Tuesday, 22 May, and determined to proceed by instigating the strategy which he had originally promoted, namely the burning of the mail coaches destined for provincial areas; their failure to arrive would be the signal to local leaders that the rebellion had been unleashed.[52] The information reaching Cooke was sporadic and confused. Military attention was focused on a rebellion that was centred on Dublin, in line with the Sheares' plan, which had been communicated by Captain Armstrong. The Smithfield and Newmarket areas had been secured and troops had been posted at key government buildings and on the bridges across the Liffey. That Neilson was countenancing a more general rising came as something of a shock. Sproule the informer was sending scribbled notes to the Castle *via* John Lees at the post office with snippets of rumour and tittle-tattle. On the 19th, he noted that Neilson's nephew, John Gordon (who had been a prisoner in Kilmainham, suspected of involvement in a number of murders in the Belfast area between 1796 and 1797), was staying in the Brazen Head public house and that a consignment of pikes was due to arrive there. Sproule expressed disappointment that a soldier in Lord Muskerry's Limerick County Militia called John McMahon, who had been prepared to give evidence against Gordon, had now reneged. Two days later, on the Monday, Sproule wrote directly to Cooke to warn him of a plan hatched the previous night to attack Newgate and release Fitzgerald. Thirty men, each armed with a dagger and a case of pistols, would form part of a party, with two men (who allegedly knew Fitzgerald's cell, if not his condition) detailed to kill any guards who stood in their way. Other rebels would attack Trinity College and force the young gentlemen there to hand over their weapons. Cooke took swift action to prevent such an attack upon the gaol, sending troops to the area and forcing the abandonment of the plan.

This did not deter Neilson, who planned to rescue Fitzgerald and Russell and was, in Sproule's words, 'mad to have it done'. Despite his concerns about the lack of arms, Neilson was 'pushing it on by every earthly means ... but determined upon the tryall [*sic*]'.[53] According to a United Irish colonel (Southwell McClune) who later made a deposition to the government, Neilson met with an assembly of fifteen colonels from Dublin and surrounding districts on the evening of Wednesday, 23 May, and assigned each to a specific part of the city.[54] He made his way to the barley fields in the Smithfield area of Dublin, where a party of rebels had gathered close to Newgate Gaol. Pakenham's account of Neilson stumbling towards Newgate, having been waylaid by a visit to a public house during his mission to co-ordinate the initial stages of the rising, is based on the problematic account of Bernard Dornin in Watty Cox's sensationalist *Irish Magazine*, published in New York in the early years of the nineteenth century. Pakenham notes that Neilson emerged drunk, having lost his sense of direction as well as the purpose of his mission, and stumbled, almost instinctively, to the prison to attempt to free Lord Edward.[55] The nineteenth-century historian, W.H. Maxwell, offers a detailed account of Neilson's arrest outside the prison. Having trodden accidentally on a child, he was abused by its drunken mother and the altercation attracted the attention of the guards, in particular Tresham Gregg, the keeper of the gaol.[56] Neilson was pounced upon and detained after a struggle, during which 'His clothes were torn off him and his body was hacked at – cut and scarred in upwards of fifty places.'[57]

Those rebels gathered at the barley fields nearby to undertake the assault on the prison dissolved into the night when no signal came. According to Sproule, John Gordon, who had somehow injured his arm, took up the struggle on behalf of his uncle.[58] In his claim to the Lord Lieutenant and Privy Council for a financial reward for his part in securing Neilson, Gregg claimed that the arrest took place 'on or about the hour of nine o'clock' and that he had risked his life in the process. He was granted the £300 reward for Neilson's apprehension.[59] According to the informer Patrick McCabe, Charles O'Hara was appointed to the command of the Dublin United Irishmen after Neilson's incarceration.[60] Within the space of a few days, those who had tasked themselves with the leadership of an insurrection irrespective of French aid were either in custody, on the run or dead. Lord Edward clung to life in Newgate until 4 June, experiencing pain and delusion as septicaemia spread throughout his injured body. His death would spare the necessity of a trial for a man from such a distinguished background, with the inevitable upset for his family, not to mention the dangers of unleashing the legal wizardry of John Philpot Curran on the prosecution's case. Lord Castlereagh instructed Adjutant Samuel Stone (later elevated to the position of paymaster to the Londonderry Militia) to guard the prisoner and restrict access to him. This even meant that Fitzgerald's attorney was prevented from having direct contact with Newgate as the aristocratic chieftain sought to settle his affairs.[61]

His final days were recorded by J. Armstrong Garnett, the doctor charged with managing Lord Edward as his condition deteriorated due to the infection. The increasingly delirious leader declared that he was dying for his country, safe in the knowledge that he would be received by God as one who had contributed to its freedom. Prescribed laudanum, Fitzgerald was barely able to recognise the few visitors who were permitted to see him, among them his brother, his aunt (Lady Louisa Connolly) and Fitzgibbon (Lord Clare), who, despite his very obvious political differences, was so moved by Fitzgerald's plight that he was 'unable to remain in the room'. The dying man wished in vain to be reunited with the Presbyterian minister of Rathfriland, Reverend Samuel Barber, and Thomas Russell, who was detained in the same gaol. Fitzgerald died at two o'clock on the afternoon of 4 June. His body was conveyed quietly to St Werbergh's church, opposite Christchurch Cathedral, where he was buried 'in the most quick manner'.[62]

The rebellion spread to the counties around Dublin over the next few days, indicating that Neilson's efforts had not been completely wasted. Carlow, Wicklow, Meath and Wexford rallied to the cause and, eventually, Ulster erupted after McCracken seized the initiative from the more cautious foreign-aid leaders, such as Robert Simms. County Antrim rose on 7 June and Down two days later. With the defeat of Monro's insurgent army at Ballynahinch on the 13th, the outburst in Ulster was over, a denouement that belied the province's reputation as the cradle of republican principles on the island. The relative quietude of the north in the days after the outbreak of the rising can be attributed to the caution of the Ulster Provincial Committee, but also to the fact that Lake's campaign of repression the previous year had its intended effect. Cooke surmised that the 'Popish tinge' of the rebellion in Wexford (which at times exhibited symptoms of naked sectarianism), combined with Presbyterian concerns about French actions against Protestant cantons in Switzerland and the actions of French privateers against American shipping, had forced Ulster Presbyterians into a fundamental rethink. There is also evidence to suggest that stories of atrocities against Protestants in Wexford had permeated north, leading to further confusion about what exactly was meant by 'the cause'.[63]

It seems remarkable that the Prime Minister, William Pitt, faced by the crises of continental war and rebellion on his doorstep, would allow himself to be distracted by a duel with the Foxite Whig MP George Tierney, who alleged that Pitt had impugned his character by questioning his loyalty to the country during an angry parliamentary exchange. As the flames of insurrection spread across the counties surrounding Dublin, Pitt and Tierney exchanged shots on Putney Heath. Both missed (the PM's marksmanship was no doubt discredited given the girth of his opponent) and retired to their duties, leaving Home Office minister William Wickham to report to Cooke that London 'is not yet recovered from the panick [*sic*]'.[64] With common sense restored to Downing Street and the military dealing with the rebellion in Ireland, the authorities in London and Dublin began to grapple with the task of preparing charges against the leaders of the conspiracy. Neilson was first in their sights, with the case against him and the other state prisoners being compiled during the next weeks.

His prospects were bleak. Not only had Neilson been caught red-handed reconnoitring Newgate prison, he was also alleged to be directing affairs even after his incarceration, circulating a letter *via* one Hanley to United Irish figures on the outside, encouraging them to persist in their efforts to assemble and rise outside Dublin, to the south of the city (believed to be Kilgobbin near Stepaside, in the shadow of the Wicklow Mountains). Neilson's orders were intercepted by Higgins, who quickly passed them on to the Castle on 8 June. In his letter, Neilson also advanced the view that Ulster would rise imminently, a forecast that was not without accuracy.[65] Neilson's conduct meant that it was likely he would face the harshest penalty if he was put on trial. The arrest of the fugitive informer William Bird on 19 June raised the possibility that Bird might, after all, be persuaded to give evidence in court.[66]

On 25 June, Neilson, John and Henry Sheares, Oliver Bond, Michael Byrne and John McCann were brought before the Special Commission for the trial of High Treason, Misprision of Treason, Murder and Manslaughter, which was presided over by Lord Chief Justice Lord Carleton, Baron George and Justices Crookshank, Chamberlain and Day. Grand juries of the city and county of Dublin were sworn and the prisoners arraigned. Neilson was charged with high treason but declined to name two counsels to represent him for reasons, he said subsequently, of financial embarrassment. He did, however, ask that his chains be removed because their weight contributed significantly to the discomfort he was enduring on a hard bed. The other prisoners chose their counsels and the court was adjourned until 4 July. Neilson's return to court saw him relieved of his chains and he waived the right to have the list of charges against him read in full because 'it was unnecessary – it would only be a waste of time'. John Philpot Curran and George Ponsonby, who were defending Oliver Bond, offered to represent him free of charge and his agent was James Crawford.

Neilson was arraigned on three different counts of high treason: for having imagined and compassed the death of the king; for having conspired with the French to dethrone him; and for having planned to subvert the constitution. When asked to plead, Neilson hesitated before replying that he was not guilty. When asked how he would like to be tried, he replied that this should be in the usual way before adding by God and his country. He also complained about the chains he had to endure and it was agreed that his legal team be allowed access to his cell.[67] Two days later, he wrote to his wife, Anne, to inform her that he was in reasonable health, despite his harsh treatment. Of the impending trial, he commented that he was certain the court would show no leniency: 'My trial comes on next Thursday; and though I have no apprehension, I am prepared for the worst, because I know the malice of my enemies is extremely keen.' As a result of the entreaties of his representatives, only one leg was now in irons, but a lack of sleep and loss of appetite were concerning.[68]

The damning evidence of Captain Armstrong at the trial of Henry and John Sheares on 12 and 13 July was enough to deliver a guilty verdict and the brothers were executed the following day. Neilson was relieved that nothing said during their twenty-two-hour trial implicated him and he reported to his wife the same day that he had recovered from a 'smart illness', his chains had been removed and he was allowed to take brief, lonely walks in the lobby. His isolation was a source of annoyance; the guards were under instructions not to allow him to communicate with his fellow prisoners. Regarding more practical matters and with an eye to what he must surely have feared to be his own fate, Neilson asked Anne to see that his mother and uncle look after the farm at Skegoniell and that Anne's father, William Bryson, tend to the Belfast properties. She was to dedicate herself to the children, Anne, Sophia, Jane, William and Mary:

> And oh! Let me entreat you once more to rear them hardily, to do everything in the house in turn. To William, reading, writing, English well – no other language, nor dancing; to the girls the same, with knitting and sewing, but no tambour nonsense. Let their dress be plain and homely, befitting their state; and of all things labour to form their minds by curbing pride and inciting to virtue and industry, not by scolding or whipping, or cajoling but by emulation, which is by far the safest and surest incentive to exertion.[69]

Crawford forewarned Neilson that Bird was once again his accuser, but the authorities were looking to secure an even better witness. John Cormick, a merchant who lived on Thomas Street, was – like Neilson – one of Lord Edward's entourage and it was in his house that the United Irish leader had been concealed in the period before his arrest and fatal wounding. Implicated in the rising, Cormick escaped from Dublin to Liverpool and then London, where he remained for a short time disguised as a sailor and assuming the name Campbell, before fleeing to Guernsey in the guise of a Captain Coppinger. Cormick was arrested there on 10 July by Anthony Fabiani, one of the king's messengers. Cormick gave a statement indicating that he was aware of large numbers of disaffected in London and offered to 'prove the sincerity of his repentance by assisting to make any discoveries which may tend to the public good'. This included continuing a correspondence with Edward Lewins, a United Irish emissary in Paris, in the hope of eliciting information on future plots. Castlereagh was hopeful that Cormick could be persuaded to give evidence against Neilson, 'his conviction being of the last importance, as he was undoubtedly one of the leading originators of the treason and one of the desperate planners of the Insurrection which was mediated on Dublin and of the rebellion which has broken out'. Castlereagh was excited about the prospect of Cormick taking the stand 'as Neilson's trial must come on speedily and our chief witness [Bird] has betrayed symptoms of unwillingness'.[70] But Cormick escaped from Fabiani's house on Ranelagh Street, Pimlico, on 23 July. While this may have been considered a serious blow, Wickham noted that it was unlikely that he would have given evidence in court and his flight would have no negative consequences since 'his reputation is gone forever within his party'.[71]

The government's attempts to prepare a case against Neilson were not proving fruitful and the absence of any significant figure to seal his fate from the witness box would make Curran's job of defending him considerably easier. Sproule, another informer who preferred anonymity, wrote to his handler, John Lees, that Neilson was among the most dangerous of the state prisoners and while a deal could be arranged to allow some of them to go into exile, such leniency should not apply to him. 'Nelson [*sic*] I would not spare. Massacre and murder was his avowed purpose throughout.'[72] The execution of John McCann on 24 July added greater urgency to the situation. With Bond, Byrne, Neilson and the other state prisoners at risk, it was time for someone to take the initiative. Neilson would be at the forefront of this development, paving the way for a remarkable deal between the prisoners and the government that would, to varying degrees, suit their very different purposes.

9

Worse Than Punic, 1798–9

Even as the government forces were still contending with the United Irish threat in Wexford during June and early July, attention was focused on those state prisoners confined in the Dublin prisons of Newgate, Kilmainham and the Bridewell. Just prior to the defeat of the rebels at Vinegar Hill (the decisive battle in the Wexford uprising) on 21 June, Neilson's tormentor, William Bird (John Smith), who had wrestled himself free from government control at the start of the year, was arrested in a ditch near Drogheda, along with his wife. They had been 'regaling themselves with wine'. His earlier reluctance to testify notwithstanding, Bird's unpredictability was such that his appearance as a witness against Neilson could not be ruled out. Writing to his wife from Newgate on 14 July, Neilson feared the worst. It was already his belief that his guard had been instructed to shoot any of his fellow prisoners who had the temerity to inquire from across the courtyard about his condition and when his attorney, James Crawford, informed him that Bird could once more be his accuser, it was a prospect the prisoner believed to be 'too ridiculous and wicked even for the present times'.[1]

The rapidity with which courts martial, trials and executions had been effected across various districts suggested that the further effusion of insurgent blood was inevitable. For many loyalists, this was a perfectly acceptable response to what had been, in their view, a violent and anarchic insurrection. As the editor of the *Northern Star* and as an agitator, Neilson had made powerful enemies and his death on the scaffold was awaited eagerly by those who felt themselves victims of his subversion. Robert Ross, the Newry MP, wrote excitedly (if prematurely) from Dublin that Neilson and Oliver Bond would follow McCann to the gallows: 'Oliver Bond to be executed on this day at 2 o'clock. Nelson [*sic*] of Belfast is to be tried in a day or two, he pretends to be mad but I hope it will not prevent him being hanged.'[2] The new viceroy, Lord Cornwallis, was less convinced about the inevitability of further convictions. The punishment of those caught red-handed in acts of rebellion was one thing; producing evidence to convict state prisoners detained before the insurrection, and who were being represented by lawyers of the ability of Curran and George Ponsonby, was quite another. The bloodlust of the ultra-conservatives might not be satisfied. Cornwallis explained his dilemma to the Home Secretary, Portland, noting that 'There is scarcely any one of the state prisoners except Neilson against whom there is any evidence that is likely to convict.'[3]

In fact, Cornwallis' concerns were assuaged by the prospect of what he called an 'extraordinary' proposition from the state prisoners, whereby they would equip the government with information about the history and nature of the United Irishmen's project (while omitting reference to specific individuals) in return for both an end to the trials and executions and an undertaking to permit them to be banished from the kingdom to settle in any country not at war with Britain. The genesis of this deal, often referred to as the Kilmainham Treaty, lay with Samuel Neilson. Concerned about the impending trials of Michael Byrne and Oliver Bond, as well as the likelihood of further executions (including, most likely, his own), Neilson mulled over a suggestion, made initially by his attorney, Crawford, that the state prisoners negotiate with the government. According to Neilson's subsequent account of the contacts, published in New York in 1802, he was reluctant to explore the possibility of discussions, such was his suspicion of an administration that had, over the previous few years, attempted to close his newspaper and deprive him of his liberty. Crawford had undertaken some of the exploratory work in the middle of July by contacting the veteran Whig Lord Charlemont to act as an intermediary, but he cited his old age and infirmity as reasons for not fulfilling the role. Instead, Francis Dobbs, a former Volunteer of the 1780s and Member of Parliament for the borough of Armagh, had agreed to conduct the delicate negotiations.

Neilson, meanwhile, had the means to communicate with prisoners at the Bridewell and received a positive initial response to the proposal from Arthur O'Connor, who was being held there. By 23 July, the possibility of an arrangement had reached Lord Castlereagh and it became necessary for Neilson to share the plan with the other prisoners. Michael Byrne was under sentence of death, while Bond's trial started that day; he was duly condemned. Both these men agreed to the idea, although they stressed that they were motivated more by the interests of the state prisoners as a group than any desire for their own personal safety. By now, the notion of talks between the prisoners and the government had gained momentum and a Castle spokesman, Henry Alexander, one of the Members of Parliament for the city of Derry (who was also a relative of Bond's), had been established as the conduit. Alexander was despatched to Newgate to ask Neilson to set out his ideas on paper and these were delivered to the Chief Secretary, complete with the names of most of the state prisoners being confined in the three gaols.[4]

For Cornwallis and Castlereagh, an accommodation would wrong-foot the ultras, save the public purse the expense of elaborate trials and hasten the banishment of men whose activities had destabilised the country for the best part of a decade.[5] Cooke, whose intelligence network had provided a flow of information, if not a stream of witnesses, saw the possibilities immediately and articulated these to Wickham: 'We get rid of 70 prisoners, many of the most important of whom we could not try and who could not be disposed of without doing such a violence to the principles of Law and Evidence as could not be well justified.'[6] Alexander informed his superiors that Neilson had offered the tantalising prospect of providing the government with a comprehensive statement on the activities of the United Irish conspiracy: 'I hold in my hand every muscle, sinew ... of the internal organisation of the United Irishmen. I will make it as plain as the palm of my hand.'[7]

Despite the advantages that these early contacts seemed to offer, there were divisions among the prisoners about the extent of any goodwill on the part of the government. While more than seventy of those detained endorsed Neilson's note, Arthur O'Connor did not sign the draft proposal, nor did William Sampson, who felt that since he had no leadership role in the organisation, any signature was, *ipso facto*, an admission of guilt. Thomas Russell, too, was reluctant to negotiate, but he was persuaded by his old friend from Belfast to fall in with the plan in order to prevent further bloodshed.[8] Roger O'Connor and William Dowdall were opposed to the plan from the outset. The former, the brother of Arthur and himself no stranger to controversy, would later assert that Neilson conceived of the deal to save himself from the gallows, while Castlereagh's willingness to countenance the treaty was based on the potential for personal embarrassment in the courtroom due to his earlier association with the cause of reform and – as O'Connor dubiously asserts – 'his former acts in connexion with the Northern Star paper'.[9]

This lack of unity was enough to persuade Cornwallis and Castlereagh not to take steps to prevent the execution of Byrne on 25 July, a smart but cynical strategy designed to panic the prisoners into action. As a consequence, Neilson was permitted to visit Arthur O'Connor and Sampson in the Bridewell and their signatures were then added to the proposal. Cornwallis was thus able to communicate to the Home Secretary that Byrne's death had 'operated very forcibly on the minds of the prisoners' and this gave Dublin Castle the confidence to manipulate the terms of Neilson's original proposal by insisting that any statement from the prisoners include the names of all persons relevant to the conspiracy, thereby effectively turning it into an informer deposition. This caused outrage among the state prisoners and Neilson, who had been permitted to visit the other detainees across the three gaols, was asked to seek a meeting with the Lord Lieutenant himself in order to apprise him of the fact that 'some unprincipled and bloody man' in the administration had surely been acting mischievously, without the knowledge of the viceroy. Cornwallis did not meet with the prisoners face-to-face, but Castlereagh, Cooke and Lord Chancellor Fitzgibbon (Clare) did accede on the condition that they engage with three of the most prominent prisoners: O'Connor, Thomas Addis Emmet and William James MacNeven. The men met in Dublin Castle on Sunday, 29 July, and a revised proposal was agreed. This included a guarantee that no information given freely by the prisoners would implicate anyone and reaffirmed that they would accept banishment as an alternative to trial. The prisoners also received confirmation that others held in custody would be offered the same terms as the state prisoners. For their part, the prisoners stated that they would relate the nature of the connections between the United Irishmen and foreign powers.[10]

Neilson declared himself satisfied with the way his proposal was being handled at this stage and he wrote excitedly to his wife from Newgate on 30 July: 'Wonderful have been the events of the last week. It is impossible for me to give them in detail; suffice it to say that we have been, in some degree, instrumental in meeting the government on the great principle of conciliation, which we hope will tranquillise the country, and on terms honourable to all parties.' Given that his and Bond's lives had been spared, he was sensitive to any charges of self-preservation: 'You will hear abominable stories about this business, for they are already afloat, but I know you will laugh at them. It will ever be the pride of my life that I was instrumental in the business.'[11]

With the terms of the compact drawn up and the government affirming its wish to act in good faith, O'Connor, MacNeven and Emmet set to work producing a memorandum explaining how the Society of United Irishmen was formed due to the unrepresentative nature of a corrupt Irish Parliament and developed as a consequence of misgovernment, repression and the deliberate attempt to infuse sectarianism into Irish politics. They argued that their activities were designed to moderate Irish politics by blunting the excesses of both Orangemen and Defenders and 'restraining them from employing a mutually destructive exertion of force'. The increasing militancy of the United Irishmen was attributed to the extreme measures taken by the government, notably the Insurrection Act, which legitimised military excess and violence. Of the links with France, the memorandum stated that the French were unlikely to abandon their commitment to separating Ireland from England 'so long as the discontents of the people would induce them to support an invasion'. True to their word, the thorough document was cleverly crafted and avoided implicating any of their colleagues, prompting the *Courier* newspaper to declare it 'a masterpiece of writing'.[12]

The early proceedings had progressed satisfactorily and *The Observer* noted the change in mood music. O'Connor, Emmet and MacNeven had been conveyed to the Castle in hackney cabs, without a guard, and the prisoners were now receiving visits from relatives. Neilson, who had been heavily chained and accompanied by troops when he was arraigned just days earlier, had walked arm in arm with Dobbs from Newgate to Dublin Castle on Wednesday, 1 August. The commission of oyer and terminer, under which a team of judges were to have met to establish Neilson's trial, had been cancelled.[13] The initial optimism would soon, however, be replaced. On 6 August, Cooke arrived at Kilmainham, where Emmet and MacNeven were imprisoned, to complain that the memorandum was regarded as a justification of the United Irishmen instead of a statement of their activities. The prisoners asserted that any attempt by the government to redact the document for public consumption would be countered by the publication of omitted sections by the prisoners and their friends outside the gaols. They promised Cooke they would look again at the wording and requested that O'Connor be permitted to confer with them the following day. As the three men started their work, MacNeven received word that he was to appear before the Secrecy Committee of the House of Lords, in what was an attempt by the authorities to isolate each of them in order to extract information that could be printed and published as parliamentary proceedings, thus providing the state prisoners with no right of reply. These summons halted the dialogue and, in the interim, courts martial continued as the remnants of the rebellion were being addressed.

Neilson regarded the tactics of the administration as duplicitous and he, along with Bond, was invited by Henry Alexander to set out their concerns on paper. They did this on the 8th:

> It is to be premised, that all communications on the present state of the country are to be confidential, explicit, and calculated to restore harmony by concessions on the part of the government and obedience on the part of the people. First then, we are of the opinion, that in order to tranquilise the public mind, there should be an immediate and *universal* amnesty, together with a general *liberation of the prisoners* in the different jails and tenders, who

> are charged with treason, or treasonable practices. Government pointing out such excepted persons as they wish to leave the country, and who may prefer emigration to imprisonment or trial. We think this step will so prepossess the people in favour of Lord Cornwallis' government that they will cheerfully listen to any proposals which may be made for the restoration and continuance, not only of tranquillity, but of mutual confidence. With respect to the persons who may be chiefly instrumental in the different counties to effectuate this desirable object, we think an immediate correspondence be opened with them, by such prisoners as approve of this measure, and will voluntarily assist in it. We, on our part, will do everything in our power to carry it into effect.

The government's response was to request that the prisoners bring their influence to bear on those insurgents who continued to fight in Wicklow. Dobbs accompanied two United Irish representatives despatched to the area to help pacify the county by offering terms to the insurgents based on those negotiated by the state prisoners.[14]

The day after Neilson and Bond took this initiative, the former appeared before the Secrecy Committee of the House of Lords. MacNeven, O'Connor and Emmet also gave evidence between 7 and 8 August. The administration intended to publish these responses, omitting any attempt by the prisoners to justify their actions or glorify the cause. Neilson's appearance before the committee came just days after John Hughes, the Belfast United Irishman-turned-informer, swore to the committee that Neilson had visited Grattan at his country house in Tinnehinch and that Neilson claimed that Grattan had been sworn into the United Irishmen, something that, as already noted, both Neilson and Grattan denied. Neilson's responses to the questions asked of him were short and factual. He stated that he had been a member of the United Irishmen since 1791, that the society's original aims had been to force the government into making a fundamental reform and that communications with France were later established alongside a military structure. Neilson stated that he had been active in the weeks leading up to the rebellion, filling vacancies in the leadership ranks, communicating Fitzgerald's orders and planning an assault on Newgate on the night he was arrested. Neilson said he believed that Fitzgerald was afraid of a French invasion lest this lead to a conquest of Ireland, and so the commander-in-chief resolved to unleash a rebellion. He stated that he, along with Bond and Sweetman, had met with Grattan twice at Tinnehinch and although he had briefed the parliamentarian on the country's affairs, he had not sworn him into the movement. Immediately after his examination, Neilson wrote to the committee through Fitzgibbon to say that he had omitted reference to a third meeting with Grattan, in the company of Hughes.

Neilson's evidence mentioned individuals, but significantly, he did not implicate anyone – Fitzgerald was dead and Sweetman and Bond were under the terms of the agreement between the state prisoners and the government. He did, however, pause to say that since the naming of Lord Edward might injure the Fitzgerald family, no further reference would be made to him. Lord Dillon interjected, asking Neilson if he knew where he was and reminding him of his responsibility to answer questions. Neilson replied, 'I do know where I am; I know you may send me back either to my cell or to the scaffold – I am indifferent; but I will answer no question tending to implicate any person.' Neilson's parting shot, in response to a question from Lord Kilwarden about the best means of quietening the country, harked back to his *Star* editorials: 'I say, then (and I speak from a knowledge of the people as well as a feeling of their sufferings), to rule this country in quiet you must complete the amnesty: in a word, you must govern by public opinion and not by force.'[15] Despite all this, damage had been done to Grattan's reputation. Moreover, the fact that Arthur O'Connor was a signatory to the prisoners' memorandum – and had been examined by the Irish Lords – provided the administration with the opportunity to embarrass his English Whig friends, such as Charles James Fox and Richard Brinsley Sheridan.

In an undated statement made by Neilson, he outlined his views in a way that reflected his political frustration, republican outlook and uncompromising character. Had these words been delivered at the gallows, a prominent place in the gallery of martyrs would have been assured.

> With respect to the progress of truth by discussion and not of arms, I agree with Godwin; but when discussion is utterly at an end, I know no means of resisting tyranny but by arms. While it was possible to persuade the people from this last appeal, I advised every man I know to exert himself to keep the country quiet. But when the horrid cruelties committed by the army – when robbery, rape and butchery and rapine of every kind had become a Custom, and when I found the country thus maddened into resistance, I did conceive neutrality a crime, and had I been at large, I would have lent my feeble aid to the common cause of my much injured and bleeding country. Death to me has no fears – slavery accompanied by barbarous cruelty I cannot endure. As to liberty for Ireland, I die for her. And so far from regretting any political act of

> my life, I look back upon the whole with intimate pleasure. I die in confidence that truth must triumph and that Ireland must be free. As to my religion, that is a matter between my maker and myself with which the community has nothing to do. As to my morals they have ever been – to do to others as I would they do to me and in this faith I shall depart without a groan.[16]

The reserved nature of the prisoners' responses to the Secrecy Committee disappointed the governments in London and Dublin. Wickham, the Under-Secretary for the Home Department, complained that the prisoners acted in bad faith and that their language 'caused very unpleasant sensations here, and given room to fear that these persons were neither correct in their principles nor sincere in their disclosures'.[17] It was at this point that Neilson asserted that the government began to move away from its earlier commitments, although, in truth, the state prisoners had been evasive during their questioning by the Lords. On 18 August, Cooke gave the impression that the administration was ready to make the arrangements for the prisoners' banishment. Neilson requested two months to settle his business affairs and see his confiscated papers returned.[18] When the government sanctioned the publication of information in the newspapers that gave a distorted picture of the evidence given to the secret committee (by the use of selective references to lengthy examinations, the clear implication was that the men had, in fact, revealed the names of their associates), the prisoners responded angrily, placing what Castlereagh referred to as an 'unbecoming advertisement' on 27 August that attempted to clarify their position, an action which resulted in their being placed once again in solitary confinement:[19]

> Having read in the different newspapers publications pretending to be abstracts of the reports of the secret committee of the House of Commons, and of our depositions before the committees of the Lords and Commons we feel ourselves called upon to assure the public that they are gross, and, to us, astonishing misrepresentations, not only unsupported by, but in many instances directly contradictory to, the facts we really stated on these occasions. We further assure our friends, that in no instance did the name of any individual escape from us; on the contrary, we always refused answering such questions as might tend to implicate any persons whatever, comfortably to the agreement entered into by the state prisoners with government.

The advertisement was signed by O'Connor, Emmet and MacNeven. Neilson stated that he too would have signed it had the colleague transmitting it to the press been given access to him.[20]

On the same day that the advertisement appeared, the London *Times* asserted confidently that 'The Rebellion may therefore be considered as wholly at an end.'[21] In fact, the Dublin government was faced with another major crisis as a small French fleet under the command of General Jean Joseph Humbert, a veteran of the Bantry campaign at the end of 1796, had arrived at Killala Bay in County Mayo on the 22nd and landed around 1,100 well-equipped soldiers. This development took the government completely by surprise, but while the loyalist yeomen on the spot retreated, there appeared to be little in the way of local support for the foreign troops, who had been convinced that they would be welcomed as liberators. The area was not historically a centre of United Irish activity, although there was a significant Defender presence, part of which had arrived in Connaught in the aftermath of the Armagh outrages of 1795. Many of these men rallied to the cause. A planned secondary invasion under General Hardy was still in the port of Brest and by the time this fleet departed under the command of Bompard and Wolfe Tone, Humbert's force had been defeated by Lake and Cornwallis at Ballinamuck in County Longford. Unsurprisingly, news of the landing was greeted with indignation in Dublin, with many loyalists further convinced that the prisoners had acted deceitfully, fully aware of French intentions. The fact that James Napper Tandy, long associated with the United cause and known to many of the state prisoners, landed briefly on Rutland Island in mid-September in command of a French corvette reinforced suspicions, leading for calls to resume the trials and executions.[22] As Neilson learned of these developments, over which neither he nor his fellow internees had any control, he was rocked by the sudden and untimely death of his great friend and cellmate Oliver Bond.

Bond was the son of a Presbyterian minister who owned a woollen drapery business on Dublin's Pill Lane and was heavily involved in United Irish politics. He and Simon Butler served a prison term in 1793 for their savage criticism of the House of Lords. Bond was a Dublin agent for the *Northern Star* and Neilson helped to support his wife, Eleanor (daughter of the leading United Irishman Henry Jackson), during his incarceration.[23] Bond's association with the society extended into its militant phase and he was a member of the Leinster Directory, leading members of which were arrested at his house on Bridge Street on 12 March 1798. The informer Samuel Turner alleged that Bond had been the society's treasurer, paying emissaries abroad, such as Edward Lewins and MacNeven, and receiving donations from sympathisers in America. Tried and found guilty of high treason on 23 July 1798, it was expected that his execution would follow those of the Sheares and John McCann. The deal between the state prisoners and the government led to the commutation of Bond's execution and he remained incarcerated, sharing a cell and bed with Neilson in Newgate. The informer Samuel Sproule alleged that Bond was still plotting at this stage and had received letters from both outside of the gaol and from supposed debtors (in reality, United Irishmen) who conspired to get themselves imprisoned with the intent of smuggling letters for Bond from cell to cell, using envelopes weighted with pennies and string. [24]

His death on 6 September 1798 was a huge personal blow to Neilson, whose wife, Anne, often stayed with the Bonds when she was in Dublin; she was there when Mrs Bond was informed of her husband's death. Neilson's friendship with him was an extremely close one: 'I was overwhelmed with the most profound grief. It was not a common acquaintance – it was not a patriot of a few months standing, whose loss I had to deplore – no – It was a man with whom the closest intimacy for seventeen years had grown into a friendship truly inexpressible.'[25] The hastily convened inquest was based on an examination carried out by the surgeon-general, with Drennan being one of four physicians who were present. The inquest heard evidence from a female prisoner, Catherine Poynton, who had witnessed Bond emerging from the cell he shared with Neilson between five and six o'clock in the morning and falling down the two steps into the courtyard, landing on his back. Neilson had not been a witness to the fall, but he stated that he, Bond and two others had dined together the previous evening on sheep's heart and other food, consuming a bottle of wine before playing ball in the prison yard until dark. The men had then drunk some punch and Bond had eaten more sweetbread and some mutton before continuing to drink with a number of others who had joined the group. Neilson proceeded to tell the inquest that he had retired around eleven and found Bond dead between five and six o'clock the following morning, fully dressed and in the position described by Poynton. Neilson was unsure whether his friend had slept in their shared bed. The inquest concluded that Bond's body was unmarked, save for a cut on the back of his head, which was likely sustained as he fell. It was possible that he had fallen on a copper ice-kettle in the cell and, in all probability, he had not been to bed. The coroner ruled that an apoplectic fit was the likely cause of death, although other, more sympathetic, accounts have disputed this verdict.[26]

Neilson's grief was interrupted when he happened upon the *Courier's* report on the preamble of the Banishment Bill relating to the state prisoners, which was being steered through the Irish Parliament. Neilson objected to the wording of the bill, which stated that the prisoners had acknowledged their crimes, retracted their opinions and implored pardon. He drafted a letter to the editor of the

Courier on 12 September, enclosing a copy of the compact and insisting that, as far as he was aware, none of the state prisoners saw themselves as having committed a crime, nor had they disowned their earlier actions; their object was to prevent the effusion of more blood. On the same day, Neilson wrote to Castlereagh of his intention to contact the *Courier*, enclosing a copy of the newspaper and his handwritten letter to the editor.

> My Lord
>
> Feeling in common with the rest of my fellow prisoners, extremely hurt at a publication which tends to brand our names with infamy, I think it incumbent on me, who commenced the negotiation, to justify our characters and motives by setting the whole in a true point of view. At the same time wishing to pay all due respect to government, I trouble you with a copy of a letter which I mean to send off by this night's mail. I also take the liberty of sending the newspaper with the offensive pages underscored.
>
> I am, my lord, your lordship's most obedient servant,
>
> Samuel Neilson.

Neilson's action prompted a hasty response from the administration. Cooke and his fellow Under-Secretary, Alexander Marsden, arrived in Newgate clutching copies of the letters and the *Courier*. Asked if he had taken leave of his senses by threatening to attack publicly the business of Parliament, Neilson replied that his judgement was intact and that he was protesting against the falsehood contained in the wording of the bill, namely that the prisoners 'neither confessed *crimes*, retracted *opinions*, nor *implored* pardon'. Unconvinced by Marsden's philosophical attempts to justify the wording of the bill, Neilson asserted that he planned to seek publication of his letter in the press. Cooke declared that this intent to publish constituted a breach of the compact between the government and the prisoners and, as a consequence, the executions would resume. Neilson, as he often did, responded bluntly: 'Why, sir; as to executions I have my mind made up; I would rather suffer a thousand deaths than permit such a false statement to be thus solemnly recorded.' When Cooke interjected to say that Neilson could be executed without much difficulty, the latter replied, 'I know your will is law; and to save you trouble, I would prefer your giving orders to Gregg [the gaoler who had detained him on the night of 23 May] this instant to hang me out the door, than acquiesce in such an abominable measure.' Cooke's rejoinder was to push Neilson into a corner; the latter had gone out on a limb without consulting his fellow prisoners. On canvassing their opinions, Neilson decided to drop the approach to the press in the interest, he maintained, of preventing the country from falling into further misery.[27] The prisoners, including detainees in gaols outside Dublin who had been offered terms similar to the state prisoners in the capital, were now to await their fate under the terms of the Banishment Bill.[28]

In October, Neilson implored Castlereagh to show humanity and 'some degree of former regard for me' by including a number of young men from Belfast on the list of prisoners entitled to the same terms of banishment as himself. A resolution seemed imminent when it was reported that the prisoners in Newgate were permitted to dine with those in Kilmainham on the 21st and, after weeks of waiting, they were told to prepare to depart from the kingdom at twenty-four hours' notice. Neilson contacted Marsden to request a place on a ship due to depart for America from Larne: 'I am ready to emigrate without delay.'[29] The plans that some of the prisoners may have had to exile themselves in the United States were, however, dashed by the American ambassador in London, Rufus King, who asked Portland in the middle of September to exclude his country from the list of states considered acceptable to the British government, noting that, 'I do not think they will be a desirable acquisition to any nation.' The Home Secretary's polite response was that the king would not permit the state prisoners to depart for any place they would not be welcomed.

Despite these assurances, the ambassador wrote again on 17 October to complain that he was aware of reports that some of the men were indeed being readied for transportation to America; if this was the case, the president would refuse residence to these 'delinquents'. Wickham was now forced to report to Castlereagh in Dublin that the United States was not an acceptable destination for the prisoners, with the ambassador threatening to seize and deport any who did manage to make the journey.[30] Neilson's version of these events stated that the day after it was announced that the prisoners would be emigrating to America, Marsden informed him that this plan had come unstuck due to the concerns expressed by the American ambassador. A week later, a dejected Neilson received the following note: 'Mr Marsden begs leave to inform Mr Neilson that in consequence of the objections which have been made to sending persons from hence to America, and which Mr M explained to Mr N at their last interview, government are now under the necessity of withholding permission for any of the prisoners to take their passage at present for America.'

With what must have been a combination of anger and resignation, Neilson took up his pen and replied to Marsden's missive: 'SIR – I received your note of yesterday, stating, in substance, that we were, after being debarred Europe, also refused emigration to America. May I take the liberty of requesting that you will have the goodness to say if there is any country to which we may depart? If there is no such place, I must consider my imprisonment as durable as my existence, and the faith of the Irish government as worse than Punic.'[31]

For the northern prisoners in particular, the attitude of the United States government must have been hugely disappointing. Former Volunteers like Neilson had been excited in their youth by the advent of representative government across the Atlantic, a process that owed much to Ulster exiles. Castlereagh, himself a northerner, noted smugly that 'I understand the leading traitors are as averse to a residence in America as Congress can be to receive them – the Directory in Kilmainham describe the Tyranny of the American government as not less grievous as their own and speak of Adams [President John Adams] and Mr Pitt in terms of equal respect.'[32] The prisoners' antipathy was based on the increasingly centripetal and tyrannical tendencies of Adams' administration, evidenced by the passage of the Alien and Sedition Acts of 1798, measures that sought to justify the extension of state power with reference to national security. While their ire was directed at the British and Irish governments, the hostility towards Rufus King would later dictate the politics of those prisoners who would eventually settle in the United States after their long captivity. Oliver Bond's father-in-law, Henry Jackson, a man of considerable enterprise and wealth, wrote to King to protest against the treatment of himself and the other state prisoners. While the ambassador later relented and permitted Jackson to emigrate to the USA, he was critical of an Irish propensity for supporting 'malcontents' in his country and asserted that while there were many fine Irishmen in the US, he was concerned that there would also be 'the indigent and illiterate, who, entertaining an attachment to freedom, are unable to appreciate those salutary restraints without which it degenerates into anarchy'. Thomas Addis Emmet, deprived at the last minute of his agreed right to find solace in America, a deprivation which led to his continued detention in both Dublin and then Fort George, Scotland, vented his fury at Rufus King's intervention years later as a resident in the United States embarking on a distinguished legal career. In a powerfully worded letter, he lambasted King for his meddling:

> Your interference was then, sir, made the pretext of detaining us for four years in custody ... The misfortunes which you brought upon the objects of

> your persecution were incalculable. Almost all of us wasted four of the best years of our life in prison ... I have been prevented from saving a brother, from receiving the dying blessings of a father, mother and sister, and from soothing their last agonies by my cares; and this, Sir, by your unwarrantable and unfeeling interference.[33]

Even before King's dramatic interposition, however, Cornwallis was searching for creative solutions to the problem of the most senior state prisoners as the likelihood that they would comply with the terms of their exile was considered to be low. Writing to Portland in the middle of September, he outlined a solution to his dilemma: 'It has occurred to me that perhaps they might be safely stationed at Fort George and other of the forts in the Highlands of Scotland.' Conscious of the reputations of the prisoners, he acknowledged the need to avoid scaring the locals.[34] General Sir Ralph Abercromby, who had resigned his duties as commander-in-chief so dramatically earlier in the year, had provided Portland with an inventory of Scottish fortifications in his new capacity as military commander in Scotland. Edinburgh Castle was deemed unsatisfactory due to the number of French prisoners contained therein, the lack of an effective command ('the duty done in a slovenly manner') and its proximity to the city, with all the risks this entailed. Stirling Castle was overlooked for the same reasons, while Dumbarton Castle was considered too close to the Irish Channel to be completely secure; besides, the castle was occupied 'by a few old drunken invalids and some boys enlisted for the 65th Regiment'. The islands of Bass Rock and Inch Colm in the Firth of Forth were considered possible destinations for the prisoners but, in the end, passed over. Fort George, built in the immediate aftermath of the Jacobite Rebellion of 1745/46, was a secure fortification close to Inverness on the Moray Firth, described by Abercromby as having 'no connections with any town or disaffected Country – possesses good accommodation – has a resident Lieutenant Governor and Fort Major, is healthy, and has a respectable garrison'. Wickham's check for a suitable location for the prisoners was still in progress in early March.[35]

It would take some time before Neilson and the other state prisoners considered to be the most dangerous would be shipped to Fort George. Other internees were permitted to exile themselves or, in some cases, were sent into Prussian military service under the terms of the Banishment Act.[36] The government was preoccupied with other matters, not least the fallout from the last gasp of the 1798 Rebellion, when Wolfe Tone, holding the rank of Chef de Brigade and serving on board the French ship *Hoche*, was arrested in October after a small invasion fleet was engaged by the Royal Navy in Lough Swilly. Tone's subsequent court martial in the Royal Barracks, Dublin, delivered the inevitable guilty verdict and he was sentenced to hang after his request to be shot as an officer was refused. Tone avoided the gallows by cutting his throat and dying, several days later, on 19 November. There is no record of Neilson's reaction to Tone's demise. The man referred to by Tone in his journal as 'The Jacobin' had worked closely with him during the heady days of 1791 and 1792, collaborating to forge the Society of United Irishmen and outmanoeuvre the more cautious reforming instincts of many Belfast Presbyterians and Volunteers. Despite Neilson's frustration with Tone (as a spokesman for the Catholics) about Catholic caution and political secrecy over the following years, he would also surely have remembered the compact between the leading radicals at McArt's Fort in the summer of 1795 and the days he and his family had spent in Tone's company just prior to the latter's exile. His death would not have impacted Neilson to the extent that Bond's had, but his fellow prisoner Thomas Russell was deeply affected.[37]

The government's attention was also turning to the issue of a political union between Ireland and Britain, not a new idea, but one that had, for some time, excited the imaginations of Pitt and Castlereagh. Persuading the Irish legislature to vote itself out of existence would not be accomplished easily and Castlereagh was devoting a large amount of time to the task. The administration was also occupied by the worrying state of the country. The rebellion was over but the prospects of re-ignition loomed large in the minds of the conservative interest; Dublin Castle was inundated with reports of incipient revolution. A determined rearguard action in the Wicklow Mountains distracted the military until November, when Joseph Holt abandoned a campaign that had sapped the military's resources for months after the end of the rebellion. One of Holt's colleagues, Michael Dwyer, held out until 1803 in the largely inaccessible highlands.

Beyond this resistance, the Castle was receiving almost daily information in late 1798 and early 1799 from worried loyalists. In August, Major-General Wilford of the Reay Fencibles alerted Castlereagh that a new rebellion was planned for the end of the month; notices had been distributed widely 'to induce people to rise'. In County Down, Lord Downshire's land agent, George Stephenson, warned in September of the very real possibility of a rising in the neighbourhood of Loughinisland, close to Downpatrick. Robert Ross, admittedly something of a scaremonger, attempted to convince Downshire of a sinister plot, one that the Lord Lieutenant's apparent lenity was likely to encourage: 'Everything seems to indicate an intention of laying the groundwork of a second rebellion ... For heaven's sake do not let poor Ireland fall a sacrifice to the madness and dotage of a very silly old Indian bitch [i.e. Cornwallis].' Richard Annesley, the former member for Newtownards and MP for Blessington from 1798, wrote anxiously that the rebellion was merely smothered and would erupt again with greater severity. Moreover, he suggested 'that those persons who are now confined are going on as usual with their diabolical schemes'. Annesley had it on good authority that Arthur O'Connor was co-ordinating a renewed United Irish organisation.

In February 1799, it was reported that O'Connor had been moved from Kilmainham to Newgate 'in consequence of some new discovery against this person and some of his connexions [*sic*]'. MacNeven was also removed and placed in a room in Dublin Castle. Cornwallis himself was aware of the threat. In December, he informed Portland that Antrim and Down were being disturbed by robberies and assassinations, with secret meetings being convened and trees cut down for the manufacture of pike handles. Antrim magistrates declared in March that the county was in 'a state of disturbance' and General Nugent would soon declare martial law across the region. Nocturnal meetings in Dublin and clandestine activity in Carlow, Wicklow, Kildare, Tipperary and Wexford suggested that something significant was afoot. There was intelligence suggesting a rebellion on either Christmas Day or St John's Day (27 December) and concerns were expressed by Cooke about the 'unpleasant' atmosphere in Limerick, Tipperary and Cork, where 'the lower classes [were] ripe for mischief in the extreme'.[38]

Concerns about the security of Ireland undoubtedly convinced the administration to effectuate the plan to convey the most dangerous of the state prisoners to Fort George. Castlereagh had long held the view that Neilson and the other state prisoners would likely prove an embarrassment to the government and that future confinement in Dublin would be both risky and expensive.[39] Intelligence suggesting that detainees had been orchestrating the unrest across various parts of Ireland led to cells being searched and papers confiscated in January 1799. Neilson complained that his personal papers were taken from him by a Castle 'ruffian' by the name of Carleton. Just days earlier, his wife, Anne, had appealed to Castlereagh for clemency, noting that their property had been sold in an attempt to meet the demands of creditors – debts incurred at least in part by the destruction of the *Northern Star* presses. Despite several requests, Neilson's papers were not returned to him.[40]

Rumours that the state prisoners were to undertake forced labour on the River Thames proved false; the next phase of their incarceration would be in Scotland.[41] Dublin's police chief, Henry Sirr, was asked on 18 March to convey Neilson, Russell, Matthew Dowling, William Dowdall and Arthur O'Connor from Newgate to the Pigeon House on the South Wall, near Ringsend, at the entrance to Dublin port. The other prisoners – Thomas Addis Emmet, John

Sweetman, John Chambers, Joseph Cuthbert, John Cormick, John Sweeney, Edward Hudson, William James MacNeven, Roger O'Connor, Hugh Wilson and George Cumming – were also to be readied for imminent departure. The men were informed that evening that they were being embarked the following morning, but their destination was not revealed. Letters complaining of the scandalously late notice of their departure were sent to Cornwallis and Castlereagh, but to no avail. Neilson wrote to the Lord Lieutenant to protest that this latest order was yet another violation of the agreement between the prisoners and the government:

> I have received a message this moment from Mr Cooke through our jailor [Gregg], that 'I am to be removed to a ship tomorrow morning at six o'clock'. I am astonished at this notice so contradictory to the faith of the government, solemnly pledged: for tho' I wish to go abroad, yet I would desire to settle, as agreed upon, the place of exile and accommodation on board. It must occur to Your Lordship, that at any rate two or three days are necessary to prepare for an eternal adieu to my native country – my wife and my children! – I thought the treatment I had received for the last seven years from government, might have satiated any revenge, without this additional severity, and this additional breach of a most solemn engagement.[42]

At 6.30am on Tuesday, the 19th, the prisoners were escorted to the Pigeon House by a heavily armed detachment of the Buckinghamshire Regiment. They were brought by small boat to the *Ashton Smith* and set to sea that evening, 'whether for Botany Bay, Siberia or to be scuttled and sunk', as Neilson later recorded.[43] Guarded by Captain Ewing and a party of troops from the Angusshire Fencibles, the prisoners were taken into Belfast Lough where four additional detainees confined on the prison ship *Postlethwaite*, 'capable of doing infinite mischief in the North', were brought on board: Reverend William Steel Dickson (alleged adjutant-general of the United Irishmen in County Down before his arrest on 5 June 1798), William Tennent, Robert Hunter (a Belfast shipbroker) and Robert Simms.[44] The pastoral care dispensed by Dickson to other prisoners on board the tender included leading periods of contemplation and prayer. A fellow prisoner in Belfast, the merchant John Caldwell, remembered how Dickson, the dissenting minister in Portaferry (County Down), kept the men on their knees for long periods – no doubt, this practice was a feature of the journey to Fort George.[45]

For Neilson, the time spent on board the *Ashton Smith* was arguably his most difficult experience to date. Significant periods spent in cold, dark prisons – often heavily chained – had reduced him to a shadow of the man taken into custody back in September 1796. Rheumatic pains and fevers combined to weaken his physical condition and recourse to alcohol had perhaps been a form of escapism.[46] Contemporary accounts of the voyage testified to the fact that Neilson was seriously unwell and there were fears that he would not survive the journey. John Sweetman was a former soldier-turned-brewer who had housed Neilson upon his release from Kilmainham in the months before the rebellion. His diary recorded the drama of Neilson's illness, which came on even before the ship had reached Belfast Lough to take on the northern prisoners. In his diary, Sweetman recounted Neilson's delirium in graphic detail as worried friends took it in turns to watch him day and night:

> He darted from his bed, and ran around the hold, in search of robbers who had plundered his house; his manner, looks and conversation evince delirium. It is difficult to restrain him from going upon deck ... He continues speaking, raving, and starting, in the most frightful manner during our watch; the prisoners cannot sleep and the hold is in a state of the greatest confusion. Thomas Russell is called, being the next on the watch. He reported next morning, as did those who succeeded him, that Neilson continued as first stated, raving, starting and using strong efforts to get up. About half past nine we were all alarmed by a fit which seized him, being the second since his coming on board. This fit was not so violent as the former. Feeling the dreadful effects of Neilson's situation, we agreed that a representation should be made of his case to government, declaring that his life was in danger; and Macneven [*sic*], as a medical man, was instructed to write a letter to Lord ________ [probably Castlereagh] on the subject.

On the morning of the 25th, Neilson experienced another violent fit lasting two hours and it was thought that he would expire by nightfall. MacNeven requested that the stricken man be taken off the ship. Reverend William Steel Dickson noted that Neilson had been 'barbarously' forced to make the journey and his condition 'silenced every tongue and wounded every heart'. As the prisoners continued their journey across the Irish Sea and into the Firth of Clyde, Neilson's condition settled somewhat. On Saturday, 30 March, after eleven days at sea and having been delayed by heavy winds, the state prisoners were taken off the *Ashton Smith* at Gourock and met by three messengers and soldiers of the North York Militia. The prisoners were put into four carriages and brought to Greenock a few miles away, where they had originally been scheduled to berth until the weather prevented them from doing so. That Abercromby's aide-de-camp, Major Hay, was their escort said much about the importance of the newly arrived detainees. In Greenock, they dined opulently, drinking ale, stout and port, served by waiters, in front of a roaring fire and slept in the town hall under heavy guard. Two traders, acquainted with Simms and Tennent, were allowed to converse with them. Dickson took great pleasure in informing them that, contrary to the impression deliberately given by the government, what had just occurred was not a 'popish' rebellion. He wrote down the names of the prisoners to show that of the twenty men who had been sent to Scotland, only four were, in fact, Catholics.

After a comfortable night's sleep, with each man resting on a dressed feather bed, they travelled to Bishopton, where they breakfasted before proceeding through Renfrew, Govan and the Gorbals district of Glasgow, attracting crowds of curious onlookers. The *Glasgow Courier* presented a vivid – but hostile – depiction of the scene: 'The public curiosity was naturally excited to see the hellish authors of the diabolical scenes of rebellion, devastation and murder that now disgrace the sister kingdom. They all wore a very modest Jacobinical smile on their faces.' Emmet was described as shortsighted and O'Connor was dressed in green, the rebel colour of choice: 'Happy would it have been for this country and the peace of Ireland had he been clothed with green turf six years ago.' Dickson, in his mid-50s, received little sympathy: 'They are, in general, good looking men (particularly Sweetman, the two O'Connors and Swiney [*sic*]) with the exception of Steel Dickson, whose countenance will, at any time recommend him to the gallows, and is, in all appearances, better adapted to the office of Jack Ketch than the pulpit.'[47]

When the men reached the town of Hamilton in Lanarkshire, they were again hosted lavishly and Dickson noted that the meal provided in Aberdeen 'was equal to anything of the kind I have ever seen or tasted, in variety and elegance', with over twenty-seven dishes on offer, along with both red and white wine. At different stages of the journey, the prisoners were permitted to place orders for warm clothes to alleviate the expected effects of the harsh weather they would experience at Fort George.[48] While Neilson's perilous condition had improved since the traumatic first few days of his journey, his spirits would no doubt have been dampened further had he been aware that his *Northern Star* office had finally been purchased by the printers John Doherty and David Simms, who were set to embark on business in what had been the hub of the United Irishmen's propaganda machine.[49]

The long journey ended on 9 April, when the prisoners reached the imposing edifice of Fort George. The man in charge of securing the dangerous new inmates was the lieutenant-governor of Fort George, Colonel James Stuart, half-brother of the Earl of Moray. Aware of the lack of a precedent, Abercromby inquired of Portland whether the prisoners were to enjoy a diet 'such as people in the middling class are accustomed to' and if wine was to be provided. The authorities in Scotland were concerned about who was going to foot the bill for the prisoners' detention. Stuart scribbled down a list of questions for his superiors. Were the prisoners to be locked up at all times except during meals? Was solitary confinement to be the norm? Were they to be allowed newspapers or pen and ink? Should the prisoners' money be taken from them?[50] Despite the generosity extended to them during the journey, Cooke wrote from Dublin that the prisoners were to be guarded very carefully: 'I fear they are so rooted in bad principles and so pledged to each other that no confidence can be placed in them whatever.' He advised Wickham to see to it that they should be granted as little access to pen and ink as possible, although Thomas Whinnery, the Belfast postmaster who had long been a useful informant, reported to his Dublin master, John Lees, on the day of their arrival that the prisoners had already started to write to their Belfast friends; he offered to make a note of the letters that came through his office.[51]

Neilson wasted little time in making his frustrations known to the Home Secretary. He wrote to Portland on 27 April to complain that he had fulfilled his side of the agreement with the government only to be removed from Dublin in haste and in the midst of a fever before finding himself 'a close prisoner in a fortress at the extremity of the Empire'. Removed from his helpless family, he demanded redress 'as may seem consistent with Justice and humanity'.[52] Dickson's *Narrative* detailed his apprehension that incarceration in Fort George would bring a worsening situation for the prisoners, more negative even than the cold, damp and oppressive conditions experienced in Newgate, Kilmainham and on board the *Postlethwaite*. He was, however, pleasantly surprised by the state of the barracks and the provision made for the inmates: 'The change in our situation and treatment was so great and so pleasing that sometimes I could not restrain my imagination from playing with the thought that I had been transported not only to a *new heaven and a new earth*, but the society of spirits more perfect, than those, by which I had been haunted, for months before.'

The prisoners were received warmly by Lieutenant-Governor Stuart, who had the capacity to show a great level of humanity even while laying out the strict conditions of their confinement. Dickson, who continued to record his experience of the food served to the detainees, wrote approvingly of the five dishes that had been prepared for the new arrivals, served by two servants who offered up a dozen jugs of ale and porter and ten bottles of port. Supper and ale was available for later. The accommodation for the prisoners would be lavish in comparison with what had been endured hitherto; twenty rooms were allocated by ballot, each generous in size and 'clean, dry, airy, well plastered and ceiled'. There was glass in the windows and the beds were comfortable and dressed. Four invalid soldiers at the fort were assigned to the prisoners, carrying out duties such as cleaning the rooms, making beds and ensuring that candles were maintained and replaced. The prisoners had access to a physician when required and, for a time, the men were permitted to walk the ramparts of the fort, exorcising the effects of their Dublin gaols and the difficult voyage to Scotland. In response to a request that books and newspapers be made available, Stuart sought the government's approval and confirmed that this request would, in the end, be granted. The men were also permitted to write to their friends and families – letters were to be sent, unsealed, to the lieutenant-governor on Saturdays for checking. No reference to politics was allowed.[53]

It is likely that reports of the more benign conditions at Fort George had filtered into the public domain, leading to pressure for a more austere approach to be taken. *The Times* made reference to the effectiveness of the strict regime that had existed in Dublin due to fears that prisoners would escape and within days Stuart had, on the orders of Portland, curtailed the detainees' allowance, opportunities for mixing and letter-writing.[54] Despite their confinement, the prisoners' diet was good. Dickson noted how salmon caught within sight of the fort was eaten twice weekly, while mutton, lamb, beef, veal and, on occasions, crab and lobster were provided by their cook, Mrs McGregor. By May 1800, Portland himself had consented to the request that the state prisoners be permitted to swim in the sea thrice weekly; Stuart later extended this to six days a week.[55] In time, they were able to congregate more freely, walk the ramparts and spend long periods out of their cells. The liberal conditions experienced by the prisoners at Fort George were appreciated and a healthy respect developed between the prisoners and Stuart, described by one of them as 'a gentleman by birth, education and habits'.[56]

Stuart's humanitarianism was recognised by those on the outside. Working tirelessly for his brother William's release, Robert Tennent acknowledged the governor's role in enabling his sibling's return to health from a serious throat complaint:

> for the recovery of your health and the re-establishment of a broken constitution depends upon that person to whom you and your fellow prisoners, and the cause of humanity itself, are already so much indebted. And on my honour, if there is a person in the world above another whom

> I think worthy of that trust, Governor Stuart is the man, and I know not another in whose hands I would sooner have it placed.[57]

Some prisoners took full advantage of the generous conditions of their confinement to maintain their intellectual and academic interests. MacNeven, a physician with a keen interest in Gaelic culture, worked on translations of *Ossian*, while the formerly promiscuous Tennent read the Bible and practised writing in Greek and Latin.[58] As far as Neilson's experience of Fort George is concerned, the publication by Madden of a selection of prison letters to his wife offers some understanding of how he was affected by his long captivity. These published letters, though valuable, are edited versions of fuller correspondence. Only a few of his complete letters are extant and there are no copies of Anne's replies. Nonetheless, Neilson's words offer an insight into his anxieties as a prisoner far away from his devoted wife and children. In his writings, he offered business guidance to Anne in her new enterprise, parenting advice, updates on his physical condition, religious insights and even – despite the orders of the government – brief references to the politics of the day.

Anne Neilson lived and worked in Belfast and was about to open a small shop selling silk, hosiery, buttons and ribbons.[59] The business and family matters would have kept her in Belfast for the duration of her husband's confinement, although we do know that she spent some time in Dublin with her friend Eleanor Bond, the widow of Oliver Bond, Neilson's long-time friend.[60] Neilson's concern for his wife's enterprise was often charming, albeit sometimes patronising: 'Of all things remember not to buy too much of any one article, be it even so cheap – this is ruin to a young beginner.'[61] In June 1799, as he was settling into the more relaxed regime in Fort George, he offered more counsel to Anne, expressing concern at the high price and inconvenient location of the new shop:

> I much fear you have let some much more desirable places slip thro' your fingers for want of decision at the moment they were in your power. I mention this, not as a subject of regret but as a caution to you in business – when you meet the very thing you want, buy it without delay and never buy the thing you don't want be it even so cheap. Many a young beginner has been ruined by bargains ... I wish I had it in my power to give you more minute advice, but three years absence from the world has left me far behind the fashion of the day which you know I never studied much ... It gives me no little pain to state to you that in all your dealings you must be on your guard: long experience has convinced me that, situated as society now is, self

> is the ruling principle of the human heart and a despicable principle it is: but those who are to live by the world are forced to match and in some sort, shape their conduct by its habits and manners. The friendship of those who have proved themselves exceptions to this rule you should cultivate above all earthly things. Remember that dispatch is the life of trade, sell quick, be your profits small and let no old shopkeepers by-past you.[62]

Neilson would repeat his advice of buying small and selling quickly on a regular basis and he was eager to point out that excessively fancy or luxurious goods would not be profitable. Anne was being assisted in her endeavours by two of her daughters, Anne and Sophia. In early August, he inquired about the nascent business, pointing out that 'You have never yet mentioned to me who are your most industrious and steady friends since you began, nor what kinds of goods you succeed best in, nor do you say whether Anne or Sophia makes the best shopkeeper.' He was concerned about the location of the new shop and agreed with his wife that searching for a more convenient place, closer to home, would be advantageous.[63] As the winter approached, he advised Anne to procure a small lantern for one of the children to carry before her on the way to and from the shop. He also reminded her to wear suitable shoes to prevent her feet from becoming damp: 'You will remember how apt you were always to catch cold when you neglected the necessary precaution.' His fears were confirmed when he discovered, by a letter from William Simms, that she was unwell: 'No doubt you have caught cold going between the house and shop during the late tempestuous weather. I hope this will stimulate your friends in their exertions to get you fixed in some comfortable situation before the winter sets in. As you are at present it will be impossible to go on.'[64]

Neilson's helplessness in the face of his wife's difficult situation – running a business and bringing up the children alone – was a constant anxiety and his advice was likely redolent of his own inner voice:

> I was exceedingly vexed to find by yours of the 14th which I received two days ago that your illness had left such a depression in your spirits. If you permit yourself to fall into despondence the situation of our affairs is hopeless indeed, but I cannot think that possible after the singular fortitude you have so long displayed under the most seizing afflictions. I conjure you my dear Nancy by the conjugal affection which has been the delight of our lives – by the love you bear to our offspring as well as by the sure hope of a protecting providence not to give up to melancholy. It is true – a heavy hand has been laid upon us but what are our sufferings compared to those of others?[65]

The pain of separation was also obvious in Neilson's references to his children. By the end of 1799, Agnes (Anne) was 11 years of age, Sophia 9, Jane 8, William 5 and Mary 3 or 4. Neilson's letters reveal that he was strict with his children, but desirous that they receive a good education and ambitious regarding the development of their principles and morals. He was rarely short of domestic advice for Anne, particularly concerning her parenting. He asked her to use larger sheets of paper when writing to keep him informed of the children's progress and requested that they write a few lines on each letter sent. If, for some reason, these were missing or perfunctory by nature, Neilson would admonish his wife. When one letter was deemed too short, he responded by stating that he would 'expect to hear minutely from yourself and from the children a little of *their own* thoughts, conveyed in their own manner without prompting. Otherwise I would rather not hear from them at all.' In another instance, he suspected that Sophia's lines were dictated to her and hoped this would not be repeated. In late July, he wrote that, 'It gives me much pain to inform you that the few lines written by the girls was [*sic*] far from satisfactory. The writing was very indifferent but what was inexcusable, several words were ill-spelled.'[66] A subsequent letter pointed out that the girls 'both seem to write rather in a hurry – I am persuaded that if they took time they would be less liable to error, don't allow them when speaking of themselves to write "i" instead of "I".'[67] Neilson's advice from afar included the suggestion that the children receive support in their learning:

> I think it would be an amusement for John in his leisure hours to bring the children forward in their spelling, and I am sure he could with very little trouble put the girls into the way of Arithmetic. They would one and all learn with his care, for an hour per day, than in all the time they spend in school ... With respect to William I would recommend you take special care to prevent him from being bullied, or stupefied by the superior quickness of his sisters – let him take a good deal of his own way, and keep the control over him in your own hands still however permitting the girls to reason him into proper behaviour.[68]

Writing specifically to the older girls, Anne and Sophia, Neilson requested that they furnish him with more information on their and their siblings' situation. His letter of 17 August reveals his genuine concern for their welfare and conveys the personal pain felt by an absent father:

> In your next I expect you will tell me how you are employed before breakfast, how between that and dinner and how you spend your evenings. I will expect to hear that you help your mother very much, for you know I am locked up here in prison and can do nothing for either of you. Tell me also what sort of children Jane, William and Mary are – do they obey their mother and behave like good children? Let me also know who of you sleep together and which is always up first in the morning.[69]

When Anne sent him details of the children's ages and heights, he marked these on the wall of his prison cell and looked at them regularly, 'mixed with both pain and pleasure'. He often emphasised the importance of education in his advice: 'It is therefore necessary above any other thing to keep the young mind employed: not to forced tasks or unreasonable attention, but to something (either of ability or amusement and these can be easily united) so that the mind is not left to wander amongst the giddy youth of the age, for then it will certainly take a wrong direction.'[70] Warming to his theme, Neilson wrote to Anne advising her to ensure that Anne Jun. and Sophia be exposed to reading those books that would lead to their improvement. He had agreed with his fellow prisoner, the Dublin bookseller John Chambers, that the girls receive books sent to Belfast through the auspices of a mutual friend.[71] His anxiety that the girls would be easily distracted from their studies was revealed as the dark evenings set in: 'These long nights have reminded me to impress upon you a particular duty respecting the children; I mean to guard them against the foolish nonsense to which they might otherwise be subjected about hobgoblins, fairies, ghosts, and such other fantasies as girls are accustomed to conjure up.'[72] Despite Neilson's concerns, his children's education was proceeding satisfactorily. Anne and Sophia received premiums in their classes at the Belfast Second Academy, while young William was a prizewinner in English.[73]

As far as Neilson's physical health was concerned, the more benign conditions at Fort George were having a positive effect. The dark days of his confinements in both Kilmainham and Newgate, not to mention the plunge into sickness that had so worried his companions during the voyage, were ameliorated somewhat under Lieutenant-Governor Stuart's regime. Despite this, however, Neilson and the other prisoners suffered bouts of mental and physical anguish as continued incarceration and the separation from family and friends took their toll. It is unknown whether Anne was aware of the full extent of her husband's malady on board the *Ashton Smith*, but during his early days at Fort George he informed her that he was 'still ailing less or more, cough, rheumatism and weakness in my limbs are what chiefly attack me and mostly in turn. On the other hand I have a tolerable appetite and sleep a few hours every night.'

By May, he reported that his cough and rheumatic pains were 'but slight compared to what they were'.[74] By early June, he could walk for a couple of hours each day on the ramparts and was benefiting from the pure air. While pain endured, he was 'indeed nearly in my usual state'. He had been affected temporarily by an inflammation of the eyes, a condition contracted by several of the prisoners. By July, his optimism was tempered by a realisation that physical weakness was now to be expected: 'In point of bodily pain I am much at ease but my appetite has considerably declined. I find no return of vigour to my limbs and a general lassitude pervades my whole frame, but in a much less degree than last year.' Nonetheless, the following month, Neilson reported that:

> I cannot say that I am quite stout and probably never will have that satisfaction whilst a prisoner but I have no particular cause of complaint save bad sleep and even that does not rest so heavy on me as might be expected, for during my doses, I am transported home among those I love. This you will have learned from experience, greatly tends to lessen the grief attendant upon separation.

Other prisoners lapsed into ill health; Roger O'Connor suffered a severe fit upon the ramparts and Joseph Cuthbert, the Belfast tailor, suffered from a fever.[75] The summer air produced an improvement and Anne would have been heartened by her husband's opinion that 'I am fully as well as I have been at any period these two years', although he complained of a weakness in his ankles.[76]

Neilson's prison correspondence offers further insight into his religious outlook. While his political activities in the period before the rebellion revealed a willingness to deploy violent methods in order to achieve his political objectives, a strong sense of personal faith pervades his writing and this devoutness seems far removed from the ferocity of the rebellion he helped to construct. His letters suggest an aversion for institutions, including, it would seem, his own Presbyterian congregation, which was distracting itself from the principles of the scriptures by concentrating on the search for an assistant:

> A profession instead of a practice of Christianity with them (as with most of the world) but too predominant. In such cases the sound generally passes for the substance. It would be a happy change in the world if men would learn to pursue the process and example of Christ instead of those abominable

> superstitions, rites and ceremonies which have been imposed by priests upon mankind in their stead.[77]

Neilson's religious individualism was Calvinistic. His suspicion of Catholics, in the context of faith, was derived from his opinion that they were obstructed from truly knowing God by the distractions of institutions. This concern extended to his own denomination:

> I hope you will all learn the important lesson (that tho' Sam Law, Dick Moon or Jack Gardiner may choose your Pastor) yet you will yourselves educate your children in the true principles of Christianity which believe me are not to be acquired by a mere Sunday show. No! they are to be instilled in the life and conversation and only that precept and example. An ignorant creature may think penance necessary. A less ignorant person may confide in stated public duties as they are called; but for my part, I think the real Christian, whose foundation is seen is he who follows the example of Jesus and smiles upon the puny institutions of man ... but my trust is still kept up by the hope that an All wise Providence will bring light out of all this darkness and that the day is by no means remote when these important truths shall be made manifest to all who will believe.[78]

As the year neared its end, Neilson found solace in reading, hearing his fellow prisoners play a range of musical instruments through the night and taking time to reflect on his devoted family. The length, tone and content of his letters home caused Anne to speculate on his mood and condition, a practice which irked Neilson and 'call[ed] to my mind the days when *mania* and *cunning*, servility and *unprecedented boldness*, terror of death and *unfeeling hardihood*, were ascribed to me all at the same moment'. With no prospect of release, the state prisoners prepared themselves for a new century and the harshness of a Fort George winter.[79]

10

This Dreary Mansion: From Fort George to the New World, 1800–3

While the state prisoners' conditions in Fort George were less brutal than those in the Dublin and Belfast gaols, their continuing incarceration and their remoteness from families and friends combined to bring an air of resignation to their existence. The concession of newspapers did, however, allow the prisoners to follow the most vexing political question of the post-rebellion period as the Union Bill was being debated at both Westminster and College Green. Regarded by its architects, Pitt, Cornwallis and Castlereagh, as a means of bringing cohesion to the empire, providing stability for Irish politics in the wake of such a destructive insurrection and addressing England's strategic vulnerability, a political union between the two kingdoms was provoking intensive discussions in London and Dublin – and not just in the respective legislatures.

Attitudes to the Union were complex. Some Irish MPs, conscious of the disdain that many of the English political class felt for even the most refined of Irishmen, resisted the threat to the parliamentary independence of College Green (such as it was), which was believed to have been won by the efforts of Grattan and his supporters in 1782. Advocates of a Union, on the other hand, theorised that an independent Irish Parliament was actually a threat to the stability of the empire, raising the possibility that the two legislatures could clash on fundamentals of policy, with the concomitant potential for chaos. Castlereagh asserted that a Union would be good for Ireland's commercial prospects, with co-operation supplanting competition in a settlement that would be as beneficial for Ireland's economy as the Union between England and Scotland had been for the latter's in the years after 1707. The abolition of the Irish Parliament would, however, require MPs to vote themselves out of existence, with only 100 being eligible to represent Ireland in a Union parliament in London. For opponents of the measure, the impact on Dublin's cosmopolitan life would, it was feared, be huge and the city where Members of the Irish Parliament and their families would converge during legislative sessions to contribute wholeheartedly to the economic, social and cultural wealth of the capital would be deprived of its status as the second city of the empire. The Protestant establishment feared the dilution of its power, since College Green reflected the hegemony of the Anglican minority, many of whom thrived on the spoils system that had been the basis for legislative–executive relations for decades.

The Orange Order was officially neutral on the Union, with fears that it would diminish the power of the Ascendancy and many of the institution's members expressing concern that Cornwallis was planning to make Catholic emancipation an integral part of the project, even though a Catholic minority within the Union could have been viewed as preferable to the continuation of a disgruntled Irish Catholic majority on the island. The question of Catholics and the Union was among the most controversial elements of the proposal. To create an umbilical link between the Union Bill and emancipation would have raised Catholic expectations to the level reached in 1794, when Fitzwilliam embarked upon his short-lived viceroyalty. Figures like Fitzgibbon (Lord Clare), a convinced unionist, baulked at the idea of tying the Catholic issue to the bill. Pitt, too, was cautious, although he hoped to address the Catholic Question at a later stage, from a position of strength, and he was successful in persuading the Catholic hierarchy to endorse this strategy.

In the north, meanwhile, Presbyterian attitudes had not been entirely sobered by the carnage of the rebellion. Nonetheless, the prospect of dissolving an Ascendancy parliament that had long scorned the claims of Dissenters was not exactly unpopular and both the Synod of Ulster and the Presbytery of Antrim, representing the admittedly diverse range of opinions within Presbyterianism, had lost their more vocal republicans to the gallows, prison or exile. There was, in some circles, a sense that Presbyterians would be better treated in a more tolerant Union setting, with fewer restrictions on the practices and pretensions of the dissenting tradition.[1] Many United Irishmen would have seen the connection with England as injurious to Ireland's prospects, something Tone made quite clear in his statement of the aims of the United Irishmen back in 1791. Bizarrely, such opposition to any political union gave a common cause to the most unlikely of allies, with Thomas Russell and Pat Byrne alleging in 1799 that Orangemen in Dublin 'have offered terms to the U.I. and are going about in order to destroy all party faction and to have a common cause'.[2]

Pitt had presented the case for a Union with Ireland to the British House of Commons in January 1799 and subsequent debates were reported widely in the newspapers of the day. Divided into two groups, the prisoners at Fort George were permitted to interact during two separate meal sittings and the proposals for the Union would certainly have been a topic of conversation. While the detainees were forbidden to include political opinions in their letters, Neilson did pass comment on the issue in July when he set out his views to Anne:

> I see a union is determined on between Great Britain and Ireland. I am glad of it. In a commercial point of view, it cannot be injurious: and I can see no injury the country will sustain from it politically. So decidedly am I of this opinion, that I would purchase or rent land in Ireland at this moment in preference to any country on earth, had I it in my power. Many persons, however, of great knowledge differ from me on this subject, but time will show who is right. You will say this is a point with which you have no concern. Very true. But as I know it will make a bustle with you, I wish you to be in possession of my opinion, in order that any person may have it, who thinks it worth the asking for. If I had possessed the means, I would have published my sentiments on this subject, in a short, nervous pamphlet; so deeply am I impressed with its national utility.

Neilson's sentiments at this juncture would indeed have surprised many of his countrymen, since the United Irishmen, angered by the recall of Fitzwilliam and the sanctioning of repressive policies in Ireland in the period leading up to and during the rebellion, would have been hostile to London's political and military policy, especially at a time when the republican cause in Ireland had nailed its colours to the French mast. Through the columns of the *Northern Star*, Neilson had once been one of the most significant opinion formers in Ireland. Any pamphlet would, indeed, have encouraged nervousness in him, to the extent that Madden later attempted to deny that the views expressed were actually Neilson's true feelings at all, given that all correspondence was censored by the authorities before being forwarded to the intended recipient.[3] It is, however, important to note that public opinion was being bombarded with different arguments, both for and against the Union, and positions on the proposal were always in a state of flux. For many radicals, the situation in the middle of 1799 was shaped by a number of factors. A legislative union would have brought trade benefits at a time when Irish commerce was in a state of turmoil and the newspapers were full of advertisements advising the public of dissolving business partnerships. The demise of an unrepresentative Irish parliament was never going to be anathema to excluded Irish radicals and such a scenario would deliver the best chance of securing the long-held objective of Catholic emancipation.

In another of his letters, unpublished by Madden, Neilson articulated his position further:

> In my last I stated my opinion of the intended union between these countries. I am still more and more convinced by its utility in a commercial point of view; and in a political. I again say it is preferable to the present deplorable state of Ireland – any state is preferable to that in which the benevolence of Government had been counteracted and perverted by the rancorous and bloody Orange system which at this moment leaves the Crown and tramples upon the people; such are my fixed opinions in this subject and I care not who knows them: they may be unpopular with some but that is of no consequence to me for I do know that those men who now billow so loudly against this measure are the very men who stood in the way of that liberal ground of reconciliation which would have stopped torrents of blood in Ireland and which would have been equally for the interest of the Government and the governed.[4]

Neilson's position was stated clearly and it was not entirely inconsistent with his earlier anti-Ascendancy views. The Union was, after all, opposed by conservatives such as John Foster and other advocates of political exclusivity, the sort of men whose intransigent objections to reform had alienated many Presbyterians and Catholics to the point of rebellion. Had the Irish Parliament become more representative of the population in 1782, it may have been worth defending, but the exclusion of the vast majority made it difficult for Neilson to argue for saving it. A Union legislature, with a more sympathetic understanding of Catholic and Dissenter grievances, would have more potential for the securing of those principles of religious equality and representation upon which the United Irishmen had been founded. Of course, the Union did not address the extent to which England had become a brake on Ireland's political freedom, but the development of the revolution in France had, for some, made such an alternative less desirable.[5] As a businessman, he would have seen the livelihoods of those he operated with ruined by commercial arrangements that favoured English manufacturers; a new dispensation would, in theory at least, allow Irish enterprises to compete on equal terms.

Neilson's attraction to the possibilities of a Union did not mean he had changed his political views irrevocably; rather that in mid-1799, with the debate still raging, he was considering the most likely means of achieving his long-held ambitions. Fitzgibbon's intervention the following year, when he buried any prospect of Catholic emancipation, may well have persuaded Neilson to reject the constitutional shift being proposed after all. As time went on, he would again reveal his subversive outlook, evidenced by information contained in a later letter written by his fellow prisoner, Thomas Russell. Russell continued to promote the cause of insurrection and would, upon his release, be the most active of the Fort George prisoners, playing a role in the planning and effecting of Robert Emmet's rising in 1803. Writing to his friend John Templeton in Belfast, Russell proclaimed his thirst for action, avoiding the ire of his captors by stating his political aspirations in a letter conveyed to Ireland by a sympathetic visitor:

> so far from conceiving the cause of Ireland lost, or being weary of its pursuit, I am more than ever, if possible, inflexibly bent on it, for that, I stay (if I can stay) in Europe; all the faculties I possess shall be exercised for its advancement; for that, I wished to go to Ireland, not to reside, but to see how I will be able to serve it, and that I can only know when at large. Every motive exists to serve the generous mind, – the widows and orphans of my friends, the memory of the heroes who fell, and the sufferings of the heroes who survive. My very soul is on fire; I can say no more.

Russell ended his letter by stating that his fellow prisoner, Neilson, 'participates in my sentiments' – as did many of the other prisoners since these principles were 'almost universal among us'.[6] The involvement of Russell, Thomas Addis Emmet, MacNeven and William Dowdall in continuing revolutionary intrigue would suggest that incarceration at Fort George did not dampen enthusiasm for the cause among some of those interned. Indeed, Emmet's young brother Robert, who had emerged as a serious proponent of renewed insurrection and was a member of the new United Irish executive that formed to fill the leadership vacuum, was plotting actively in Ireland, England, and on the continent. On his way to Hamburg in the summer of 1800, Robert Emmet and his brother-in-law John Patten apparently visited Fort George. A cousin, St John Mason, another United Irishman, visited the prisoners there before proceeding to Hamburg while John Palmer and the indefatigable William Putnam McCabe also travelled to the fortress.[7] The knowledge and consent of the state prisoners in the project, combined with the ongoing negotiations with the French (despite the misgivings of many United Irishmen), undermines the view that the Emmet rebellion, which erupted on the streets of Dublin in July 1803, was a doomed quixotic adventure.

One who did not, however, share the lingering enthusiasm for the revolutionary cause was Robert Hunter, the Belfast shipbroker who had been arrested in 1798 and sent, along with Dickson, Tennent and Cuthbert, to Fort George. Hunter had renounced his earlier militancy and cut a somewhat aloof and dejected figure in Scotland. In 1801, Hunter, who had started to provide the authorities with evidence of the prisoners' opinions and behaviour, wrote to the Belfast magistrate Cortland Skinner about the continuing intrigue at Fort George, alleging that Neilson, along with Russell, was attempting to spread republican principles throughout Scotland, especially among the militia regiments that had been raised to protect the country from invasion. Hunter recounted to Pelham, Portland's successor as Home Secretary, how an earlier letter detailing these allegations had been opened in the usual way on the orders of Governor Stuart and its contents leaked among the guards, one of whose wives (an Irish woman) had related the details to Thomas Emmet's wife, who had by that stage been permitted to stay at the fort.

Hunter, who was regarded with suspicion, was followed to his room one evening and tackled on the issue. He stated that he believed he was treated with suspicion by the authorities and was writing to clear his name. Hunter was afraid for his safety: 'I kept my head, and did not know the moment my life would be attempted, because they knew well it was not this new occurrence in Scotland, but the whole of their doings, I could reveal.' Hunter was aware that some of the prisoners had been broken by their incarceration, but some were intent on continuing their cause, with Russell and Neilson at the head of the new conspiracy: 'They are at present crazy in consequence of Peace coming on, and you are a God to Bonaparte and the French government; but the consolation is it's only an armed truce and will last no time. At all events, it may put back their liberty for Ireland for some time, but in the end they know and are certain their Union [that is, the United Irish conspiracy] will triumph.'[8]

Neilson's continued links to the radical cause would manifest themselves more fully after his release in 1802. It is clear, however, that there was some flexibility in his thinking during the Fort George years, a flexibility that was typical of the shifting sands of public opinion more generally. The Union with Britain may have offered some commercial and religious opportunities, but the fact remained that London had directed operations in Ireland and provoked the enmity of many with the overall direction of its policy. The prisoners' release would, for some, signal a renewal of their earlier republicanism. In a letter to Anne delivered by the son of his fellow prisoner, John Sweetman, Neilson asserted that his political conduct was 'out of the range of forgiveness' and that he looked forward to the liberation of Ireland 'with as much confidence as I ever did'.[9]

The years of confinement inevitably caused divisions among the prisoners, some of them petty and others deep-rooted. The most divisive figures were the O'Connors, Arthur and Roger, viewed by some of their fellow prisoners as firebrand demagogues, whose belated attachment to the cause and determination to unleash a rebellion without French assistance encouraged a bitter feud with Thomas Addis Emmet and his entourage. Arthur O'Connor's arrest and trial in Maidstone back in early 1798 had allowed the Emmet wing of the United Irish leadership to regain the ground it had lost at that time, although Fitzgerald and his allies had pushed ahead with their plans for a rising, with Neilson, recently released from prison, aligning himself with the charismatic lord. At Fort George, tensions between Emmet and O'Connor were renewed, with the former later alleging that O'Connor had been sent to Fort George to serve as a government agent charged with the task of securing evidence to convict him.[10] Neilson was certainly friendly with Emmet at Fort George, any strategic difference between them in 1798 having been resolved.

As Emmet's wife and children applied to take up residence in the fortress (this was eventually granted towards the end of 1800), Neilson noted that the negative attitude of the authorities to this family was somewhat different to that afforded to the O'Connors. Roger, who had not signed the agreement between the government and the prisoners and was not, therefore, subject to the Banishment Act, had suffered very poor health in the months after his arrival in Scotland and his wife and three of their children were permitted to live with him in September 1799. He would also be given what were regarded by the other prisoners as extra privileges.[11] Neilson confided in his wife that 'I feel very sensibly how different is the plan proposed for the lady of my friend [Emmet].'[12] Thomas Emmet had requested that his wife be allowed to join him too, but this seemed to have fallen on deaf ears and Neilson observed how 'there appears to be a *marked* difference: so it was in days of yore'.[13] This concern over Roger O'Connor's preferential treatment was reaffirmed when Neilson noted pointedly that: 'Mrs O'Connor and her children remain with Mr O'Connor, and they all have the liberty of ranging the Fort and neighbourhood, the other nineteen of us are closely confined as usual.'[14]

The obvious enmity between Emmet and the O'Connors cannot have helped the atmosphere in Fort George. Arthur O'Connor had found William Tennent to be detached from the feud and believed that he intended to endeavour to end 'the spirit of faction, and the malignity that has taken such deep root in the minds of some of the men in this prison'. Believing faction to be an abhorrence, O'Connor

– seemingly with no awareness of irony – accused Emmet in a letter to Tennent of 'underhand techniques'. Aspersions about him were spread by Emmet's friends outside of the gaols, as was a misrepresentation of what O'Connor had stated before the secret committee. He alleged that Emmet used his influence to create 'such perfidy, intrigue and cowardice' and that he 'brought the infection with him to this prison, that on our arrival, flattery and slander and every vile act was set on foot to make proselites [*sic*] and to embody a faction'. O'Connor believed these actions to be a betrayal of the United Irish oath of union and brotherly love and that Emmet's behaviour was unworthy of a republican, since individual passions were to be sacrificed in favour of the public interest. O'Connor continued to vituperate about his fellow prisoners:

> I could not forget that from the moment I perceived the infection had shewn itself here, I instantly cut off all communication with the infected, and that from that time, stung with the contempt their disgraceful conduct had brought on them; goaded by the worst passions of the human mind, they have passed their time in an uninterrupted practice of slander and calumny a prey to the blackest malignity, galled to find themselves deemed unworthy of society by a man actuated by honor [*sic*], what room have they left unbesieged to destroy all intercourse between the man who had dismissed them from his society and the rest of the prisoners. To cover their own disgrace by the appearance of numbers what means however infamous have they left untryed [*sic*]? Flattery, bullying, and brutality, slander, and every means that intrigue and faction usually practice and which can be played off with most effect in the narrow focus of a prison, I can not forget that they have sent their calumnies to Ireland, of which my letters inform me and that they have night and day disseminated the same calumnies among the different regiments that have been in this garrison, of which I have been informed of several of the soldiers, and as if to prove that the violence of those malignant passions ... some of them have avowed that this attempt to assassinate my character, was but a prelude to assassinate my person; dastardly crimes that ever go hand in hand.[15]

O'Connor was convinced he had been ostracised because he refused to engage in intrigue and observed that he was described by others as aristocratic, proud and ambitious, suggesting that there was a disdain for his privileged origins among the bourgeois leaders of the United Irish conspiracy confined there. The divisions among the prisoners were the subject of rumour and gossip in Ireland. Lady Moira exchanged news with Lady Granard and wrote dismissively of the feuding that had become a feature of life in the fort:

> They are all quarrelling at Fort St George [*sic*] of the 20 – 16 are on one side 4 on the other[.] [T]he four O'Connor and his Br Roger, Dowling who was Secretary to the Whig Club and Hudson nephew to the dentist – Russell ... knocked Dowling down. O'Connor says L[or]d Ed[ward] was a coward, and had neither nerves or spirit, that Emmet was and is a sensualist & voluptuary – & McNevin [*sic*] is a paltry mixture of duplicity and meanness.

She went on to cite a verse that had been circulated around the internees:

> O'Connor his mind I'm bound to confess,
> He writes well, he spoke well and printed the Press
> The faults of O'Connor I will also maintain,
> He's Envious, malignant, a liar and vain
> Of O'Connor in power then Erin beware
> For O'Connor in power woud [*sic*] act Robespierre.[16]

Neilson's friendship with both Russell and Emmet meant that he would certainly have sided with them in their suspicion of the O'Connorite wing. He wrote to Anne that while he maintained good relations with his fellow prisoners, 'only there is *one* or *two* I don't choose to be very intimate with. I am but a plain man myself, and I don't like those who affect to be otherwise.'[17] By the end of 1801, O'Connor's position had deteriorated further. Neilson noted that 'A certain gentleman has ceased to have mischief in his power here. Hudson, Chambers, Tennent, and Dowling alone, are on speaking terms with him.'[18] The dispute lasted for the duration of the prisoners' incarceration at Fort George and attempts by John Sweetman, John Chambers and others to reconcile the two men were only partially successful on board the *Ariadne*, the ship that would eventually carry the detainees to Europe in 1802. O'Connor was persuaded to withdraw his challenge to a duel with Emmet; the latter would say that he had never intended to cause O'Connor any injury. For his part, O'Connor retracted comments on Emmet's character. After a handshake on the foredeck, the two men retreated, but there would be no reconciliation between them.[19]

Aside from the disagreements, Neilson tried to keep himself occupied. Having requested that he forego supper in the hope that this saving would enable him to cover the costs of laundry and other services, he spent the early days of 1800 framing and glazing profile sketches of the children, which were hung up over his fireplace. Reflecting on all he had lost and his inability to shape the lives of those he held dear, Neilson wrote pitifully to Anne that 'I cannot forget that I once had a home. I cannot help feeling that I have a family.' As morale sank further, Neilson mused that he and his fellow prisoners would be the last to be freed: 'We are put like old debts in the back of the book, and may lie so until chance or some incident shall bring a curious eye to overhaul the musty pages which enclose us; although God knows how the selection was hit upon, for many in this place were never calculated to set the Liffey on fire.'[20] As the better weather approached, the prisoners bathed in the sea three days a week at the foot of the fort's ramparts and Neilson availed of this opportunity. The possibility of Emmet's wife and children joining him was still being pursued, but Neilson was at pains to point out that such an arrangement was out of the question for Anne. Certainly, the cost of this would have been well beyond the means of a man who had become impoverished over recent years. He may also have remembered his falling-out with Henry Joy McCracken in Kilmainham on the issue of how such arrangements could affect the prisoners' morale and solidarity. The most likely explanation, however, is that he was reluctant to expose Anne to the cold and harsh conditions in what he referred to as 'this dreary mansion'.[21]

By the middle of the summer of 1800, Emmet's wife and three of their children had arrived and the family was permitted access to all areas of the fort in the company of a guard. After the release of Roger O'Connor at the end of that year, Mrs Emmet and the children had more space and privacy and Neilson observed that the delightful Emmet children would make excellent company for his son, William. The advantages of having his son with him were not lost on Neilson. While the young Emmets would prove perfect friends ('I never saw children I would so soon have him with'), William would bond with his father and learn from the array of intellectual and practical talent possessed by the prisoners. The idea that William, by now aged six, would join his father took root in early September 1800 and Neilson hoped that the authorities would 'not debar me the duty of assisting to educate my only son'. The visit shortly afterwards of Dr Robert Tennent, brother of Neilson's fellow prisoner William, was another reminder that the presence of family could do much to ameliorate his 'dreary solitude'. Thus began a campaign to bring the boy to the fort.

Robert Tennent, who would meet with Anne Neilson and her four daughters in Belfast at the start of the following year, was working tirelessly for his brother's liberation, as well as applying pressure so young William Neilson would be permitted to join his father. It was originally hoped that Emmet's brother-in-law,

John Patten, who was negotiating to deliver another of the Emmet children to Fort George, might be able to bring William there as well, but this opportunity was missed.[22] Meanwhile, Neilson continued to insert occasional letters to his children and as the new year dawned, he wrote positively about their 'great progress in writing'. He also offered advice that sheds some light on his outlook, declaring that while reading and writing were intrinsically pleasurable, the children should earn the right to do what they enjoy and not benefit simply 'by the fruits of another's industry'. In another letter addressed to his girls, Neilson explained, in geographical terms, the location of Fort George in relation to Belfast. Praising Sophia on a piece of writing recently sent to him, Neilson wrote that all of the prisoners were suitably impressed, so much so that Thomas Emmet had used it in the education of his eldest son, Robert.[23]

In July 1801, Neilson's efforts to secure William's passage to Fort George took on a new urgency when it transpired that his fellow prisoner, Joseph Cuthbert, had been successful in an application for his wife and niece (Jane Park) to join him in Scotland, presenting the opportunity for William to travel with them. Robert Tennent was still working on Neilson's behalf. Neilson had written to Pelham in the hope that ministerial backing would be given to the request. He also wrote to the Duke of Portland and provided instructions to Tennent to call with the Home Secretary to stress the urgency of the situation. The indomitable doctor, who was also under instruction from his brother to request that the now destitute wife and family of Robert Hunter be allowed to reside at Fort George, could transmit the news to his brother that the decision had been left to Lieutenant-Governor Stuart, whose benevolence was such that Robert Tennent 'was so confident of his concurrence that I wrote to Mrs Neilson on Friday evening the 24th informing her of the circumstances, and advising her to make use of the opportunity that offered for sending her son to FG'.[24] Tennent's intercession was successful; Portland had in fact informed Stuart two days before that Neilson's request had been granted.[25] William arrived in August, but only after a very serious illness prior to his departure. Neilson wrote words of support to his anxious wife in late July in a way that reflected his strong Christian values:

> As to the possible event, I am happy to find that your mind is made up and prepared for the worst. This is the true frame of mind which reason and religion equally point out. The loss of a much loved child is no doubt one of the most afflicting trials that can befall a human being; but when we consider the mass of wickedness and of sorrow from which he is snatched away, and when we look forward to the well-founded hopes of glorious eternity, we

> should bow to the stroke, and say with reverence, 'The Lord giveth, and the Lord taketh away, blessed be the name of the Lord.'[26]

Thankfully, young William recovered and was able to make the journey from Belfast to Fort George in the company of Mrs Cuthbert and her niece, who (he informed his mother on arrival) 'took great care of me' during what was a peaceful voyage. William reported that his father, who had been incarcerated for most of the child's life to date, was in good health and had prepared a small bed and a little chair for his arrival. Despite the separation from his father, William recognised him from a miniature portrait kept at home. As he settled into his new surroundings, William assured his mother that his health was improving and that he was bathing in sea water every morning, even plucking up the courage to dive. As far as schooling was concerned, he was receiving instruction in mathematics from Matthew Dowling, reading and grammar from Dickson and writing, reading and geography from his father. Evenings were spent playing with the Emmet children before retiring at nine o'clock, an hour before his father. Surrounded by instructors, William informed his mother that he was receiving lessons for ten hours each day 'and I think it not enough'. Neilson had praised him, saying he was 'in a fair way of being a good scholar'.[27] William had spent time away from his mother before; indeed, he was not with her in Belfast when Robert Tennent had visited her earlier that year, being instead in the country. However, it was natural that she would worry about his welfare and Neilson was keen to assuage any anxieties. It was clear that he was enlivened by young William's presence in Fort George:

> he evinces every day new powers of mind, which excite in me the most lively presages of his capacity, when it shall be matured by instruction and experience ... His instruction is so mingled with agreeable conversation, that he always prefers it to play, and my company to that of any other person, young or old. As to wine you may be at your ease, he will never taste anything here, liquid, but milk and water while he has his health ... It is not very easy for me to describe the pleasure I feel in the boy, who far exceeds my most sanguine expectations, and I suppose I possess as much rational affection for him as ever a father did for his son.

For someone who eschewed pride, Neilson's warmth towards his son is touching, but he warned Anne to refrain from attaching herself to him to such an extent that his loss would be unbearable. He chided her for expressing her devotion to

William in a way that 'borders on being sinful'. Should William, for any reason, be taken from them, 'I really do not know how you would be able to meet such a stroke, and yet it is one for which we should always be prepared, being, as it is, in the ordinary course of human events.' Despite his own love for his son, Neilson admitted to his wife that it was duty 'to be prepared to resign him to his Maker, whenever shall be demanded, without repining'.[28]

The bond between father and son developed further over the next weeks and months, and Neilson's letters to Anne reveal both his love for the boy and the high expectations he had of him:

> his propensities seem to lead towards everything that is good already. The worst a cool observer could say of him is, that he is a little forgetful; and he has some timidity, which, though some people think it is likely to keep the young out of danger's way, is generally the most direct to it – at least, if not the most direct, the most certain. This last, I am confident will be easily removed; the former is perhaps constitutional, and I should be the last person living to be censorious respecting it, for I never was blessed with a tenacious memory, especially respecting trivial matters.

Neilson kept notes on his wall of the occasions when William's forgetfulness led to minor faults in his conduct, erasing these incidents once corrective behaviour had been noted. Their contentedness in each other's company and the games they played were conducted within clear boundaries: 'On the slightest word, or even look, of seriousness, he is all attention and obedience.' Another part of William's rounded education was his learning of the flute, under the tutelage of John Cormick. William was on the way to becoming proficient, being able quite quickly to 'turn a tune with a good deal of taste'. Neilson was at pains to assure his wife that the boy's music tuition was 'stolen from his play hours'. In December, William informed his mother that he and young Robert Emmet (Thomas' son) had entertained the prisoners with a little recital and they had – in William's rather precocious words – 'the approbation of the whole company'. He was also learning Latin, insofar as Neilson's limited resources were able to procure the appropriate books. The level of education William was receiving was quite advanced; he informed his mother that he was reading Erasmus in Latin with Reverend Dickson and that he was 'in the rule of five of fractions' with Matthew Dowling. His learning was interrupted by a bout of illness at Christmas when he was laid low, much to the concern of the prisoners and the various family members who had been permitted to reside at Fort George. On Christmas Day,

Neilson reported that the boy had been cared for most assiduously by Mrs Emmet and by Jane Park, Cuthbert's niece. Fruits, sweetmeats and jellies were provided to maintain his health and spirits.[29]

During the latter part of 1801, the prisoners were optimistic that a peace deal between England and France was imminent, a development that would offer the prospect of release. With the publication of a tentative agreement in early October, Neilson wrote to Anne to express hope of a reunion and regret at a war which he felt had 'occasioned so much human misery'. By the middle of the month, he was expecting news of his release and outlined his plans:

> As for myself, I have learned (as I have often told you) to be easy in my mind, and prepared fully for any event; anxious to be restored to my family, for the purpose of exercising my abilities and industry for their maintenance, I am by no means wedded to a spot. Love of country is a natural feeling, and no one ever possessed it more than myself; yet I am able to endure a separation from it, rather than continue here a living burthen to my friends, wasting away that life which might be so usefully devoted to the comfort of my wife and the independence and education of my children. In case of expatriation, I will of course prefer going to a country where liberty and property appear to be best secured by mild government, emanating from the public will; – such a country is America.[30]

The earlier attitude of the American ambassador, Rufus King, to the state prisoners notwithstanding, Neilson had identified the fledgling United States as a destination that was in tune with his liberal and bourgeois outlook. Interestingly, though, he added to Anne that he had other ties to America that would pull him to that country if he were to be unable to repatriate himself in Belfast. These ties may have been his old colleagues from the *Northern Star*, John Rabb or perhaps Samuel Kennedy or William Kean, all of whom had reached the United States and were involved – in one way or another – in the newspaper industry.

Within a month, Neilson's initial optimism had turned to cynicism and he noted sadly that he entertained few hopes of being reunited with Anne in Ireland. He believed England was being somewhat disingenuous in its attempts to negotiate a settlement and that the hostilities would resume when the weather improved or when Britain felt less anxious about a French invasion. In a letter delivered to Anne outside of the usual official channels, Neilson acknowledged that the government was reluctant to liberate any prisoner because there was a risk that 'that the Irish wish to shake off their yoke when the opportunity occurs [and

London] will not be hasty in sending away those who might be the most ready to concur in any similar operation ... I know, for my own part, I will embrace almost any honourable offer to get out of their hands, well knowing a prison is no place to accomplish either public or private purposes'. Neilson stressed that he needed to avoid giving the authorities cause for concern over his intentions: 'You will easily see that I could not wish to put Government in possession of my apprehensions on this subject, and of course I am constrained to blink this point as much as I can in my regular correspondence.' This might suggest that Neilson did see a role for himself in any continuing radical project, as suggested by Hunter and stated by Russell in his earlier smuggled note.

He was able to send letters to Anne through a Mrs Elizabeth Risk of Dublin, a visitor to Fort George with whom he was acquainted in 1798 and who was a conduit of information from the prisoners.[31] Covert correspondence indicated that Neilson was planning for the future. He was also thoroughly disillusioned with the French, believing that Bonaparte had usurped the liberty which had emerged in 1789 and been the cause of 'nearly all the calamities of my country for the last four years'. The French general had 'trampled all justice, and all liberty, under foot in his own' and felt that it was unfortunate that so many Irishmen, including those in his own milieu, had placed their trust in such a man: 'With such politicians for my friends, and with my enemies the Orangemen in power, Ireland would have no attractions for me beyond the circle of my own family.'[32]

While Neilson's prospects for release were on hold, the news reached them that those prisoners who were not subject to the terms of the Banishment Act were due to be released on bail. These included Tennent, William Dowdall, Robert Simms, Reverend William Steel Dickson and Robert Hunter. Earlier reports had indicated that the men would be returned to Carrickfergus for trial. Tennent was still regarded as a 'dangerous man', but legal question marks meant that they remained in Scotland for the time being.[33] William Tennent's health, meanwhile, had been deteriorating. His brother, Robert, wrote alarmingly: 'Good God! If my father and mother knew your situation what might be the consequence? ... I dare not even imagine the probable effect of acquainting them that they are likely to see their son no more.'[34] When his throat became inflamed in November, Dr MacNeven lanced his tonsils, but to no great effect. Robert Tennent's exertions had taken him to Dublin, where he had lobbied Under-Secretary Cooke, whose non-committal response was irksome. Neilson would have been familiar with Cooke's tendency to utilise 'one of those judicial evasions which are never wanting to a person of Mr Cooke's unholy disposition'.[35] Tennent, Dowdall, Simms, Dickson and Hunter were eventually released and this would have created additional space at the fort for the remaining prisoners and their families.

Neilson's continuing incarceration worsened his financial woes. He was, however, able to pay William's living expenses by making a number of personal sacrifices, such as refraining from drinking his daily allowance of wine (about two-thirds of a pint) and selling it to some of the prisoners at 3*s* and 6*d* per bottle. Neilson's predilection for alcohol was no secret, so such an arrangement was, no doubt, a difficult one to sustain. Despite this, he displayed typical fortitude and was confident that he would return to successful business after his release:

> I don't feel the slightest inconvenience from this privation; and though it looks a little awkward to sit at table while others are taking their glass, yet my fellow prisoners cannot but esteem me more for the motive; indeed I feel a good deal pinched about the usual expenses of mending, washing, paper, quills, &c., &c., not having, at present, a crown in the world. But then I do not owe a farthing to any person, and I have learned to make a little go very far. If my liberation were once accomplished, I am not at all afraid of being soon out of these difficulties, provided my health continues.[36]

Neilson's final year as a prisoner began with him in reasonable spirits, happy about William's recovery and hopeful that his liberation would be assured once Britain and France finally came to a peace arrangement.[37] In the meantime, William's education continued, with Matthew Dowling replacing the departed Steel Dickson as the boy's Latin teacher. Young Neilson seems to have been a welcome presence in the fort. He dined with the cook, Mrs McGregor, on a regular basis and became friendly with her son, who gave William a pigeon to adopt. For a boy far away from his mother, sisters and all he had grown up with, William took to his new environment with ease and informed his mother that 'My father and I are very snug here; we sometimes play shinney together.'[38]

As May dawned, Neilson's patience was being tried. The peace treaty of Amiens, however temporary, had been in place since the end of March, but still nothing had happened to the Fort George prisoners 'on this outskirt of the world'. Despite his frustration, he acknowledged that he and his fellow inmates would have to be patient: 'I should ... have made an ill use of my five years and three-quarters' imprisonment, if I were not able to endure even this tantalising suspense.' Neilson reported that he had recovered from all of his ailments and was enjoying a state of health that was as good as anything he had enjoyed during his life.[39] At the end of May, the prisoners finally received the news they had been waiting for through the good offices of the benevolent Stuart.[40] They would be conveyed to the free city of Hamburg as soon as convenient and thence travel to their respective destinations. For Neilson, this would be the United States and he now faced a dilemma regarding William: 'He can't bear the idea of parting with me, and has been in tears this hour past, because I won't promise to take him with me. I am indeed a good deal divided in my own opinion on the subject. I see much to say on both sides of the question, and therefore I leave it entirely for you [that is, Anne] to decide.' The prisoners had hoped to persuade the authorities not to sail to Hamburg as none of them desired to go there, France and America being the preferred options. A request to have a short stop in Ireland was lodged, although this was never going to be viewed positively by the government.[41]

As the date of their departure approached, Neilson wrote lovingly to his daughter, Sophia, instructing her to be guided by biblical principles and by her mother, 'whose example will be a model for your imitation'. Neilson had decided, after much soul-searching, that William would return to Ireland for the sake of Anne and offer comfort to the family. His faith came to the fore, as it often did, but so did a sense that their separation would not be permanent.

> Your mother will tell you where I am going, and what are my objects; I hope our separation will not be of long duration; and when our meeting, by the blessing of Divine Providence, shall take place, how much will my happiness be crowned by learning that all my little darlings have made goodness and virtue the pursuit of their lives ... May I not be disappointed in my fond hopes respecting you! And may the Father of all mercies frame your hearts, so as that you may love one another![42]

On 13 June 1802, Neilson informed Anne that the vessel due to transmit the prisoners to Hamburg, a twenty-gun frigate called the *Ariadne*, was anchored offshore, within sight of Fort George. He had hoped to receive a letter from Robert Simms or another of the Belfast coterie with news and a means of securing money to allow him to make the voyage to the United States. He asserted that any credit he could get would be used sparingly, 'the most rigid economy being what I conceive a moral duty to every one, in my situation: nay, if I could work my passage to the new world I would prefer it to the thoughts of being burthensome to any one'. Neilson finished his last letter from Fort George by telling Anne his health was good (it was certainly better than it had been during the journey to Scotland three years before). He stated that imprisonment had taught him 'that all human wisdom is folly and vanity, and that there is no happiness but in virtue; no rest but in the grave'.[43]

The king's pardon for all treasons committed by the prisoners was signed on 31 May and transmitted to the relevant legal authorities. The remaining state prisoners were permitted to leave on the condition that they would not set foot in Ireland or any of the king's dominions. If they did, the pardon would be rendered void.[44] The *Ariadne* departed for Hamburg on 30 June under the command of Post Captain Patrick Campbell, whose valour at Dunkirk two years previously had led to his elevation to the command of the frigate.[45] Three years of absence from his native land and the enforced separation from all those he held dear would certainly have been uppermost in Neilson's thoughts as the vessel sailed out of the Moray Firth and into the open sea.

On 4 July 1802, the former state prisoners reached the northern port of Cuxhaven, at the mouth of the mighty River Elbe, where Neilson had originally intended on disembarking, leaving the others to proceed by boat to the free city of Hamburg, where they would arrange for a vessel to transmit him to America. In the end, however, he accompanied them to Hamburg, a journey of around 50 miles by sea.[46] Neilson remained in the neighbouring district of Altona for a month, residing at 248 Little Fisher Street, in the home of a Jacob Heuserman. There, he and some of the other released prisoners made contact with the veteran United Irishman Archibald Hamilton Rowan, who, after spending a period of time in exile in the United States, had gone to Hamburg in August 1800 in the hope of obtaining permission to return to his homeland. Rowan wrote to Neilson, among others, offering his services and, while there was a degree of trepidation in engaging with him lest the former's application be endangered, Neilson felt obliged to strike up their old acquaintance, accepting the loan of a number of political texts and exchanging views on their common vision for Ireland..[47] In a letter to Rowan, Neilson again expounded his ideas on his country's struggle for liberty, suggesting an unreconstructed republican, albeit one who had been disappointed by the unfortunate outworking of the revolution in France:

> In the New World, however, I hope to find *the people* as I ever found them at home, honest and sincere. I am not afraid of pushing my way among a people who, I may say, have sprung from ourselves. In the propagation of truth I know there is nothing but pain and trouble, and he who embarks in that cause with any other view, will, I am confident, find himself mistaken ... Neither the eight years' hardship I have endured, the total destruction of my property, the forlorn state of my wife and children, the momentary failure of

> our national exertion, nor the still more distressing usurpation in France, has abated my ardour in the cause of my country and of general liberty ... Christ was executed upon a cross, but his morality has been gaining ground these eighteen hundred years, in spite of superstition and priestcraft. You and I, my dear friend, will pass away, but truth will remain.[48]

William Sampson, one of the attorneys who had successfully defended Neilson and the other proprietors of the *Northern Star* back in 1794, was also in Altona at this time (having previously been in Portugal and then France). Sampson had been a regular contributor to the newspaper and was, in all likelihood, the author of the satirical series *The Lion of Old England* and *The Trial of Hurdy Gurdy*, published over a number of editions in 1794.[49] He was residing in Belfast at the time of Neilson's arrest in September 1796 and the two men were well acquainted. Sampson had, however, been critical of the Kilmainham Pact in 1798 while a prisoner in Dublin and there may have been some residual resentment about the negotiations that Neilson had initiated. It is unknown whether the two men met in Hamburg, but it is possible that they did. We know something of Neilson's stay in the city from the information provided by George Wood, a native of Cork who had served in the 27th Regiment of Foot and latterly in the Buckingham Militia before taking on duties as a clerk in Whitehall, London. According to government intelligence, Wood left his lucrative employment and returned to Ireland in 1800 before travelling to Hamburg to recover money that he lost as a result of speculation. It was considered that Wood was a man of some ability, but of 'little sense and at all times of bad politicks [*sic*]'.[50] Wood had seen Neilson dining with some of the other Fort George prisoners in a public house in Hamburg on several occasions. Political issues were not discussed during mealtimes, but Wood did note that 'Neilson seemed deranged from the wildness of his discourses.' He observed that Neilson 'drank much, never saw him perfectly sober – quite enthusiastic in his friendships and wild'.[51]

Meanwhile, those who had been incarcerated together at Fort George began to go their separate ways, some into exile and others to begin the next phase of the United Irish project. Joseph Cuthbert and William Cumming boarded a ship for Portsmouth, New Hampshire; Sweetman, Matthew Dowling, Hudson and MacNeven departed for Dresden; O'Connor and Chambers travelled overland to Holland and Thomas Emmet, Russell, John Cormick, John Sweeney and Hugh Wilson sailed for the same country.

Neilson's plans altered and he arranged to return secretly to Ireland before progressing to his chosen destination, the United States. His reasons for this incredibly risky detour may be inferred as threefold: firstly, he hoped to redeem his reputation, which would have been impugned to some extent both by rumours of his careless behaviour at the time of Lord Edward Fitzgerald's arrest and by the imputed motives behind his initiation of talks with the government in the aftermath of the rebellion; secondly, he wished to see Anne, the children and his mother before his exile and, thirdly, he was in some way still playing a part in the developing conspiracy. So, having stayed in Hamburg for around one month, Neilson was on the move. He had made contact with Anthony McCann, a native of Drogheda and an active United Irishman, who had left Ireland hurriedly in the summer of 1797, around the time that Alexander Lowry, John Magennis and others had gone on the run after the abortive uprising in County Down. McCann lived in Hamburg and was, in 1802, engaged in a business partnership with a Thomas Ridgeway, who was originally from Lancashire. The two jointly owned a vessel, the *Providence*, which operated a smuggling trade between that city and various locations in the British Isles.[52] Ridgeway had been in Hamburg for five years and had co-purchased the *Providence* (formerly known as *The Sisters*) that June. Under examination in Dublin the following year, he stated that the arrangement to bring Neilson to Ireland had been made before he even purchased the vessel and that he did not receive any money for transporting him. Ridgeway said that he would not have knowingly brought the exile to Ireland and Neilson had travelled under the alias of Netherton. Ridgeway also claimed that the man he subsequently discovered to be Neilson dined in his cabin during the voyage, and intimated an intention to go to Belfast as he disembarked in Dublin. Concerned about his liberty, Ridgeway asserted that he would never have allowed Neilson on board had he known who he was, although he was fully aware that the Fort George prisoners were in Hamburg.[53] For a man who wrote so regularly about divine intervention during his imprisonment, Neilson's means of transport must have seemed entirely appropriate. The *Providence* anchored at Cuxhaven after a tortuous few days being buffeted in the Elbe estuary. Neilson wrote cryptically to Anne to explain that since a direct passage to America had been impossible to obtain, he had 'been obliged to take one by a circuitous route'. This would see him return clandestinely, after three years of absence, to his native land.[54]

Details of Neilson's movements in Ireland are incomplete, but some information is contained in reports that made their way to the authorities after Robert Emmet's failed rising in 1803, an event that caused consternation in government circles due to the intelligence failures that preceded it. Back in Hamburg, McCann had told a government informer known as Roberts (who passed the information to Sir George Rumbold, the British minister there) that

Ridgeway's boat had landed him and Neilson around 4 miles from Dublin. According to information provided by the ship's mate, Jacob Kindton, the men actually landed in broad daylight at the public quay in Dublin. The ship would return to Hamburg in October, laden with porter, spirits and butter, but only after its crew, who were offered higher wages elsewhere, had been replenished.[55] Madden noted that Neilson lodged with Bernard Coile at 13 Lurgan Street on his arrival in Dublin. Coile was a leading Defender and textile manufacturer from County Armagh who had a long association with northern republicans such as Neilson and McCracken. That Neilson stayed there for a week would suggest that Coile required little reassurance about his past motives and actions.[56]

James (Jemmy) Hope, a leading northern republican, who was well known to Neilson, was brought to Coile's to meet up with his old friend. Hope had been among those who swore a solemn pact on the top of the Cave Hill days before Tone's departure from Ireland in 1795, pledging to work to achieve their country's liberation. He had played a leading role as a United Irish emissary in 1798 and had been part of McCracken's force at the Battle of Antrim. In the aftermath of the rebellion, Hope was forced into itinerancy, working for various employers, often under an alias, but he always maintained close links with senior conspirators such as Charles Teeling, the leading Defender. Teeling had employed Hope as an overseer at his bleach green in Naul, north of Dublin, until he was forced to flee in 1802 after a dramatic encounter with one of his co-workers, a John McCarroll, who threatened to give evidence against him. With Teeling's assistance, Hope set up a haberdasher's shop in the Coombe district of Dublin, where he remained until the spring of 1803, when he was again forced to leave after being approached by the Belfast attorney James McGucken, who had abandoned his sympathies for the republican cause and was in the pay of the government. McGucken offered Hope money to dissociate himself from the United Irishmen. The latter pulled two pistols on his former friend before McGucken defused the situation and shared a drink with him. Hope knew it was time to move on and departed that evening, thereby evading an arresting party that appeared at the house the following morning. Hope established himself in Butterfield Lane near Rathfarnham, where he assisted Robert Emmet in his endeavour to raise the standard of rebellion once again.[57] It was while Hope was running his small business in the Coombe that he was summoned to Coile's to renew his friendship with Neilson. Hope's mission was to accompany Neilson to Belfast and serve as his bodyguard and companion. According to Hope, Neilson stressed the dangers inherent in such an exercise: 'Do not mistake; this is not a party of pleasure; if we are discovered the event will be banishment to you and death to me.'

On the first night of the journey, early in September 1802, the men stayed with the aforementioned Charles Teeling, who had been arrested in Lisburn on the same day as Neilson and Russell in Belfast six years before. The men had been imprisoned together in Kilmainham, with both experiencing ill health as a consequence of their confinement in that damp gaol. While they must have spent time reminiscing, they must also have discussed the current state of the country and the appetite for another rising. Early the next morning, Hope intimated to Neilson that it was time to recommence their journey and the latter resumed his disguise of a wig and spectacles before the two men set out for Belfast. There, Hope proceeded to the home of Neilson's mother to tell her that her son was in town; Neilson, meanwhile, was reunited with Anne and spent three days with his family, reputedly meeting only one person who was not a relation. It would be the last time he saw his beloved Anne.

Madden asserts that associates of the town sovereign, Reverend William Bristow, were aware of the clandestine visit but decided against taking any action, being firm in the belief that he was in the town purely for familial reasons.[58] Alexander Marsden in Dublin received news of his sojourn in a letter from Belfast dated 10 September. Marsden was apprised of the fact that the celebrated Samuel Neilson had been in Belfast 'in Cog' [*sic*] for some days. Significantly, the letter added:

> on further inquiry today I understand he is gone to Dublin ... From his returning here its [*sic*] surmised that there is a conspiracy ... to raise the people ... I fear [it] will have a bad tendency. James Hope, an emigrant from this part was also here and clearly some system is again about to be agitated. A great number of emigrants are daily returning to this county.[59]

It must certainly have pained Neilson to leave his family after such a short period. No public mention was made of his surreptitious return, with the *Belfast News-Letter* making no reference to the former editor of its one-time rival. Rather, the locals were waiting expectantly for the arrival of the famous actress Mrs Siddons, who was due to play her most famous role, that of Lady Macbeth, in the town's theatre once again.[60]

Returning to Dublin, Neilson and Hope made a detour through Creeve, Ballybay, in County Monaghan, the home of John Jackson, brother of the veteran United Irishman Henry Jackson. Neilson was well acquainted with the Jacksons; Henry's daughter, Eleanor, was married to his great friend and Newgate cellmate, Oliver Bond. Neilson's eldest daughter, Anne, was staying with John Jackson's family at Creeve House. Neilson then met with some of his former friends in Dublin and was satisfied that he had convinced any doubters of the correctness of his conduct, which led to 'different proofs of continued or renewed friendships'. Neilson wrote to his wife to declare that he felt very glad of the opportunity to 'vindicate my character from the foul aspersions which had been cast upon it behind my back'. He acknowledged that men like Coile and Jackson had harboured him in the knowledge that his discovery would have catastrophic consequences for them.[61]

Mrs Elizabeth Risk was also involved in harbouring Neilson during his stay in Dublin. She was the widow of an insurgent who had died in the year of the rebellion and at whose house in Sandymount, it was later asserted, Lord Edward Fitzgerald was to have been lodged on the day he was captured. This aptly named woman, a client of the lawyer William Dowdall, who was detained along with Neilson and the others in Fort George, had been one of those permitted to visit the state prisoners and on at least one occasion she smuggled letters to Ireland that were political in nature and not, therefore, passed through the official channels established by Lieutenant-Governor Stuart.[62] It was later suggested that among the documents smuggled out of the fortress 'sewed up in her under-dress, to avoid discovery, and ... conveyed to Mrs Neilson' was the initial draft of Neilson's pamphlet detailing the events surrounding the negotiations between the United Irish state prisoners and the government.[63]

Mrs Risk's name emerged in August 1803 during the examination of Ross McCann (no relation to Anthony), a United Irishman detained hastily in the aftermath of the Emmet rising. McCann, the agent of the veteran Whig Henry Grattan, had sent money to William Dowdall when the latter had been detained at Fort George but subsequently told Mrs Risk to avoid contact with him, since he was 'active' in treacherous activity upon his release. McCann's hostility may have been attributable to Dowdall having allegedly 'discarded his wife' in the hope of marrying McCann's stepdaughter, who had a personal fortune of £5,000. McCann professed ignorance of Neilson's presence in the capital the previous year but later became aware that Dowdall had escorted Neilson during his time in Dublin. Dowdall had been one of the first detainees to be freed (along with the northern prisoners, such as William Tennent, who were also not subject to the Banishment Act) and his release boosted the efforts of the continuing conspiracy. He was involved in organising the United Irishmen in Dublin as well as developing links (alongside William Putnam McCabe) with republicans based in England, such as the infamous Colonel Edward Despard, whose arrest in November 1802 thwarted any prospect of a combined rebellion across the British Isles.

Ross McCann suggested that Neilson had collected money in Dublin. While it is possible that this was intended to be used to pay for Neilson's expenses (which included his fare to America and the upkeep of his family), it is also conceivable that Neilson was involved in a process of moving money around to pay for the secret return of exiled United Irishmen from the continent in preparation for another uprising. A letter presented to McCann during his examination implied that Mrs Risk's maidservant had overheard Dowdall speaking of plans for another rising. This would imply that Neilson was aware of such a scheme, but McCann did not, at the time, think that Neilson's appearance in Dublin was in any way sinister, even though he was frequently in the company of Dowdall and reportedly stayed briefly with John Stockdale, who, like Neilson, was a one-time printer of a United Irish newspaper (*The Press*). Another informant, Mrs Usher, suggested that Neilson had stayed at 41 Gordon Lane during his brief spell in Dublin; she claimed that he had been unwell and that she had been sent to seek medical help.[64]

Madden's account of Neilson's last days in Ireland, based on his interviews in the 1840s with surviving United Irish veterans such as James Hope, holds that Neilson also resided at the Irishtown retreat of the publican and grocer Charles O'Hara of High Street, a northerner who had been active in Dublin in 1798, succeeding Neilson as the effective leader of the conspiracy in the capital after his arrest outside Newgate. O'Hara was again active when the military committee of the United Irishmen re-formed under men such as Philip Long, the surgeon Thomas Wright and, eventually, Robert Emmet. Neilson allegedly visited Robert Emmet at his family home outside Dublin sometime after his arrival in Ireland, again suggesting that he was at least sympathetic towards (and perhaps complicit in) the plans for a further insurrection.[65] He also met with James Dixon, the 76-year-old tanner and veteran of Irish radical politics who lived near the gaol at Kilmainham. Dixon had been a regular visitor and close confidante of Neilson during the latter's incarceration there between 1796 and 1798. Anne Neilson had often stayed in his house when she was in Dublin to visit her husband. Later confined and questioned about Neilson's reappearance in Ireland in 1802, Dixon asserted that he had happened to see Neilson 'by mere accident' and believed that his old friend had returned to Ireland only to say farewell to his wife and family. Chief Secretary William Wickham, fully aware of Dixon's involvement in the conspiracies of 1798 and 1803, was dismissive of his claims.[66] The renewal of Neilson's links with O'Hara and Dixon is suggestive of a continuity in military matters between the two outbursts of United Irish activity and Neilson's knowledge of, and support for, the Emmet conspiracy. While it would seem that

O'Hara had, for a short time at least, provided 'a most useful intelligence' to the authorities in 1800, he was now back firmly on the side of the insurgency.[67]

His final goodbyes said, Neilson prepared to depart for the United States in late October 1802 and he was accompanied to Ringsend by Hope and the veteran radical John Palmer of Catpurse Row, one of whose sons, also called John, was an associate of Emmet who had accompanied William Putnam McCabe to France in 1800. Madden recounts an emotional farewell as Neilson prepared to embark. Grateful to his protector, he placed a guinea in Hope's hand and assured him, 'Never despair, man! The enemy have it all their own way, and they will do injury only to themselves.' As Neilson boarded the ship, Hope asked Palmer to purchase provisions for the three-week journey and have them taken on board. Leaving Ireland for the last time, Neilson commenced his voyage to the United States, the latest in a long line of United Irish exiles determined to make their mark on the New World.[68] An anonymous poem published in the *Belfast News-Letter* in November may have been submitted on Neilson's behalf by his friends in the town. It echoes both his espousal of liberty and his concerns about the way in which the French Revolution developed, with its attendant dangers for Ireland:

> Oh friends, enslaved, but dear, I sigh farewell!
> An exile seeking freedom o'er the wave.
> Beneath the Gallic scourge I will not dwell;
> But live with Liberty, or share or grave![69]

Not for the first time, an arduous voyage played havoc with Neilson's health and he wrote to Anne from New York on 8 December, not long after his arrival in the United States, declaring that he had not enjoyed a day of good health since he had reached his country of exile. He was, however, able to secure the publication of his pamphlet detailing the 'faithless conduct of the Irish government' during the negotiations with the state prisoners in 1798, in which he defended himself and his colleagues from any lingering suspicions that they had, in some way, made their associates vulnerable while protecting themselves from the gallows. Eager for news from home, Neilson seems to have been contemplating a move to Charlestown in New Hampshire, a small settlement free from the crowds and ill health associated with the large cities. He wrote to Anne again at the start of the new year to say he was living frugally and that he had been approached to start a newspaper relating to Irish interests in New York, something he was uncertain about at that stage, 'both on account of my delicate health and my incapacity still of judging the true state of parties and of the country'.[70]

Neilson's fears for his health were well founded. The eastern seaboard was once again in the grip of an outbreak of yellow fever, a viral disease caused by a mosquito bite. An outbreak in Philadelphia in 1793 resulted in the deaths of approximately 10 per cent of the city's population. Fears of a similar plague reportedly saw 30,000 inhabitants leave the city in late 1802.[71] By the beginning of February, Neilson had accepted an invitation to escape from the metropolis, visiting the town of Peekskill on the Hudson, around 70 miles from New York. This period of recuperation was at the behest of his doctors. Neilson stayed with a friend, a Mr Owens.[72] He informed Anne that, having received considerable encouragement from the resident Irish community, the plan to establish a newspaper was more advanced. Neilson was also keen to be reunited with his son, William, and hoped that the boy would soon be able to make the journey and assist with preparations for the arrival of the family.[73]

By April, Neilson had visited Newburgh in Orange County and was received warmly by Isabella Tennent, sister of William Tennent, and her husband John Shaw. Shaw wrote to his brother-in-law to inform him of Neilson's three-day stay, describing him as 'so lively and healthy', compared to the ill health that had plagued him when Shaw had first welcomed the new arrival in New York the previous autumn.[74] From Newburgh, Neilson travelled to Philadelphia, where he established contact with William Kean, his former colleague from the *Northern Star*, who had been confined with him in Kilmainham, released, was then active in the rebellion in both counties Antrim and Down and captured again, only to make a dramatic escape from a Belfast prison. Neilson met with Kean and his former United Irish friend John Caldwell to discuss the process of setting up a newspaper. He also corresponded with Dr John Campbell White, a Belfast physician and United Irishman who had emigrated to Baltimore and become, in the words of Caldwell, 'an enthusiastic American'. The outcome of these contacts convinced Neilson to establish an evening newspaper in New York and he wrote to Anne to request again that young William be sent out to join him. While he was able to write without pain, he remarked that his eyesight was deteriorating and that he had to hold paper three or four inches from his eyes in order to read.[75] The last extant letter home was written on 19 May. Addressing his son, Neilson thanked him for looking after the family and requested that he communicate his affection to them. It seems that Neilson expected William to be ready to board a ship bound for New York. The short letter, written in what Neilson described as a 'scrawl', had taken nearly an hour to write 'and that in torture, owing to a terrible rheumatism'.[76]

In an effort to escape once again from the yellow fever, he boarded a boat and sailed up the Hudson River in search of solace, but fell ill and was taken off at

Poughkeepsie, then a small town, on Sunday 28 August. In cases of yellow fever, the afflicted exhibit signs of jaundice and can experience multiple organ failure. Given his long history of ill health, it is likely that Neilson's resistance levels were low. He died the following morning. He was interred with decency in the Dutch Presbyterian burying ground, located on Market Street in Poughkeepsie.[77] While many of his conspiratorial associates, such as Haslett, the two Simms, Hope, Charles Teeling, Tennent, MacNeven and Thomas Addis Emmet lived long into celebrated middle age and the tragic demises of others, like Tone, McCracken, Fitzgerald and Russell, resulted in their names becoming part of national folklore, Neilson's personal dénouement was a lonely one, isolated as he was from the friends and family who had sustained him during the difficult years of imprisonment and financial impoverishment. He was laid to rest in a town that was not his place of residence, nor even his intended destination. For someone whose political importance has been understated, the anonymous nature of his passing seems strangely appropriate.

POSTSCRIPT

The redevelopment of Poughkeepsie in the early years of the nineteenth century led to the removal of Neilson's remains from the Dutch Presbyterian burying ground in 1830 by the editor of the *Telegraph* newspaper in the town, Egbert B. Killey, who arranged for the body to be buried in the Episcopal cemetery at Christ Church. However, Neilson's contribution to the United Irish project was not to be forgotten and, in September 1880, a plot was purchased in Poughkeepsie's newer Rural Cemetery by Father James Nilan of St Peter's church in the town, who was a member of a Neilson Monument Association which had been established the previous year. A committee, consisting of John O'Brien, James Mulrein, John Moore, Chas Cooke and James Toland, was appointed to oversee the arrangements for transferring Neilson's remains once again, this time to the new cemetery.

Soon afterwards, the remains were exhumed and conveyed, in a newly made urn designed by a Mr Crook, for re-interment on Wednesday, 15 September, of that year. The urn was placed in a metal box containing a copy of each of the local newspapers, the names of subscribers to the burial fund, a list of the officers and members of the association and a copy of its prospectus and minutes. The small headstone, which had marked the earlier burial site, was also removed, restored (by the wonderfully named Mr Asa Tomb) and placed on the new grave. It read: 'If the memory of a man who discharged all the duties of his station in life as a father, husband and persecuted patriot, claims a tear, here the tribute is due.' Invited to the ceremony were Jane Neilson McAdam, Samuel's third daughter, then aged ninety and residing in Yonkers (New York), and his granddaughter, Mrs Drake. A sizeable crowd had gathered in inclement weather to mark the occasion and the pallbearers were men of significant local rank, including the mayor, William Harloe, who addressed the gathering: 'The cause of civil and religious liberty has risen and spread in many lands during the last 100 years, and whenever we find a true lover of that cause we will find one who will honor the name and memory of Samuel Neilson.'[1]

Following representations by the indefatigable Belfast antiquarian Francis Joseph Bigger, a new memorial was built on the grave and this was dedicated formally on 29 August 1905. The task of producing a new marker was undertaken by the Poughkeepsie branch of the Ancient Order of Hibernians, Division 2. Made from Quincy granite, the impressive 5-foot-high memorial was completed by James Lynch and a large crowd assembled on the 102nd anniversary of Neilson's death to listen to music and addresses, one of which was given by the priest of St Peter's, Father William Livingstone. A further oration was delivered by Father Francis J. O'Hare, an Irish priest who had, at one time, been a curate in the parish of Hilltown in County Down, not far from Neilson's birthplace at Ballyroney.[2]

* * * *

Neilson's family in Ireland would mourn the loss of a son, husband and father. His mother, Agnes Neilson (*née* Carson), died in April 1804 at the age of seventy-four.[3] Samuel Neilson's wife, Anne, who had visited her husband regularly when he was in the gaols of Kilmainham and Newgate and had written so assiduously to him at Fort George, was left to bring up the five children from the meagre profits of the haberdashery on Ann Street. The records of Rosemary Street (Third) Presbyterian Church show that an Anne Neilson married Bernard McClune on 26 December 1805 and the ceremony was conducted by Reverend Samuel Hanna.[4] Madden cites Mary Ann McCracken's fond description of Anne, whom she knew well, having worked with her to mediate in the dispute between Samuel and Henry Joy McCracken when they were prisoners in Kilmainham:

> Mrs Neilson was a very superior woman, a most exemplary wife and mother; for whom I had the highest esteem, and continued in terms of intimacy and friendship, from 1795, when I first became acquainted with her, and her death. I never saw a family so well regulated, such order and neatness, on such a limited income; and such well-trained children, most amiable and affectionate to each other, and so respectful to their mother, and all so happy together – it was quite a treat to spend an evening with them.

Anne died on 2 November 1811 and was buried in the Neilson plot in the graveyard of Knockbreda parish church, adjacent to the resting place of Samuel's older brother John and his family. The inscription on the grave describes her as 'A woman who was an ornament to her sex; who fulfilled, in the most exemplary manner, the duties of a daughter, wife, and mother.'[5]

William Bryson Neilson would live a short but distinguished life, excelling at the Belfast Academy of Reverend William Bruce and gaining employment in

1807, at the age of fourteen, in the Belfast counting house of John Martin and Co., a position that saw him despatched to Lisbon at the end of his apprenticeship to manage the import of goods from the Portuguese colonies. It was there that he learned of the death of his mother. He wrote to his sisters in a way that bore a striking resemblance to the tone of his father's letters to Anne:

> The loss of such a mother as ours is one which can never be repaired, but this much you will allow me to remark, that inordinate grief will not only be pernicious to your health, but is also displeasing to the Almighty, whose will it has been to take her to Himself. I am sure my dear girls, your reason will concur with me in this, and do not let your feelings get the better of you.

On returning to Belfast, William participated in the civic life of the town, supporting the newly established Belfast Academical Institution (the brainchild of William Drennan, among others) and the Belfast Historic Society, through which he acquired a reputation as a fine orator. In March 1816, William Neilson was at the centre of a remarkable controversy that engulfed the Academical Institution. Following a St Patrick's Day dinner held there and attended by leading members of the institution's management, toasts were drunk that were offensive to the government, which had contributed a significant amount of the money required to administer the college. These toasts proclaimed support for parliamentary reform, Catholic Emancipation, the will of the people, the fall of the Bastille, Lazare Carnot (who had sponsored the French mission to Ireland in December 1796), Marshal Michel Ney (the Napoleonic war hero who had been executed by firing squad the previous year) and 'the exiles of Erin – may they find that protection under the wing of the republican eagle, which was denied them by the monarchical lion'. The resignation of Robert Tennent (senior) and others was the price paid by the Academical Institution to preserve its financial status. William Bryson Neilson, who was at the dinner as a member of the school board, was also forced to resign, although it was not his desired course of action.[6]

He left Martin and Co. in 1813 to commence business in Belfast, but this was unsuccessful and he departed Ireland in November 1816 to establish himself in Jamaica. He wrote to his sister, Anne (who was then unmarried), to express his regret at having to borrow money for his fare from a friend and for being unable to fulfil his obligations towards her. He did, however, make financial plans for her through the auspices of a friend, William Shaw. Just as his enterprise in the West Indies was launching, however, he too succumbed to yellow fever and died on 7 February 1817, five days after taking ill. Unlike his father, William Neilson died in the company of friends; Howard Grimshaw of Belfast (a son of Nicholas Grimshaw, an Englishman who had settled in Belfast and helped pioneer the town's cotton industry) observed his friend's descent into a raving restlessness. While William did not utter any final words of farewell, he did call repeatedly for his sister, Anne, until the very end. Grimshaw, writing to his brother Robert in Belfast, noted that the doctors stated that Neilson, 'being too stout and full of blood', was poorly suited to the Jamaican climate.[7] In a eulogium delivered in Belfast by Robert Tennent (the nephew of William Tennent), a member of the Belfast Historic Society, the time William Neilson spent in the company of his captive father during his youth was recounted and mention was made of the quality of the education he received at Fort George from men whom Tennent believed Ireland should have listened to more sympathetically. Neilson kept company with a generation of young men whose fathers had pioneered the liberal spirit that prevailed in Belfast in the last quarter of the eighteenth century and their deliberations in the Historic Society and at the Academical Institution kept Presbyterian radicalism alive after the Act of Union, due to which, according to Tennent, 'Ireland has fallen from the proud name of Country to the humiliating title of Province.' Tennent saw in young Neilson the spirit of his father and this convinced him that the cause of Ireland had not been totally extinguished:

> When I witnessed the growing genius of a man such as Neilson, my mind was never conquered by despair. I did feel a hope still lingering, that the curtain had not fallen for ever on my country; that the last solemn office was not yet to be performed, and that her eyes were not to be eternally closed on her liberties and her character.[8]

William Neilson's last will and testament, dated 27 December 1816, was registered on 8 September 1818, with Robert Grimshaw, Robert Neilson and William Shaw as executors. Its terms were that his unmarried sisters (Anne and Mary) would have joint share of his estate unless one of them were to marry, in which case the whole was to be settled on the other. He requested that his aunt (Martha, the wife of Samuel Neilson's brother John) and his four sisters should accept rings as a sign of his gratitude. The will was to become invalid in the event of William marrying; Robert Grimshaw was aware of the object of his affection and the young woman was to receive a locket with some of his hair.[9]

William Neilson's sisters would live long and fulsome lives. As the eldest child, Anne's short – and at times ill-spelt – letters were sent to her father at Fort George. Samuel Neilson had written to his wife to indicate that he expected his eldest daughter to help her mother to run the shop. After her brother's death, Anne married a Mr D. Magenis from Armagh on 1 May 1818 and took up residence in Philadelphia.[10] Sophia, the second daughter (born August 1790), married John McAdam on 5 March 1811 and the couple lived in Belfast. The Neilson gravestone at Knockbreda records her death as 5 February 1872 at the age of eighty-one. When Thomas Moore's life of Lord Edward Fitzgerald was being readied for publication in 1831, Sophia Neilson wrote to William James MacNeven, the Catholic physician, United Irishman and prisoner at Fort George who later emigrated to the United States, imploring him to speak out in favour of her father and contradict the suggestion of Fitzgerald's betrayal that appeared in the book. Sophia was horrified at the 'unjust and abominable insinuation', telling MacNeven that, 'Tis hard indeed! After sacrificing property, liberty and life in the cause – to have so foul a stain cast on his memory by an Irish Catholic.' Years later, she wrote to congratulate Madden for his efforts in doing 'justice to the memory of our father'.[11] The third daughter was Jane Neilson, born on 9 September 1791. She married George McAdam of Belfast on 4 May 1813 and emigrated to New York in 1836. It was Jane who, at the ripe old age of ninety, attended the interment ceremony for her father at the Rural Cemetery in Poughkeepsie in 1880.[12]

The youngest child, Mary Neilson, is not recorded in the birth register of Rosemary Street Presbyterian Church. She married William John Hancock, the agent of Charles Brownlow's Lurgan estate before his appointment as assistant commissioner under the Irish Poor Law Act of 1838. A gravestone inside the abbey at Howth near Dublin marks Hancock's resting place and lists Mary's death as 27 July 1857, aged sixty-one. Mary was, therefore, born some time in 1795 or 1796, just prior to Samuel Neilson's arrest and subsequent detention in Kilmainham Gaol. It is known that Anne Neilson stayed frequently in Dublin to be close to her imprisoned husband (usually with the tanner James Dixon, who lived near the prison) and was even permitted on occasion to sleep with her husband in the cell. It is very probable that the infant Mary was, on occasion, brought to the gaol as well.[13] Like her older sister Sophia, Mary was anxious to preserve her father's reputation and legacy. When Madden's volumes on the lives and times of the United Irishmen were advertised in 1842, Mary had also exhorted him to avoid making the same errors about her father as Moore, who had, in her view, confused the government's attempts to blacken the name of the state prisoners at the time of the Kilmainham Treaty with a connection between Neilson and the betrayal of Lord Edward Fitzgerald.[14] The torch of liberalism in Ulster was held by Mary and her husband. Against a backdrop of loyalist antipathy towards Daniel O'Connell's campaign for Catholic Emancipation in 1828, Hancock sought to disarm the yeomanry infantry in Lurgan, which, as Allan Blackstock notes, was 'thoroughly Orange'. Hancock thus provoked the hostility of the loyalist population, earning him the epithet William 'Papist' Hancock.[15]

* * * *

Samuel Neilson's Belfast was the epicentre of political radicalism in Ireland from 1791 to 1796. His arrest in September of 1796, along with that of other notables, shifted the leadership of the United Irishmen towards Dublin. But with the north subdued before, during and after the rebellion, the roots of the liberty tree would soon be disturbed as alternative, conservative forces were at work. The story of Belfast's political, theological and cultural development in the years after the Union has been analysed expertly in recent times by historians such as Allan Blackstock and Jonathan Jeffrey Wright. Contrary to popular belief (or, in some cases, wish), Presbyterian attitudes changed neither unanimously nor instantly after 1798, with evangelical and unionist outlooks competing with liberal and radical visions.[16] As early as 1806, however, it was Nelson, not Neilson, who was high in the town's consciousness. Following the death of the celebrated naval hero at Trafalgar the previous October, a Nelson Club was established in Belfast to promote both patriotism and loyalty during what became a critical phase in the war against France. Its membership included two men associated with the radical set a decade before, Cunningham Greg and Gilbert McIlveen Jun., the latter a founder member of the Society of United Irishmen.[17]

One aspect of Neilson's historical legacy, the *Northern Star*, was not quite extinguished. Writing from Bath in April 1803, John Robertson, describing himself as a good friend to the *News-Letter*, wrote anxiously to John Lees at the post office in Dublin to relay information from a Mr Black in Belfast. Dougherty, the printer, had travelled to Dublin to seek a licence to publish a second newspaper in the town. While it was not known who the partners were, it was thought that they were associated with the *Star* and that the aim was to 'rekindle the flame of dissension and rebellion'. Reports indicated that the proposed new venture was not designed to make a profit; the aim was to injure the *News-Letter* for its part in supporting government policy. Robertson reminded Lees that William Simms had been denied a licence some years earlier, 'it being easier to prevent a fire being kindled than to extinguish it after it is once begun', and suggested that the new attempt should be dealt with in a similar fashion. The plan failed to take off, although a second newspaper, the *Belfast Commercial Chronicle*, did materialise two years later. Martha McTier noted dryly that the new venture, with the conservative Belfast postmaster Thomas Whinnery as one of the several proprietors, was not destined to inspire: 'half a dozen such would not make a poor Neilson'.[18]

McTier's assessment was accurate. Samuel Neilson's contribution to the United Irish project had been enormous. Not only was he critical to the formation of the society in 1791, his editorship of the *Northern Star* provided a means of popular politicisation that was quite remarkable, feeding an audience of thousands with twice-weekly accounts of public mobilisation, philosophical arguments, satirical insights and savage condemnations of government-inspired assaults on the advocates of political change and innovation. His control of nascent Belfast republicanism and strategic military planning until his arrest in late 1796 makes him a crucial influence on the trajectory of the United Irishmen; he continued to exert this influence during his imprisonment and after his eventual release in February 1798. His role in orchestrating the early stages of the rebellion and in negotiating the settlement that prevented further loss of blood (while preserving elements of the organisation's basic structure) makes him a figure of the first rank. Neilson's accomplishments confirm him as an undeniable heavyweight in the development of Belfast, Ulster and Irish radicalism.

Subsequent events derailed the idealistic vision of the United Irishmen, namely, to end religious division and establish a form of national government that owed more to the spirit of participation and democracy and less to social or religious self-interest. The 1798 Rebellion had unleashed a spiral of violence and sectarian toxicity that the United Irishmen could scarcely have predicted. However, despite this ultimate failure, the sometimes shadowy figure whom Wolfe Tone nicknamed 'the Jacobin' deserves, without question, to be viewed as central to any understanding of the momentous decade of the 1790s.

ENDNOTES

Introduction

1 T. Bartlett (ed.), *Life of Theobald Wolfe Tone: Memoirs, Journals and Political Writings, Compiled and Arranged by William T.W. Tone* (Dublin: The Lilliput Press, 1998), pp. 47–8; 120.

2 Tone's use of the term 'Blefescu' was a nod to the fictional island of Blefuscu in Jonathan Swift's *Gulliver's Travels*, which was considered to be a reference to France. Belfast's Francophile tendency at this time may have prompted Tone to christen the town thus. It is possible that Tone's reference to MacDonnell as 'the Hypocrite' was a pun on Hippocrates, the acknowledged father of medicine. In 1803, the physician, who was well acquainted with most of the radical set in Belfast, subscribed to the fund raised to reward anyone providing information that would lead to the apprehension of Thomas Russell, who had attempted to raise Ulster in support of Robert Emmet's failed uprising. MacDonnell's act of betrayal earned him the opprobrium of his former friends.

3 NAI, Frazer MSS II/40, information of William Bird, n.d., late 1796.

4 T. Moore, *The Life and Death of Lord Edward Fitzgerald*, 2 (London: 1831), pp. 78–87; TCD, Madden MSS 873/534, Sophia McAdam (Neilson) to William James MacNeven, 31 August 1831; 873/189 Mary Hancock (Neilson) to R.R. Madden, 11 April 1842.

5 J. Wills, *Lives of Illustrious and Distinguished Irishmen*, 4, 1 (Dublin: McGregor, Polson and Co., 1845), pp. 62–3; J. Lindsey, *The Shining Life and Death of Lord Edward Fitzgerald* (London: Rich & Cowan, n.d.), pp. 133–6. Lindsey's hostile account of Neilson's 'utter folly' refers to him as a 'giant' whose 'gigantic' frame was conspicuous at a time when Lord Edward was the most wanted man in Ireland.

6 T. Pakenham, *The Year of Liberty: The Great Irish Rebellion of 1798* (London: Hodder and Stoughton, 1969), p. 103.

7 J. Kelly, Review article, *Studia Hibernica,* 28 (1994), p. 173. Kelly notes that Neilson is a figure of importance 'whose fragmented biography represents the key to unlocking the secrets of radicalism in Ulster in the 1790s'.

8 NA, Kew HO100/34/50, Prospectus of the *Northern Star*, 18 November 1791; B. Inglis, *The Freedom of the Press in Ireland 1784–1841* (London: Faber and Faber, 1954); J. Gray, 'A Tale of Two Newspapers: The Contest Between the Belfast News-letter and the Northern Star in the 1790s' in J. Gray and W. McCann (eds), *An Uncommon Bookman: Essays in Memory of J.R.R. Adams* (Belfast: Linen Hall Library, 1996); G. O'Brien, 'Spirit, Impartiality and Independence – the Northern Star 1792–7', *Eighteenth Century Ireland*, 13 (1998), pp. 7–23.

9 R.R. Madden, *The United Irishmen – Their Lives and Times*, 4th Series, 2 (Dublin: J. Mullany, 1860), p. 156.

10 J. Quinn, *Soul on Fire: A Life of Thomas Russell 1767–1803* (Dublin: Irish Academic Press, 2002); J. Gray, 'Thomas Russell: Millennial Vision: Thomas Russell Reassessed', *Linenhall Review*, 4 (1989).

11 See Madden, *The United Irishmen – Their Lives and Times*, 4th Series, 2, Samuel Neilson to Anne Neilson, 5 September 1799, pp. 107–8.

12 See Bartlett, *Life of Theobald Wolfe Tone*, p. 63.

Chapter 1

1 K. Muhr, *Place Names of Northern Ireland*, 6, County Down IV (Belfast: QUB, 1996), p. 153.

2 Presbyterian Historical Society of Ireland, *A History of Congregations in the Presbyterian Church in Ireland 1610–1982* (Belfast: PHS, 1982).

3 PRONI, T/1013/2/B/#257, Marriage records, Carnmoney Presbyterian Church, donated by Miss McKinney of Sentry Hill; J.W. Lockington, *Ballyroney: Its Church and People* (1979), pp. 7–8; *Fasti of the Presbyterian Church in Ireland*, 639; 'Entries from Rev Alexander Neilson's Family Bible' in *The Irish Ancestor*, 1, 2 (1969), pp. 76–7.

4 PRONI, T/1013/2/B/#257; *The Irish Ancestor*, 1, 2 (1969), p. 77.

5 See Lockington, *Ballyroney: Its Church and People*, p. 15.

6 *Ordnance Survey Memoirs of Ireland – Parishes of County Down 1 1834–35 (South Down)* 3 (Belfast: Institute of Irish Studies, 1990), pp. 10–18.

7 See Fasti, *Records of the General Synod*, 3, 1778–1820 (Belfast, 1898); see PRONI, T/1013/2/B/#257. Lockington gives the date of his death as 31 May 1782. Reverend Neilson was buried in the same grave as his predecessor, Reverend Robert Thompson. Presbyterian Historical Society of Ireland, *A History of Congregations in the Presbyterian Church in Ireland 1610–1982* (Belfast: PHS, 1982); 'Reverend Neilson's Grave', *Ulster Journal of Archaeology*, 14 (1908), p.142; PRONI, D/654/A3/1B, Freeholder Poll Book, 1783. See also *Belfast News-Letter*, 9 November 1798.

8 The year of Samuel Neilson's birth has generally been cited as 1761, although the marriage records of Carnmoney Presbyterian Church and a reference in the family Bible state that he was born in 1762. Reverend King was succeeded as minister in Dromara by James Jackson Birch, the brother of Reverend Thomas Ledlie Birch, the dissenting minister in Saintfield who would be an influential United Irishman in the 1790s and a regular contributor to Samuel Neilson's *Northern Star*. A sister of the two reverends Birch – Mary – would marry the son of Reverend King.

9 See PRONI, T/1013/2/B/#257; *The Irish Ancestor* 1, 2 (1969), p. 77. The best account of Neilson's life was compiled by R.R. Madden, the Young Ireland sympathiser who recorded details of the leading United Irishmen in a series of volumes. Madden erroneously gives Samuel's date of birth as 17 September 1761 and this has been quoted frequently since. R.R. Madden, *The United Irishmen – Their Lives and Times*, 4th Series, 2 (Dublin: J. Mullany, 1860), p. 2. See also Madden, *The United Irishmen – Their Lives and Times*, 2nd Series, 1, I (Dublin: J. Mullany, 1860) for additional information on Neilson.

10 J.J. Monaghan, 'A social and economic history of Belfast 1790–1800', (unpublished PhD thesis, Queen's University Belfast, 1936).

11 H. Joy, *Belfast Politics or a Collection of the Debates and Resolutions, and other Proceedings of that Town* (Belfast: 1794), pp. 94–7.

12 G. Chambers, *Faces of Change: The Belfast and Northern Ireland Chambers of Commerce and Industry 1783–1983* (Belfast: NI Chamber of Commerce and Industry, 1984), p. 3.

13 H. Joy, *Historical Collections Relative to the Town of Belfast: From the Earliest Period to the Union with Great Britain* (Belfast, 1817), pp. 225–7.

14 A.T.Q. Stewart, *A Deeper Silence: The Hidden Origins of the United Irishmen* (London: Faber and Faber, 1993), p. 4.
15 For a masterly treatment of Irish parliamentary politics, see E.M. Johnston-Liik, *History of the Irish Parliament*, 6 Volumes (Belfast: Ulster Historical Foundation, 2002).
16 G. Benn, *A History of the Town of Belfast from the Earliest Times to the Close of the Eighteenth Century* (London: Marcus Ward & Co., 1877), p. 625; *Belfast News-Letter*, 17–21 March 1780. In 1791, there would be 167 licensed publicans in Belfast; see Joy, *Belfast Politics*, p. 97.
17 UM, 603–1914 Minute book of the Rathfriland Volunteers.
18 *Belfast News-Letter*, 21–24 July 1778.
19 See G. Benn, *A History of the Town of Belfast*, p. 754–5.
20 *Belfast News-Letter*, 18–22 June 1779.
21 *Belfast News-Letter*, 30 January–2 February 1781; 2–6 February 1781.
22 PRONI, T654/2 Rosemary Street Church Register of Baptisms and Marriages.
23 D. Armstrong, *Rev Sinclare Kelburn 1754–1802: Preacher, Pastor, Patriot* (Belfast: Presbyterian Historical Society, 2001), p. 8; Rev. J.W. Nelson, 'The Belfast Presbyterians 1670–1830: An analysis of their political and social interest' (unpublished PhD thesis, Queen's University, Belfast, 1985).
24 PHS, MIC/IP/7 Third Belfast Congregation Committee Minute Book.
25 *Belfast News-Letter*, 24–27 July 1781.
26 See H. Joy, *Historical Collections*, pp. 208–9.
27 Ibid., pp. 211–12.
28 *Belfast News-Letter*, 1–5 August 1783.
29 *Belfast Mercury*, 9 January 1784; 23 January 1784.
30 Ibid., 30 April 1784.
31 Ibid., 14 May 1784.
32 See H. Joy, *Historical Collections*, pp. 295–6.
33 *Belfast Mercury*, 9 July 1784.
34 Ibid., 13 July 1784.
35 Ibid., 4 May 1784. It is likely that some of these new recruits were Catholic. This dramatic development prompted savage criticism from conservatives who believed that invitations to Catholics to become members of Volunteer companies blatantly undermined the constitution and the laws under it.
36 Ibid., 8 and 15 October 1784.
37 PRONI, T654/2 Rosemary Street Church Register of Baptisms and Marriages. The church records spell Anne Bryson's name as 'Mrs Ann Neilson' in the marriage record, although her name is spelt 'Anne' on the family gravestone in Knockbreda graveyard, Belfast. Agnes (called Anne) was born on 8 March 1788; Sophia on 5 August 1790; Jane on 9 September 1791; William Bryson Neilson in 1794 and Mary in 1795 or 1796. Mary Neilson is buried in the old abbey at Howth. She was married to William John Hancock of Lisburn. Her year of birth has been calculated from the gravestone inscription. *Ulster Journal of Archaeology*, 7 (1901).
38 *Belfast News-Letter*, 18–21 July 1786.
39 *Belfast News-Letter*, 30 June–4 July 1786; 11–14 July 1786.
40 *Belfast Mercury*, 17 January 1786; 20 March 1786; 21 December 1786.
41 *Belfast News-Letter*, 17–21 November 1786; 21–24 November 1786.
42 PRONI, T654/2 Rosemary Street Church Register of Baptisms and Marriages.
43 *Belfast News-Letter*, 6–10 July 1787.
44 *Belfast News-Letter*, 17–20 July 1787.
45 *Belfast News-Letter*, 19–22 February 1788; 9–13 May 1788.

46 See R.R. Madden, *The United Irishmen – Their Lives and Times*, 4th Series, 2 (Dublin: J. Mullany, 1860), p. 2.

47 See *Records of the General Synod*, 3, 1778–1820 (Belfast: 1898).

Chapter 2

1 *Belfast News-Letter*, 3–6 February 1789.

2 Martha McTier of Belfast, sister of William Drennan, noted: 'All the weighty interest in the kingdom except the Hillsboroughs are united for appointing the Prince regent with unlimited power.' J. Agnew (ed.), *The Drennan–McTier Letters 1776–1819*, 1, 1776–1793 (Dublin: Irish Manuscripts Commission, 1998), Martha McTier to William Drennan, undated, p. 325.

3 *Belfast News-Letter*, 13–17 March 1789.

4 *Belfast News-Letter*, 17–20 March; 24–27 March 1789.

5 *The Patriot Soldier: or Irish Volunteer. A Poem, Written by a Member of the Belfast First Volunteer Company* (Belfast, 1789); *Belfast News-Letter*, 17–21 April 1789. Neilson did write poetry and song. A five-stanza commemoration of the French Revolution written for the celebrations of July 1792, with Neilson's signature below it, can be found in the Rebellion Papers at the National Archives in Dublin. NAI, Rebellion Papers 620/19/87.

6 *Belfast News-Letter*, 21–24 July 1789.

7 *Belfast News-Letter*, 8–11 September 1789.

8 *Belfast News-Letter*, 21–25 August; 25–28 August 1789.

9 H. Joy, *Historical Collections Relative to the Town of Belfast* (Belfast: 1817), pp. 341–2.

10 *Belfast News-Letter*, 20–23 April 1790.

11 *Belfast News-Letter*, 9–12 March 1790.

12 PRONI, D/654/A3/1B Poll Book Ballybrick townland; *Belfast News-Letter*, 9–13 November 1798 (list of Neilson's assets at public auction); see E.M. Johnston-Liik, *History of the Irish Parliament 1692–1800*, 2, pp. 163–4.

13 *Belfast News-Letter*, 31 March–2 April 1790.

14 *Belfast News-Letter*, 27–30 April; 7–11 May 1790. Most accounts of Neilson assert erroneously that he was active in supporting the independent cause in County Down. See W.T. Latimer, *Ulster Biographies Relating to the Rebellion of 1798* (Belfast: Presbyterian Historical Society, 1998 ed.), p. 28.

15 J. Agnew (ed.), *The Drennan–McTier Letters*, 1, William Drennan to Samuel McTier, 3 May 1790, p. 349; W.S. Dickson, *A Narrative of the Confinement and Exile of William Steel Dickson D.D.* (Dublin: Stockdale, 1812), p. 20.

16 *Belfast News-Letter*, 2–6 April 1790.

17 *A Collection of all the Authenticated Public Addresses, Resolution, and Advertisements Relative to the Late Election of Knights for the Shire of County Antrim Together with a Correct List of the Poll. By a member of the Independent Committee* (Belfast, 1790).

18 *Belfast News-Letter*, 28 May–1 June 1790.

19 *Belfast News-Letter*, 25–29 June 1790; Samuel Neilson's first 'biographer', Bernard Dornin of 150 Pearl Street, New York, asserted that Neilson began to take upon himself the direction of a newspaper in 1790: B. Dornin, *Sketch of the Life of Samuel Neilson of Belfast Ireland, Editor of the Northern Star and Member of the Irish Directory* (New York: 1804). A copy of this brief sketch can be accessed in the Madden Papers at Trinity College, Dublin: TCD, Madden MSS 873/191.

20 See *A Collection of all the Authenticated Public Addresses*, pp. 142–5. For Caldwell, see PRONI, T/3541/5/3 Particulars of History of a North County Irish Family – an autobiographical account, c. 1850; *Belfast News-Letter*, 15–18 June 1790.
21 *Belfast News-Letter,* 11–15 June 1790.
22 E.M. Johnston-Liik, *History of the Irish Parliament 1692–1800*, 6, p. 348.
23 PRONI, Sharman Papers D856/D/5, William Sharman to Samuel Neilson, 28 August 1790.
24 *Belfast News-Letter*, 29 June–2 July 1790.
25 *Belfast News-Letter*, 20–23 July 1790.
26 *Belfast News-Letter*, 23–26 November; 10–14 December 1790.
27 *Belfast News-Letter*, 22–26 October 1790.
28 LHL, Belfast Charitable Society Committee Book 5 February 1791; 12 March 1791.
29 *Belfast News-Letter*, 15–18 March; 29 March–1 April 1791.
30 *Belfast News-Letter*, 14–17 June 1791.
31 A.T.Q. Stewart, *A Deeper Silence: The Hidden Origins of the United Irishmen* (London: Faber and Faber, 1993), p. 155. John Robb (Rabb) would later be Neilson's printer at the *Northern Star* office in Wilson's Court. Lowry was from Linen Hill, near what is now Katesbridge in County Down, and played a very significant role within the United Irish organisation. Lowry's relative youth in 1791 places a question mark over whether he would have been in the company of such older and well-established radicals. He was, however, considered a significant enough figure to accompany Neilson and Tone to the trouble spot of Rathfriland the following year. In a letter from Elizabeth Lowry to the Chief Secretary Lord Pelham dated 1797, in which she asked him to permit her son to return to Ireland whence he had fled in June, Mrs Lowry claims that her son was by that time in his twenty-second year (letter in the possession of the current owners of Linen Hill, Katesbridge). McCabe, meanwhile, was a watchmaker and cotton manufacturer who was very friendly with Neilson and was a founder member of the Society of United Irishmen. McCracken was the son of the prosperous merchant Captain John McCracken and was himself a cotton manufacturer who would later command the United Irish forces at the Battle of Antrim in June 1798.
32 A.T.Q. Stewart, 'A Stable Unseen Power: Dr William Drennan and the Formation of the United Irishmen', in M. Roberts, J. Bossy and P. Jupp (eds), *Essays Presented to Michael Roberts: sometime professor of Modern History in the Queen's University of Belfast* (Belfast: Blackstaff, 1976), pp. 84–5.
33 See Agnew, *The Drennan–McTier Letters*, 1, William Drennan to Samuel McTier, 21 May 1791, pp. 357–8. Neilson's name was spelt 'Nelson' in the letter. This is a common misspelling of his name in the primary sources. It is clear that Drennan was writing about Samuel Neilson.
34 Ibid., McTier to Drennan, 2 July 1791, p. 360.
35 *Belfast News-Letter*, 11–15 June 1790.
36 J. Quinn, *Soul on Fire: A Life of Thomas Russell* (Dublin: Irish Academic Press, 2002), p. 22.
37 C.J. Woods (ed.), *Journals and Memoirs of Thomas Russell* (Dublin: Irish Academic Press, 1991), p. 42.
38 Ibid., pp. 53–6.
39 See T. Bartlett (ed.), *Life of Theobald Wolfe Tone* (Dublin: The Lilliput Press, 1998), pp. 118–19.
40 *Belfast News-Letter*, 15–19 July 1791.
41 N. Rodgers, *Equiano and Anti-Slavery in Eighteenth Century Belfast* (Belfast: The Belfast Society, 2000), pp. 6–12; *Belfast News-Letter,* 16–20 December 1791; O. Equiano, *The Interesting Narrative and other Writings* (London: Penguin, 2003 ed.), p. 235. Neilson was a subscriber to the Irish edition of Equiano's narrative, taking five copies (p. 380). LHL, Belfast

Charitable Society Committee Book, 17 December 1791. At this meeting, the committee's plans to forbid a publican from opening a public house in the vicinity of the poor house were dropped in favour of accepting securities that he would not sell spirits to any inmate.

42 *Belfast News-Letter*, 15–19 July 1791; 6–9 September; 9–13 September 1791.

43 M. Elliott, *Wolfe Tone: Prophet if Irish Independence* (New Haven and London: Yale University Press: 1989), pp. 126–33.

44 See T. Bartlett, *Life of Theobald Wolfe Tone*, p. 47.

45 L.H. Parsons, 'The Mysterious Mr Digges', in *William and Mary Quarterly*, 22, 3 (1965), pp. 486–92. Digges was reputedly threatened with prison for failing to return a set of silver spurs loaned to him by Neilson. James Quinn believes it more likely that Digges' freedom was in doubt due to debt. In 1792, he was arrested during a shopping trip to Glasgow after stealing from shops and from his travelling companions. J. Quinn, *Soul on Fire: A Life of Thomas Russell* (Dublin: Irish Academic Press, 2002), pp. 38–9.

46 See T. Bartlett, *Life of Theobald Wolfe Tone*, pp. 119–23.

47 Historical Manuscripts Commission – Thirteenth Report, Appendix Part VIII, *The Manuscripts and Correspondence of James, First Earl of Charlemont*, 2 (London: 1894), Haliday to Charlemont, 5 November 1791, p. 160.

48 NAI, Rebellion Papers 620/15/8/1, *Northern Star* minute book.

49 NAI, Rebellion Papers 620/19/42/1–4; replies to Neilson, Simms and Caldwell, correspondence from Thomas Walsh of Armagh, David McComb of Dromore, Will Forsythe of Larne and Thomas Armstrong of Richill (all October 1791).

50 NAI, Rebellion Papers, 620/19/42/5, Nicholas Browne (Dungannon) to proprietors, 8 October 1791.

51 NAI, Rebellion Papers 620/19/42/15,16,21 and 27, John Moore of Carrickfergus, John Boyd of Ballymoney, Alexander Crawford of Lisburn and Reverend Thomas Ledlie Birch of Saintfield to the proprietors, all October 1791.

52 NAI, Rebellion Papers, 620/19/42/24, R. Hyde to proprietors, 12 October 1791.

53 NAI Rebellion Papers, 620/19/42/18, G. Dickson to proprietors, 10 October 1791.

54 NAI, Rebellion Papers 620/15/8/1, *Northern Star* minute book.

55 See J. Agnew, *The Drennan–McTier Letters*, 1, William Drennan to Samuel McTier, Thursday, n.d., November 1791, p. 371.

56 NA Kew, HO/100/34/50, Printed prospectus of the *Northern Star*, 18 November 1791.

57 *Belfast News-Letter*, 9–13 December 1791.

58 *Belfast News-Letter*, 20–23 December 1791; 27–30 December 1791; 31 December 1791–3 January 1792.

Chapter 3

1 Until late 1793, the *Northern Star* would be published on Wednesdays and Saturdays.

2 NAI, Rebellion Papers 620/15/8/1, *Northern Star* minute book, 1791–2.

3 Ibid. Meeting held on 2 February 1792. *Northern Star*, 28 January–1 February 1792.

4 See R.R. Madden, *The United Irishmen – Their Lives and Times*, 4th Series, 2, pp. 20–1.

5 *Northern Star*, 11–14 January 1792.

6 NAI, Rebellion Papers 620/15/8/1, *Northern Star* minute book, 1791–2.

7 See Madden, p. 18.

8 *Northern Star*, 8–11 February 1792.

9 Ibid., 31 March–4 April 1792.

10 Ibid., 4–7 April 1792.
11 For an excellent analysis of the philosophical influences on the Patriot and United Irish traditions, see S. Small, *Political Thought in Ireland* 1776–1798 (Oxford: Clarendon Press, 2002).
12 *Northern Star*, 5–8 December 1792.
13 *Northern Star*, 24–28 November 1792.
14 *Northern Star*, 30 March–3 April 1793; 14–18 November 1793.
15 Ibid., 17–21 November 1792.
16 Ibid., 27–30 June 1792; 9–13 June 1792; 20–23 June 1792.
17 Historical Manuscripts Commission – Thirteenth Report, Appendix Part VIII, *The Manuscripts and Correspondence of James, First Earl of Charlemont*, 2, (London: 1894), Charlemont to Haliday, 15 December 1791, p. 182.
18 *Northern Star*, 21–25 January 1792.
19 *Northern Star*, 25–28 January 1792.
20 H. Joy, *Historical Collections Relative to the Town of Belfast: From the Earliest Period to the Union with Great Britain* (Belfast: 1817), pp. 363–4; H. Joy, *Belfast Politics or a Collection of the Debates and Resolutions, and other Proceedings of that Town* (Belfast: 1794), pp. 3–22; *Northern Star*, 8–11 February 1792.
21 See Joy, *Belfast Politics*, p. 22. Interestingly, Robert Getty, one of those who had called for the meeting in the first place, sided with the moderates.
22 *Northern Star*, 18–21 April 1792.
23 Ibid., 5–9 May 1792.
24 *Belfast Mercury*, 16 March 1786.
25 *Northern Star*, 2–5 May 1792.
26 J. Agnew (ed.), *The Drennan–McTier Letters 1776–1819*, 1, 1776–1793, William Drennan to Samuel McTier, 2 April 1792, p. 404.
27 *Northern Star*, 23–27 June; 4–7 July 1792.
28 *Northern Star*, 4–7 July 1792.
29 M. Elliott, *Wolfe Tone: Prophet of Irish Independence* (New Haven and London: Yale University Press, 1989), pp. 173–5.
30 T. Bartlett (ed.), *Life of Theobald Wolfe Tone*, pp.133–5.
31 *Northern Star*, 11–14 July 1792; 14–18 July 1792. In the latter issue, it was noted rather acerbically that the *Belfast News-Letter* quoted only the opinion of its editor and not the majority view as expressed by Kelburn and Neilson.
32 See T. Bartlett (ed.), *Life of Theobald Wolfe Tone*, p. 135.
33 NAI, Rebellion Papers 620/19/87. The song is in Neilson's hand and includes the line ''Mong the sons of the North may its glow soon be found.'
34 For a list of the harpers, see H. Joy, *Belfast Politics or a Collection of the Debates and Resolutions, and other Proceedings of that Town*, p. 51. The oldest player was 86 years old and the youngest 15 years old. Six of the players were blind. The female harper was Rose Mooney from Meath, whose age was not given.
35 T. Bartlett (ed.), *Life of Theobald Wolfe Tone,* pp. 131–2.
36 *Northern Star*, 14–18 July 1792.
37 G. O'Brien, 'Spirit, Impartiality and Independence: The Northern Star, 1792–1797', in *Eighteenth Century Ireland*, 13 (1998) p. 13.
38 For an insight into the Defenders, see L.M. Cullen, 'The Internal Politics of the United Irishmen', and M. Elliott, 'The Defenders in Ulster', both in D. Dickson, D. Keogh and K. Whelan (eds), *The United Irishmen, Radicalism and Rebellion* (Dublin: The Lilliput Press,

1993), pp. 176–96; pp. 222–33: L.M. Cullen, 'The Political Structures of the Defenders', in H. Gough and D. Dickson (eds), *Ireland and the French Revolution* (Dublin: Irish Academic Press, 1989), pp. 117–38.

39 *Belfast News-Letter*, 31 March–3 April 1789.

40 Sir R. Musgrave, *Memoirs of the Different Rebellions in Ireland* (Dublin, 1801), p. 105. Despite the anti-Catholic nature of the work, Musgrave's collection of evidence was praised by R.B. McDowell and the detail acknowledged by Dr David Dickson in his foreword to the fourth printing of the book (Indiana: Round Tower Books, 1995).

41 *Northern Star*, 12–16 May 1792. Neilson's editorial in this edition expressed his serious concern about events in the area. The raising of sectarian tensions would undermine the United Irish aspiration both at this time and later.

42 PRONI, Downshire Papers D/607/B/359, Robert Ross Rowan to Downshire, 16 May 1792; D/607/B/361, Downshire to Westmoreland, 18 May 1792.

43 PRONI, Downshire Papers D/607/B/364, Lord Annesley to Downshire, 1 June 1792.

44 Fletcher's subscription to the *Northern Star* was one of several in the vicinity, along with those of the leading Defender Roger Magennis and Alexander Lowry of Linen Hill. Fletcher's lease of the 28-acre farm at Ballybrick is noted in a list of Neilson's assets in the *Belfast News-Letter*, 9–13 November 1798.

45 Lowry's Volunteer role was identified by T.G.F. Paterson, 'The Irish Volunteers of Ulster 1778–1793; County Down', in *Irish Sword*, 7, 28 (1966), pp. 204–30. He was on the list of Neilson's secret Volunteer committee in Belfast in 1791 (see note 31, Chapter 2). He would flee Ireland in 1797, ending up in Stavanger, Norway, where he married. Lowry returned to Ulster in 1806. I am indebted to the work of Mr John McCabe of Stoneyford, County Antrim, for information relating to Lowry, a much under-researched figure in the United Irish movement.

46 Probably John Cowan of Carnew, captain of the Waringsford Volunteers (see T.G.F. Paterson above). Cowan later acted as a colonel in the military structure of the United Irishmen in Down. See K.L. Dawson, 'The Military Leadership of the United Irishmen in County Down 1796–8', in M. Hill, B. Turner, K. Dawson (eds), *1798 Rebellion in County Down* (Newtownards: Colourpoint Press, 1998), pp. 20–39; T. Bartlett (ed.), *Life of Theobald Wolfe Tone*, pp. 137–8.

47 *Northern Star*, 18–21 July 1792.

48 T. Bartlett (ed.), *Life of Theobald Wolfe Tone*, pp. 142–4.

49 Ibid., pp. 146–7. Details of the meeting with Downshire were submitted to the *Northern Star* under the pseudonym 'XY'. *Northern Star*, 25–29 August 1792. Unrest in the south Down area was not confined to Rathfriland and the surrounding district. The Men of Mourne Volunteers in Kilkeel reconstituted themselves in August 1792 'to help maintain peace in the neighbourhood'. UM,188/Zg3662, Minute book of the Men of Mourne Volunteers.

50 *Northern Star*, 5–8 September 1792; 29 September–3 October 1792; 3–6 October 1792; 6–10 October 1792; 17–20 October 1792.

51 T. Bartlett (ed.), *Life of Theobald Wolfe Tone*, Neilson to Tone, 21 November 1792, p. 184. Teeling was a leading Catholic with impeccable Defender connections. Two of his sons, Bartholomew and Charles, were heavily implicated in the United Irish conspiracy. Teeling was also the father-in-law of the leading Defender in Down, John Magennis.

52 Ibid., Neilson to Tone, 29 November 1792, pp. 185–6.

53 J. Agnew (ed.), *The Drennan–McTier Letters*, 1, Drennan to Martha McTier, 25 November 1792; Martha McTier to Drennan, (undated) late 1792, pp. 428–431.

54 T. Bartlett (ed.), *Life of Theobald Wolfe Tone*, Neilson to Tone (undated), p. 186.

55 *Northern Star*, 5–8 December 1792; 8–12 December 1792.
56 Historical Manuscripts Commission – Thirteenth Report, Appendix Part VIII, *The Manuscripts and Correspondence of James, First Earl of Charlemont*, 2 (London, 1894), Haliday to Charlemont, 16 December 1792, p. 208.

Chapter 4

1 *Northern Star*, 12–15 December 1792.
2 KHLC, Camden MSS U840/0147/4/2, (n.d.). See also N. Curtin, 'The Transformation of the Society of United Irishmen into a Mass Based Revolutionary Organisation', *Irish Historical Studies*, 24, 96 (November 1985, pp. 471–3.
3 J. Agnew (ed.), *The Drennan–McTier Letters 1776–1819*, 1, 1776–1793, Martha McTier to William Drennan, 25 December 1792, p. 452.
4 *Northern Star*, 25–28 July; 8–11 August; 10–13 October; 17–21 November 1792. Scottish radical activity is analysed in E.W. McFarland, *Ireland and Scotland in the Age of Revolution: Planting the Green Bough* (Edinburgh: Edinburgh University Press, 1994).
5 Ibid., 1–5 December 1792. Henry and John Sheares, both of whom would be hanged in 1798 for their role in promoting rebellion in Ireland, were also at this meeting. L. Swords, *The Green Cockade: The Irish in the French Revolution 1789–1815* (Dublin: Glendale Press, 1989), p. 66.
6 J. Agnew (ed.), *The Drennan–McTier Letters 1776–1819*, 1, 1776–1793, Drennan to Sam McTier, 31 December 1792, p. 455.
7 H. Joy, *Historical Collections Relative to the Town of Belfast: From the Earliest Period to the Union with Great Britain* (Belfast: 1817), pp. 396–8.
8 S. McSkimin, *History of the Irish Rebellion in 1798 particularly in Antrim, Down and Derry* (Belfast: Cleeland and Co., 1853), p. 28.
9 *Northern Star*, 1–5 December 1792.
10 J. Agnew (ed.), *The Drennan–McTier Letters 1776–1819*, 1, 1776–1793, Drennan to Sam McTier, 31 December 1792, pp. 455–6; NAI, Rebellion Papers 620/20/42, anon. to correspondence committee, Dublin, January 1793.
11 H. Joy, *Historical Collections Relative to the Town of Belfast: From the Earliest Period to the Union with Great Britain* (Belfast: 1817), p. 399.
12 Historical Manuscripts Commission Thirteenth Report, Appendix Part VIII, *The Manuscripts and Correspondence of James, First Earl of Charlemont*, Vol. II (London: 1894), Haliday to Charlemont (undated, probably December 1792), p. 394.
13 PRONI, Tennent Papers D/1748/D/1/5/19, Rev. John Tennent to his son John Tennent, 19 October 1792.
14 J. Agnew (ed.), *The Drennan–McTier Letters*, 1, Drennan to Sam McTier, 28 December 1792, pp. 454–7; Martha McTier to Drennan, 31 December 1792; *Northern Star*, 29 December 1792–2 January 1793.
15 *Northern Star*, 31 December 1792–2 January 1793.
16 *Northern Star*, 9–12 January 1793.
17 *Northern Star*, 30 January–2 February 1793. The full list of offending publications appeared in the paper in July and included the resolutions of the Belfast meeting of 26 December 1792; the Irish Jacobins' resolutions of 15 December 1792; the resolutions of a meeting of Dublin United Irishmen, 19 December 1792; the Masonic Lodge 730 resolutions, 19 December 1792; the resolutions of Newtownards Volunteers, 29 December 1792; a letter from Carrickfergus, published on 12 January 1793. Another article deemed offensive was one respecting the

results of a reform of Parliament that appeared on 5 December 1792. *Northern Star*, 3–6 July 1793.

18 J. Agnew (ed.), *The Drennan–McTier Letters*, 1, Drennan to Martha McTier, (n.d.) January 1793, p. 462. *Northern Star*, 23–26 January 1793.

19 *Northern Star,* 16–20 February 1793.

20 J. Agnew (ed.), *The Drennan–McTier Letters*, 1, Samuel Neilson to William Drennan, 17 February 1793, pp. 491–2.

21 T. Bartlett (ed.), *Life of Theobald Wolfe Tone*, Neilson to Tone, 28 February 1793, p. 223.

22 *Northern Star*, 20–23 January 1793.

23 A.T.Q. Stewart, 'The transformation of Presbyterian radicalism in the North of Ireland 1792–1825' (unpublished MA thesis, Queen's University, Belfast) pp. 35–50. See also Stewart, *A Deeper Silence: The Hidden Origins of the United Irishmen* (London: Faber and Faber 1993), pp. 183–4.

24 *Northern Star*, 9–13 February 1793.

25 *Northern Star*, 27 February–2 March 1793.

26 T. Bartlett (ed.), *Life of Theobald Wolfe Tone*, Robert Simms to Tone, 12 February 1793, p. 222.

27 *Northern Star*, 10–13 April 1793.

28 *Northern Star*, 9–13 March 1793.

29 NA Kew, HO/100/46/35, Evan Nepean to Robert Hobart, 18 February 1793.

30 NA Kew, HO/100/43/152, General Whyte to Hobart, 29 March 1793.

31 NA, Kew HO/100/43/155 Report by Belfast Committee, 10 March 1793.

32 J. Agnew (ed.), *The Drennan–McTier Letters*, 1, Martha McTier to William Drennan (undated, probably Wednesday 13 March 1793), pp. 502–3; T. Bartlett (ed.), *Life of Theobald Wolfe Tone*, Robert Simms to Tone, (n.d.) March 1793, pp. 224–5; Neilson to Tone, 11 March 1793, p. 224.

33 *Northern Star*, 9–13 March 1793.

34 NA Kew, HO/100/43/103, General Whyte to Edward Cooke (Dublin Castle), 17 March 1793.

35 NA Kew, HO/100/43/44, copy of printed critique of the House of Lords by Bond and Butler, 1793.

36 *Northern Star,* 16–20 March 1793; 3–6 April 1793; 6–10 April 1793. General Whyte, commanding officer in the town, noted that there was not a word from the multitude who flocked to see Cuthbert in the pillory. NA Kew, HO/100/46/59, Whyte to Evan Nepean, 8 April 1793.

37 *Northern Star*, 23–27 March 1793.

38 *Northern Star*, 8–11 May 1793.

39 J. Agnew (ed.), *The Drennan–McTier Letters*, 1, William Drennan to Martha McTier, 1 July 1793 pp. 549–50. At the February trial of the newspaper owners, an affidavit named Neilson, William Simms, Robert Simms, Henry Haslett and John Rabb as the sole proprietors, suggesting that some of the original ones had indeed drawn back. A Barrister (i.e. William Sampson), *A Faithful Report of the Trial of the Proprietors of the Northern Star; at the bar of the King's Bench, on the Twenty-Eighth of May 1794, on an Information Filed ex-officio, by the Attorney General* (Belfast: 1794), p. 9.

40 NAI, Rebellion Papers 620/15/8/1, Northern Star minute book entry for 18 June 1793.

41 C.J. Woods (ed.), *Journals and Memoirs of Thomas Russell* (Dublin: Irish Academic Press, 1991), journal entries for 16–24 April, 8 July 1793; p. 72; p. 81.

42 *Northern Star*, 13–17 April 1793.

43 NA Kew, HO/100/46/59, General Whyte to Evan Nepean, 8 April 1793.
44 *Northern Star,* 25–29 May 1793.
45 J. Agnew (ed.), *The Drennan–McTier Letters*, 1, Martha McTier to William Drennan, 1 April 1793, p. 510.
46 C.J. Woods (ed.), *Journals and Memoirs of Thomas Russell*, p.72; J. Agnew (ed.), *The Drennan–McTier Letters,* 1, William Drennan to Samuel McTier, 20 April 1793, p. 515. The underlying loyalty of Catholics was demonstrated by the granting of £2,000 for a statue of the king. At the same dinner, Tone was rewarded with £1,500 for his services. NA Kew, HO/100/43/238, Sackville Hamilton (Under-Secretary Dublin Castle) to Hobart, 25 April 1793.
47 J. Agnew (ed.), *The Drennan–McTier Letters,* 1, William Drennan to Samuel McTier, (undated) late May 1793, p. 532.
48 PRONI, D516/1, Samuel Neilson to William Drennan, 10 June 1793.
49 *Northern Star*, 29 May–1 June 1793.
50 *Northern Star*, 1–5 June 1793; 29 May–1 June 1793.
51 C.J. Woods (ed.), *Journals and Memoirs of Thomas Russell*, entry for 21 August 1793, p. 108.
52 The dinner was held at Daly's in Dublin on 20 August. If Russell and Tone were in daily communication, it is possible that the former informed Neilson of the proceedings, prompting Neilson to write to the leading Catholic Richard McCormick. See note 48, T. Bartlett (ed.), *Life of Theobald Wolfe Tone*, Samuel Neilson to Richard McCormick, 26 August 1793, pp. 226–7. See also D. Mansergh, *Grattan's Failure* (Dublin: Irish Academic Press, 2005), p. 169.
53 T. Bartlett (ed.), *Life of Theobald Wolfe Tone*, Richard McCormick to Theobald Wolfe Tone (undated), p. 227. Russell's journal for 5–9 September suggests that he and Tone were approved of in Belfast. This might indicate that Neilson had been placated and the northern Presbyterians now had a more positive attitude towards the radical Catholic leadership of Tone, Keogh and McCormick. C.J. Woods (ed.), *Journals and Memoirs of Thomas Russell,* p. 123.
54 The *Star*'s print run was over 4,000. G. O'Brien, 'Spirit, Impartiality and Independence; The Northern Star 1792–1797', *Eighteenth Century Ireland,* 13 (1998), p. 16.
55 NAI, Rebellion Papers 620/15/8/1, *Northern Star* minute book entries for 25 January and July 1793. Smith would act as Neilson's attorney during his troubled time as a prisoner in Kilmainham Gaol, 1796–98.
56 *Northern Star*, 12–15 June 1793.
57 *Northern Star*, 14–17 August 1793.
58 *Northern Star*, 30 December 1793–2 January 1794.
59 Sampson, *Faithful Report*, p. vii.
60 *Northern Star*, 6–10 February 1794.
61 The proprietors were listed as William McCleery, William Tennent, John Haslett, Henry Haslett, William Magee, Samuel Neilson, John Boyle, William Simms, Robert Simms, Gilbert McIlveen, John Tisdall, John Rabb and Robert Caldwell. This number had been reduced by the trial. See note 50, Sampson, *Faithful Report*, p. 2.
62 J. Agnew (ed.), *The Drennan–McTier Letters, 2*, William Drennan to Samuel McTier, 16 May 1794, pp. 53–5; PRONI, Tennent Papers D/1748/D/1/8/4, William Tennent to John Tennent, 26 May 1794.
63 Sampson, *Faithful Report*, p. 8.
64 Ibid., pp.18–22.
65 Ibid., pp. 27–31.
66 Ibid., pp. 35–40.

67 It would later be asserted that the offending article was due to appear in the *Belfast News-Letter* and the only reason it did not was because its editor had doubts about whether the costs of the advertisement would be paid. *Northern Star*, 4–8 December 1794.
68 PRONI, Tennent Papers D/1748/D/1/8/5, William Tennent to John Tennent, 28 May 1794; M. Durey, *Transatlantic Radicals and the Early American Republic* (Kansas: University Press of Kansas, 1997), p. 117.
69 J. Agnew (ed.), *The Drennan–McTier Letters*, 2, William Drennan to Samuel McTier, 31 May 1794, pp. 61–2.
70 *Northern Star*, 14–17 July 1794.
71 *Northern Star*, 28–31 July; 31 July–3 August; 4–7 August 1794.
72 A Barrister (i.e. William Sampson), *A Faithful Report of the Second Trial of the Proprietors of the Northern Star; at the bar of the King's Bench, on the Seventeenth of November 1794, on an Information Filed ex-officio, by the Attorney General* (Belfast, 1795), hereafter Sampson, *Second Trial*, p. 5.
73 Sampson, *Second Trial*, p. 14. This point had already been asserted in the *Star* before the trial. *Northern Star*, 30 October–3 November 1794.
74 Sampson, *Second Trial*, pp. 14–53.

Chapter 5

1 The Neilson plot lies adjacent to that of John Neilson and close to other graves, such as those of the Hasletts, Waddell Cunningham and the wealthy merchant Thomas Greg.
2 *Northern Star*, 8–12 May 1794; 12–15 May 1794; 8–11 September 1794. Alexander Gordon and his brother John were nephews of Neilson who were implicated in United Irish activities in the period before the 1798 Rebellion. The *Belfast News-Letter*'s tribute to Thomas Neilson was extensive, referring to his 'pious disposition, steady patriotism, filial and fraternal affection, sincere friendship, integrity and uprightness in trade, a feeling for the distressed'. This last comment no doubt refers to the fact that Thomas Neilson, like his brother, was a member of the committee governing the operation of the Belfast Charitable Society; LHL, Belfast Charitable Society Committee minute book.
3 *Northern Star*, 4–8 September 1794.
4 NAI, Rebellion Papers 620/15/8/7, pocket book detailing deliveries and payments relating to the *Northern Star*.
5 *Northern Star*, 23–26 October 1793.
6 Ibid., 23–26 December 1793.
7 J. Agnew (ed.), *The Drennan–McTier Letters*, 2, William Drennan to Samuel McTier, 3 March 1794, pp. 25–6. The *Star* could boast that the 'Lion of Old England' was being printed in 'almost all the American papers'. *Northern Star*, 22–25 September 1794.
8 *Belfast News-letter*, 1–5 December 1794. The editor added the following at the end of the notice: 'The above was sent us in the name of 14 gentlemen who ordered its insertion two times.' *Northern Star*, 4–8 December 1794; TCD, Sirr MS 868/2f6, Samuel Owens to Thomas Russell, 7 December 1794. C.J. Woods noted that Owens was an officer in the Donegore Volunteers. He emigrated to the USA in 1797. C.J. Woods (ed.), *Journals and Memoirs of Thomas Russell* (Dublin: Irish Academic Press, 1991), p. 176 footnote.
9 *Northern Star*, 14–18 December 1794.
10 J. Gray, 'A Tale of Two Newspapers: The Contest Between the *Belfast News-Letter* and the *Northern Star* in the 1790s', in J. Gray and W. McCann (eds), *An Uncommon Bookman – Essays in Memory of J.R.R. Adams* (Belfast: Linen Hall Library, 1996), p. 184.

11 *Northern Star*, 28–31 July; 8–11 September 1794.
12 See J. Gray, 'A Tale of Two Newspapers', pp. 179–80; *Belfast News-Letter*, 15–19 December 1794. The notice for sale referred to the *News-Letter*'s circulation figures (which stood at 2,975 in January 1794 and 3,225 in July). Noting that each paper would be read by six people, Joy stated that the July readership stood at 19,300.
13 J. Agnew (ed.), *The Drennan–McTier Letters*, 1, William Drennan to Samuel McTier, 20 July 1793, p. 556.
14 *Northern Star*, 7–11 September 1793. See also E.W. McFarland, 'Scottish Radicalism and the "Belfast Principle"', in *Cultural Traditions in Northern Ireland – Varieties of Scottishness* (Belfast: Queen's University, 1997) pp. 65–89.
15 *Dictionary of National Biography*; Sir J. Ferguson, *Balloon Tytler* (London: Faber and Faber, 1972). Tytler, aka Donaldson, features in the journals of Thomas Russell for 1794 as someone who was well connected with the radicals. C.J. Woods (ed.), *Journals and Memoirs of Thomas Russell* (Dublin: Irish Academic Press, 1991), pp. 151–76.
16 NAI, Rebellion Papers 620/27/1; NAI, Frazer MSII/39, information of William Bird alias John Smith, hereafter cited as William Bird, 1796. Tytler left Ireland for the United States, settling in Salem, Massachusetts. He published a pamphlet in the US, entitled *Rising of the Sun in the West*, which had been composed on his voyage. In this, he argued that Scotland and Ireland, living under tyranny, need not delay in their national endeavours – foreign aid would be problematic, so more urgent and independent action was required. He concluded: 'Till this inactivity ceases and these nations make some *real* struggle for liberty, they not only must expect to remain destitute of foreign aid, but merit the contempt and detestation of the entire world.' NAI, Rebellion Papers 620/22/62, James Tytler, *The Rising of the Sun in the West, or, The Origin and Progress of Liberty* (printed). Additional information on Tytler and his links with the Belfast radicals can be found in E.W. McFarland, *Ireland and Scotland in the Age of Revolution: Planting the Green Bough* (Edinburgh: Edinburgh University Press, 1994), p. 137.
17 NAI, Frazer MS II/40, information of William Bird, n.d., 1796.
18 Information of Thomas Collins, quoted in R.B. McDowell, *Proceeedings of the Dublin Society of United Irishmen* (Reprinted Dublin: Irish Manuscripts Commission, 1998), pp. 107–9.
19 LHL, Joy MS Volume IV, 306–7; 313.
20 J. Agnew (ed.), *The Drennan–McTier Letters*, William Drennan to Samuel McTier, 6 February 1794, pp. 14–15.
21 NA (Kew), HO/100/46/65–66, anonymous (Molesworth Street) to ________, 4 May 1793.
22 *Report of the Secret Committee of the House of Lords* (Dublin: 1798), Appendix V Examination of Samuel Neilson, 9 August 1798. See also N. Curtin, 'The Transformation of the Society of United Irishmen into a Mass-based Revolutionary Organisation 1794–96', *Irish Historical Studies*, 24, 96 (1985), p. 475.
23 *Northern Star*, 30 June–3 July 1794.
24 *Northern Star*, 22–26 May 1794.
25 L. Cullen, 'The "Suppression" of the Volunteers and United Irishmen: Sources and Interpretations 1792–94', in B. Browne (ed.), *The Wexford Man, Essays in Honour of Nicky Furlong* (Dublin: Geography Publications, 2007), pp. 62–5.
26 For an excellent analysis of the Defenders, see J. Smyth, 'Popular Politicisation, Defenderism and the Catholic Question', in H. Gough and D. Dickson (eds), *Ireland and the French Revolution* (Dublin: Irish Academic Press, 1990), pp. 109–16.
27 NA (Kew), HO/100/43/145–55, report from Westmorland to ______, 29 March 1793.
28 PRONI, Pelham Transcripts T/755/2, General Dalrymple to Chief Secretary Pelham, 9 August 1794.

29 In a letter to Sam McTier, Drennan asserted that Presbyterians and Catholics were at odds with each other because 'the former love the French openly and the Catholics almost to a man hate them secretly – and why? Because they have overturned the Catholic religion in that country and threaten to do it throughout the world'. Drennan failed to distinguish between the Catholic Church and rural Catholics. J. Agnew (ed.), *The Drennan–McTier Letters*, 2, Drennan to McTier, 21 January 1794, pp. 5–7; C.J. Woods (ed.), *Journals and Memoirs of Thomas Russell*, entries for 18–19 January 1794.

30 NA (Kew), HO/100/46/184, Cooke to Thomas Broderick, 16 August 1794.

31 For excellent analyses of the nature of the Fitzwilliam viceroyalty, see D. Mansergh, *Grattan's Failure: Parliamentary Opposition and the People in Ireland 1779–1800* (Dublin: Irish Academic Press, 2005), pp. 176–90; R.B. McDowell, *Ireland in the Age of Imperialism and Revolution 1760–1801* (Oxford: Clarendon Press, 1979), pp. 445–61.

32 *Northern Star*, 4–8 September 1794; 22–25 September 1794.

33 NA (Kew), HO/100/46/259, Fitzwilliam (Dublin) to Portland, 8 January 1795.

34 *Northern Star*, 2–5 February 1795.

35 Ibid., 26–30 March 1795.

36 J. Agnew (ed.), *The Drennan–McTier Letters*, 2, William Drennan to Samuel McTier, 8 April 1795, pp. 145–7.

37 *Northern Star*, 26–30 March 1795.

38 *Northern Star*, 2–6 April 1795.

39 PRONI, T/755/2 Pelham Transcripts, Portland to Pelham, 28 June 1795.

40 *Northern Star*, 26–30 March 1795.

41 Ibid., 23–27 April; 30 April–4 May 1795.

42 There is evidence to suggest that the northern United Irishmen were countenancing both revolution and French assistance before Jackson's mission. A County Antrim weaver named John Mitchell deposed that 'in or abouts March 1794' he was taken to a house of a publican, James McAllister, in Ballynashee and sworn in as a United Irishman. Among the principles of the society, he recalled 'several articles the subject of which was to overthrow the present Government and Constitution of this country by force'. He deposed that in meetings it was stated that the society would rise in the event of an invasion by the French. NAI, Frazer MS II/16, examination of John Mitchell, n.d.

43 KHLC, Camden MSS U840/0147/4/1, Rowland O'Connor to Sackville Hamilton, 7 June 1795.

44 T. Bartlett, *Life of Theobald Wolfe Tone*, pp.105–9.

45 TCD, Sirr MS 868/2f182, James Tytler to Thomas Russell, 7 September 1795.

46 NAI, Rebellion Papers 620/16/3/3, Tone to Russell, 1 September 1795. Tone asked for this communication to be shown to his friends, among them Samuel Neilson.

47 T. Bartlett, *Life of Theobald Wolfe Tone*, letter to Tone from one of the United Irish leaders in Belfast, probably Russell, 21 September 1795, pp. 239–40.

48 R.R. Madden, *Antrim and Down in '98*, Memoir of James Hope (Glasgow: Cameron, Ferguson and Co., n.d.), pp. 98–9.

49 NAI, Rebellion Papers 620/10/121/26, McNally to Edward Cooke, n.d. 1795.

50 E.M. Johnston-Liik, *History of the Irish Parliament 1692–1800*, 3, pp. 296–7.

51 PRONI, Pelham Transcripts T/755/2, Dalrymple (Dungannon) to Pelham, 13 July 1795.

52 Quoted in K. Whelan, *The Tree of Liberty: Radicalism, Catholicism and the Construction of Irish Identity 1760–1830* (Cork: Cork University Press, 1996), J. Short to G. Geraghty, 6 January 1796, p. 122.

53 R.R. Madden, *Antrim and Down in '98*, p. 14.

54 McGucken was, by his own account, admitted into the United Irishmen at this time. NAI, Rebellion Papers 620/3/32/13, information of James McGucken, n.d. 1798; *Northern Star*, 14–18 January 1796; 18–21 January 1796; 4–8 February 1796; 29 July–1 August 1796.
55 NA (Kew), HO/100/62/145, information of William Bird, 29 July 1796.
56 PRONI, Pelham Transcripts T/755/2, Cooke to Pelham, 31 August 1795; Dalrymple to Pelham, 25 September 1795; Cooke to Pelham, 29 October 1795.
57 KHLC, Camden MSS U840/0150/3, information relating to Michael Phillips, 4 February 1795.
58 NAI, Rebellion Papers 620/22/47, examination of Michael Phillips, n.d.; 620/22/48 examination of Peter Kearney. Kearney, a member of the Dublin Militia, asserted that Phillips had aroused the suspicion of other Defender figures. Another source of information claimed that Campbell had issued Defender tickets to a Thomas McCaffery in Ballyshannon, County Donegal. These were playing cards, with the initials 'R.C.' on them. This information was provided by Harry Major, the town provost, who inserted the tickets in his note to the authorities. He also stated that the Defenders had sent an agent to France and the society's plan 'seemed to be for a general massacre of Protestants'. KHLC, Camden MSS U840/0149/4/2, Harry Major to ____, 29 July 1795; U840/049/4/2, W. Knott (Battlefield) to James Fleming (Dublin), 17 July 1795. Notification of Magennis' marriage to Miss Teeling in Lisburn appeared in the *Northern Star*, 9–13 May 1796.
59 Phillips claimed that John Magennis was 'the real head of the Defenders', noting that he had acknowledged himself to be the movement's Grand Master. NAI, Frazer MSS II/13, anonymous and undated jottings on Defender activities. The information contained in these notes echoes other statements from Phillips and it is almost certain that he was the source. For Phillips' view that Neilson was the head of the United Irish conspiracy in Belfast, see PRONI, Pelham Transcripts, T755/2, Cooke to Pelham, 4 December 1795. Neilson gave Magennis a letter, allegedly from the leading Catholic Richard McCormick, which urged the people to 'take the law unto themselves for they can expect no justice from the government'. NAI, Frazer MSS II/2, examination of Michael Phillips, 5 December 1795.
60 PRONI, Downshire Papers D/607/F/293, James McKey to Downshire, 1 July 1798.
61 *Belfast News-Letter*, 4–8 January 1796; *Northern Star*, 4–7 January 1796.
62 PRONI, Downshire Papers D/607/E/28, Carhampton to Downshire, 13 January 1797.
63 NAI, Rebellion Papers 620/10/121/26, J.W. (Leonard McNally) to Edward Cooke, n.d. 1795; KHLC Camden MSS U840/0146/7, Andrew MacNevin to John Patrickson, 9 May 1795; U840/0144/15, Nathaniel Johnston to John Lees (Dublin), 22 April 1795; U840/0144/21/1, same to same, 27 April 1795.
64 KHLC, Camden MSS U840/0147/17, Nathaniel Johnston to John Lees (Dublin), 2 July 1795; U840/0147/13/2 Rev. Snowden Cupples to Rev. Dobbs and Francis Dobbs, 27 June 1795.
65 J. Agnew (ed.), *The Drennan–McTier Letters*, 2, William Drennan to Martha McTier, 29 August 1795; Martha McTier to William Drennan, n.d. September 1795; 7 February 1796, pp. 174–6; pp. 180–2; pp. 200–3.

Chapter 6

1 *Northern Star*, 31 Dec 1795–4 Jan 1796.
2 PRONI, Tennent Papers D/1748/D/1/2/1, James McCleery to John Tennent, 17 Nov 1795; NAI, Frazer MSS II/36, William Bird (John Smith) to Edward Cooke, 30 August 1796.

Bird reported that Belfast republicans were drinking with disloyal members of the artillery company when they acclaimed, 'May the hair of the Queen's c____ be manufactured into ropes to hang the King and all the Royal Family' and 'May the King be flead [*sic*] alive and his skin made into a drum head.'

3 *Northern Star*, 21–25 May 1795.

4 *Northern Star*, 28 April–2 May 1796; 17–20 June 1796; 25–29 July 1796.

5 *Northern Star*, 2–5 May 1796.

6 *Northern Star*, 21–25 January 1796.

7 J. Agnew (ed.), *The Drennan–McTier Letters*, 2, William Drennan to Martha McTier, 24 February 1796, p. 206.

8 Ibid., Martha McTier to William Drennan, 7 February 1796, p. 203.

9 *Northern Star*, 2–5 September 1796; 3–6 June 1796; 26–29 August 1796; 1–15 June 1796.

10 NA Kew, HO/100/86/134, Edward Cooke to William Wickham, 11 March 1799.

11 NAI, Frazer MSS II/17, Charles Skeffington to Edward Cooke, 25 April 1796.

12 NAI, Frazer MSS II/18, William Bird information, May 1796; II/23A, Bird to Edward Cooke, 19 July 1796; II/32 Thomas Whinnery [Belfast] to _____, 18 August 1796.

13 PRONI, McPeake Papers T/3048/A/9, Thomas Pelham (Dublin) to John King (London), 10 May 1796.

14 NAI, Frazer MSSII/18, William Bird information, May 1796; II/37, 30 August 1796.

15 NAI, Rebellion Papers 620/25/131, W.S. to _____, 13 September 1796.

16 *Belfast News-Letter*, 8–11 December 1789.

17 NA Kew, HO/100/64/21–25, Lord Camden to the Duke of Portland (with enclosure from Alexander Crawford), 7 April 1796.

18 NAI, Frazer MSS II/22, Bird to Edward Cooke, 15 July 1796; NAI, Rebellion Papers 620/25/197, Thomas Whinnery (Belfast Postmaster) to John Lees (Dublin Postmaster), 29 October 1796; PRONI, Pelham Transcripts T/755/3, John Brown to General Nugent, 29 October 1796.

19 NAI, Frazer MSS II/40, Bird's notes on United Irish prisoners in custody, n.d. late 1796.

20 NAI, Frazer MSS II/36, Bird (Liverpool) to Cooke, 30 August 1796.

21 *Northern Star*, 18–21 May 1795; 22–25 June 1795; 1–4 July 1796; 27 June–1 July 1796.

22 NAI, Frazer MSS II/37, Bird information, 30 August 1796; II/24 no date; II/18 Bird information, May 1796; NA Kew, HO/100/62/141, Bird statement, 23 July 1796.

23 NAI, Rebellion Papers 620/10/121/38, J.W. (Leonard McNally) to ____, 5 October 1796.

24 PRONI, Pelham Transcripts T/755/3, Edward Cooke to Henry Pelham, 27 July 1796; Duke of Portland to Pelham, 26 September 1796; General Nugent to Pelham, 6 October 1796.

25 NAI, Rebellion Papers 620/33/72, Edward Newell (Belfast) to Edward Cooke, n.d. 1797. It is likely that this was Alex Kennedy, a close associate of Cuthbert, who was implicated in assassination plots in Belfast at the end of 1796.

26 NLI, Lake Correspondence MSS/56/143, General Lake to Thomas Knox, 5 March 1797; MSS/56/141, Lake to Knox, 17 February 1797.

27 The United Irishmen would always deny that acts of assassination were sanctioned by the leadership. Dublin 'moderates' such as Thomas Addis Emmet and William James MacNeven viewed assassination as an act of criminality. See 'Memoir, or Detailed Statement of the Origin and Progress of the Irish Union; Delivered to the Irish Government, by Messrs Emmet, O'Connor and MacNeven 4 August 1798', in W.J. MacNeven, *Pieces of Irish History, Illustrative of the Condition of the Catholics of Ireland of the Origin and Progress of the Political System of the United Irishmen; and of their Transactions with the Anglo-Irish Government* (New York: 1807), p. 213.

28 NA Kew, HO/100/62/143–44, William Bird information, July 1796.

29 NAI, Frazer MSS II/40, Bird's notes on the Belfast prisoners in custody, n.d. late 1796; Frazer MSS II/22, Bird to Cooke, 15 July 1796.

30 NAI, Frazer MSS II/25, Bird to Cooke, 29 July 1796; NAI, Frazer MSS II/22, Bird to Cooke, 15 July 1796.

31 NAI, Rebellion Papers 620/27/1, Information of William Bird, n.d. 1796; NAI, Frazer MSS/ II/19, Information of Bird, 26 May 1796.

32 *Northern Star,* 17–20 June 1796.

33 NAI, Rebellion Papers 620/27/1, Information of Bird, n.d. 1796; NAI, Frazer MSS/II/19, Information of Bird, 26 May 1796,

34 NAI, Rebellion Papers 620/25/155, James McKey to Lord Downshire, 9 October 1796. Neilson's suspicions would also have been aroused because Bird had written to him on a number of occasions, pleading poverty and asking for financial assistance. J. Agnew (ed.), *The Drennan–McTier Letters*, 2, Martha McTier to William Drennan, 25 September 1796, pp. 265–7.

35 NAI, Frazer MSS II/40, Bird information on the United Irish prisoners, n.d. late 1796.

36 See for example, the resolutions passed by Lodge 539 (Randalstown, Co Antrim, in January 1793, the month of the execution of the French king, Louis XVI): 'As we are well convinced that taxation without representation is tyranny and nothing can save the country from the devouring vultures of the present Administration, but a full and equal representation of all the people in parliament ... we should be wanting in gratitude, did we not thus publicly return our sincere thanks to those guardians of liberty, the Volunteers of Ireland for their spirited exertions in the cause of the people.' Freemasons from Clough in County Down published the following resolution the previous year: 'We will indiscriminately promote the interest of mankind in general, the dignity of Masonry in particular and always look forward to the day when the chains of oppression will be loosed off the people of Ireland, and each individual, of every persuasion, taste the sweets of freedom, and enjoy the Rights of man.' *Northern Star*, 9–12 January 1793; 18–21 January 1792.

37 *The Constitutions of Freemasonry, or Ahiman Rezon*, Rule 115, published by the Grand Lodge of Ireland (Dublin, 1858 edition). The nexus between United Irish politics and Freemasonry is documented in works by A.T.Q. Stewart, *A Deeper Silence: The Hidden Origins of the United Irishmen* (London: Faber and Faber, 1993); N. Curtin, *The United Irishmen: Popular Politics in Ulster and Dublin 1791–1798* (Oxford: Clarendon Press, 1994) and J. Smyth, 'Freemasonry and the United Irishmen' in Dickson, Keogh, Whelan (eds), *The United Irishmen: Republicanism, Radicalism and Rebellion* (Dublin: The Lilliput Press, 1993). Recent work by Petri Mirala has demonstrated that loyalist Freemasonry was a feature of the complex politics of County Armagh in the 1790s. P. Mirala, 'Freemasonry, Conservatism and Loyalism in Ulster 1792–9', in R. Gillespie (ed.), *The Remaking of Modern Ireland 1750–1950* (Dublin: Four Courts Press, 2004).

38 NAI, Frazer MSS II/31, Bird to Cooke, 17 August 1796; II/35, Bird (Liverpool) to Cooke, 29 August 1796. The commander-in-chief would arrest Joseph Cuthbert, a leading conspirator, in November 1796. He did this when 'I visited several public houses, where were assembled meetings of freemasons'; PRONI, Pelham Transcripts T/755/3, Carhampton (Belfast) to Pelham, 15 November 1796.

39 Grand Masonic Lodge of Ireland (Molesworth Street, Dublin), Members Register.

40 NAI, Rebellion Papers, 620/25/187 Knox to _____ , 25 October 1796.

41 J. Agnew (ed.), *The Drennan–McTier Letters*, 2, Martha McTier to William Drennan, 25 September 1796, pp. 266–7.

42 NAI, Frazer MSS II/33, 34. Brown Square (built 1791) was located in the Millfield area of Belfast, which was then on the fringe of the town. See R. Gillespie and S. Royle, *Belfast Part 1, to 1840*, Irish Historica Towns Atlas, 12 (Dublin: Royal Irish Academy and Belfast City Council, 2003), p. 12.

43 NA Kew, HO/100/62/137–8, information of William Bird, 15 July 1796; NAI Frazer MSS II/32, Thomas Whinnery to Cooke, 18 August 1796; II/37, Bird (Isle of Man) to Cooke, 30 August 1796; T. Bartlett (ed.), *Revolutionary Dublin 1795–1801: The Letters of Francis Higgins to Dublin Castle* (Dublin: Four Courts Press, 2004), p. 36.

44 KHLC, Camden MSS U840/0148/2/1, Andrew MacNevin to Pelham, 6 July 1795. A number of contemporary accounts make reference to an important steering committee in Belfast. For example, a deposition given by John Mitchell, a weaver from the townland of Ballynashee in County Antrim, mentioned a general committee in the town (consisting of Neilson, Russell, Haslett and Sinclaire). Subscriptions would be sent to this committee to pay for the legal costs of those imprisoned and to underwrite the political evangelism that saw United Irish emissaries traverse the north. NAI, Frazer MSS II/4; 16, examinations of John Mitchell, n.d., presumed 1796.

45 NAI, Rebellion Papers 620/36/227, J.W. (McNally) to Cooke, 7 June 1796; 620/10/121/31, McNally to Cooke, 11 July 1796. Hope referred to this mission in his information to Madden. R.R. Madden, *Antrim and Down in '98* (Glasgow: n.d.), pp. 108–9. Brief information on William Metcalf can be found in the Rebellion Papers, 620/7/74/23, James McGucken to Cooke, n.d. Metcalf was imprisoned in the artillery barracks in Belfast after the rebellion, although he was active as a United Irish emissary in the period between 1800 and Emmet's rising in 1803. NAI, Frazer MSS I/12, 2 September 1798; NAI, Rebellion Papers 620/49/11, James McGucken to Cooke, 9 March 1800.

46 E.W. McFarland, *Ireland and Scotland in the Age of Revolution: Planting the Green Bough* (Edinburgh: Edinburgh University Press, 1994), p. 139.

47 NA Kew, HO/100/62/153–63, Camden to Portland, 6 August 1796; PRONI, Pelham Transcripts T/755/3, Camden to Pelham, 6 August 1796.

48 *Northern Star*, 2–5 September 1795; 5–9 December 1796; NAI, Rebellion Papers 620/24/166, Dalrymple to Cooke, 27 August 1796.

49 *Belfast News-Letter*, 6–10 February 1797; 10–13 February 1797; 13–17 February 1797. These attacks occurred in the aftermath of the arrests of Robert and William Simms and an attack upon the office of the *Northern Star*. The brothers had taken over the running of the newspaper after Neilson's arrest in September 1796.

50 *Northern Star*, 5–9 May 1796.

51 *Northern Star*, 13–16 May 1796; *Belfast News-Letter*, 16–20 May 1796.

52 *Northern Star*, 20–23 May 1796.

53 *Northern Star*, 5–8 August 1796.

54 R.R. Madden, *The United Irishmen – Their Lives and Times*, 3rd Series (Dublin: J Mullany, 1846), p. 180. In his evidence to the House of Commons Secrecy Committee on 9 August 1798, Neilson dated the military organisation of the United Irishmen from the autumn of 1796. He and Russell were arrested on 16 September 1796, giving the historian some idea of sequence. *Report from the Committee of Secrecy of the House of Commons in Ireland as Reported by the Right Honourable Lord Viscount Castlereagh*, Appendix XXXL, p. 69.

55 NAI, Rebellion Papers 620/25/9, Andrew Newton (Coagh) to J. O'Connor (Castleknock – enclosure to Edward Cooke (Dublin), 3 September 1796; PRONI, Downshire Papers D/607/D/102, Thomas Lane to Lord Downshire, 16 July 1796; D/607/D/110, Camden to Downshire, 3 August 1796; D/607/D/146 Robert Ross to Downshire, 2 September 1796.

56 NAI, Rebellion Papers 620/10/121/79, J.W. (McNally) to Cooke, 2 October 1797.
57 NAI, Frazer MSSI/49, information of Michael Lowry (Lissue, near Lisburn) to Rev. Philip Johnson, 19 and 26 August 1796; II/37, Bird to Cooke, 30 August 1796.
58 PRONI, Pelham Transcripts T/755/3, Camden to Chief Secretary Henry Pelham, 28 August 1796; Camden to the Duke of Portland, 20 August 1796.
59 NAI, Rebellion Papers 620/24/130, resolutions passed at a meeting in Derriaghy Church, 10 August 1796; 620/24/176, Rev. Philip Johnson to Lord Castlereagh, 30 August 1796.
60 NAI, Rebellion Papers 620/24/172, examination of James Manson, 29 August 1796.
61 R.R. Madden, *The United Irishmen – Their Lives and Times*, 4th series, 2, p. 44.
62 *Northern Star*, 12–16 September 1796. For the apparent emergence of a new informer, see note 97.
63 NAI, Rebellion Papers 620/25/56, Nugent to Edward Cooke, 14 September 1796; 620/25/56A, Pollock to Cooke, 13 September 1796.
64 *Northern Star*, 16–19 September 1796.
65 *Northern Star*, 12–16 September 1796.
66 NAI, Rebellion Papers 620/25/60/1–17, arrest warrants for United Irish suspects, September 1796; 620/25/65/1, arrest warrant for John McCabe; 620/18A/3, copies of warrants with amendment made to the warrant for the arrest of Thomas McCabe.
67 *Northern Star*, 12–16 September 1796.
68 J. Agnew (ed.), *The Drennan–McTier Letters*, 2, Martha McTier to William Drennan, 25 September 1796, p. 267.
69 *Northern Star*, 12–16 September 1796.
70 NAI Rebellion Papers 620/25/103, anon (Belfast) to ____, 24 September 1796.
71 *Belfast News-Letter*, 16–19 September 1796; *Northern Star*, 19–23 September 1796.
72 NAI Rebellion Papers 620/25/82, digest of an intercepted letter from Martha McTier to Drennan, n.d. 1796.
73 J. Agnew (ed.), *The Drennan–McTier Letters*, 2, William Drennan to Martha McTier, 19 September 1796, p. 263.
74 Ibid.
75 NAI, Frazer MSS I/49, examination of Michael Lowry, 19 and 26 August 1796.
76 N. O'Sullivan, *Every Dark Hour: A History of Kilmainham Jail* (Dublin: Liberties Press, 2007), pp. 30–1.
77 C.H. Teeling, *Personal Narrative of the Irish Rebellion of 1798* (London: H. Colburn, 1828), p. 35.
78 J. Agnew (ed.), *The Drennan–McTier Letters*, 2, William Drennan to Martha McTier, 19 September 1796, p. 264.
79 NAI, Rebellion Papers 620/18A/3, anonymous, probably John Pollock to Cooke, 17 September 1796.
80 *Northern Star*, 28 November–2 December 1796.
81 *Faulkner's Dublin Journal*, 15 November 1796.
82 NAI, Rebellion Papers 620/25/144, 'A.B.' to Thomas Pelham, 3 October 1796. Two large bundles of papers had been taken from Russell's lodgings while other evidence was taken by Westmeath from Samuel Kennedy's house. Rebellion Papers 620/25/33, Pollock to Camden, 17 September 1796.
83 NAI, Rebellion Papers 620/25/109, Neilson to Cooke, 24 September 1796; 620/25/110 Haslett to Cooke, 24 September 1796.
84 J. Agnew (ed.), *The Drennan–McTier Letters*, 2, William Drennan to Martha McTier, n.d. October 1796, pp. 270–1. The informer McNally would report that Dixon was a regular

visitor to Kilmainham, where he conferred with the northern radicals. Dixon was, he stated, 'very intimate with Neilson'. There is no doubt that Dixon, a well-connected Dublin United Irishmen, would both assist the prisoners and ensure that their views were communicated to those outside the confines of the gaol. The informer and editor of the *Freeman's Journal*, Francis Higgins, later asserted that Dixon had held on to a supply of pikes that Neilson deposited on the night of the rebellion's outbreak in May 1798. NAI, Rebellion Papers 620/10/121/35, J.W. (McNally) to presumably Cooke, 26 September 1796; 620/10/118/8, Higgins to Cooke, 27 February 1801.

85 NAI, Rebellion Papers 620/25/144, Andrew MacNevin (Carrickfergus) to Cooke, 5 October 1796.

86 NAI, Rebellion Papers 620/18/14/15, Francis Higgins to Edward Cooke, 27 September 1796.

87 KHLC, Camden MSS U840/0154/1, Camden notes to Portland, 22 September 1796.

88 NA Kew, HO/100/69/397, Camden to Portland, 17 June 1797.

89 TCD, Madden MSS 873/344, certificate of entry for Henry Joy McCracken.

90 RR Madden, *Antrim and Down in '98* (Glasgow: n.d.), p. 10.

91 NAI, Frazer MSS II/13, undated statements on Defender activity, most likely provided by Friar Phillips.

92 *Belfast News-Letter*, 5–8 August 1796; PRONI, Pelham Transcripts T/755/3, General Nugent to Henry Pelham, 30 September 1796; NAI Rebellion Papers 620/32/60, Colonel Prendergast to Edward Cooke, 19 August 1797. Prendergast cited the private's name as Joseph Connell. The colonel and Major Gough had actually travelled to Belfast in the aftermath of the murder to identify the body and were permitted by the town sovereign, William Bristow, to view the corpse. Bristow and Prendergast agreed that Connolly had been murdered, but felt it prudent not to publicise this at the time. The Corporal Burke referred to here was John Burke, a deserter who had taken the United Irish oath. On 6 September, Nugent reported that he had been apprehended in Belfast. NAI, Rebellion Papers 620/25/27, Nugent to Cooke (with enclosure signed by Thomas Boyd of the 21st Militia and Lt-Colonel Mackey of the Reay Fencibles), 6 September 1796. An anonymous source in Belfast in 1799 made reference to Burke as a prisoner who had escaped while he was awaiting transportation. William Tennent and Henry Haslett had apparently been raising money on his behalf. NAI, Rebellion Papers 620/3/32/1, anonymous to Pelham and Cooke, 25 February 1798. For Nugent's concerns about Connolly's death, see NAI, Rebellion Papers 620/24/143, Nugent to Cooke, 9 August 1796. Nugent enclosed a note signed by an officer in Lisburn, which made reference to the original verdict of accidental death.

93 NA Kew, HO/100/69/202–5, confession of E.J. Newell, 13 April 1797.

94 NAI, Rebellion Papers 620/25/81, Reverend Lambart to Edward Cooke, 18 September 1796. See also C. Reilly, *Edenderry, County Offaly and the Downshire Estate 1790–1800* (Dublin: Four Courts Press, 2007). It is possible that Delaney was related to James Delaney, another member of the same regiment, who had been charged with the murder of a Mr McMurdie. He was found guilty of the lesser charge of manslaughter and released after being branded on the hand and dismissed. The Queen's County Militia was certainly experiencing a degree of United Irish infiltration. Thomas Callaghan and Pat O'Brien were conveyed to Carrickfergus Gaol in September on a charge of high treason and William Higgins, a deserter, was also detained there. In what was an act of contrition, the regiment later declared its willingness to serve as fencibles in Britain or anywhere else in defence of the king and constitution. *Belfast News-Letter*, 18–22 July 1796; 26–30 September 1796; 3–7 October 1796; 7–10 October 1796.

95 PRONI, Downshire MSS D/607/A/511, Reverend William Lambart (Edenderry) to Lord Downshire, 14 October 1796. Reverend Philip Johnson was the Anglican vicar of Derriaghy and a noted loyalist and magistrate who had taken an active role in thwarting United Irish activity in the Lisburn area. There had been several attempts on his life, the most serious being on Saturday, 8 October 1796, between 8 and 9pm, when he was shot in the shoulder while mounting his horse in Castle Street, Lisburn. Henry Joy McCracken was arrested that very evening, although he did not fire the shot. In early November, a William Grimes was arrested, charged with the attempted murder of Johnson and conveyed to Carrickfergus Gaol. *Belfast News-Letter*, 7–10 October 1796; 31 October–4 November 1796.

96 NAI, Rebellion Papers 620/25/156, Portarlington (Blaris) to ______, 10 October 1796.

97 NAI, Rebellion Papers 620/25/137, Thomas Whinnery (Belfast) to ______, 1 October 1796. Richardson was arrested on 27 October; *Belfast News-Letter,* 24–28 October 1796. The examinations of Delaney and Butler reveal that they were briefed on their mission for a few days and that they met with Thomas Richardson and Henry Joy McCracken. The men were given civilian clothes and McCracken issued them a guinea each before they departed on their mission. NAI, Frazer MSS II/6, examination of Denis Delaney, 21 October 1796. Delaney's deposition stated that he was told that there was a plan to assassinate Reverend Philip Johnson when he was next due to come to Belfast.

98 NAI, Rebellion Papers 620/25/154, Reverend William Bristow to Lord Downshire, 9 October 1796.

99 NAI, Rebellion Papers 620/24/117, John Lee to Edward Cooke, 13 August 1796.

100 *Belfast News-Letter*, 19–22 August 1796. NAI, Rebellion Papers 620/24/134, Lee to Cooke, 22 August 1796.

101 NAI, Rebellion Papers 620/25/166, examination of Bell Martin before Dean Dobbs, 12 October 1796. Lee alleged that the attackers included Spears, McCracken, Cuthbert, Storey 'and a clerk of [John] Tisdall's late an editor of the Star, also a relative of Sam Neilson's'. Lee stated that Smith's alias was McGarra. It is possible that the attacker was, in fact, the United Irishman William McGaw. When arrest warrants were produced in September, the sought-after William Gaw was nowhere to be found. NAI, Rebellion Papers 620/24/148, Andrew McNevin (Carrickfergus) to Cooke, 23 August 1796; 620/18A/3, arrest warrant, 17 September 1796. There is evidence to suggest that Bell Martin also spent time in Dublin during the period before the rebellion. A Belfast United Irishman called Harry McNamee, who had been in contact with McCracken, wrote to the leading radical Thomas Potts to inform him that he and Martin were in Chapelizod in June 1797. It is possible that she was using her charms to elicit information from soldiers based in the barracks there. NAI, Rebellion Papers 620/31/127, Harry McNamee to Thomas Potts, 19 June 1797.

102 PRONI, Madden MSS (copies) T/1210/7, Mary Ann McCracken to Henry Joy McCracken, 16 March 1797.

103 NA Kew, HO/100/62/312–16, Camden to Portland, 1 November 1796; HO/100/65/105 Camden to Portland, 7 November 1796.

104 PRONI, Pelham Transcripts T/755/3, Carhampton to ___, 9 November 1796; Carhampton to Pelham, 12 November 1796.

105 *Belfast News-Letter*, 14–18 November 1796; 18–21 November 1796; 21–25 November 1796; 25–28 November 1796.

106 *Northern Star*, 14–18 November 1796; 18–21 November 1796; 21–25 November 1796. *Dublin Journal*, 19 November 1796.

107 PRONI, Downshire MSS D/607D/396, Camden to Downshire, 12 December 1796; D/607/E/63, Annesley to Downshire, n.d. January 1797.

Chapter 7

1 *Northern Star*, 17–21 October 1796; 14–17 October 1796.
2 Ibid., 7–10 October 1796.
3 Ibid., 3–7 October 1796.
4 Ibid., 21–24 October 1796.
5 PRONI, Downshire MSS D/607/D/286, Bishop of Dromore to Lord Downshire, 5 November 1796.
6 NA Kew, HO/100/62/342, G. Hill to Edward Cooke, n.d. October 1796.
7 PRONI, Pelham Transcripts T/755/3, Lord Carhampton to Pelham, 15 November 1796.
8 *Northern Star*, 11–14 November 1796; 18–21 November 1796; S. McSkimin, *Annals of Ulster from 1790 to 1798* (Belfast: Elizabeth J. McCrum, 1906), p. 40.
9 PRONI, Downshire MSS D/607/D/257, Charles Gordon to Lord Downshire, 26 October 1796.
10 NAI, Rebellion Papers 620/25/205, Matthew Smith to A. Blackwell, 5 October 1796; *Northern Star*, 6–9 January 1797; 13–16 January 1797. Writing to Matthew Smith from his prison cell, Neilson asked that arrears be sought from, among others, William McCracken (the older brother of Henry Joy McCracken) and a local tailor named Bannon, who owed rent of around £6. Conscious of his own debts, Neilson asked Smith to check whether he owed his contribution towards the paving of the town's streets. NAI, Rebellion Papers 620/28/156, Neilson to Matthew Smith, 28 January 1797.
11 *Northern Star*, 28 November–2 December 1796; 21–25 November 1796.
12 Ibid., 23–26 December 1796; 23–27 January 1797.
13 PRONI, Abercorn MSS T2541/1B3/6/2, Galbraith to the Marquis of Abercorn, 16 January 1797.
14 Ibid., 24–28 October 1796.
15 J.H. Hames, *Arthur O'Connor, United Irishman* (Cork: The Collins Press, 2001), p. 122; 135.
16 PRONI, T/3541/5/3, Particulars of a History of a North County Irish Family, autobiographical account of John Caldwell Jr., (c.1850).
17 For a discussion of the Belfast yeomanry meeting, see A. Blackstock, *Double Traitors? The Belfast Volunteers and Yeomen 1778–1828* (Belfast: The Belfast Society, in association with the Ulster Historical Foundation, 2000) pp. 21–30.
18 J. Agnew (ed.), *The Drennan–McTier Letters*, 2, Martha McTier to William Drennan, 13 January 1797, p. 284.
19 PRONI, Pelham Transcripts T/755/4A, T/755/4A/106–7, Lord Camden to Pelham, 2 February 1797.
20 NAI, Rebellion Papers 620/28/199; 200; 221, Barber to Cooke, 3 February 1797 and 6 February 1797.
21 NAI, Rebellion Papers 620/28/233, Robert and William Simms to Cooke, 7 February 1797; 620/1/2/1, 25 February and 13 March 1797.
22 NAI, Frazer MSS/1/16, declaration of Neilson, Haslett and Simms, n.d. 1797.
23 NAI, Rebellion Papers 620/28/248, Barber to Cooke, 10 February 1797.
24 *Northern Star*, 24–27 February 1797. Corbett was the registered printer of the *Northern Star* and its editor, but another source refers to Matthew Smith, Neilson's chief clerk, as editor. Humphrey Galbraith identified John Hughes (the Belfast bookseller-turned-informer) as 'the rascal who edited the *Northern Star* for Neilson', while Madden identifies Reverend James Porter (author of the series *Billy Bluff and the Squire*) as editor of the paper. NAI, Rebellion Papers 620/10/121/151, J.W. (Leonard McNally) referred to Smith as the editor, nd. 1797;

PRONI, Downshire MSS D/607/E/344, Galbraith to Downshire, 21 October 1797; R.R. Madden, *The United Irishmen – Their Lives and Times*, 4th Series, 2nd edition (London: J. Mulanny,1860), pp.19–20.

25 *Belfast News-Letter*, 13–17 February 1797.

26 *Northern Star*, 13–17 March; 17–20 March 1797.

27 Ibid., 6–10 March 1796.

28 Ibid., 24–27 March; 3–7 April; 7–10 April 1797.

29 PRONI, Pelham Transcripts T/755/4A/34–6, Lake to Pelham, 5 January 1797.

30 NLI, Lake MSS 56/25, Lake to General Knox, 8 February 1797.

31 NA Kew, HO/100/69/126–7, Camden to Duke of Portland, 1 March 1797.

32 PRONI, Pelham Transcripts T/755/4B/168, Lake to Pelham, 13 March 1797.

33 K. Whelan, 'United and Disunited Irishmen', in *The Tree of Liberty: Radicalism, Catholicism and the Construction of Irish Identity 1760–1830* (Cork: University of Notre Dame Press, 1996) pp. 126–9. In areas such as Armagh, Presbyterian allegiance to the United Irishmen could never be taken for granted. The shows of Defender strength were as likely to push Presbyterians into the conservative camp. By the summer of 1797, Lord Gosford, through whose demesne the Orange Order had paraded on 12 July 1796, could report that a 'wonderful change for the better' was taking root in his neighbourhood and that 'the United men are dying away'. Abercorn informed Camden that the Orangemen were active in the county and that many of them were 'formerly united'. KHLC, Camden MSS U840/0173/12, Lord Gosford to Camden, 19 June 1797.

34 J. Agnew (ed.), *The Drennan–McTier Letters*, 2, Martha McTier to William Drennan, 29 March 1797, pp. 306–8.

35 PRONI, Pelham Transcripts T/755/4B/268, Lake to Pelham, 16 April 1797.

36 E.J. Newell, *The Apostasy of Newell* (London, 1798), pp. 7–69; NAI, Kew HO/100/69/201–5, confession of E.J. Newell, 13 April 1797; PRONI, Pelham Transcripts T/755/5/5, Lake to Pelham, 1 May 1797; T/755/5/70, Lake to Pelham, 16 May 1797. The similarities between Newell's account and the details within a notebook in the Rebellion Papers attributed to a John Maxwell would suggest that they were the same person. NAI, Rebellion Papers 620/34/54/1, notebook of 'John Maxwell', n.d.

37 NAI, Kew HO/100/69/245, Camden to Portland, 20 April 1797.

38 *Northern Star*, 28 April–1 May 1797.

39 PRONI, Downshire MSS D/607/E/262, Thomas Lane to Lord Downshire, 21 May 1797.

40 PRONI, D/1751/1/5, article by F.J. Bigger for the *Ulster Journal of Archaeology* (undated).

41 NLI, Lake MSS 56/79, Lake to General Knox, 21 May 1797; J. Agnew (ed.), *The Drennan–McTier Letters*, 2, Martha McTier to William Drennan, 22 May 1797, pp. 314–15. Martha McTier would record that the decision not to print the advertisement was taken by Francis Jordan, whom she described as one of its proprietors. Jordan was suspected by the Belfast postmaster, Thomas Whinnery, of being a leading United Irishman and a conduit for communicating with radicals in England. Lake had his suspicions about Jordan and another prominent Belfast businessman, Cunningham Greg, who was suspected of subscribing significant amounts of cash for the United Irish prisoners in Dublin. When troops in Belfast acted to force people to take the oath of allegiance, Lake reported that Francis Jordan had done so, although suspicions were harboured that some republicans were feigning loyalty by taking the oath in the knowledge that their United Irish vows were more binding. Jordan was communicating letters to Dublin in order to evade Whinnery's snooping. The postmaster was known to open mail and report suspicious contents to the authorities. Drennan received some of Martha McTier's correspondence *via* Jordan. It was, however, his error which presented Lake

with information about the United Irish conspiracy in Belfast and Dublin, for he dropped a packet of letters destined for the prisoners in Kilmainham and these fell into Whinnery's possession. Jordan discovered his mistake and returned hastily to Belfast. Cunningham Greg's sister Jenny (Jane) was implicated and this cast further suspicion on him. I have not managed to locate the enclosure of letters that Whinnery sent to Dublin, although Mary Ann McCracken was able to tell her brother that none of the captured letters was from any member of the McCracken family. Lake described Jenny Greg as 'the most violent creature possible ... [who] has certainly done very great mischief in this town'. The general wished to execute Jordan and Cunningham Greg to set an example as he felt they were encouraging the lower orders to take the oath of allegiance because it was not binding. Jordan would later deny his United Irish links in a letter to the historian R.R. Madden, especially the suggestion by the informer John Hughes that he was the treasurer to the United Irishmen in County Antrim. PRONI, Pelham Transcripts T/755/5, Lake to Pelham 9 June 1797; Ibid., 2 July 1797; Ibid., 3 July 1797; PRONI, McCracken Transcripts T/1210/16, Mary Ann McCracken to Henry Joy McCracken (Kilmainham), 2 July 1797; TCD Madden MSS 873/184, Jordan to Madden n.d.

42 N. O'Sullivan, *Every Dark Hour: A History of Kilmainham Jail* (Dublin: Liberties Press, 2007), p. 31.

43 NAI, State Prisoner Petitions MFS58/1/SPP24, Haslett to Pelham, 6 December 1797; 22 December 1796; *Northern Star*, 12–16 December 1796; 16–19 December 1796.

44 PRONI, Madden MSS (transcripts) T/1210/28, Henry Joy McCracken to Mary Ann McCracken, 1 September 1797. Mary Ann was shocked at the brutal behaviour 'of one who has always been reckoned a tyrant and who has still been so universally disliked'. T1210/30, Mary Ann McCracken to Henry Joy McCracken, 11 September 1797.

45 PRONI, Madden MSS (transcripts) T/1210/32, Mary Ann McCracken to Henry Joy McCracken, n.d. October 1797

46 Ibid., T/1210/12, Henry Joy McCracken to Mary Ann McCracken, 24 April 1797; *Northern Star*, 17–21 April 1797; 28 April–1 May 1797; *Belfast News-Letter*, 1 May 1797. The eldest son of Samuel Neilson's late brother John was called Robert and was born on 2 January 1781. I cannot prove that this is the Robert Neilson arrested in Belfast and detained in Kilmainham. A petition sent to the Castle on his behalf indicated that he was destitute and prepared to go into voluntary exile but unable to afford the cost of emigration. PRONI, T654/2, Rosemary Street Church Register of Baptisms and Marriages; NAI, State Prisoner Petitions MFS58/1/SPP34.

47 PRONI, Madden MSS (transcripts) T/1210/12, Henry Joy McCracken to Mary Ann McCracken, 24 April 1797.

48 C.H. Teeling, *Personal Narrative of the Irish Rebellion of 1798* (London: 1828), p. 39.

49 NAI, Rebellion Papers 620/14/218/5, unknown, n.d., probably March 1797.

50 PRONI, Madden MSS (transcripts) T/1210/20, Henry Joy McCracken to his sisters, 27 June 1797; NAI, Rebellion Papers 620/36/38, Joseph Nugent to Edward Cooke, 21 March 1798.

51 NAI, Rebellion Papers 620/28/49, Thomas Whinnery to John Lees, 10 February 1797.

52 PRONI, Madden MSS (transcripts) T/1210/17, William McCracken to Mary Ann McCracken, 9 June 1997.

53 Ibid., Mary Ann McCracken to Henry Joy McCracken, 10 August 1797. Robert Simms admonished Thomas Russell for the same excess; TCD, Sirr MSS 868/2f307, Robert Simms to Russell, 10 August 1798.

54 The letters dropped accidentally by Francis Jordan in Belfast were destined for the prisoners. McCracken was able to write to his sisters *via* Anne Neilson; PRONI, Madden MSS (transcripts) T/1210/4, Henry Joy McCracken to his sisters, 10 January 1797.

55 C.H. Teeling, *Personal Narrative of the Irish Rebellion of 1798* (London, 1828) p. 48.
56 PRONI, Dobbin Papers T/316/4, Neilson to Orr, Cochran and Fitzgerald, 15 March 1797.
57 NAI, Rebellion Papers 620/30/87, Cleland to Castlereagh, 16 May 1797.
58 W.A. Maguire, 'Arthur McMahon, United Irishman and French Soldier', in *Irish Sword*, IX (36). Hughes's mother was a Carson, making him a cousin of Neilson's.
59 *Report From The House of Lords (Ireland) Secrecy Committee* (London, 1798).
60 M. Elliott, *Partners in Revolution: The United Irishmen and France* (New Haven: Yale University Press, 1982), pp. 134–44; R. Wells, *Insurrection* (London: Beviary Press, 2013 ed.), pp. 81–95.
61 PRONI, Pelham Transcripts T/755/4B/302, Lake to Pelham, 23 April 1797; NA Kew, HO/100/69/418, Cooke to Grenville, 26 June 1797.
62 NAI, Rebellion Papers 620/31/128, 'Farmer' to George Anderson, 20 June 1797; NLI Musgrave MSS 4156, information communicated by Farmer, 6 June 1799. Farmer was an anonymous informer in County Down who furnished the Marquis of Downshire with details of United Irish and Defender activity in the area. According to Lord Shannon, the doctor who stood up to Magennis on Dechomet (named by Farmer as a Dr Mecomson [Malcolmson]) later turned informer, having spoken out to say that he was for reform and not murder. PRONI, Shannon Papers D/2707/A3/3/41, Lord Shannon to his son Henry Boyle, 23 June 1797.
63 R.R. Madden, *Antrim and Down in '98* (Glasgow, n.d.), p. 121; S. McSkimin, *History of the Irish Rebellion in 1798 Particularly in Antrim, Down and Derry* (Belfast: 1853) pp. 85–7.
64 PRONI, Pelham Transcripts T/755/5, Lake to Pelham, 1 June 1797. The authorities were aware of the unfolding plans because an informer, Nicholas Mageean (a Catholic farmer from the townland of Lessans, near Saintfield in County Down), was providing high-grade information as a delegate to the provincial committee and colonel in the military structure of the United Irishmen in Down. Mageean's information was given before Reverend Cleland and is presented in the Lytton White Papers at the Public Records Office of Northern Ireland and (without specific names) in the *Report From The House of Commons (Ireland) Secrecy Committee* (London, 1798).
65 Hastings Mason would return to Ulster – probably in early 1798. He was subsequently described by James McKey, one of Downshire's correspondents, as 'a very bad boy'. PRONI Downshire MSS D/607/F/98, McKey to Downshire, 16 March 1798. Mason had enrolled as a United Irishman when the Downshire Militia was posted there. Interesting sidelights on Mason's life can be accessed in the memoirs of the loyalist gentleman and yeomanry officer, Morgan Jellet, a distant relative and close friend of Mason; PRONI T2777/1A, The Anecdotal Recollections of Morgan Jellet. Robert Rollo Reid landed at Girvan in Ayrshire and settled in Kirkoswald. A well-known radical, he was placed under strict surveillance. See E.W. McFarland, *Ireland and Scotland in the Age of Revolution* (Edinburgh: Edinburgh University Press, 1994), p. 145.
66 NAI, Rebellion Papers 620/14/285/5, n.d. 1797.
67 PRONI, Downshire MSS D/607/E/300, Bishop of Dromore to Downshire, 20 August 1797; PRONI, Lytton-White Papers D/714/2/6a, report by Nicholas Mageean, 31 July 1797.
68 KHLC, Camden MSS U840/0173/12, Lord Gosford to Camden, 19 June 1797.
69 C.H. Teeling, *Personal Narrative of the Irish Rebellion of 1798* (London, 1828), p. 59; R.R. Madden, *The United Irishmen – Their Lives and Times*, 4th Series, 2nd Edition (London, 1860), p. 25.
70 See Madden, *The United Irishmen – Their Lives and Times*, 4th Series, 2nd Edition, p. 44.

71 NAI, Rebellion Papers 620/14/218/5, anonymous account, March 1797. O'Neill's visit to the prison was considered 'a great triumph to the republican party'. O'Neill was warned that his continuing calls for parliamentary reform would be viewed with suspicion in the light of the visit to see the Kilmainham prisoners, the implication being that he was being used by them. See D. Mansergh, *Grattan's Failure*, p. 213.

72 PRONI, Madden MSS (transcripts) T/1210/27, Henry Joy McCracken to Mary Ann McCracken, 24 August 1797; Ibid., T/1210/28, Henry Joy McCracken to Mary Ann McCracken, 1 September 1797.

73 NAI, Rebellion Papers 620/32/176, prisoners to ______, 20 October 1797.

74 NAI, State Prisoner Petitions SPP/35, 14 October 1797 and 28 October 1797; J. Agnew, (ed.), *The Drennan–McTier Letters*, 2, William Drennan to Martha McTier, 14 November 1797, pp. 342–3; NAI, Rebellion Papers 620/32/187, Surgeon George Stewart to Cooke, 28 October 1797.

75 NAI, Rebellion Papers 620/32/179, William Kean to Robert Kean, 16 October 1797.

76 NAI, State Prisoner Petitions SPP/35, Matthew Smith memorial, 4 November 1797; written submission by William Simms, 4 November 1797, Neilson to Pelham, 7 November 1797; J. Agnew (ed.), *The Drennan–McTier Letters*, 2, William Drennan to Martha McTier, 14 November 1797, pp. 342–3. On 9 December, William McCracken informed his parents that Neilson's condition had deteriorated again, which suggests that any concession had been suspended: PRONI, Madden MSS (transcripts) T/1210/39, William McCracken to Mr and Mrs J. McCracken, 9 December 1797. The informer Francis Higgins was aware of Neilson's excursions outside the gaol, suggesting that he 'rides about the environs of the city'. T. Bartlett (ed.), *Revolutionary Dublin 1795–1801: The Letters of Francis Higgins to Dublin Castle* (Dublin: Four Courts Press, 2004), p. 217.

77 NAI, State Prisoner Petitions SPP/35, Neilson to Cooke, 24 December 1797; 30 December 1797; NAI, State Prisoner Petitions SPP/245 (Microfilm MFS58/2), Anne Neilson to Cooke, 3 January 1798; Neilson to Cooke, 6 January 1798.

78 C.H. Teeling, *Personal Narrative of the Irish Rebellion of 1798* (London, 1828), pp. 110–14; NAI, Rebellion Papers 620/18/14/59, Francis Higgins to Edward Cooke, 29 August 1798. The work of Professor Thomas Bartlett in publishing and annotating the full text of the letters by the Dublin informer Francis Higgins is invaluable for any study of this period. T. Bartlett (ed.), *Revolutionary Dublin 1795–1801: The Letters of Francis Higgins to Dublin Castle*, p. 178.

79 NAI, Rebellion Papers 620/32/179, William Kean to Robert Kean, 16 October 1797.

80 Letter from William Bird to Cooke, published in O'Connor's *The Press* in January 1798 and quoted in Madden, *The United Irishmen – Their Lives and Times*, 4th Series, 2nd Edition, p. 48.

81 T. Bartlett (ed.), *Revolutionary Dublin 1795–1801: The Letters of Francis Higgins to Dublin Castle*, p. 217.

82 Bird's letter to Neilson is quoted in Madden, *The United Irishmen – Their Lives and Times*, 4th Series, 2nd Edition, p. 50. His letter to Camden was published in the (Dublin) United Irish newspaper *The Press* on 20 February 1798 and quoted in Madden, p. 51. See also KHLC, Camden MSS U840/0197/2, Bird to Camden, 3 February 1798. Bird's missive asserted that he would pass information to the Whig politician Lord Moira that would 'strike your boldest orators dumb and raise through the three kingdoms such a tornado of execration as will penetrate the formost [*sic*] recesses of the cabinet of St James and the castle of Dublin'. Camden's fortunes were hit further by Newell's reversion to the side of the United Irishmen. In a note to the viceroy, Newell vented his spleen: 'The people execrate you – your very guards

are the friends of freedom and they detest you ... I assure you that your government has at present not long to exist – the fall of royalty and the birth of liberty is near at hand.' KHLC, Camden MSS U840/0197/3, Newell to Camden, 21 February 1798.

83 J. Agnew (ed.), *The Drennan–McTier Letters*, 2, William Drennan to Martha McTier, 8 February 1798, pp. 362–5.

84 H. Reid, 'The Battle of Ballynahinch', in Hill, Turner, Dawson (eds), *1798 Rebellion in Down* (Newtownards: Colourpoint Press, 1998), p. 139.

85 TCD, Sirr MSS 868/2f245; 868/2f266, Rowley Osborne to Thomas Russell, 4 February 1798; 22 February 1798.

86 NLI, Lake MSS 56/104, Lake to Knox, 18 October 1797. The United Irishman Robert Rollo Reid, lying low in Ayrshire following his hasty exit from Ireland in June 1797, was depressed by the naval defeat. He is alleged to have uttered, 'Damn it!, then we will have no invasion this season.' See E.W. McFarland, *Ireland and Scotland in the Age of Revolution*, p. 174.

87 J. Hayter Hames, *Arthur O'Connor: United Irishman* (Cork: The Collins Press, 2001), p.158.

Chapter 8

1 T. Pakenham, *The Year of Liberty: The Bloody Story of the Great Irish Rebellion of 1798* (London: Hodder and Stoughton, 1969), pp. 47–58.

2 NA, Kew HO/100/75/223–228, Camden to Portland, 15 March 1798; KHLC, Camden MSS U840/0156/28, Camden to Pitt, 17 March 1798.

3 PRONI, Downshire MSS D/607/F/82, Robert Ross to Lord Downshire, 5 March 1798; Downshire MSS D/607/F/108, Ross to Downshire, 27 March 1798.

4 KHLC, Camden MSS U840/0186/6, Lord Abercorn to Camden, 12 March 1798.

5 KHLC, Camden MSS U840/0156A/29–30, Camden to Pitt, 26 March 1798 and 7 April 1798; NA, Kew HO/100/75/29–32, Camden to Wickham, 22 January 1798.

6 T. Graham, 'The Shift in United Irish Leadership from Belfast to Dublin, 1796–1798', in J. Smyth (ed.), *Revolution, Counter-Revolution and Union: Ireland in the 1790s* (Cambridge: Cambridge University Press, 2000,) pp. 59–60.

7 Thomas Reynolds' career as an informer is outlined in T. Bartlett (ed.), *Revolutionary Dublin 1795–1801: The Letters of Francis Higgins to Dublin Castle* (Dublin: Four Courts Press, 2004) pp. 57–8.

8 NA, Kew HO100/75/110–112, Portland to Camden, 23 February 1798; HO100/75/130–132, J.W. (McNally) to Pelham, 25 February 1798; M. Elliott, *Partners in Revolution: The United Irishmen and France* (New Haven: Yale University Press, 1982), pp. 144–50.

9 *Dublin Journal*, 17 March 1798; *Belfast News-Letter*, 30 March 1798; PRONI, Shannon Papers D/2707/A3/3/61, Earl of Shannon to his son Viscount Boyle, 19 April 1798; NA Kew, HO/100/75/281, Wickham to Cooke, 24 March 1798 and HO/100/75/283–284, Wickham to Camden, 24 March 1798; NAI, Rebellion Papers 620/36/59, anonymous report, 24 March 1798; NA Kew, HO/100/66/101, Lord Balkley to Portland, 13 May 1798.

10 NA, Kew HO/100/76/130, Camden to Portland, 24 April 1798.

11 See T. Bartlett (ed.), *Revolutionary Dublin 1795–1801: The Letters of Francis Higgins to Dublin Castle*, Francis Higgins to Cooke, 21 February 1798, p. 222. Drennan was of the view that Neilson's release was attributable either to a quarrel among the informers or to his conversations with Castlereagh and Chief Secretary Pelham. It is likely that he was correct, to varying degrees, on both counts. See J. Agnew (ed.), *The Drennan–McTier Letters*, 2, Drennan to Martha McTier, 8 February 1798, p. 363.

12 R.R. Madden, *The United Irishmen – Their Lives and Times*, 4th Series, 2nd Edition, Samuel Neilson to Anne Neilson, 17 March 1798, p. 100.

13 *House of Lords (Ireland) Report from the Secrecy Committee* (Dublin, 1798), evidence of Samuel Neilson before the Secrecy Committee of the Irish House of Lords, 7 August 1798.

14 NA, Kew HO/100/76/178–179, information of Thomas Reynolds, 11 May 1798; NAI, Rebellion Papers 620/3/32/23, information provided to the government by the informer Thomas Reynolds, 9 May 1798.

15 NA, Kew HO/100/76/132–133, information provided by the Saintfield informer Nicholas Mageean, a colonel in the military structure for County Down and sometime representative on the Ulster Provincial Committee, 17 April 1798.

16 R.R. Madden, *The United Irishmen – Their Lives and Times*, 1st Series, Vol. 1, (London: 1860), pp. 216–17. Madden's account is based on that of Thomas Reynolds Jun., who presented this version in response to one that appeared in T.J. Howell's account of state trials, which included reference to a confrontation between Neilson and Reynolds that depicted the former as superior in physical strength to Reynolds. The younger Reynolds refuted this completely, accusing Howell of believing an embellished account with an inaccurate anecdote from the memoirs of the barrister John Philpot Curran. T. Reynolds, *The Life of Thomas Reynolds Esq by his Son*, Vol. 1 (London: Henry Hooper, 1839), pp. 198–202.

17 T. Reynolds, *The Life of Thomas Reynolds Esq by his Son*, p. 198.

18 R.R. Madden, *The United Irishmen – Their Lives and Times*, 4th Series, 2, p. 153.

19 T. Bartlett (ed.), *Revolutionary Dublin*, Francis Higgins to Cooke, 15 March 1798, p. 230; Higgins to Cooke 15 May 1798, pp. 235–6; Higgins to Cooke, 25 May 1798, p. 242.

20 NAI, Rebellion Papers 620/36/50, Neilson to Cooke, 23 March 1798.

21 R.R. Madden, *The United Irishmen – Their Lives and Times*, 4th Series, 2, Samuel Neilson to Anne Neilson, 17 March 1798, p. 100. Northern leaders were informed that Neilson was at the forefront of United Irish activity in Leinster and that 'he was riding almost day and night organising the people and no person almost knew where he dined or where he slept'. PRONI, Lytton-White Papers D/714/2/20a, information provided by the Saintfield informer, Nicholas Mageean, March or April 1798.

22 NAI, Rebellion Papers 620/51/145, Boyle to Cooke, n.d. 1798; PRONI, Madden MSS (transcripts) T/1210/40, Henry Joy McCracken to Mary Ann McCracken, 8 May 1798; PRONI, Lytton-White Papers D/714/2/20a, information provided by the Saintfield informer, Nicholas Mageean, March or April 1798. The loyalist historian Richard Musgrave stated that McCracken had been sent to Dublin in February 1798 on United Irish business and that he stayed there some time before bringing news to the north about Leinster's plans for an uprising. See R. Musgrave, *Memoirs of the Different Rebellions in Ireland,* (Dublin, 1801), p. 27.

23 NAI, Rebellion Papers 620/18/3/41, Thomas Boyle to Edward Cooke, 10 March 1798.

24 NAI, Rebellion Papers 620/52/145, information of Dennis Ryan, n.d. 1798; 620/51/145, Thomas Boyle to Edward Cooke, n.d. 1798.

25 NAI, Rebellion Papers 620/36/228, Thomas Boyle to Cooke, 3 April 1798. Evans was implicated by Boyle, who would allege that the landowner would be intimate with Father Teeling of Donabate in a plot to assassinate Lord Carhampton. Evans was apprehended at his townhouse in North Great George's Street in July 1798 and exiled to France. Representations were made to Cooke by Evans's cousin Charles Henry Coote but to no immediate avail. Evans would return to Ireland in 1811. *Freeman's Journal*, 21 July 1798. P. Bates, *1798 Rebellion in Fingal: Preparation, Outbreak and Aftermath* (Loughshinny: P. Bates, 1998) p. 75, 100, 138.

26 *House of Commons (Ireland) Report from the Secrecy Committee* (Dublin, 1798), Appendix XIV, p. 128, information supplied by Mageean; T. Graham, 'The Shift in United Irish Leadership from Belfast to Dublin 1796–98', in J. Smyth (ed.), *Revolution, Counter-revolution and Union* (Cambridge: Cambridge University Press, 2000), pp. 55–66.

27 NAI, Rebellion Papers 620/52/136, anonymous letter, 29 April 1798; 620/52/149, Anthony Richardson to Thomas Reynolds, n.d. 1798; K.L. Dawson, 'Henry Monro; Commander of the United Irish Army of Down', in *Down Survey; The Yearbook of Down County Museum* (Downpatrick: 1998), p. 20; PRONI, T2777, The Anecdotal Recollections of Morgan Jellet. Jellet, a member of the loyalist yeomanry during the rebellion, encountered Kean in the US and heard this account first-hand.

28 NA, Kew HO/100/76/130, Camden to Portland, 24 April 1798. As early as 21 March, Drennan was telling Martha McTier that Neilson was being sought and that he was trying to evade capture. J. Agnew (ed.), *The Drennan–McTier Letters*, 2, Drennan to Martha McTier, 21 March 1798, p. 383.

29 TCD, Sirr MSS 869/9f9, Deposition of J.H.E. McG., n.d. 1798.

30 NAI, Rebellion Papers 620/36/196, Magan to Cooke, 22 April 1798.

31 NAI, Rebellion Papers 620/10/121/151, J.W. (McNally) to Cooke, n.d. 1798; T. Bartlett, *Revolutionary Dublin*, Higgins to Cooke, 15 May 1798, pp. 235–6; R.R. Madden, *The United Irishmen – Their Lives and Times*, 4th Series, 2, p. 53. William Drennan, who was perplexed by Neilson's release, was equally confused by reports of this meeting. Neilson had not been arrested and yet was defying the authorities. 'I do not know how or why all this happens.' J. Agnew (ed.), *The Drennan–McTier Letters*, 2, Neilson to Martha McTier, n.d. May 1798, p. 406.

32 For an excellent analysis of the Grattanite position, see D. Mansergh, *Grattan's Failure: Parliamentary Opposition and the People in Ireland 1779–1800* (Dublin: Irish Academic Press, 2005), pp. 211–41.

33 NA, Kew HO/100/76/11–14, informer A.B. to ____, n.d. 1798.

34 *House of Lords (Ireland) Report from the Secrecy Committee* (Dublin, 1798), Appendix 1, pp. 146–51 and pp. 158–59; R.R. Madden, *The United Irishmen – Their Lives and Times*, 1st Series, 2 (Dublin, 1857), p. 408; M. Durey, 'John Hughes, Reluctant Agent Provocateur and Millenarian: a note and new documents', in *Eighteenth Century Ireland*, VII, 1992, pp. 141–6. It is worth noting that the published evidence in the House of Commons Secrecy Report differs to that presented by the Lords. Grattan's son, also called Henry, attributes this to the fact that John Foster, the Speaker of the Commons (and certainly no friend of the United Irishmen), refused to listen to what Hughes had to say. An interesting footnote on the reports from the two houses of the Irish Parliament comes from the MP for Newry, Robert Ross, one of Downshire's correspondents. While Ross's strident conservatism should be treated with some circumspection, he claimed that a defective copy of the Lords evidence was placed in the version that was sent to the House of Commons. The difference between the two reports was discovered after they were completed and the defective copy was found to be in the hand of a clerk in Castlereagh's office. The relationship between the House of Downshire and the Stewarts of Mount Stewart was never cordial and it may be that Ross was keen to discredit the new Chief Secretary. H. Grattan (Jun.), *Memoirs of the Life and Times of the Rt Hon Henry Grattan*, Volume IV (London: Henry Colburn, 1842), p. 373.

35 NA, Kew HO/100/66/365, Castlereagh to William Wickham, 5 September 1798.

36 H. Grattan (Jun.), *Memoirs of the Life and Times of the Rt Hon Henry Grattan*, Volume IV, pp. 409–11.

37 NA, Kew HO/100/78/379, Cornwallis to Portland, 24 September 1798; HO/100/78/373, Castlereagh to Wickham, 24 September 1798; HO/100/78/414, Wickham to Castlereagh,

29 September 1798; *Belfast News-Letter*, 19 October 1798; 9 November 1798; 16 November 1798.

38 *Belfast News-Letter*, 28 December 1798.

39 NA, Kew HO/100/76/220–221, Samuel Sproule to John Lees (and passed to the Home Office in London), n.d. May 1798.

40 NA, Kew HO/100/76/208–9; PC 1/41/A136 Copy of pocket book notes found at the home of Lord Edward Fitzgerald. HO/100/76/170–177, Camden to Portland, 11 May 1798; *Faulkner's Dublin Journal*, 5 May 1798.

41 *Belfast News-Letter*, 14 May 1798.

42 *Dublin Journal*, 10 May 1798; *Freeman's Journal*, 12 May 1798; NAI, Rebellion Papers 620/51/39, Samuel Sproule to John Lees, 15 May 1798.

43 T. Bartlett (ed.), *Revolutionary Dublin*, pp. 234–8.

44 Gallagher was arrested the same night as Fitzgerald was captured and was sentenced to death for his part in a conspiracy to rescue him. NAI, Rebellion Papers 620/39/144, anonymous information, 3 August 1798. The *Freeman's Journal* (22 May 1798) asserted that Sirr's assailant was arrested and was surly and uncooperative when detained. He was rumoured to be a member of the London Corresponding Society.

45 T. Pakenham, *The Year of Liberty* (London: Hodder and Stoughton, 1969), pp. 92–5. Pakenham accused Neilson of being careless about his and Fitzgerald's security and asserted that the capture of the rebel leader required only luck on the part of the authorities 'and the complete recklessness of Samuel Neilson'. T. Moore, *The Life and Death of Lord Edward Fitzgerald*, 2, (London, 1831) pp. 78–87.

46 NAI, Rebellion Papers 620/51/29, Sproule to Cooke, 23 May 1798; PRONI, McPeake Papers T/3048, Elizabeth, Lady Holland to _____, September 1801.

47 TCD, Madden MSS 873/189, Mary Hancock Neilson to Madden 11 April 1842; 873/534, Sophia McAdam to W.J. McNeven, 31 August 1831; 873/535, W.J. McNeven to Sophia McAdam, 19 October 1831.

48 NA, Kew HO/100/76/203–5, Camden to Portland, 20 May 1798; HO/100/76/208–9, papers found on Lord Edward Fitzgerald.

49 The use of codes and cyphers by the United Irishmen would have made many written notes unintelligible to the authorities. Gradually, however, a clearer picture would emerge. When Arthur O'Connor was arrested in 1798, code words were discovered in his razor case: 'Belfast' became 'Boston'; 'France' was 'Williams'; 'Ireland' was 'Patrickson' and 'Dublin Bay' was 'Honduras Bay'. John Cormick, the Dublin feather merchant in whose house Fitzgerald would take refuge, would later declare that the United Irishmen would use words related to business to protect against government interception. Cormick, who escaped capture as he was being prepared as a witness against Neilson, revealed that the Executive was referred to as the 'Trustees' and £5000 meant 5,000 men. NA, Kew PC1/41/A136, papers found in Arthur O'Connor's razor case, n.d. 1798; HO/100/77/246, Castlereagh to Wickham with notes on the declaration of John Cormick, 17 May 1798.

50 NA, Kew HO/100/76/217–9, evidence of Captain Armstrong against the Sheares, 17 May 1798.

51 R.R. Madden, *The United Irishmen – Their Lives and Times*, 1st Series, Vol. 2 (London: 1842), pp. 135–7.

52 T. Bartlett (ed.), *Revolutionary Dublin*, Francis Higgins to Edward Cooke, 25 May 1798, p. 242.

53 NAI, Rebellion Papers 620/51/17, Sproule to Lees, 19 May 1798; 620/32/15, Lord Muskerry to Cooke, 5 August 1797; 620/51/23, Sproule to Lees, 21 May 1798; Sproule to Lees, 23 May

1798; TCD, Sirr MSS 869/9f9, deposition of J.H.E. McG., n.d. 1798. The deponent declared that Neilson stated he had collected fourteen men to rescue Lord Edward on the night he was taken.

54 W.H. Maxwell, *History of the Irish Rebellion in 1798*, 4th ed (London: H.G. Bohn, 1854), p. 57.

55 See T. Pakenham, *The Year of Liberty*, p. 103; B. Dornin, 'A Sketch of the Life of Samuel Neilson of Belfast, Editor of the Northern Star, and member of the Irish Directory', *The Irish Magazine and Monthly Asylum for Neglected Biography*, September 1811, pp. 396–402. Pakenham repeats Dornin's mistake of stating that Neilson had earlier been a prisoner in Newgate.

56 See W.H. Maxwell, *History of the Irish Rebellion*, pp. 58–9.

57 *Memoirs of the Life and Times of the Rt Hon Henry Grattan*, Vol. 4, by his son Henry Grattan Esq MP, p. 369.

58 NAI, Rebellion Papers 620/51/26, Sproule to Cooke, 23 May 1798. Gordon's subsequent role is difficult to ascertain. Martha McTier noted that 'one of the Gordons' (John or perhaps his brother Alexander) had been 'taken up and whipping expected, he was, however, pardoned and even allowed a guard to convoy him out of town'. J. Agnew (ed.), *The Drennan–McTier Letters*, 2, Martha McTier to William Drennan, 31 May 1798, p. 409. This raises the possibility that Gordon had turned approver. Another source, the Belfast attorney and informer James McGucken, wrote to Cooke that Gordon had departed for Belfast after the burning of the mail coaches and left thereafter for Liverpool. NAI, Rebellion Papers 620/7/74/1, McGucken to Cooke, n.d. 1798.

59 NAI, Rebellion Papers 620/38/116, memorial of Tresham Gregg, 4 June 1798; 620/39/131, Gregg's deposition, 31 July 1798; 620/39/143, Council Chamber of Dublin, 2 August 1798.

60 R.R. Madden, *The United Irishmen – Their Lives and Times*, 1st Series, 2 (Dublin: J. Mullany, 1857), p. 493.

61 PRONI, D/584/3, Robert Marshall to Stone, 26 May 1797; D/584/4, Castlereagh to Stone, n.d. May 1798. Castlereagh, the Chief Secretary, allowed Fitzgerald to be attended by a private physician (Dr Lindsay) and by the Surgeon-General, George Stewart.

62 NA, Kew HO/100/77/52–3, Edward Cooke to William Wickham, 6 June 1798. J. Armstrong Garnett's account of Fitzgerald's worsening condition can be found in the Camden Papers in the Kent History and Library Centre in Maidstone, Kent. KHLC, Camden MSS U840/0199/5. The small, private burial was not to the satisfaction of Lady Louisa Connolly, who complained to Camden that while two of the peer's oldest servants were present, his agent, Mr Leeson, was not and there was also a mix-up over the funeral escort. Camden MSS U840/0199/3, Lady Louisa Connolly to Camden, 10 June 1798.

63 NA, Kew 100/77/20–22, Cooke to Wickham, 2 June 1798; HO/100/77/143–5, Castlereagh to Camden, 12 June 1798; NAI, Rebellion Papers 620/38/36, Rev. Snowden Cupples to Rev. Foster Archer, 3 June 1798. During the rebellion, Leonard McNally countered the view that the rising was, in some ways, a Catholic plot. The day before the insurrection broke out in Ulster, he declared that Jackson, Bond, Neilson and Sampson would, in no way, sanction a plot 'the object of which was to subvert the Protestant religion and establish popish bigotry'. Indeed, he noted that the middle-class Catholics held the Pope in contempt – only the wealthier Catholics were pious; 'others are deists'. NAI, Rebellion papers 620/10/121/111, J.W. (McNally) to Cooke, 6 June 1798.

64 NA, Kew HO/100/76/304–5, Wickham to Cooke, 28 May 1798.

65 T. Bartlett (ed.), *Revolutionary Dublin*, Francis Higgins to Edward Cooke, 8 June 1798, p. 251. A copy of Higgins's letter was sent to Home Secretary Wickham in London. NAI, Kew HO/100/77/20–23.

66 *Belfast News-Letter*, 21 June 1798.
67 *Belfast News-Letter*, 29 June 1798; 10 July 1798.
68 R.R. Madden, *The United Irishmen – Their Lives and Times*, 4th Series, 2, p. 101.
69 Ibid., p.102.
70 *Memoirs and Correspondence of Viscount Castlereagh, Second Marquesse of Londonderry, edited by his brother Charles Vane, Marquesse of Londonderry*, Vol. 1 (London: 1848), p. 242. Letter from General Dalrymple to Wickham, 17 July 1798; NAI, Kew HO/100/77/244, Castlereagh to Wickham, 16 July 1798; M. Durey, *Transatlantic Radicals and the Early American Republic* (Kansas: University Press of Kansas, 1997), p. 139.
71 *Memoirs and Correspondence of Viscount Castlereagh*, Wickham to Castlereagh, 23 July 1798, pp. 228–9, and NAI, Kew HO/100/77/278; *The Observer* (London), 29 July 1798.
72 NAI, Rebellion Papers 620/39/102, Sproule to Lees, 21 July 1798.

Chapter 9

1 *Belfast News-Letter*, 22 June 1798; R.R. Madden, *The United Irishmen – Their Lives and Times*, 4th Series, 2, p. 101.
2 PRONI, Downshire MSS D/607/F/339, Robert Ross to Lord Downshire, 26 July 1798.
3 NA, Kew HO100/66/350, Cornwallis to Portland, 26 July 1798. Castlereagh was still hopeful that Neilson would be convicted, even though Bird had always resisted inducements to testify and Cormick had retracted his earlier statements. In the event of the Attorney General proceeding with Neilson's trial, Castlereagh believed that he would be able to convince two United Irish colonels to give evidence. NA, Kew HO100/77/369, Castlereagh to Wickham, 28 July 1799. Bearing in mind that William Orr had been executed the previous year for administering a United Irish oath, the case against Neilson was strong. He had been arrested reconnoitring Newgate on the day the rebellion broke out and was found to have an incriminating letter from John Sheares in his pocket. The merchant John Caldwell, who had been detained in Belfast, had confessed under examination to John Pollock that he had been sworn into the movement by Neilson, although he later retracted this statement. NAI, Rebellion Papers 620/39/203, list of Belfast prisoners who had been offered the benefit of General Nugent's proclamation respecting the state prisoners, 24 August 1798.
4 S. Neilson, *Brief Statement of a Negociation* [*sic*] *between Certain United Irishmen and the Irish Government in July 1798* (New York: 1802), pp. 9–10. Neilson's account asserted that O'Connor received the early outline of the plan 'in warm terms of approbation'. The prisoners' statement can be found in the Home Office papers in London, with Neilson's name at the head of the list of prisoners who signed. NA, Kew HO100/77/305. While Neilson's account of the agreement between the state prisoners and the government stated that the process was initiated in July 1798, he indicated that the first contact was in June when writing to the Duke of Portland from Fort George in 1799. NRS, RH2/4/85ff.63–5, Neilson to the Duke of Portland, 27 April 1799.
5 KHLC, Camden MSS U840/98/2, Castlereagh to Camden, 9 July 1798.
6 NA, Kew HO100/77/311–12, Cooke to Wickham, 28 July 1798.
7 T. Pakenham, *The Year of Liberty*, p. 288.
8 *Arthur O'Connor's Letter to Lord Castlereagh* (Dublin: 1799), p. 4; *Memoirs of William Sampson* (New York: George Forman, 1807), p. 25; J. Quinn, *Soul on Fire: A Life of Thomas Russell*, p. 207. O'Connor did not sign the Neilson draft on the 24th, such was his mistrust of the Irish administration. Sampson was visited by Oliver Bond's wife and although she did

not plead with him to sign in order to save the life of her husband, the visit did convince Sampson that supporting the process was, in fact, the right thing to do. W. Sampson, *Memoirs of William Sampson*, p. 25.

9 NAI, Rebellion Papers 620/14/211/2, Roger O'Connor to ___, 13 September 1811.

10 NA, Kew HO100/77/307, Cornwallis to Portland, 26 July 1798; Neilson, *Brief Statement*, pp. 10–11. MacNeven's account stresses his distrust of Cooke and stresses that he, O'Connor and John Sweetman had suggested a meeting with Castlereagh with the aim of catching the eye of Cornwallis. W.J. MacNeven, *Pieces of Irish History, illustrative of the condition of the Catholics of Ireland of the origin and progress of the political system of the United Irishmen; and of their transactions with the Anglo-Irish government* (New York: W.J. MacNeven, 1807), pp. 172–6.

11 R.R. Madden, *The United Irishmen – Their Lives and Times*, 4th Series, 2, pp. 102–3, Samuel Neilson to Anne Neilson, 30 July 1798. While Madden quotes much of Samuel Neilson's prison correspondence, the version provided is edited. Papers deposited in the library of the University of Rhode Island by one of Neilson's descendants, Katherine Burt Jackson, contain fuller versions of his 1799 letters, copied by one of his daughters in the years after his death. I am grateful to the staff at the university for furnishing me with a copy of this archive. Neilson's pride in the part he played at this time was reaffirmed in a letter sent to Anne from Fort George on 15 September 1799: URIL, Samuel Neilson Collection, 1799–1977, Mss. Gr. 72.

12 Memoir of the Union, 4 August 1798. The memorandum is produced in full in Neilson, *Brief Statement*, pp. 13–28. The quotation from the *Courier* was quoted disapprovingly in *Faulkner's Dublin Journal*, 30 August 1798.

13 *The Observer*, 5 August 1798; *Belfast News-Letter*, 3 August 1798. One hostile source asserted that Neilson was not, in fact, chained all of the time in Newgate and that he told John Philpot Curran he wore them only for the inspector. The gaoler claimed that Neilson was chained to protect the life of his guard. J. Wells, *Lives of Illustrious and Distinguished Irishmen*, Vol. VI (i) (Dublin: 1825), p. 62.

14 Neilson, *Brief Statement* pp. 30–1. According to the newspapers, Dobbs was accompanied to Wicklow by 'a Mr McCabe, late a leader of the rebels'. This was William Putnam McCabe. *The Times*, 20 August 1798.

15 *House of Lords (Ireland) Report from the Secrecy Committee* (Dublin, 1798), evidence of Samuel Neilson before the Secrecy Committee of the Irish House of Lords, 7 August 1798; Neilson, *Brief Statement*, p. 33–5.

16 NAI, Rebellion Papers 620/52/112, statement of Samuel Neilson, undated.

17 See *Memoirs and Correspondence of Viscount Castlereagh*, Vol. 1, p. 259–64. Wickham was irked by the failure of the committee to press O'Connor about his journey to Switzerland in the company of Lord Edward Fitzgerald in 1796. MacNeven's contacts with the Spanish minister in Hamburg had not been addressed, nor were any of the names of French agents being declared. Wickham believed, understandably, that the state prisoners were being economical in their answers and sticking to a prepared script.

18 Neilson, *Brief Statement*, pp. 30–1; NAI, State Prisoner Petitions SPP/245, Neilson to Cooke, 21 August 1798.

19 *Faulkner's Dublin Journal*, 23 August 1798; *The Freeman's Journal*, 28 August 1798. The *Dublin Journal* vented its fury – and that of many loyalists – in its editorial of 30 August: 'So utterly unworthy have the imprisoned Traitors proved themselves of the lenity which they have late experienced, and so obviously was their last outrage intended to encourage and foment a new Rebellion, that Government is not only justified, but entitled to the thanks of the kingdom of Ireland, in having them remanded to their former strict imprisonment.'

The prisoners were criticised not only for the advertisement but for distributing thousands of handbills at Donnybrook Fair. The editorial continued: 'Now are the murders of the last six years, and the massacres of 1798, not only defended – but the Prime Murderers – the Arch Traitors – the Chief Assassins, talk of JUSTIFICATION.' Charles Cornwallis Marquis Cornwallis, *Correspondence of Charles, First Marquis Cornwallis*, Vol. 2 (London: 1859), Castlereagh to Wickham, 27 August 1798, p. 390.

20 Neilson, *Brief Statement*, pp. 31–2. As lawyers, O'Connor and Emmet were obvious choices to represent the prisoners' position. MacNeven, too, was a United Irish leader of considerable standing and his involvement would have mollified the Catholics. That Neilson was not pushed forward as one of the three spokesmen may indicate a lack of faith in his judgement. In the light of the advertisement, Castlereagh noted soberly that the prisoners' statement had angered supporters of the government. His tone suggested that the entire nature of the compact with the state prisoners was at risk. NA, Kew HO100/78/207, Castlereagh to Wickham, 28 August 1798.

21 *The Times*, 27 August 1798.

22 Members of Parliament such as Edmund McNaghten (Antrim) and 'virulent barristers' Francis Hely-Hutchinson (Naas) and William Conyingham Plunket (Charlemont) were particularly vocal in calling for the resumption of treason trials and executions. W.J. MacNeven, *Pieces of Irish History*, p. 192.

23 *Northern Star*, 31 December 1795.

24 Madden asserts that Neilson had seen the coffin sent to Newgate for Bond and had assessed that the rope to be used was of sufficient strength to carry his weight. R.R. Madden, *The United Irishmen – Their Lives and Times*, 4th Series, 2, p. 163; NAI, Rebellion Papers 620/39/190, Samuel Sproule to John Lees, 21 August 1798.

25 Neilson, *Brief Statement*, p. 35.

26 *Faulkner's Dublin Journal*, 8 September 1798. A biographical sketch of Thomas Addis Emmet, written in 1915 by one of his relations, alleges that Bond was poisoned. Madden cites an account by one of Bond's friends, James Davock, who insisted that Bond was killed by one Simpson, the under-gaoler at Newgate. Only the surgeon-general had a clear sight of Bond's body at the inquest and Poynton later accused Simpson of killing Bond (contrary to her evidence), prompting the under-gaoler to kick her in the back, causing her death through injury. Madden also references a newspaper article of 1843, written by an informed source, which alleges that Bond was struck on the back of the head by one of the turnkeys. The newspaper editor was the veteran United Irishman John Binns. See R.R. Madden, *The United Irishmen – Their Lives and Times*, 4th Series, 2, pp. 164–5.

27 Neilson, *Brief Statement*, pp. 36–8

28 For example, some prisoners in Belfast were offered the benefit of a proclamation by General George Nugent, the commander in Ulster, which granted them a similar chance to leave Ireland in return for information. Many of the Belfast prisoners, including leading figures such as William Tennent, Rev. William Steel Dickson, Luke Teeling, John Magennis and Robert Simms, did not accept the terms. NAI, Rebellion Papers 620/39/203, list of prisoners in Belfast, 24 August 1798.

29 NAI, State Prisoner Petitions SPP/245, Neilson to Castlereagh, 11 October 1798. The men mentioned by Neilson were William Thompson, John Thompson and Samuel McCauley; Neilson to Marsden, 20 October 1798; *Belfast News-Letter*, 26 October 1798.

30 NA, Kew HO100/79/328, Rufus King to Portland, 13 September 1798; HO100/79/330, Portland to Rufus King, 22 September 1798; HO100/79/336, Rufus King to Portland, 17 October 1798; HO100/79/55, Wickham to Castlereagh, 19 October 1798.

31 Neilson, *Brief Statement*, pp. 38–9.
32 NA, Kew HO100/79/65, Castlereagh to Wickham, 29 October 1798.
33 See MacNeven, *Pieces of Irish History*, Rufus King to Henry Jackson, 23 August 1799; Thomas Addis Emmet to Rufus King, 9 April 1807, pp. 235–48.
34 NA, Kew HO100/66/387–8, Cornwallis to Portland, 13 September 1798.
35 NRS, RH2/4/85ff.7–9, R Dundas (Lord Advocate) to Portland, 6 March 1799; RH2/4/85ff.11, memo of Sir R. Abercromby, 6 March 1799. Part of Abercromby's communication with Portland is cited in D. Douglas, *The Only Safe Place: The Irish State Prisoners at Fort George* (Perth: Braehead Publishers, 2000), pp. 29–30; NA, Kew HO100/86/10, Wickham (draft) to Cornwallis, 3 March 1799.
36 *The Times*, 15 April 1799.
37 See J. Quinn, *Soul on Fire*, pp. 211–13.
38 NA, Kew HO100/78/211, R.R. Wilford to Castlereagh, 27 August 1798; PRONI, Downshire MSS D/607/F/427, George Stephenson to Lord Downshire, 24 September 1798. (Interestingly, Thomas Russell attempted to raise Loughinisland in his effort to support Robert Emmet's insurrection in July 1803.) PRONI, Downshire MSS D/607/F/526, Robert Ross to Downshire, 8 November 1798; PRONI, Downshire MSS D/607/G/41 and 54, Richard Annesley to Downshire, 30 January 1799 and 9 February 1799; *Belfast News-Letter*, 12 February 1799; NA, Kew HO100/79/276–279, Cornwallis to Portland, 21 December 1798; NA, Kew HO100/86/142, Cooke to Wickham, 14 March 1799; *Belfast News-Letter*, 12 March 1799. The view that the United Irishmen continued to pose a threat was communicated to Dublin from different parts of the country. Reverend Snowden Cupples warned that the situation in the vicinity of Lisburn was 'worse than this time last year' and that a number of strangers were organising clandestine operations. Men of property were being frozen out of the movement as a result of their timidity during the rising and 'the form of obligation is altered and approaches nearly to Defenderism'. NA, Kew HO100/86/244, Castlereagh to Wickham, 3 April 1799. An anonymous source in Belfast reported that Henry Haslett, a founder member of the United Irishmen and former prisoner at Kilmainham, had re-entered the republican ranks and was holding secret meetings at his home with 'ruffians' and that they were prepared to print papers with the blood of Mr (Edward) Cooke. NAI, Rebellion Papers 620/3/32/1, anonymous to Pelham and Cooke, 25 February 1799.
39 NA, Kew HO100/66/377, Castlereagh to Wickham, 29 October 1798.
40 PRONI, Downshire MSS D/607/G/132, Robert Johnston to Lord Downshire, 23 March 1799. In his letter, Johnston expressed criticism at the government's handling of the state prisoners, asserting that they had been agitating in the Dublin gaols: 'They have shipped them off after having kept them here till they did almost all the mischief that could be done.' Madden asserted that a prisoner called Ivers had passed information relating to a continued United Irish conspiracy to the government in the autumn of 1798, leading to searches of the prisoners' cells. R.R. Madden, *The United Irishmen – Their Lives and Times*, 4th Series, 2, p. 87. NAI, Rebellion Papers 620/56/136, Anne Neilson to Castlereagh, 12 January 1799; Neilson, *Brief Negotiation,* p. 40. Neilson's assets were advertised for sale in the *Belfast News-Letter*. The business of Alexander, Neilson and Gordon would be let to a suitable bidder and the current stock sold at a reduced cost for cash. Leases for properties in Skegoniell, High Street, the house and stable that was the *Star* office and Waring Street were advertised, along with a horse and cart and shares in London and Liverpool Traders. *Belfast News-Letter*, 12 October 1798; 9 November 1798.
41 NAI, Rebellion Papers 620/7/74/5, information of James McGucken (United Irishman, lawyer and informer), 29 January 1799.

42 Neilson, *Brief Statement*, p. 41.
43 TCD, Sirr MSS 869/6f9, Castlereagh orders, 18 March 1799; R.R. Madden, *The United Irishmen – Their Lives and Times*, 4th Series, 2, extract from John Sweetman's diary, p. 93; Neilson, *Brief Statement*, p. 41.
44 NA, Kew HO100/86/163, Castlereagh to Wickham, 19 March 1799.
45 PRONI T/3541/5/3, *Particulars of History of a North County Irish Family,* John Caldwell c. 1850.
46 Madden's view was that Neilson did not consume excessive amounts of alcohol before his confinement. His sufferings were such, however, that 'the old ruinous remedy for alleviating such troubles' became increasingly a feature of his existence in gaol, during his brief period of freedom after his release in February 1798 and in the period before the state prisoners were transported to Scotland. Madden defended Neilson's drinking by saying that business – political or otherwise – was conducted in public houses. Madden, *The United Irishmen – Their Lives and Times*, 4th Series, 2, p. 160.
47 Quoted in *Belfast News-Letter*, 9 April 1799. Jack Ketch was the renowned executioner for the restored Charles II, famed for his less than efficient executions of Lord Russell and the Duke of Monmouth.
48 See Madden, *The United Irishmen – Their Lives and Times*, 4th Series, 2, extract from John Sweetman's diary, pp. 170–4; Rev. W.S. Dickson, *A Narrative of the Confinement and Exile of Reverend William Steel Dickson D.D.* (London: 1812), pp. 100–22.
49 *Belfast News-Letter*, 5 April 1799.
50 NRS, RH2/4/85ff.19, Abercromby to Portland, 1 April 1799; RH2/4/85ff.55, list of questions asked by Stuart, 22 April 1799.
51 NA, Kew HO100/66/414, Cooke to Wickham, 23 March 1799; HO100/86/264, Whinnery to Lees, 9 April 1799.
52 NRS, RH2/4/85ff.63–65, Neilson to Portland, 27 April 1799.
53 See Dickson, *Narrative*, pp. 125–34. By October, John King, an Under-Secretary at the Home Office, ruled that letters being sent to Fort George would be directed undercover to the secretary for the Civil Department in Dublin before being conveyed to London and thence to the prisoners in Scotland. NRS, RH2/4/222ff.43, John King to Lt-Gov. Stuart, 31 October 1799. It may not be beyond the bounds of possibility that the prisoners were treated benevolently because Governor Stuart was the son of a former Grand Master of the Freemasons in Scotland, while his half-nephew also filled the same position between 1796 and 1798. Some of the state prisoners, including Neilson and Tennent, were Freemasons.
54 The *Belfast News-Letter* had noted that 'Those already arrived are very merry, as they mostly employ their time with music.' *Belfast News-Letter*, 24 May 1799; *The Times*, 26 April 1799; Dickson, *Narrative*, pp. 134–5.
55 NRS, RH/2/4/222ff.70, King to Stuart, 5 May 1800.
56 Dickson, *Narrative*, pp. 147–8.
57 PRONI, Tennent Papers D/1748/B/1/319/41, Robert Tennent to William Tennent (Fort George), 16 July 1801.
58 See Madden, *The United Irishmen – Their Lives and Times*, 3rd Series, 2, Memoir of William James MacNeven (Dublin: 1860); PRONI, Tennent Papers D/1748/B/3/3/4; D/1748/b/3/10/1, diary entries and pocket book, 1801.
59 Neilson's letters indicate that the shop was in the centre of Belfast. Later directories of Belfast for 1807 and 1808 list her business premises as 56 High Street and 99 High Street respectively. *Merchants Aplenty: Joseph Smyth's Belfast Directories of 1807 and 1808* (Belfast: Ulster Historical Foundation, republished 1991).

60 J. Agnew (ed.), *The Drennan–McTier Letters*, 2, Martha McTier to William Drennan, 7 June 1799, p. 508.
61 University of Rhode Ireland Library (hereafter URIL) Mss.Gr.72, Samuel to Anne Neilson, 11 May 1799.
62 URIL, Mss.Gr.72, Samuel to Anne Neilson, 1 June 1799.
63 Ibid., Samuel to Anne Neilson, 4 August 1799; 17 August 1799.
64 Ibid., Samuel to Anne Neilson, 5 September 1799; 15 September 1799.
65 Ibid., Samuel to Anne Neilson, 22 September 1799; 22 September 1799.
66 Ibid., Samuel to Anne Neilson, 21 July 1799; 28 July 1799.
67 Ibid., Samuel to Anne Neilson, 8 September 1799.
68 Ibid., Samuel to Anne Neilson, 21 July 1799; 4 August 1799. 'John' may refer to his nephew, John Neilson Jun., son of his late brother, or perhaps John Gordon (his nephew and business partner, who had been imprisoned in Kilmainham with Neilson).
69 Ibid., Samuel to Agnes (his wife, Anne) and Sophia Neilson, 17 August 1799.
70 Ibid., Samuel to Anne Neilson, 17 August 1799.
71 Ibid., Samuel to Anne Neilson, 5 September 1799.
72 Ibid., Samuel Neilson to Anne, 17 November 1799.
73 *Belfast News-Letter*, 2 July 1799; 31 December 1799.
74 URIL, Mss.Gr.72, Samuel to Anne Neilson, 11 May 1799; 25 May 1799.
75 Ibid., Samuel to Anne Neilson, 6 July 1799; 4 August 1799.
76 Ibid., Samuel to Anne Neilson, 25 August 1799; 28 September 1799.
77 Ibid., Samuel to Anne Neilson, 21 July 1799.
78 Ibid., Samuel to Anne Neilson, 5 September 1799.
79 Letters from Samuel to Anne Neilson, quoted in Madden, *The United Irishmen – Their Lives and Times*, 4th Series, 2, 13 October 1799; 20 October 1799; 5 November 1799, pp.111–12.

Chapter 10

1 T. Bartlett, 'An Union for Empire'; I. McBride, 'Ulster Presbyterians and the Passing of the Act of Union', in M. Brown, P.M. Geoghegan and J. Kelly (eds), *The Irish Act of Union, 1800* (Dublin: Irish Academic Press, 2003).
2 NAI, Rebellion Papers 620/7/74/5, information provided by the Belfast United Irishman Robert Hunter, 29 January 1799. The informer Leonard McNally made the same observation: 'The Orange and Green are making rapid approaches towards each other'. NAI, 620/10/121/124, J.W. (McNally) to Cooke, 20 January 1799.
3 URIL, Mss.Gr.72, Samuel to Anne Neilson, 21 July 1799; R.R. Madden, *The United Irishmen – Their Lives and Times*, 4th Series, 2, pp. 105–6. It is likely that some of the letters to and from Neilson were smuggled in and out of Fort George by visitors or by insiders.
4 URIL, Mss.Gr.72, Samuel Neilson to Anne, 28 July 1799.
5 The derailing of the revolution in France and the emergence of the Bonaparte dictatorship was viewed with increasing alarm by some of the United Irishmen, who had pinned their hopes on the attractiveness of French liberty. By 1802, that flame had been extinguished. See, for example, a letter written from Fort George by Thomas Russell to his friend in Belfast, John Templeton: 'What has occasioned the temporary miscarriage of the Cause, is useless to dwell on. Providence orders all for the best. I am sure the people will never abandon that cause, and I am equally sure it will succeed. But I fear that many were led so far astray, as to think favourably of the usurpation of Bonaparte, which tramples on liberty in France, suspends its progress in

the world, and madly attempts its total destruction. If that predilection was extensive, it was certainly very fortunate that no revolution took place; for there would have been no change but a change of masters.' Russell to Templeton, 5 June 1802, quoted in Madden, *The United Irishmen – Their Lives and Times*, 3rd Series, 2, p. 201.

6 Ibid., pp. 202–3.

7 R. O'Donnell, *Robert Emmet and the Rebellion of 1798* (Dublin: Irish Academic Press, 2003), pp. 165–8. Madden noted that these visits took place and stated that Mason spent ten days at Fort George, meeting regularly with prisoners on the ramparts, though not with Emmet, with whom he communicated by letter through Lt-Col. Stuart. R.R. Madden, *The United Irishmen – Their Lives and Times*, 3rd Series, 2, pp. 97–102; pp. 287–8. Given the suspicions cast on Robert Emmet at the time of his expulsion from Trinity College in April 1798 and William Putnam McCabe, due to his obvious association with the insurrection, it is difficult to believe that even someone as tolerant as Stuart would be so accommodating.

8 M. MacDonagh, *The Viceroy's Postbag: Correspondence hitherto unpublished of the Earl of Hardwicke First Lord Lieutenant of Ireland after the Union* (London, John Murray, 1904), pp. 260–2.

9 See Madden, *The United Irishmen – Their Lives and Times*, 4th Series, 2, Samuel Neilson to Anne Neilson, 1 January 1802, p. 131.

10 Thomas Addis Emmet (a descendant of Emmet), *Memoir of Thomas Addis and Robert Emmet with their ancestors and immediate family*, Vol. 1 (New York: 1915), pp. 318–19.

11 NRS, RH2/4/85ff.91–92, Lt-Gov. Stuart to Portland, 13 June 1799. Stuart believed that Roger O'Connor's medical complaint 'lies more in Mr O'Connor's mind than his body', but an enclosure by Dr Thomas Stephen (RH2/4/85ff.95) noted some of his symptoms; headaches, anxiety, depression of mind and an inability to speak coherently, with a wandering imagination. The following month, Stuart would recommend that O'Connor be permitted to take some air in a carriage outside of the fort, accompanied by a guard. NRS, RH2/4/85ff.101, Stuart to Portland, 19 July 1799.

12 URIL, Mss.Gr.72, Samuel Neilson to Anne, 8 September 1799; 15 September 1799.

13 See Madden 4, 2, Samuel Neilson to Anne, 18 May 1800, p. 115.

14 See Madden, Samuel Neilson to Anne, 30 March 1800, p. 114.

15 PRONI, Tennent Papers D1748/B/1/238/1, Arthur O'Connor to William Tennent, n.d. 1801.

16 PRONI, Granard Papers T/3765/J/9/2/8, Lady Moira to Lady Granard, 13 October 1800.

17 See Madden, Samuel Neilson to Anne, 20 April 1800, pp. 114–15.

18 Ibid., 4 November 1801, pp. 128–9. In the summer of 1801, Stuart was in no doubt about the bickering among the prisoners: 'I understand they have fallen out among themselves and that Mr O'Connor is now the object of their dislike – they say they wonder how they could be so deceived by a fellow without Science or arts to entitle him to take any lead, on the other hand, he treats them with the most sovereign contempt.' By the time the prisoners left the fort, the disputes were common knowledge. Lt-Governor Stuart informed Pelham that relations between the men had been strained: 'For a considerable time past, the prisoners have been on very bad terms with one another. Several of them not speaking to the other – O'Connor speaking only to Hudson.' NRS, RH2/4/87ff.89, Stuart to E.F. Hutton, 24 July 1801; RH2/4/88ff.185, Stuart to Pelham, 30 June 1802.

19 TCD, Madden MSS 873/577, document passed to Madden by the son of John Sweetman. Thomas Emmet's disdain for O'Connor led him to request a set of duelling pistols. See R. O'Donnell, *Robert Emmet*, I, p. 166; Madden, 3rd series, 2, p. 288. Another significant fall-out at Fort George was the fallout between Edward Hudson and William Dowdall. Hudson

accused his fellow prisoner of siding with the others against him, despite having earlier shown himself to be supportive of Hudson's more moderate position. In a bitter letter to Dowdall, Hudson stated that he no longer regarded him as a friend and any future intercourse 'cannot exceed the civility of the table'. He felt that some of his fellow inmates were endeavouring 'to intimidate those whom they cannot otherwise influence to join their cabal' and was critical of the 'hideous deformity of their conduct'. Hudson's opinion of the others was damning: 'They may pretend to be anything else, but United Irishmen: that honourable appellation, the premise of our country – they have disgraced – have forfeited ... I do not think that I shall ever be so much of a Christian as to forgive these men.' NAI, Rebellion Papers 620/12/43/5, Hudson to Dowdall, 24 September 1801.

20 See Madden, Samuel Neilson to Anne, 26 January 1800; 30 March 1800, pp. 113–14.

21 Ibid., Samuel Neilson to Anne, 15 June 1800, p. 116.

22 Ibid., 6 December 1800; 28 December 1800, pp. 118–19; PRONI, Tennent Papers D1748/B/1/319/31, Robert Tennent to William Tennent, 29 January 1801.

23 See Madden, Neilson to his daughters, 18 January 1801; 5 April 1801, pp. 119–20.

24 PRONI, Tennent Papers D1748/B/1/319/42, Robert to William Tennent, 29 July 1801.

25 NRS, RH2/4/222ff.136, Portland to Stuart, 22 July 1801.

26 See Madden, Samuel Neilson to Anne Neilson, 26 July 1801, p. 123.

27 Ibid., William Neilson to his mother, 30 August 1801 and 14 September 1801; William Neilson to his sisters, 7 September 1801, pp. 124–5.

28 Ibid., Samuel Neilson to Anne, 14 September 1801, p. 125.

29 Ibid., Samuel Neilson to Anne, 28 September 1801; 5 October 1801; 18 October 1801; 22 November 1801; 25 December 1801; William Neilson to his mother, 6 December 1801, pp. 125–30

30 Ibid., Samuel to Anne Neilson, 18 October 1801, pp. 127–8.

31 Mrs Risk and a Mr B. Worthington were permitted to access Fort George to speak with William Dowdall, a lawyer, about two disputed wills that he was a witness to. NRS, RH2/4/222ff.148, G. Shee to Lt-Gov. Stuart, 11 September 1801. It seems likely that this was a ploy to secrete information in and out of the fort. See note 60.

32 See Madden, Samuel Neilson to Anne, 4 November 1801, pp. 128–9.

33 PRONI, Tennent Papers D1748/B/1/319/33, Robert Tennent to William Tennent, 16 March 1801. These legal difficulties were caused by an error on the original warrant signed by Portland, which accused the state prisoners of high treason against the king. This opened the possibility of a challenge, since the right of *habeas corpus* was protected better in the Scottish jurisdiction under the Act of Settlement of 1701 than it was south of the border, something that was recognised by the Scottish Lord Advocate Robert Dundas (as well as by William Dowdall, one of the state prisoners, who was also a lawyer). The prisoners not subject to the Banishment Act (including Dowdall) were well aware of their rights and wrote to Stuart to ask him to remind the Home Secretary of this fact. Stuart, meanwhile, panicked when he discovered a grammatical error in the warrant. The document recited the names of the prisoners but then went on to order the Lord Advocate to detain 'him' (singular) rather than 'them' (plural). Stuart wrote to Dundas of his concerns, 'recollecting how very strict law is, and how tenacious of the smallest inaccuracy Gentlemen of the law are apt to be, I thought it best to send you the warrant that it may be corrected if necessary'. Stuart made the correction on copies of the warrant and informed Portland that the mistake was known only to Dundas, the Fort Major (Baillie) and his trusted clerk. NRS, RH2/4/87ff.19–20, Tennent, Dowdall, Simms and Hunter to Lt-Gov. Stuart, 12 March 1801; RH2/4/87ff.27–28, Stuart to Dundas, 19 March 1801; RH2/4/87ff.29–30, Stuart to Portland, 29 March 1801.

34 PRONI, Tennent Papers D1748/B/1/319/41, Robert Tennent to William Tennent, 16 July 1801. Tennent had been assessed by the resident physician, Dr James Roy, whose report mentioned a soreness of the throat and an anxiety that was a consequence of being confined. Though a sympathetic man, Stuart was sceptical of Tennent's condition, believing him to be angling for an early end to his captivity. The prisoners were allowed to exercise, swim and play ball and cricket. John Chambers was allowed to leave the fort in a carriage, accompanied by a guard, something that was seen as an act of partiality by the other detainees. While the climate was harsh, Stuart maintained, 'I do not know a more healthy place in His Majesty's dominions than Fort George.' NRS, RH/2/4/87ff.89, Lt-Gov. Stuart to E.F. Hutton, 24 July 1801.

35 PRONI, Tennent Papers D1748/B/1/319/45, Robert Tennent to William Tennent, 6 October 1801.

36 See Madden, Samuel Neilson to Anne, 4 November 1801, pp. 128–9.

37 While the possibility of liberation raised expectations among the prisoners, Lt-Gov. Stuart was anxious about the implications of this for his own financial position. He wrote to Portland in October to point out that once he was no longer responsible for the state prisoners, he would be reduced to very narrow economic circumstances. He asked about the possibility of either resuming his half-pay entitlement with the 121st Regiment or taking on a company of invalids. NRS, RH2/4/87ff.114–115, Stuart to Portland, 15 October 1801.

38 See Madden, Willam B. Neilson to Anne Neilson, 17 January 1802, p. 132.

39 Ibid., Samuel to Anne Neilson, 16 May 1802, p. 134.

40 Lt-Gov. Stuart to the state prisoners, 31 May 1802, quoted in Thomas Addis Emmet, *Memoir of Thomas Addis and Robert Emmet with their ancestors and immediate family*, Vol. 1 (New York: 1915), p. 314. Stuart's humanity is shown by his style of communication: 'Although I am not warranted to give this information officially, I am very certain of the fact, and the gentlemen will make what use they judge proper of the communication.'

41 See Madden, Samuel to Anne Neilson, 31 May 1802, pp. 134–5.

42 Ibid., Samuel to Sophia Neilson, 5 June 1802, p. 135.

43 Ibid., Samuel to Anne Neilson, 13 June 1802, pp. 135–6.

44 NA, Kew KB33/37, pardon of Samuel Neilson and ten others for treasons relating to the Rebellion in Ireland, 31 May 1802.

45 J. Allen, *Battles of the British Navy*, Vol. 2 (London: Henry G. Bohn, 1852), p. 11.

46 See Madden, Samuel to Anne Neilson, 4 July 1802, p. 137.

47 P. Weber, *On the Road to Rebellion: The United Irishmen and Hamburg* (Dublin: Four Courts Press, 1997), p. 172. Weber cites a letter to Rowan from Thomas Addis Emmet, who expressed concern that any dealings between the former prisoners and Rowan might produce unwanted consequences: 'We are in some measure apprised of your situation, and of the injury you might possibly sustain by holding intercourse with us; we therefore voluntarily deprive ourselves of the pleasure we should enjoy in your society, and declined calling on you directly on our arrival. For my part it would give me the utmost pain if your friendship towards me were to lead you into any embarrassment, or subject you to any misrepresentation on a point of such material importance to yourself and family.'

48 W.H. Drummond (ed.), *The Autobiography of Archibald Hamilton Rowan* (Dublin: 1840), pp. 435–6; Neilson to A. Hamilton Rowan, 12 July 1802.

49 *Memoirs of William Sampson* (Belfast: Atholl Books, reprinted 2007), introduction by K. Robinson, p. 7.

50 NAI, Rebellion Papers 620/67/203, anonymous information about George Wood, 25 August 1803.

51 NA Kew, HO100/117/93-7, examination of George Wood, 18 October 1803. In his examination, Wood stated that he had arrived in Hamburg in October 1801.

52 See Weber, *On the Road to Rebellion*, p. 173.

53 NAI, Rebellion Papers 620/12/140, examination of Thomas Ridgeway, 18 August 1803. Ridgeway was still in custody in Kilmainham in December 1803. NAI, SPP 1A/17A/5/3954. George Wood, who had been in Hamburg at this time, stated that Neilson, McCann and Ridgeway were often together. The latter's denial that he knew his passenger's identity is not credible. See NA Kew, HO100/117/93-7, examination of George Wood, 18 October 1803.

54 See Madden, Samuel to Anne Neilson, 5 August 1802, p. 137.

55 NAI, Rebellion Papers 620/11/130/18, examination of Ross McCann, 20 August 1803; 620/11/160/26, J. Foster (Customs House, Drogheda) to Alexander Marsden, 10 September 1803. The Roberts alluded to here may well have been the informer Samuel Turner who was still in Hamburg in 1802 and who used the names Roberts and Richardson over the years to avoid being exposed as a government agent. See Weber, *On the Road to Rebellion*, p. 179.

56 See R.R. Madden, *The United Irishmen – Their Lives and Times*, 4th Series, 2, p. 152. Wood later stated that Anthony McCann told him that Neilson had not altered his political opinions. See NA Kew, HO100/117/93-7, examination of George Wood, 18 October 1803.

57 See R.R. Madden, *Antrim and Down in '98*, pp. 137–43.

58 See Madden, *The United Irishmen – Their Lives and Times*, 4th Series, 2, p. 152.

59 Ibid., p. 152; NAI, Rebellion Papers 620/10/121/16, ______ (Belfast) to Alexander Marsden, 10 September 1802.

60 *Belfast News-Letter*, 19 October 1802.

61 See Madden, Samuel to Anne Neilson, n.d. October 1802, pp. 138–9.

62 Ibid., Samuel to Anne Neilson, 4 November 1801 and note, pp. 128–9. Mrs Risk was accompanied to Fort George by 'young Mr Worthington' and remained there for a week. NAI, Rebellion Papers 620/11/138/3, examination of Ross McCann, 11 August 1803. It was alleged by McCann that the County Down United Irishman Reverend William Steel Dickson had dined at least once with Mrs Risk since his release from Fort George. A selection of confiscated letters to and from Mrs Risk are in the Rebellion Papers in the National Archives of Ireland. Her prison exchanges with the lawyer William Dowdall were centred on a legal dispute between her and a Mrs Beere over a will. She seemed to be staying at different stages in Temple Street and Werbergh Street in the capital. NAI, Rebellion Papers 620/12/148/1–15. Risk and Worthington were given permission to visit Fort George by the Home Office official in London, George Shee. NRS, RH2/4/222ff.148, G Shee to Lt-Gov. Stuart, 11 September 1801.

63 *The Phoenix* (New York), 29 December 1860.

64 NAI, Rebellion Papers 620/11/138/3; 620/11/138/5, examinations of Ross McCann, 11 and 20 August 1803; 620/11/138/5A, examination of Mrs Usher, 22 August 1803; see R. O'Donnell, *Robert Emmet and the Rebellion of 1798*, pp. 125–6; R. O'Donnell, 'The Military Committee and the United Irishmen', in M.T. Davis and P.A. Pickering (eds), *Unrespectable Radicals? Popular Politics in the Age of Reform* (London: Routledge, 2007), pp. 125–45. While Grattan thought highly of Dowdall, he was concerned by the prisoner's continued support for republicanism. Grattan wrote to McCann in March 1802, asking him to convey to Dowdall that he would be ruined if he were to persist. Grattan would not recommend him for employment unless he was convinced that Dowdall had rejected sedition. NAI, Rebellion Papers 620/12/143/8, Grattan to Ross McCann, 6 March 1802. Neilson had admitted to his

wife that he was suffering from ill health, due to 'perpetual night riding and anxiety of mind'. See Madden, Samuel to Anne Neilson, n.d. October 1802, pp. 138–9.

65 NAI, Rebellion Papers 620/11/130/18, secret information, 20 August 1803; see O'Donnell, *Robert Emmet and the Rebellion of 1798*, pp. 125–6; for the reputed meeting between Neilson and Robert Emmet, see O'Donnell, *Robert Emmet and the Rebellion of 1798*, p. 190; see O'Donnell, 'The Military Committee and the United Irishmen', in Davis and Pickering (eds), *Unrespectable Radicals? Popular Politics in the Age of Reform*, p. 137.

66 NAI, Rebellion Papers 620/10/121/35, J.W. (McNally) to Edward Cooke, 26 September 1796; 620/12/141/24, James Dixon to Wickham, 26 September 1803.

67 NAI, Rebellion Papers 620/10/121/132, J.W. to Cooke, 29 September 1800.

68 See Madden, *The United Irishmen – Their Lives and Times*, 4th Series, 2, pp. 153–4. In a short article by Katherine Burt Jackson (Neilson's great-great-great-granddaughter), located in the Neilson archive in the University of Rhode Island, it is asserted that Neilson arrived in New York on board *The Ohio*, commanded by a Captain Hall. URIL, Mss.Gr.72 Neilson 72/1/1/8, copybook in Neilson Collection, written by one of his daughters. On his return to Hamburg, Anthony McCann had told George Wood that he too had seen Neilson board the ship to take him to America, and while he received no news from him, it was said that Neilson had become more sober during his final voyage. NA Kew, HO100/117/93-7.

69 'The Helvetians Farewell to his Country', *Belfast News-Letter*, 16 November 1802.

70 See Madden, Samuel to Anne Neilson, 8 December 1802 and 1 January 1803, p. 139; S/ Neilson, *Brief Statement*.

71 M. McCarthy, 'Yellow Fever', *The Lancet*, 357 (June 2001); *Belfast News-Letter*, 2 November 1802.

72 It is likely that this was Samuel Owens from the Holestone in County Antrim. Back in late 1794, Owens had raised a subscription to support the proprietors of the *Northern Star*, who had incurred financial losses as a consequence of their lengthy legal disputes with the government. Owens had emigrated to the United States in 1797 or 1798. See C.J. Woods (ed.), *Journals and Memoirs of Thomas Russell*, p. 176.

73 See Madden, Samuel to Anne Neilson, 4 February 1803, pp. 139–40; Neilson's contacts with known United Irish exiles may indicate a continuing attachment to the cause. It is known that he had been in contact with William Dowdall from the United States. NAI, 620/11/138/4, examination of Philip Long, 18 August 1803.

74 PRONI, Tennent Papers D/1748/C/1/184/6, John Shaw to William Tennent, 27 April 1803. The former United Irishman John Caldwell, who had settled in the United States, was later critical of William Tennent's pursuit of Shaw for the repayment of money owed. In May 1806, Caldwell wrote that, 'Shaw has a large family, and tho' he is unfortunate, is honest, but can do nothing for himself or his family unless he gets a discharge for the debt due by him to William Tennent, which at any rate, he is unable to pay.' PRONI, D/1759/3B/6, John Caldwell Letters from New York addressed to Robert Simms, 15 May 1806.

75 See Madden, Samuel to Anne Neilson, 4 February 1803, pp. 139–40; PRONI, D/1759/3B/6. John Caldwell (NY) to Robert Simms (Belfast), 18 October 1802.

76 See Madden, Samuel to William B Neilson, 19 May 1803, p. 140.

77 *Political Barometer*, 6 September 1803. The newspaper offered a brief and sympathetic survey of Neilson's life, with some inaccuracies, such as mentioning Grattan as one of those who headed the United Irishmen and identifying only two children. Neilson is likely to have died of the yellow fever; his death is often attributed to apoplexy and this is consistent with the final symptoms of yellow fever. The *Belfast News-Letter* recorded Neilson's death as 27 August 1803. *Belfast News-Letter*, 25 October 1803.

Postscript

1 *Poughkeepsie Daily Eagle*, 4 September 1880; 15 September 1880; 16 September 1880.
2 *Poughkeepsie Evening Star*, 29 August 1905. F.J. Bigger was the editor of the *Ulster Journal of Archaeology* and was descended from the Belfast United Irishman, David Bigger, a cousin of Samuel Neilson.
3 PRONI, T/1013/2/B/#257, marriage records of Carnmoney Presbyterian Church; *Belfast News-Letter*, 20 April 1804.
4 PRONI, T654/2, births and marriage records of Rosemary Presbyterian Church. Bernard McClune was the proprietor of a tavern on Edward Street in the town.
5 Madden, *The United Irishmen – Their Lives and Times*, 4th Series, 2, pp. 156–7.
6 J.J. Wright, *The Natural Leaders and their World* (Liverpool: Liverpool University Press, 2012), pp. 85–7; R. Tennent, *Eulogium on William Bryson Neilson, Esq* (Belfast: n.d.).
7 URIL, Mss.Gr.72/1/1/8, copybook in Neilson Collection, written by one of his daughters; biographical notes compiled by William Bryson Neilson's friend Robert Grimshaw; information provided by Robert McDowell for John Martin & Co., 9 February 1843; W.B. Neilson (Lisbon) to his sisters, 4 December 1811; Howard Grimshaw (Kingston, Jamaica) to his brother Nicholas, 9 February 1817; W.B. Neilson to Anne Neilson, 25 January 1812; 14 November 1816.
8 R. Tennent, *Eulogium on William Bryson Neilson.*
9 PRONI, D395/3, will of William Bryson Neilson, 27 December 1816.
10 URIL, Mss.Gr.72/1/1/3, genealogical notes; *Belfast News-Letter*, 5 May 1818.
11 *Belfast News-Letter*, 8 March 1811; TCD, Madden MSS 873/534, Sophia McAdam to W.J. MacNeven, 31 August 1831; 873/424, Sophia McAdam to Madden, 4 October 1843.
12 *Belfast News-Letter*, 18 May 1813. Jane was married in St Anne's Parish Church, Belfast, by Rev. William Bruce, a leading moderate and her headmaster at the Belfast Academy some years earlier; URIL, Mss.Gr. 72/1/1/3, genealogical notes on Jane Neilson McAdam.
13 *Ulster Journal of Archaeology*, 7, 1901; J. Agnew (ed.), *The Drennan–McTier Letters*, 2, William Drennan to Martha McTier, n.d. October 1796, p. 270.
14 TCD, Madden MSS 873/189, Mary Hancock Neilson to Madden, 11 April 1842; 873/190, same to same, n.d., 1842.
15 A. Blackstock, *Loyalism in Ireland 1789–1829* (Woodbridge, Boydell and Brewer, 2007), pp. 221–2; 267.
16 See Blackstock, *Loyalism in Ireland 1789–1829*; J.J. Wright, *The Natural Leaders and Their World:* Politics, Culture and Society in Belfast, c.1801-1832 (Liverpool: Liverpool University Press, 2012).
17 *Belfast News-Letter*, 14 January 1806.
18 NAI, Rebellion Papers 620/66/232, John Robertson to John Lees, 5 April 1803; J. Agnew (ed.), *The Drennan–McTier Letters*, 3, Martha McTier to William Drennan, 10 March 1805, pp. 331–2.

Bibliography

PRIMARY SOURCES

Manuscripts

Northern Ireland

Public Record Office of Northern Ireland, Belfast
Rev. Robert Black Correspondence (T/3041)
Freehold Records (D/654/A3/1B)
Pelham Transcripts (T/755)
Leonard Dobbin Papers (T/316/4)
Tennent Papers (D/1748/A/1/5/18)
McCance Papers (D272)
Lytton White Papers (Cleland MSS) (D714)
Downshire Papers (D607)
Letters concerning the confinement of Lord Edward Fitzgerald (D/584)
McPeake Papers (T/3048)
Granard Papers (T/3765)
The Anecdotal recollections of Morgan Jellet (T/2777/1A)
Particulars of History of a North County Irish Family (John Caldwell Jr) (T/3541/5/3)
Shannon Papers (D/2027/A3/3/)
Copies from Madden MSS (T/1210/1–46)
The Will of William Bryson Neilson 1818 (pre-1858 wills and admons)

Linen Hall Library, Belfast
Belfast Charitable Society Committee Book 1791–1794
Joy MSS

Presbyterian Historical Society, Belfast
Third Belfast Presbyterian Church Committee Minutes (MIC IP7/5)

Republic of Ireland

National Archives of Ireland, Dublin
Rebellion Papers 620 collection
State Prisoners Petitions
Frazer MSS

Trinity College, Dublin
Madden MSS
Sirr Papers (MSS 868/1–2)

National Library of Ireland, Dublin
Lake MSS (56)
Musgrave MSS (4156)

Scotland
National Records of Scotland, Edinburgh
Lord Advocate Correspondence (RH2/485–89 and 222)

England
Kent History and Library Centre, Maidstone
Camden MSS (U840)

National Archives, London
Home Office Papers (HO/100)

Other
University of Rhode Island
Samuel Neilson Collection Mss. Gr.72

Newspapers and Periodicals
Belfast News-Letter
Northern Star
The Belfast Mercury; Or, Freeman's Chronicle
Faulkner's Dublin Journal
Freeman's Journal
The Press
The Observer
The Times

Collections of Official Documents
Report of the Secret Committee of the Irish House Commons (1798)
Report of the Secret Committee of the Irish House of Lords (1798)

Published Papers and Correspondences
Agnew, J. (ed.), *The Drennan–McTier Letters*, Vol. I, 1776–1793; Vol. II, 1794–1801 (Dublin, 1999).
Bartlett, T. (ed.), *Memoirs and Journals of Theobald Wolfe Tone* (Dublin, 1998).

Bartlett, T. (ed.), *Revolutionary Dublin 1795–1801: Letters of Francis Higgins to Dublin Castle* (Dublin, 2004).

Historical Manuscripts Commission – Thirteenth Report, Appendix, Part VIII, *The Manuscripts and Correspondence of James, First Earl of Charlemont Vol. II 1784–1799* (London, 1894).

McDonagh, M., *The Viceroy's Postbag: Correspondence hitherto unpublished of the Earl of Hardwicke, First Lord Lieutenant of Ireland after the Union* (London, 1904).

Memoirs and Correspondence of Viscount Castlereagh, Second Marquess of Londonderry, edited by his brother Charles Vane, Marquess of Londonderry, Volume 1 (London, 1848).

Records of the General Synod of Ulster, Volume 3, 1778–1820 (Belfast, 1898).

Thomas Russell Journals and Memoirs (Edited by C.J. Woods).

Contemporary Works and Pamphlets

The Belfast Politics Enlarged – Being a Compendium of the Political History of Ireland for the Last Forty years; Compiled by John Lawless Esq (Belfast, 1818).

A Collection of all the Authenticated Public Addresses, Resolutions, and Advertisements Relative to the late Election of Knights for the Shire of County Antrim Together with a Correct List of the Poll, By a member of the independent committee (Belfast, 1790).

Curran W.H., *The Life of the Right Honourable John Philpot Curran, Late Master of the Rolls in Ireland*, in two volumes (London, 1819).

De Latocnaye, *A Frenchman's Walk Through Ireland 1796–7* (reprinted Belfast, 1984).

Dickson, W.S., *A Narrative of the Confinement and Exile of William Steel Dickson D.D.* (Dublin, 1812).

A Faithful report of the Trial of the Proprietors of the Northern Star; at the King's Bench, on the twenty-eighth of May 1794, on an Information, filed ex-officio, by the Attorney General, For the Insertion of a Publication of the Irish Jacobins of Belfast 15 December 1792. By A Barrister (Belfast, 1794).

A Faithful report of the Second Trial of the Proprietors of the Northern Star; at the King's Bench, on the seventeenth of November 1794, on an Information, filed ex-officio, by the Attorney General, For the Insertion of The Society of United Irishmen's Address to the Volunteers of Ireland, on the 19th December 1792 (Belfast, 1795).

MacNeven, W.J., *Pieces of Irish History, Illustrative of the Condition of the Catholics of Ireland of the Origin and Progress of the Political System of United Irishmen; and of their Transactions with the Anglo-Irish Government* (New York, 1807).

Merchants in Plenty: Joseph Smyth's Belfast Directories of 1807 and 1808 (reprinted Belfast, 1991).

Musgrave, Sir Richard, *Memoirs of the Different Rebellions in Ireland from the arrival of the English: Also, Particular Detail of that which Broke Out the 23 May 1798; with the History and Conspiracy which Preceded it* (4th ed., Indiana, 1995).

Neilson, S., *Brief Statement of a Negotiation between Certain United Irishmen and the Irish Government in July 1798* (New York, 1802).

O'Connor, A., *The State of Ireland in 1798* (London, 1798).

O'Connor, A., *Letter to Lord Castlereagh* (Dublin, 1799).

Paddy's Resource being a select collection of original patriotic songs for the use of the people of Ireland (Belfast, 1795).

The Patriot Soldier: or Irish Volunteer. A Poem Written by a Member of the Belfast First Volunteer Company (Belfast, 1789).

Sampson, W., *Memoirs of William Sampson* (New York, 1807).

'A Sketch of the Life of Samuel Neilson of Belfast, Editor of the Northern Star, and Member of the Irish Directory', *The Irish Magazine and Monthly Asylum for Neglected Biography* (September 1811), pp. 396–402.

Tennent, R., *Eulogium on William Bryson Nelson [sic], Esq late member of the Belfast Historic Society, born in Belfast, May 14 1794...died in Jamaica Feb 7 1817* (Belfast, no date).

Secondary Works

Books

Bartlett, T., Dickson, D., Keogh, D., Whelan, K., *1798: A Bicentenary Perspective* (Dublin: Four Courts Press, 2003).

Benn, G., *History of the Town of Belfast* (Belfast: A. McKay, 1823).

Bew, J., *Castlereagh: Enlightenment, War and Tyranny* (London: Quercus, 2011).

Blackstock, A., *Loyalism in Ireland 1789–1829* (Woodbridge: Boydell Press, 2007).

Brown, M., Geoghegan, P.M., Kelly, J., *The Irish Act of Union: Bicentennial Essays* (Dublin: Irish Academic Press, 2003).

Carroll, D., *The Man from God Knows Where: Thomas Russell 1767–1803* (Dublin: Columba Press, 1995).

Chambers, G., *Faces of Change: The Belfast and Northern Ireland Chambers of Commerce and Industry 1783–1983* (Belfast: Century Books, 1984).

Concannon, (Mrs) T., *Women of '98* (Dublin: Gill, 1919).

Curtin, N., *The United Irishmen: Popular Politics in Ulster and Dublin* (Oxford: Clarendon Press, 1994).

Davis, M.T., and Pickering, P.A., *Unrespectable Radicals? Popular Politics in the Age of Reform* (Aldershot: Ashgate Publishing Ltd., 2008).

Dickson, C., *Revolt in the North: Antrim and Down in 1798* (Dublin: Clonmore & Reynolds, 1960).

Dickson, D., Keogh, D., Whelan, K., *The United Irishmen – Republicanism, Radicalism, Rebellion* (Dublin: The Lilliput Press, 1993).

Drummond, W.H., *Autobiography of Archibald Hamilton Rowan, Esq* (Dublin: Thomas Tegg & Co., 1840).

Durey, M., *Transatlantic Radicals and the Early American Republic* (Kansas: University Press of Kansas, 1997).

Elliott, M., *Partners in Revolution: The United Irishmen and France* (New Haven: Yale University Press,1982).

—, *Wolfe Tone: Prophet of Irish Independence* (New Haven: Yale University Press, 1989).

Ferguson, J., *Balloon Tytler* (London: Faber and Faber, 1972).

Fisher, J.R., and Robb, J.H., *Royal Belfast Academical Institution: Centenary Volume* (Belfast: McCaw, Stevenson & Orr, 1913).

Fitzpatrick, W.J., *A Note to the Cornwallis Papers; Embracing with other revelations, A Narrative of the Extraordinary Career of Francis Higgins, Who Received the Government Reward for the Betrayal of Lord Edward Fitzgerald* (London: J. Murray, 1859).

—, *Secret Service Under Pitt* (London: Longmans, Green & Co., 1892).

Geoghegan, P.M., *Robert Emmet: A Life* (Dublin: Gill and Macmillan, 2002).

Gough, H., and Dickson, D., *Ireland and the French Revolution* (Blackrock: Irish Academic Press, 1990).

Grattan, H., *Memoirs of the Life and Times of the Rt Hon Henry Grattan by his son Henry Grattan Esq. MP*, Volume 4,(London: Colborn, 1842).

Hayter Hames, J., *Arthur O'Connor: United Irishman* (Cork: The Collins Press, 2001).

Hill, M., Turner, B., and Dawson, K.L., *1798 Rebellion in County Down* (Newtownards: Colourpoint, 1998).

Hyde, H.M., *The Rise of Castlereagh* (London: Macmillan & Co. Ltd., 1933).

Inglis, B., *The Freedom of the Press in Ireland 1784–1841* (London: Faber and Faber, 1954).

Jacob, R., *The Rise of the United Irishmen* (London: George C. Harrop, 1937).

Latimer, W.T., *Ulster Biographies Relating to the Rebellion of 1798* (Belfast: Cleeland, Mullan & Son, 1897).

Lindsey, J., *The Shining Life and Death of Lord Edward Fitzgerald* (London: Rich & Cowan, 1949).

McComb, W., *McComb's Guide to Belfast* (Belfast: William McComb, 1861).

McDowell, R.B., *Ireland in the Age of Imperialism and Revolution 1760–1801* (Oxford: Clarendon Press, 1979).

—, *Proceedings of the Dublin Society of United Irishmen* (Dublin: Irish Manuscripts Commission, 1998 reprinted).

—, *Grattan – A Life* (Dublin: The Lilliput Press 2001).

McFarland, E.W., *Ireland and Scotland in the Age of Revolution: Planting the Green Bough* (Edinburgh: Edinburgh University Press, 1994).

McNeill, M., *The Life and Times of Mary Ann McCracken 1770–1866 – A Belfast Panorama* (Dublin:Alan Figgis and Co. Ltd., 1960).

McSkimin, S., *History of the Irish Rebellion in 1798 Particularly in Antrim, Down and Derry* (Belfast: John Mullan, 1853).

—, *Annals of Ulster from 1790 to 1798* (Belfast: John Henderson, 1906).

Madden, R.R., *Antrim and Down in '98* (Glasgow: Cameron, Ferguson & Co.n.d.).

—, *The United Irishmen – Their Lives and Times*, 1st Series, 1st Edition (London: J. Mullany, 1842).

—, *The United Irishmen – Their Lives and Times*, 1st Series, 1st Edition, Volume (ii) (London: J. Mullany, 1842).

—, *The United Irishmen – Their Lives and Times*, 2nd Series, 1st Edition, (London: J. Mullany, 1842).

—, *The United Irishmen – Their Lives and Times*, 3rd Series, 2nd Edition (London, J. Mullany, 1860).

—, *The United Irishmen – Their Lives and Times*, 4th Series, 2nd Edition (London: J. Mullany 1860).

Mansergh, D., *Grattan's Failure: Parliamentary Opposition and the People in Ireland 1779–1800* (Dublin: Irish Academic Press, 2005).

Millin, S.S., *Sidelights on Belfast History* (Belfast: W. & G. Baird, 1932).

Moore. T., *The Life and Death of Lord Edward Fitzgerald* (Dublin: Longman, Rees, Orme, Brown, & Green 1831).

Muhr, K., *Place Names of Northern Ireland*, Vol. 6: County Down (Belfast: Queen's University Belfast, 1996).

Murray, W., *A Photographic Record of 1798 Memorials on the Island of Ireland and Beyond* (Wexford: Carrigbyrne Film Productions Ltd., 2002).

O'Donnell, R., *Robert Emmet and the Rebellion of 1798* (Dublin: Irish Academic Press, 2003).

—, *Robert Emmet and the Rising of 1803* (Dublin: Irish Academic Press, 2003).

O'Sullivan, N., *Every Dark Hour: A History of Kilmainham Jail* (Dublin: Liberties Press, 2007)

Ordnance Survey Memoirs of Ireland: Parishes of County Down I 1834–5 (South Down), Vol. 3 (Belfast: Institute of Irish Studies 1990).

Pakenham, T., *The Year of Liberty* (London: Panther, 1969).

Palliser, F.W., *The Irish Rebellion of 1798* (London: Simpkin, Marshall & Co. 1898).

Patterson, J.G., *In the Wake of the Great Rebellion: Republicanism, Agrarianism and Banditry in Ireland after 1798* (Manchester: Manchester University Press, 2008).

Presbyterian Historical Society of Ireland, *A History of Congregations in the Presbyterian Church in Ireland 1610–1982* (Belfast: P.H.S., 1982).

Quinn, J., *Soul on Fire: A Life of Thomas Russell* (Dublin: Irish Academic Press, 2002).

Reilly, C., *Edenderry, County Offaly, and the Downshire Estate, 1790–1800* (Dublin: Four Courts Press, 2007).

Small, S., *Political Thought in Ireland, 1776–1798: Republicanism, Patriotism and Radicalism* (Oxford: Clarendon Press, 2002).

Smyth, J., *The Men of No Property: Irish Radicals and Popular Politics in the Late Eighteenth Century* (Dublin: Gill & Macmillan, 1992).

— (ed.), *Revolution, Counter-Revolution and Union: Ireland in the 1790s* (Cambridge: Cambridge University Press, 2000).

Stewart, A.T.Q., *A Deeper Silence: The Hidden Origins of the United Irishmen* (London: Faber and Faber, 1993).

—, *The Summer Soldiers: The 1798 Rebellion in Antrim and Down* (Belfast: Blackstaff Press, 1995).

Strain, R.W.M., *Belfast and its Charitable Society: A Story of Urban Social Development* (London: Oxford University Press, 1961).

Swords, L., *The Green Cockade: The Irish in the French Revolution 1789–1815* (Dublin: Glendale Press1989).

Teeling, C.H., *Personal Narrative of the Irish Rebellion of 1798* (London: R. & T. Washbourne 1828).

—, *Sequel to the Personal Narrative of the Irish Rebellion of 1798* (Belfast: John Hodgeson, 1832).

Thuente, M.H., *The Harp Restrung: The United Irishmen and the Rise of Irish Literary Nationalism* (New York: Syracuse University Press, 1994).

Tillyard, S., *Citizen Lord: Lord Edward Fitzgerald 1763–1798* (London: Chattow and Windus 1997).

Weber, P., *On the Road to Rebellion: The United Irishmen and Hamburg 1796–1803* (Dublin: Four Courts Press, 1997).

Wells, R., *Insurrection: The British Experience 1795–1803* (London: A. Sutton, 1983).

Whelan, F., *God-Provoking Democrat: The Remarkable Life of Archibald Hamilton Rowan* (Dublin: New Island, 2015).

Whelan, K., *The Tree of Liberty* (Cork: Cork University Press 1996).

Wills, J., *Lives of Illustrious and Distinguished Irishmen*, Vol. VI, Part 1 (Dublin: A. Fullarton & Co., 1845).

Wilson, D., *United Irishmen, United States: Immigrant Radicals in the Early Republic* (New York: Cornell University Press, 1998).

Wright, J.J., *The Natural Leaders and their World: Politics, Culture and Society in Belfast, c. 1801–1832* (Liverpool: Liverpool University Press, 2012).

Young, R.M., *Historical Notices of Old Belfast and its Vicinity* (Belfast: Marcus Ward & Co., 1896).

Articles

Armstrong, Rev. D., 'Reverend Sinclare Kelburn 1754–1802' (Belfast: Presbyterian Historical Society of Ireland 2001).

Bailie, W.D., 'William Steel Dickson DD', in *The Bulletin of the Presbyterian Historical Society* (vi, 1976).

—, 'The Reverend Samuel Barber 1738–1811: National Volunteer and United Irishman', in J.L.M. Haire, *Challenge and Conflict: Essays in Irish Presbyterian History and Doctrine* (Belfast: W.G. Baird 1981).

Cole, Francis J., 'John Wesley and his Ulster Contacts', in *Proceedings of the Belfast Natural History and Philosophical Society* (Belfast: 1845).

Cullen, L., 'The Political Structures of the Defenders', in Gough, H., and Dickson, D. (eds), *Ireland and the French Revolution* (Dublin: Irish Academic Press, 1990).

—, 'The "Suppression" of the Volunteers and United Irishmen: Sources and Interpretations 1792–1794', in Browne, B. (ed.), *The Wexford Man, Essays in Honour of Nicky Furlong* (Dublin: Geography Publications, 2007).

Curtin, N.J., 'The Transformation of the Society of United Irishmen into a mass-based Revolutionary Organisation 1794–6', in *Irish Historical Studies*, Vol. 24, No. 96 (1985).

—, 'Symbols and Rituals of United Irish Mobilisation', in Gough, H., and Dickson, D. (eds), *Ireland and the French Revolution* (Dublin: Irish Academic Press, 1990).

Davies, S., 'The Northern Star and the Propagation of Enlightened Ideas', in *Eighteenth Century Ireland*, Vol. 5 (1990).

Durey, M., 'John Hughes, reluctant agent provocateur and millenarian: a note and new documents', in *Eighteenth Century Ireland*, Vol. 7 (1992).

Elliott, M., 'The Kent Treason Trials of 1798: A Window on the United Irishmen', in Wichert, S., *From the United Irishmen to Twentieth Century Unionism: A Festschrift for A.T.Q. Stewart* (Dublin: Four Courts Press, 2004).

Graham, T., 'The Transformation of the Dublin Society of United Irishmen into a Mass-Based Revolutionary Organisation 1791–96', in Bartlett, T., Dickson, D., Keogh, D., and Whelan, K., *1798 – A Bicentenary Perspective* (Dublin: Four Courts Press, 2003).

—, 'The Shift in United Irish Leadership from Belfast to Dublin 1796–1798', in Smyth, J. (ed.), *Revolution, Counter-Revolution and Union: Ireland in the 1790s* (Cambridge: Cambridge University Press, 2000).

Gray, J., 'A Tale of Two Newspapers: The Contest Between the *Belfast Newsletter* and the *Northern Star* in the 1790s', in Gray, J., and McCann, W. (eds), *An Uncommon Bookman – Essays in Memory of J.R.R. Adams* (Belfast: Linen Hall Library, 1996).

Hudson Parsons, H., 'The Mysterious Mr Digges', in *William and Mary Quarterly*, Vol. 22 (1965).

Kennedy, W.B., 'The Irish Jacobins', in *Studia Hibernica*, Vol. xvi (1976).

MacDonald, B., 'Distribution of the Northern Star', in *Ulster Local Studies, The Turbulent Decade: Ulster in the 1790s*, Vol. 18, No. 2 (1997).

Maguire, W.A., 'Arthur McMahon, United Irishman and French Soldier', in *Irish Sword*, Vol. 9 (1957).

Maher, M., 'Oliver Bond', in *Dublin Historical Record*, Vol. xi, No. 4 (1950).

Muir, A., 'The Eighteenth-Century Paper-Makers of the North of Ireland', in *Familia*, Vol. 20 (2004).

O'Brien, G., 'Spirit, Impartiality and Independence: The Northern Star, 1792–1797', in *Eighteenth Century Ireland*, Vol. 13 (1998).

O'Donnell, R., 'The Military Committee and the United Irishmen, 1798–1803', in Davis, M.T., and Pickering, P.A., *Unrespectable Radicals? Popular Politics in the Age of Reform* (Aldershot: Ashgate Publishing Ltd., 2008).

Onsborough, W.N., 'Legal Aspects of the 1798 Rising, its suppression and the Aftermath', in Bartlett, T., Dickson, D., Keogh, D., and Whelan, K., *1798 – A Bicentenary Perspective* (Dublin: Four Courts Press, 2003).

Paterson, T.G.F., 'The Irish Volunteers of Ulster 1778–1793 County Down', in *Irish Sword*, Vol. 7, No. 26 (1966).

Quinn, J., 'The Kilmainham Treaty', in Bartlett, T., Dickson, D., Keogh, D., and Whelan, K., *1798 – A Bicentenary Perspective* (Dublin: Four Courts Press, 2003).

—, 'The United Irishmen and Social Reform', in *Irish Historical Studies*, Vol. 31, No. 122 (1998).

Smyth, J., 'Popular Politicisation, Defenderism and the Catholic Question', in Gough, H., and Dickson, D., *Ireland and the French Revolution* (Dublin: Irish Academic Press, 1990).

Unpublished Theses

Monaghan, J.J., 'A social and economic history of Belfast 1790–1800', MA thesis, QUB (1936).

Nelson, Rev. J.W., 'The Belfast Presbyterians 1670–1830: An analysis of their political and social interest', PhD thesis, QUB (1985).

Stewart, A.T.Q., 'The transformation of Presbyterian radicalism in the North of Ireland 1792–1825', MA thesis, QUB (1956).

Index